NEW APPROACHES
TO PERSONALITY CLASSIFICATION

NEW APPROACHES
TO PERSONALITY CLASSIFICATION

EDITED BY ALVIN R. MAHRER

COLUMBIA UNIVERSITY PRESS
NEW YORK AND LONDON
1970

Alvin R. Mahrer is Professor of Psychology and Director of the Clinical Psychology Program at Miami University, Oxford, Ohio.

Copyright © 1970 Columbia University Press
Standard Book Number: 231-03296-X
Library of Congress Catalog Card Number: 73-96313
Printed in the United States of America

CONTRIBUTORS

Alvin R. Mahrer, Ph.D.
Miami University
Oxford, Ohio

George W. Albee, Ph.D.
Case Western Reserve University
Cleveland, Ohio

Raymond B. Cattell, Ph.D.
University of Illinois
Champaign, Illinois

Hans J. Eysenck, Ph.D.
University of London
London, England

Reuben Fine, Ph.D.
New York, New York

Molly Harrower, Ph.D.
University of Florida
Gainesville, Florida

John L. Horn, Ph.D.
University of Denver
Denver, Colorado

Timothy Leary, Ph.D.
Berkeley, California

Maurice Lorr, Ph.D.
Catholic University of America
Washington, D.C.

Steve Pratt, Ph.D.
Jacksonville State Hospital
Jacksonville, Illinois

Arthur B. Sweney, Ph.D.
Texas Technological College
Lubbock, Texas

Frederick C. Thorne, M.D., Ph.D.
Journal of Clinical Psychology
Brandon, Vermont

Jay Tooley, Ph.D.
Jacksonville State Hospital
Jacksonville, Illinois

CONTENTS

Introduction   1
    Alvin R. Mahrer

STRUCTURAL APPROACHES TO PERSONALITY
CLASSIFICATION   5

A Factor Analytic System for Clinicians   7
1 The Integration of Functional and Psychometric Requirements
in a Quantitative and Computerized Diagnostic System   9
    Raymond B. Cattell

A Factor Analytic System for the Individual Patient   53
2 The Dynamic Calculus Model for Motivation and Its Use in
Understanding the Individual Case   55
    John L. Horn and Arthur B. Sweney

Factor Analysis, Natural Types, and Hospitalized Psychotics   99
3 A Typological Conception of the Behavior Disorders   101
    Maurice Lorr

FUNCTIONAL APPROACHES TO PERSONALITY
CLASSIFICATION   117

   A Diagnostic Dimension for the Psychoanalyst   119
 4 Therapeutic Accessibility as a Basis for Diagnosis   121
      Reuben Fine

   The Scaling of Mental Health Potential   137
 5 Projective Classification   139
      Molly Harrower

COMPREHENSIVE APPROACHES TO PERSONALITY
CLASSIFICATION   165

   A Behavior Modification Approach   167
 6 A Dimensional System of Psychodiagnostics   169
      Hans J. Eysenck

   Existential-Transactional Preface to a Classification System   209
 7 The Diagnosis of Behavior and the Diagnosis of Experience   211
      Timothy Leary

   Motivational Needs, Hospitalization, and a Classification
   System   237
 8 Motivational Theory: Foundations of Personality Classification   239
      Alvin R. Mahrer

 9 Motivational Theory: A System of Personality Classification   277
      Alvin R. Mahrer

   Existential Psychological States, Integration, and a Clinical
   Diagnostic Approach   309
10 Diagnostic Implications of Integrative Psychology   311
      Frederick C. Thorne

Beyond Disorder, toward Transactions   347

11   Toward a Metataxonomy of Human Systems Actualization:
The Perspective of Contract Psychology   349
     Steve Pratt and Jay Tooley

SUMMARY   381

The Question of Psychodiagnosis   383

12   Notes toward a Position Paper Opposing Psychodiagnosis   385
     George W. Albee

Present Trends and Future Directions   397
     Alvin R. Mahrer

Index of Names   415

Subject Index   423

INTRODUCTION

ALVIN R. MAHRER

The purpose of this book is, simply and straightforwardly, to introduce ten new approaches to the classification of personality. The ten proposed approaches are not presented as exhaustive, but they are nevertheless a comprehensive sample of what has so far been proposed. These approaches offer new personality models and new ways of categorizing persons derived from these models. All can be usefully examined in terms of their relative positions on two continua. One concerns their development, which ranges from beginning and tentative foundations to more or less finished and defined sets of categories. The other ranges from modifications and extensions of the conventional psychiatric nosology to substantively new and different approaches to categorization. Some of the personality models and associated classification schemata are significant variations on the traditional psychiatric medical model; some are strikingly different.

The problem is to devise a way of categorizing persons or a set of personality dimensions by which to meet all the theoretical and practical demands under which the present standard psychodiagnostic system is crumbling. We stand almost helpless to understand and categorize persons who populate our hospital system. A classification system is needed to incorporate entire new bodies of personality conceptions and to evolve appropriate categories and dimensions based upon, for example, emerging and developing existential and transactional notions of personality and the new factor analytic methodologies. The broad spectrum of psychotherapeutic techniques demands a new

1

system to provide meaningful and useful categories and personality dimensions. Personality theorists, experimental methodologists, psychological and psychiatric researchers, cadres of mental health workers, clinics, hospitals, and even professional organizations of psychologists and psychiatrists call for new modes of systematizing, organizing, categorizing, taxonomizing in general, indicating dimensions of personality.

There is a long history to what Menninger terms "the urge to classify" people, their problems, and their potentials. The conventional psychiatric nosology is merely one response to the issue of identifying meaningful categories, groups, classes, or types. Robbins (1966), Menninger (1963), and Zilboorg and Henry (1941) are representative of those who tell the histories of classificatory endeavors. These endeavors culminated, in 1917, in the acceptance of a classification of mental diseases by the American Psychiatric Association (then called the American Medico-Psychological Association). Revision was begun in 1948 by the Committee on Nomenclature and Statistics of the American Psychiatric Association, and officially adopted in 1952 as the standard classification of mental disorders (American Psychiatric Association, 1952). Three major categories were utilized: (1) Disorders caused by or associated with impairment of brain tissue function. These are divided into brain disorders of an acute and of a chronic nature. (2) Disorders of psychogenic origin or without clearly defined clinical cause or structural change in the brain. This category includes psychoneurotic disorders, personality disorders, transient situational disorders, psychophysiologic autonomic and visceral disorders, and psychotic disorders. (3) Mental deficiency.

The 1952 classification has recently been replaced by a more complicated nomenclature officially adopted by the American Psychiatric Association in 1968. Instead of the former three major groups, the new system includes 164 psychiatric diagnoses organized into ten major groups: (1) Mental retardation. (2) Organic brain syndromes, psychotic and nonpsychotic. (3) Psychoses not attributable to mental retardation or organic brain conditions. (4) Neuroses. (5) Personality disorders and other nonpsychotic disorders. (6) Psychophysiologic disorders. (7) Transient situational disturbances. (8) Special symptoms not classified elsewhere. (9) Behavior disorders of childhood and adolescence. (10) Conditions without manifest psychiatric disorders and nonspecific conditions.

This volume offers the most recent trends in attempts to express "the urge to classify," going beyond criticism of an existing approach to offer constructive alternatives or modifications. The contributors are representative of a constructive upheaval of psychological-psychiatric thought which, building upon meaningful criticisms, is now prepared to take some positive, constructive steps.

The upheaval is occurring as a part of the professionalization of such disciplines as clinical psychology (Tyler and Speisman, 1967), dynamic psychiatry, social psychology, sociology, and social work. For example, clinical psychologists trained within the last twenty years in a variety of schools and approaches to personality theory were thrust into practical mental hospitals and clinics where they, along with other disciplines, were expected to speak the language of Kraepelinian psychiatry. They learned there to employ nineteenth-century psychiatrese, both in their conceptualizations and their psychodiagnosis. But clinical psychologists are beginning to develop their own personality classification approaches. Similar changes and trends are occurring within other disciplines.

The essays here offer various emphases from philosophical consideration of the process of diagnosis to factor analytic methods, from basic personality theory to practical considerations of the private practitioner, yet each contributor responds to these questions: What are constructive, positive supplements, complements, or alternatives to the present system? What is a meaningful and useful system for the classification of personality?

REFERENCES

American Psychiatric Association. *Diagnostic and statistical manual of mental disorders.* Washington: American Psychiatric Association, 1952.
Menninger, K. A. *The vital balance.* New York: Viking, 1963.
Robbins, L. L. A historical review of classification of behavior disorders and one current perspective. In L. D. Eron (Ed.), *The classification of behavior disorders.* Chicago: Aldine, 1966. Pp. 1–37.
Tyler, F. B., and Speisman, J. C. An emerging scientist-professional role in psychology. *Amer. Psychologist,* 1967, **22**, 839–47.
Zilboorg, G., and Henry, G. W. *A history of medical psychology.* New York: W. W. Norton, 1941.

STRUCTURAL APPROACHES TO PERSONALITY CLASSIFICATION

Structural approaches to psychodiagnostic classification work within the personality framework of the standard psychiatric nomenclature. For example, a structural approach might fully accept the concept of acute functional psychosis and seek essentially to reorganize the kinds or types of acute functional psychoses; factor analytic methods are applied and the writer finds new subgroups or types under the general heading of acute functional psychosis. The aim is to probe into the structure of personality, to uncover the underlying contours of organization, to search out the more systematically derived natural (factor analytic) groupings, factors, communalities, nexuses, and dimensions. Maurice Lorr provides a new structure for acute functional psychosis. Raymond B. Cattell seeks to explore the factor analyzed structure underlying the entire standard psychiatric nomenclature. In offering a new structural organization his building block is the source trait. John L. Horn and Arthur B. Sweney apply the overall Cattellian structure to the individual patient and show how a new structure offers a set of categories and methods of assessing motivations and drives. The following three chapters aim at systematizing the underlying structure of the present psychiatric psychodiagnostic system.

A FACTOR ANALYTIC SYSTEM FOR CLINICIANS

Cattell's avowed aim is to provide a classification system, born of factor analysis, to bridge the gap between methodologist-psychometrician and clinician-practitioner. His claim is that factor analysis is a scientific method of putting a confused theoretical house into order — without damaging the theory itself. His restructuring begins with surface traits, which simply indicate that a set of variables go together or form a correlation cluster. The factor analytic model probes beneath these surface traits to sets of source traits, which account for the source of change variance in the actual variables. The range of normal and pathological is spanned by perhaps thirty or so of these source traits which potentially will yield modal collections or types of persons, although no such typology is as yet proposed.

His approach places normality and abnormality on different levels of the same or similar source traits. Neurosis refers to a deviant pattern of ordinary (normal) source traits, i.e., an unusual degree of deviation on traits which every individual possesses to some degree. The addition of certain factors peculiar to pathology is diagnostic of psychosis. His system identifies the individual's uniqueness and idiosyncratic dynamic conflicts in terms of unique source traits and unique combinations of common traits. These are derived from extravagantly repeated measures and observations (P-technique) which sample the individual over a period of time.

Cattell's approach invites the clinician to use specific measures to assess an individual's source traits and their combination. On the other hand, the typical clinician may back away from a diagnostic approach in which he must deal with "factors" and "traits," even though Cattell offers full explanations of both terms.

Is it indeed possible to put the Kraepelinian-psychiatric house in order, using factor analytic methodology, and leave the conceptual framework intact? It seems true that the factor analytic methodology adds an internal conceptual structure to a set of theoretical observations, and the application of this methodology may well prove to be among Cattell's most enduring contributions. However, while Cattell claims that his psychodiagnostic approach leaves intact the fabric of the theoretical framework, one can make a case that he has changed nearly everything but the vocabulary. The very meaning of normality, neurosis, and psychosis is drastically altered. The basic tenet of psychiatric illness and disease is threatened. Washed away is the traditional set of psychiatric nomenclatures, replaced with sets of source traits and freely varying combinations, with a promised new typology. The traditional tenet of a single stable disease (is the patient a schizophrenic or is he suffering from a character disorder?) is replaced with flexible combinations. One wonders if imposing internal conceptual order by means of factor analysis does not invite a thoroughgoing factor analytic psychodiagnostic approach.

1

THE INTEGRATION OF FUNCTIONAL AND PSYCHOMETRIC REQUIREMENTS IN A QUANTITATIVE AND COMPUTERIZED DIAGNOSTIC SYSTEM

RAYMOND B. CATTELL

Factors: The Universal Model

Like all failures in human communication, the misunderstandings between psychometrists on the one hand and psychiatrists on the other—often the despair of research workers over the last two generations —have undoubtedly been due to a lack of certain kinds of imagination on both sides. There are now, fortunately, countless signs that the gap is closing and that we stand at the beginning of a period of very fertile interaction and growth of measurement and functional, dynamic thinking. All too many psychometrists—especially those in the educational and ability fields and those whose concentration on mere item properties has caused me to dub them itemitrists—seem to the psychiatrist to have been preoccupied with rituals of scaling and rigidities of simple models which have little bearing on his complex problems. To the psychometrist on the other hand, the psychiatrist has seemed content with the flimsiest experimental bases for his concepts and the crudest and most unreliable of means for evaluating them in individuals. Freud and Galton have thus lived very far apart in the last generation's thinking, but one could argue that men of this high degree of imagination are never so far apart as are their followers.

How is the gap to be bridged? First, one must demand of the psychiatrist a more explicit and quantitative methodology. To the general run of psychiatric theorists, one must say that if a theory is worth anything at all, it should be expressible in a mathematical model, realistically testable. To the psychometrist, one must say that if he is not prepared to measure anything more than school examinations, intelli-

9

gence, and one or two specific abilities he is neglecting by far the most important area of individual differences, and that he will have made no contribution to functional psychology. Fortunately, a few psychologically oriented psychometrists in the past twenty years have had the ingenuity to encompass the widest affective and dynamic behavior in test devices, and the mathematical clarity to incorporate the psychiatrist's traits, states, defense mechanisms, and conflicts in logical models.

Diagnosis, as every clinician recognizes, is more than description and measurement. It can also be scientifically less—if we contrast accurate description and measurement practices with diagnosis, which is subjective and ambiguous in interpretation. But diagnosis should be more, and in the sense that the descriptions and measurements should arise in terms of functionally meaningful concepts, which carry surplus meaning and predictive power beyond that obtainable merely at a descriptive psychometric level. In short, measurement must relate to definite models of personality structure. Now the models of functional meaning which I believe can be historically demonstrated to have been of most vital importance to psychology and psychiatry are those developed out of factor analysis. We must pause to ask what this means. "Developed out of" is an important phrase, for what this model can contribute does not end with the usual mathematician's factor analytic model, still less with the bare matrix algebra formulations of the computer. Let us begin by recognizing that the original factor analytic model has developed a good deal in the last thirty years. Developments have occurred, on the one hand, through greater control by the mathematical statistician and, on the other hand, through recognition by the psychologist, the economist, and other scientists of the special, additional features required in the scientific use of the model. These two kinds of developments have helped each other a little, but actually have gone out in quite different directions with different emphases. We are more concerned here with the development of the scientific model of factor analysis, which goes decidedly beyond the mathematical model as such, and which, in the dynamic calculus, in source trait theory, and in applications to typology, has branched out into further domains of models for which factor analysis is only a first foundation.

In bringing home to the psychiatrist the great relevance of the scientific factor model to the diagnostic tasks with which he is struggling, one has to recognize the unhappy historical truth that statistics has all too frequently been taught in a way which dries up the interest of the psychologist or psychiatrist who seeks its help. It is divorced from clinical evidence of structure in most cases. And if factor analysis is introduced in statistics it is taught as if it were a very recondite study and altogether different in its thinking from other statistical procedures, such as the analysis of variance. Actually, whenever a social observer says, "The factors in the situation are these," or a physician remarks, "Some unknown factors are causing such and such a change in these recordings on the patient," they are talking factor analysis. Factor analysis is simply a means of getting at the underlying influence which give us the patterns of co-varying change in variables which we observe on the surface and wish to explain. We begin by writing down these surface appearances as the computed correlations among the measured variables.

Such correlation tables need not be restricted to individual difference variation, as the educator and the ability student have commonly restricted them. They can represent longitudinal and dynamic events. For example, the clinical observer may notice in a given patient that high excitement, telegraphic speech, and a mood of elation tend to go together over time, or that in an experimental sequence increasing complaints of hunger, irritability, and measures of fall in the blood sugar go together. In one instance, the correlation is over individual differences among people, and in another it is over occasions in time, but in both cases, it is on measured variables. The only distinction between what a shrewd clinician does when he attempts to get at the underlying influence from such observations, and what a psychometrist does with the aid of a computer, is that the latter actually measures the things he believes go together, works out a correlation coefficient to show exactly how far they go together, and then applies factor analysis to the obtained square matrix of correlations among these variables. If factor analysis is skillfully carried out it will reveal the lesser number of influences underlying the changes in the variables, locate them uniquely, and describe their properties—even though the experimenter began with only the roughest hypotheses about them.

This chapter is not going to say anything more about factor analysis as such, for libraries nowadays contain many readable presentations of it (Cattell, 1966a, 1966b; Fruchter, 1954; Harman, 1960; Henrysson, 1960). But one may point out that it has happened time and again that some talented individual, untrained in factor analysis, has actually found his own way to a crude form of it by looking at matrices of correlations and picking out the visible clusters of variables that seem to correlate together. He is then inclined to infer that there are just so many different underlying functional unities or traits here— as many as there are clusters of intercorrelating things. Actually, there is a slip in this argument and we shall below define such mere clusters as *surface traits*. One must point out that factor analysis goes beyond these, though it correctly begins by looking for such clusters. For example, one might find five or six different clusters in a set of data, yet perhaps demonstrate that they arise from only two underlying factors, which are capable of accounting, by various combinations and interactions of themselves, for this larger number of clusters and for their appearing just where they do.

A quality of factor analysis perhaps even more important than its precision is its objectivity and independence of the experimenter's theoretical convictions or prejudices. For it is capable of locating the underlying influences and uniquely determining them, when many other approaches often merely perpetuate the subjective beliefs of the observers. For example, an observer might believe that there are three distinct kinds of intelligence and the factor analysis may nevertheless show him that there is only one general factor, or, conversely, he may have the idea that depression-elation is a single dimension, whereas the factor analysis shows him that there are no fewer than seven distinct varieties of depression involved (Cattell and Bjerstedt, 1966).

In the analysis of variance type of statistical analysis, on the other hand, the investigator actually begins with these subjective impressions and seeks relations to his favorite categories. That is to say, he divides up his group according to some dimension that he thinks is important and observes how the second type of measurement alters as he classifies the group on this first dimension. The limitation of such an approach is that he may have to go through countless trial and error experiments, now with this variable and now with that subjective "shot" at the effective catgories, before he hits on the basically important, unitary tendency or category which the factor analysis can discover as a pure factor at the first attempt. Tactically, it is timely to do analysis of variance after the factor analyst has found what the significant variables are.

To the researcher who has perceived the importance of first finding the natural structure of functionally unitary traits by factor analysis, there is all the difference in the world, in psychological measurement, between the man who goes home in the evening and makes up a scale for some quality which he thinks is vitally important (no matter how psychologically skillful he is in picking his items) and the man who does a piece of basic research by factor analysis into the structure of behavior or items in the given realm of interest and then emerges with certain factors for which he makes scales. The first approach might be called the "semantic omnipotence" or "idiometric" approach and the latter the "functional measurement" approach. Since what a penetrating clinician eventually sees operating as the most important functional unities are likely to be pretty close to what can be demonstrated to be functional unities by factor analysis, the bridge we have been seeking lies here. To get the integration moving we need only, on the one hand, pull the narrow psychometrist away from his itemetric scale constructions toward multivariate experimental research on natural structure as such and, on the other, convince the psychiatrist that his own unaided eye and memory are not really as good as the "microscope" of the factor analyst and the "memory" of the computer in reaching the necessary structural concept.

It is this approach through a combination of meaningful experimental measurement of behavior and sophisticated multivariate use of computer models which I and my colleagues have tried to serve for thirty years. And although a number of pure methodologists have always perceived that such measurements and models had the potentiality of bringing psychiatrists and psychometrists together, the purely abstract perception of this fact has not been able alone to effect a realization. It has needed actual research results, such as the demonstration of ego strength, superego strength, intelligence, and other source traits, as experimentally demonstrable entities, to bring about this result. Indeed, it has only been through further actual clinical use of the factor measures, showing how they meet the demands of the psychometrist for functional understanding, that the argument has at last begun to yield its fruits in mutual understanding.

To focus now briefly on the model itself, let us point out that the core features of the factor analytic model are no different from those present in the ordinary, more or less logical use of the term *factor*. Two important features in both are (1) that any single observed variable is usually to be considered accounted for by several factors. That is to say, measuring one variable can rarely be the measurement of one factor, and the causation of any symptom is nearly always multiple, and (2) that the quantitative relation is summarized by saying that various factors *add up* in their influences upon a variable. This might be implied in everyday speech when we say that a person is in a good mood partly because he gained something on the stock exchange, partly because his digestion is working well, and partly because he has just learned that a certain person appreciates him. In terms of the explicit factor analytic model, these two features are stated succinctly in these specification equations as follows:

(1) $$a_{ij} = b_{j1}T_{1i} + b_{j2}T_{2i} + \ldots + b_{jk}T_{ki}$$

where T_1, T_2, to T_k, are various traits, drives, etc., scored for the individual i and the b_1, b_2, to b_k values are the behavioral indices which show how much each trait is involved, in the situation j, in producing the action (response) a_j. The weights of the different factors are presumed to act additively, and the factors also act linearly in the sense that a given increment in a factor always brings about a given increment in the intensity of the behavior, a_j.

Doubtless, we may want later to adopt theories which assume some more complex relationship than this. For example, we may want to depart from a linear arrangement, and suppose that as trait T_x increases in the first part of its range, the behavior shows very little change, but that the latter increases much more rapidly as T gets to the upper part of its range. This might be represented mathematically by writing in T^2 instead of T. Also, one can imagine that factors might act other than additively, e.g., in some multiplicative relationship. For example, the increase in impulsiveness of behavior might be more accurately expressed as the *product* of ego weakness (C in the 16 PF Test) and high ergic tension (Q_4 in the 16 PF) factors. Or again, we might suppose that in a certain syndrome type, such as a psychopath, the interactions of traits follow a somewhat different set of principles or mathematical laws from those seen in the average person. Such improvements are to be pursued; but we must walk before we run. These further developments can only go ahead once we have mastered the simpler principles and once actual research has located enough of the factors which obey the simpler laws to be able to recognize when we are encountering any failure of those laws.

The actual outcome of a couple of generations of application of research by factor analytic methods to those sciences, e.g., psychology, sociology, economics, where a bewildering and endless array of variables demands such sophisticated methods, has actually been a remarkably successful one. In each of these fields, it has yielded enough firm, recognizable, meaningful factor structure entities to justify the statement that the factor model is one of the most universally applicable ones in science. Present factor methods are not by any means the last word, but they are a very important first word. Through the conversion of clinical speculations about structure to precise measurable and experimentally replicable patterns it has given a more worthwhile and testable basis to theory. And now this foundation promises an era of definite laws about the ways in which factors change with age, genetic influences, learning situations, conflict, etc.

Our Present Understanding of the Nature of Psychological Source Traits

Although the purpose of this chapter is to proceed to the most comprehensive, useful, and dependable set of models for the general tasks

of diagnosis, yet it would be well to spend time on some further sub-
stantiation of one of the most important elements in that armory—
namely, the *source trait* as defined by the factor model.

The term *source trait* has been suggested for a particular, more
exactly defined factor, because it is *the source of change variance* in
actual variables. Further, it offers a clear and useful contrast to the term
surface trait, which simply says that a set of variables form a correlation cluster, i.e., that they "go together" at a superficial level. Later,
we shall bring out some valuable extra "understanding" of a case which
can be obtained through contrasting surface and source trait measurements, but for the moment, we might prepare a firmer foundation for
source traits themselves, by a brief overview of the concrete findings
and their use in diagnosis and prognosis. Again, before proceeding, we
should remind the reader that not all factors are source traits, since
the mathematician plays with a great variety of factors which do not
fit the more exacting scientific model. A source trait is a factor which,
in addition to being a factor, fits certain restrictions which would be
required by any real model proposing that a source trait be identified
with an influence or an underlying cause. These specific restrictions
we can leave to the textbooks on factor analysis in scientific experiment (Cattell, 1966a, 1966b).

Granted that the investigator is using factor analysis, he can apply
it to three kinds of observation, namely, (1) specific behaviors evaluated, i.e., quantified, in the natural life situation, (2) specific behaviors quantified in a test situation, but in a test of the questionnaire
kind in which the subject subjectively, introspectively evaluates his
own behavior, as in the consulting room, and (3) test behaviors in an
objective test situation, i.e., a miniature situation, as in the laboratory,
in which the individual behaves in response to stimuli and has his
behavior recorded. These have been called (Cattell, 1957), respectively, L-, Q-, and T-data. Furthermore, we can have a cross-classi-
fication of such data according to whether it deals with (a) abilities,
(b) general personality and temperament traits, or (c) dynamic,
interest, and motivation traits. As every student knows, factor analysis
applied to cognitive performance in test situations led comparatively
early to a first solution of the ability structure problem by Spearman's
theory of general intelligence. Most psychologists are now fairly familiar
with the structuring of the cognitive domain in terms of the newly
discovered fluid and crystallized general intelligence factors (Horn,
1966), Thurstone's primary abilities, and certain creative abilities
studied by Guilford. When these methods reached out into the general
personality factor domain, as measured by questionnaire responses,

i.e., the second kind of observation above, some two dozen factors were soon recognized, and confirmed (Cattell, 1957; Cattell, Tatro, and Komlos, 1964). These have been principally expressed in the last fifteen years in two widely used scales, namely, the Guilford-Zimmerman Scales (Guilford, 1960) and the Cattell-Tatsuoka-Eber 16 PF Test (as well as the High School Personality Questionnaire [Cattell, Wagner, and Cattell, 1970], the Child Personality Questionnaire [Porter and Schaie, 1969], and other questionnaires which measure these same factors at earlier development stages).

From the work of Schaie (1963), Norman (1963), and others, it would seem that these factors in questionnaires represent the same traits as those which appear in ratings by observers, though the "mental interiors" sometimes place a different evaluative judgment and emphasis on the behavior pattern. But, essentially, this approach through ratings and questionnaires, i.e., the first two media above, has resulted in the crystallization of concepts of source traits which follow in the general clinical tradition. That is to say, one can recognize in these patterns of expression a definite concept very similar to what most psychiatrists mean by ego strength, another very similar to super-ego strength, another expressing schizophrenic tendencies, another expressing drive tension (id) level, and so on. Additionally, a number of interesting new patterns have turned up which, like many things invisible before the time of the microscope, had evidently escaped the naked eye of the clinician, despite the Q-data and L-data media being identical with those through which the doctor gets information about his patient.

To anyone familiar with the history of science, e.g., with the history of Pasteur's impact upon medicine, it is perhaps not surprising that these new experimentally based ideas have not been immediately appreciated and embraced by psychiatrists! Thus, there has been hesitation among some psychiatrists to utilize such somewhat strange new terms as premsia (I), parmia (H), ergic tension (Q_4), etc. for the factor analytically demonstrated source trait dimensions, although they have in ten years been replicated and confirmed again and again, and shown to have important predictive value for diagnosis and therapy. Doubtless, however, time and the experience of the more enterprising will take care of this.

Nothing further will be said here specifically about the number of these factors, their nature, and their predictive value in concrete clinical situations, since they are very adequately dealt with in the chapter by Horn and Sweney. However, to complete our brief illustration of the source trait model we should pause to glance at the second realm of investigation into personality, namely, that through *objective* types of personality test (T-data). Here, some twenty factors have been recognized, which have simply been given universal index (UI) numbers, as the vitamin researchers first did with their factors. Again, several of these patterns are recognizable as dimensions known earlier from quite different kinds of methodological approach, e.g., clinical hunch. For example, one of them appears to be general intelligence and another appears to be general anxiety. There is also a curious relationship between the objective test medium, on the one hand, and the rating and questionnaire medium, on the other. We should expect the same personality source traits to turn up from both media of observation, but Q-data seems to have a greater "fineness of grain" so that factors are picked up in the coarser-grained objective test realm only at what is technically, factor analytically called the second order. Some of Eysenck's MPI (Maudsley Personality Inventory) factors in the questionnaire realm seem also to be at the second order.

There is much research still needed here into remaining obscurities, but there are also the beginnings of law and clarity. Thus, the 16 PF questionnaire can be scored *either* for 16 primary personality factors *or* for 6 second-order factors, similar to those in Eysenck's analyses (1957). Second-stratum factors can be regarded as broader organizing principles among the primaries, just as, for example, one can speak either of suns and planets (primaries) or solar systems (secondaries). There is today some debate as to whether it is more effective to work with measures and concepts from first-order or second-order domains, but the argument of the present writer is that one should always work at both, i.e., that one should first know what the patient's scores are on the primary factors, and also know the broader, cruder dimensions as shown on the gross second-order factor measures. Of course, the great advantage of the media we are now discussing— T-data or objective test factor measures—is that the evaluation of the scores of the individual does not depend on observers, who themselves have a personal equation distorting the L-data (life record, in situ) evaluation, or on the questionnaire type of response which can be faked to an appreciable extent, no matter how ingenious the psychologist is in constructing the items.

The great bulk of clinical research has so far been through the questionnaire and only to a lesser degree through the objective tests, for the simple reason that a questionnaire is easier and quicker to give! In partial defense it may be said that in most cases a reasonable cooperativeness on the part of the patient can be depended upon. Nevertheless, the present writer would argue that the future lies in the realm of objective tests. Ultimately, psychiatrists and their technicians will need to become skilled in the administration and use of objective psychological tests if the full assistance of this approach is to be gained. The day may not be far off when a one- or two-hour testing by an objective test battery, with the aid of a skilled psychometric technician, will be as common in the consultation plan of the psychiatrist as is the obtaining of blood chemistry and other data through the assistance of a physiological technician to the general physician.

Let us next look at traits from the standpoint not of media of observation but of modalities. It is probably correct to say that the majority of *clinical* psychological examinations of adults do not include the first modality—*ability* measurements—though the latter may nevertheless have relevance in those cases which include maladjustments in a job. The second modality—that of general personality and *temperament* dimensions—has also been somewhat slighted by at any rate the psychoanalyst, although there is no doubt that information about these relatively fixed nondynamic characteristics of the individual could considerably improve one's evaluation of probable success of various alternative possibilities of adjustment. But the third modality —that of *motivation* and *dynamic* observations—has always been keenly appreciated by every variety of psychiatrist, and it is here that, until recently, psychometry unfortunately had the least to offer.

Progress in factor analytic structuration of this third modality of trait has admittedly been more recent than in the other two, but the last fifteen years have seen considerable progress. Putting aside interest check lists as in the Strong or Kuder interest blank, which suffer from the same liability to distortion as the self-evaluative, questionnaire approach and have been directed to occupational rather than clinical psychology, the most significant progress for the clinician is that made with *objective* tests of motivation strength. These are nonopinionnaire approaches which utilize such responses as misperception, distortion of belief, psychogalvanic response, spontaneous attention movements, blood pressure changes, etc., in relation to stimuli chosen from dynamically important life adjustment areas. Here, the big discovery has been that human drive patterns indubitably exist; these have been called ergs to avoid confusion with the instinct theories of animals though they are quite similar in number and apparent nature to those in the primates and even the higher mammals. Along with these dynamic factors have emerged factors for ego strength and superego strength already recognized in Q- and L-data but now seen and measured through their dynamic manifestations only. All important conceptual and measurement developments in this dynamic, objective motivation measurement domain are discussed thoroughly in the accompanying chapter by Horn and Sweney.

Despite the gloomy predictions of critics that multivariate analysis would not be able to catch up with the subtleties of dynamic traits, these patterns are surprisingly clear in their form. Of course, in their level they fluctuate from day to day more than do the personality traits and certainly more than do the abilities. However, they have proved even more potent than general personality source traits in relation to clinical work and have opened up a new domain of calculation which has aptly been called the dynamic calculus; it is described by Horn and Sweney.

So much for the general survey of the areas and kinds of source traits which have been discovered in this generation and which will be discussed in appropriate chapters here. A more basic question which the psychiatrist will perhaps immediately want to raise is whether it is correct to assume that these patterns, largely found through psychometric research on normal people, apply also to the pathological realm. Along with this question we must face in the next section a still bigger question, namely, how far factors which are characteristic of people in general can hope to describe the highly specific symptoms and conflicts of a particular individual.

How Far Can Source Traits Handle the Abnormal and the Idiosyncratic?

The question of whether the source traits found in the psychological investigation of structure in normal people have useful application to pathological cases, can only be answered empirically. Factor analyses have, in fact, been carried out on abnormal, pathological groups, and over most variables they have yielded the same factors as with normals (Cattell, 1957; Cattell, Delhees, Tatro, and Nesselroade, in preparation; Dubin, 1950; Dubin, Cattell, and Saunders, 1954).

Factor analyses have also been carried out in *mixed* normal and abnormal groups, when again structures recognizably the same have emerged. However, these same results have made it quite apparent that the normal and the abnormal may be, typically, at very different *levels* on these source traits (Cattell, Tatro, and Komlos, 1964). Consequently, the first and major contribution from these batteries in diagnostic use arises from indications of such substantial difference of levels. Highly significant differences have been recognized in such formerly familiar personality factors as anxiety (UI 24), regression (UI 23), ego strength (C), general inhibition (UI 17), guilt proneness (O), as well as on such still uninterpreted source traits as UI 16, UI 30, and UI 33. On the vexed question of whether neurotics and psychotics have similar or different deviations the definite answer is that some abnormal deviations they share in common and that others are peculiar to psychosis.

What brings special interest in this connection is that when a set of items dealing wholly with abnormal responses, as in the MMPI or in some of the early work with Dubin (Cattell and Specht, 1969), are factored, one finds within this abnormal material first the personality factors already seen among normals and then some new dimensions. The former imply that quite normal types of trait may pass into abnormal expressions, as more deviant scores on the trait. This "pathology as quantitative deviation" is shown again by the work of Rickels and Cattell (1965) and others demonstrating that pathological cases tend to move back to normal levels as they return to apparent normality *clinically,* through therapeutic activity.

For example, both on the anxiety factor and on the regression factor, UI 23, as the recent studies by Cattell, Rickels, and others show, neurotics are highly deviant. That is to say, they are on an extreme level on anxiety and on an extreme level on the regression dimension. But both by therapy and by spontaneous recovery they tend to move toward normal values. Similarly, the work of Tatro has shown that psychotics are highly deviant on the factors we call UI 25, UI 30, and UI 33, though here the shifts with time have not been studied. But diagnostically it is at any rate clear that as far as certain aspects of abnormality are concerned, the abnormality can be recognized instantly in psychometric terms by unusual degree of deviation on a trait which every individual possesses to some degree, regardless of deviations also on "strictly pathological" traits.

Nevertheless, it is also true that certain factors are found which seem to be peculiar to the pathological groups and represent some dimensions of divergence which are practically meaningless for most normal people, in the sense that normals are not spread out at all thereon. Presumably, much the same normal and abnormal dimensionality could be found with physical illnesses. It is possible that UI 23 is in essence an abnormal dimension in that if we take a group of individuals well selected for mental health, such as air pilots, we find practically no variation on this dimension. In a less-selected "normal" population, which includes 5 to 20 percent of neurotics (according to one's definition!), some variation can be seen, and when normals and clinical cases are mixed the range becomes quite large. Furthermore, in the recent factorization by Eber (1966) and Cattell and Specht

(1969), of the MMPI jointly with the 16 PF it is shown that there are at least four dimensions—which have been called psychasthenia, general psychoticism, hypochondria, and depression—that scarcely seem to have any variation in the normal population, but are directions of deviation over which the clinical population scatters itself rather far.

The issue as to whether new source trait dimensions are necessary adequately to describe pathology is one closely bound up with the old argument among psychiatrists as to whether mental disorders belong to the same general conceptual framework as physical disease, or whether they should be regarded as a purely functional disorder in the sense that there is some kind of imbalance among tendencies essentially normal. The "dynamic explanation" of neuroticism and mental disorder is, of course, in this latter category in that it conceives the difficulty, indeed, as something purely in the dynamic satisfaction area of the individual, i.e., as a tangle among essentially normal needs. The germ theory of disease, on the other hand, points to a pathological organism (a parasite situation) in which a specific disease process is occurring, and certain other models of physical disease also recognize some quite specific pathological agent.

As far as psychometric evidence goes, it would seem that we must be prepared to accept both of these models of mental disorder. The fact that most of the abnormality of the neurotic can be expressed as a deviant and unusual pattern in ordinary source traits, i.e., in patterns first discovered in normal ranges of the population, suggests that neurosis, at any rate, is a purely functional disorder. On the other hand, as just indicated, perhaps half a dozen new factors of an almost purely pathological kind have to be added to a measuring instrument if it is to do justice to the full description of the psychotic. Indeed, it is for this reason that the half-dozen "pathology supplement scales" have been added to the 16 PF, which initially had 16 factors entirely defined through analyses of the normal range of behavior. In regard to the latter, the schizophrenic is significantly deviant, e.g., he is more introverted on the normal personality factors on the 16 PF than is the general nonschizophrenic population. But obviously this cannot be the whole story because there are great numbers of individuals who score just as introvertedly as the schizophrenic, but who are considered entirely normal. Incidentally, one advantage of using a scale like the 16 PF, with both normal and pathological dimensions, is that it gives one a picture of the specific prepsychotic personality of the psychotic, along with the new evidence of the pathological deviations which have become superimposed.

While this is not the place to go into complex personality theories, one may yet point out that the whole pattern of the introvert-extrovert second order factor suggests the theory of "spiral action." That is to say, it suggests that once deviation reaches a certain point, there is a sort of "chain reaction" among the various components of introversion which may force it to an extreme degree. It is conceivable—and is a matter now for very careful factor analytic investigation—that some of the pathology dimensions are, in fact, secondary derivatives, through the formation initially of special relational patterns among primary source traits. That is to say, granted certain unfortunate combinations and patterns of personality traits, which bring about internal stresses and inabilities to cope with environmental situations, any further unfavorable development in the environment may suffice to bring on these imbalances and extreme scores which our measurements show to exist in the psychotic. On the other hand, such a purely functional explanation may not be sufficient to handle most of the psychotic manifestations one sees. We have to consider the possibility of specific inherited defects, and of specific environmental agencies of stress— even of brain damage, physical poisoning, etc.—which limit to a crucial degree the individual's capacity to adjust. It would be particularly interesting in this connection to research further the nature of those objective test personality dimensions which have been indexed as UI 30, UI 33, and UI 25, and which are particularly connected with psychosis.

Regardless of whether we are dealing with common traits whose structure is visible in the normal population or common traits which emerge in clear outline only in deviant, pathological populations, the approach so far described in this section would express the uniqueness of the individual as the uniqueness of a combination of common traits. Further, it would conceive the breakdown of adaptation as an "economic" matter—a failure of summation of this and that capacity to adjust (as worked out in the specification equation above) to reach a level sufficient to cope with the particular level of demand of the environmental situation. It would regard this as partly functional in the sense that some different use of the *same* average personality resources might be a very healthy adjustment, and partly as the effect of a pathological agent, either an intolerable situation in the environment or some constitutional or endocrine or neurological failure not inherent in the personality per se.

Such explanation in terms of a constellation of *common* source traits, or of common trauma, has often been regarded by various schools of pathology, e.g., the psychoanalytic, as not enough. They believe that neither diagnostic description nor therapeutic steps can be adequate unless one deals with events that are absolutely unique to the patient. And in this they are almost certainly right, though they may not have understood how far a nosology and description of the unique in terms of particular combinations of common traits can go. These critics of common trait explanations point to the obvious fact that the majority of patients are preoccupied with some symptom or source of conflict which descriptively at least is specific to that patient. For example, Charlie Smith may be brought to the Child Guidance Clinic because of the uncontrollable way in which he spits at and beats his aunt when she visits the family. Mary James may have a phobia and hysterical fit which comes on when she sits in the back seat of a particular automobile, and Phil Brown may have the delusion that every green book he picks up in the library contains a bomb. The experienced clinician (though the Skinnerian behavior therapist will not agree) at once replies on this issue that the psychiatrist who is stressing specificity is getting too fascinated with symptoms and overlooking fundamental causes, e.g., that Charlie Smith is living at a demonstrably high level in the ergic tension factor (the source trait, Q_4), that the given phobia of Mary James is only one manifestation of an abnormally high anxiety level, and that the delusion of Phil Brown is also only one manifestation of a demonstrably very deviant score on the general regression tendency, UI 23, with its associated proneness to fantasy. With apologies again to recent views in behavior therapy, the older clinician will say that curing a symptom is not curing the personality disorder.

Even though the common traits may thus represent the more important part of the unique deviation, there is no question that descriptively they fail to include these highly specific dynamic conflicts, fixations, etc., with which the patient is greatly concerned and with which many psychiatrists—both psychoanalytic and behavior-therapeutic (reflexological)—believe therapy should be concerned. Regardless of whether the emphasis on unique traits is psychoanalytic or reflexological (or merely ideographic-aesthetic as in the case of Allport), modern psychometry has a definite answer—outside and beyond common source traits—for this need. It is the unique trait pattern as revealed and defined by P-technique. In P-technique (Cattell, 1957; Harris, 1963) the patient is measured on a set of interests, emotional attitudes, and even physiological manifestations of the dynamic trait areas in which one is interested—including any known symptom. The measures or observations are repeated for the patient every day for perhaps one hundred days. The scores on the variables are then correlated over time and factor analyzed to see that functionally unitary dynamic source trait structures vary independently from day to day and how the symptoms are accounted for by those traits.

P-technique, if it can be rendered practicable by computer help, represents a signal advance in modern diagnostics, for it is nothing less than a quantitative psychoanalysis. It finds out what goes together and what causal connections exist by the same principles as clinicians have long been using less exactly and explicitly in a long series of interview sessions. They are, however, raised to a higher degree of explicitness of dynamic model, and benefited by a new precision of calculation from use of the computer. P-technique, in fact, can supplement the description of a patient in terms of the number of common source traits, by showing what the *unique connections* of source traits are in *his own particular* dynamics. For example, the general source trait of anxiety can have its level measured in a patient by a scale which depends on the chief expressions that anxiety takes in most people. But when we do a P-technique analysis, which would include these common measures of anxiety levels as "markers," we are likely to find that the expression of anxiety in that given individual has many idiosyncrasies, e.g., in the phobia of the patient cited above, against sitting in the back seat of an automobile. The strengths of these particular attachments are shown quantitatively in the factor pattern from a P-technique analysis.

At this point in research progress, we do not have to apologize for the fact that few clinics are equipped either technically, or in terms of suitable recording apparatus and computers, for making P-technique analyses. Suffice it that basic research has shown clearly enough that this is an entirely effective technique, and it is presumably only a matter of time, as with any other human invention, before it is brought into convenient form for routine work in clinics. Actually, our concern in this chapter is even more theoretical, namely, with the conceptual status of the *unique source trait pattern* (which P-technique generates) for description, classification, and other aspects of diagnosis. Our conclusion is that the greater part of the uniqueness of the individual diagnosis can be handled in common trait terms with batteries designed for the general population, and the rest in unique source trait terms, with batteries specifically tailored to a specific patient for specific diagnostic purposes.

Thus, all the specific qualities in the psychiatrist's description of the usual patient can be encompassed in psychometric measurement. It is achieved first in terms of the absolutely unique pattern provided by the profile of combinations of levels of common source traits and, secondly, in terms of the unique source traits found by P-technique and other approaches to analyzing the single individual psychometrically. Parenthetically, when we proposed this as being a comprehensive system of description, it must be remembered that we are supposing a comprehensiveness of the batteries themselves (in regard to source traits) which actually far exceeds the quite inadequate range of test resources with which the typical clinical psychologist has struggled along for the last forty years. We are proposing instead that all three modalities—abilities, general personality (temperament) traits, and dynamic structural traits—will be covered, e.g., by such batteries as Thurstone Primary Abilities, the 16 PF Test, the MMPI, or the Guilford-Zimmerman Scales, and such recent incursions into new areas of testing as the Motivation Analysis Test, covering the principal drives and dynamic structures, as described in the chapter by Horn and Sweney. This means that the resulting unique diagnostic description of the patient in terms of common source traits will cover a profile of perhaps thirty or more normal and pathological dimensions.

The Four Basic Models: Trait, State, Process, and Type

TRAIT

Many traditional psychometrists have rested content with the above schema of diagnostic description through a profile source-trait measurement. Mathematically this represents the unique individual as a point in a k-dimensional coordinate system, each coordinate corresponding to a factorially defined source trait. The modern psychometrist cannot, however, regard this mathematical model as all that he needs to describe even the essentials of the individual personality. No matter how well the original research may have been done which revealed the functionally unitary traits, and no matter how valid the batteries may have become for measuring each of these functionally distinct source traits, the psychiatrist will feel that the picture is incomplete. It is incomplete both because it has supposed a goodness of fit of this simple model to the complexities of human nature which is not always attained and because, like any other reductive abstraction, it omits a large variety of further aspects of human nature which require incorporation in any good quantitative system of dynamic diagnosis.

Without wandering afield over some of the concrete aspects which may have been missed, let us say that virtually all can be incorporated in three further models, which we shall call those of *state, process,* and *type.* These need to be added to the source trait model if our quantitative analysis is to be reasonably complete. Let us now see how each of these concepts is realizable in a definite model on which basic research can go forward to establish various concrete instances and patterns with which measurement can work.

STATE

Obviously no attempt to predict what an individual will do or to understand why he will do it can be complete without having what is popularly described as his mood, dynamic motivational condition, etc. There exist many proposed mood scales, e.g., the Clyde mood scale or those of Nowlis, but practically all of them are subjective in the sense that the test constructor has adopted popular categories, e.g., elation-depression, gregarious feeling, etc., without any demonstration of the functional unity of such states. The means for investigating the number and nature of moods and dynamic states exist, however, in the P-technique approach described above and also in what is called the differential R-technique. The latter measures perhaps two hundred people on one occasion and then either subjects them to some disturbing stimulus or allows everyday life to provide the disturbing stimuli and measures them again after a lapse of time—two or three days perhaps. The difference scores are then calculated and correlated and the factor analysis applied to these differences defines the number of independent dimensions required to describe human mood changes.

Basic progress has been made in recognizing and measuring psychological states through the work of Cattell and Scheier (1961), Nesselroade (1967), Van Egeren (1963), Karvonen (see Cattell, 1957), Williams (1959), and others. The upshot is that some nine or ten main state dimensions of a general nature have been recognized, plus a dozen more in the motivational realm. In the first realm, such dimensions as arousal vs. torpor, elation vs. depression, stress vs. relaxation, high anxiety vs. low anxiety, etc., have been recognized and rendered measurable. Even a second-order structure is known among these states (Uhr and Miller, 1961). From a practical point of view, the chief gains have been such information as that anxiety and stress are two distinct states, with a very different pattern of physiological and psychological expression, or the psychometric realization that anxiety as a state requires a somewhat different battery for its accurate measurement from that which is valid for anxiety as a trait. This last is crucial for diagnosis, permitting one to distinguish characterological anxiety—with its particular import for neuroticism—from a merely temporary state of anxiety, which can be entirely healthy and normal in response to a real life situation.

A state is operationally defined as *a particular pattern of affected variables,* with known loadings fixed for each. It is a factor analytic statement about how rapidly and in which direction each of these variables change as the state comes on. For example, we know that both anxiety and effort stress load systolic and diastolic blood pressure positively, but the factor pattern shows that anxiety affects systolic more and stress diastolic (Nesselroade, 1967). Attention has happily been drawn, by Wessman and Ricks (1966), to the importance of states in a taxonomy of human nature, but in spite of the increasing interest in the topic most writers have remained at the vague and popular level and failed to master either the technical models needed or even the clear results which have emerged from the use of those models. Just as the uniqueness of an individual's personality can be represented by a unique point in a k-dimensional space, k being at present some 20 to 30 dimensions, so now the unique blend of feeling characteristic of a mood state can be represented as a point in a 10- to 20-dimensional space—once we have discovered a few more of the dimensions! Many matters remain to be investigated here, notably as to whether the pattern of change as a certain state subsides and returns to an average position is quite the same as when it is in a rising phase. Also, it is necessary, as with source traits, to find out whether two states may sometimes act more than additively in regard to their effects on a particular variable. This investigation of state has been particularly illuminating in regard to the tie-up of physiological variables with psychological measures, and offers new insights into the way the body engineers psychosomatic symptoms.

PROCESS

The reasonable objection which a psychiatrist and, for that matter, a physiologist, might have to much which the traditional psychologist has been content to achieve in his descriptions and measurements, resides in the psychometric description being merely "a description at an instant in time." The psychiatrist, for instance, recognizes that he makes his diagnoses partly by some particular *process* which goes on in a given patient as well as by traits at a given moment. He does this, for example, in chronic undifferentiated schizophrenia, or in diagnosing a certain depression as either involutional or part of a manic-depressive syndrome. Functional personality measurement, however, does not make this mistake of classical psychometrics. It encompasses other models than traits—for example, states and processes. In linking measurement to general structural personality theory, it necessarily has developed models to describe and measure processes—and the imaginative steps in mathematical statistics to go with these models (Cattell, 1966a,

1966b). But, once again, these developments expose the great methodological gap between the subjectivity and unreliability of researches in which a single observer will describe and "score" a process and the precision which is needed in anything which can be described as a truly scientific treatment.

The first aim in process study, as in many other fields, is to lay out an agreed taxonomy. This requires an experimental attack to recognize the number and nature of processes in human personality. Considerable progress is made toward describing processes when we have succeeded in describing correctly the structure at a given moment, i.e., the individual's position on a system of states. Once this technical mastery has been achieved, the movement from Structure 1 to Structure 2 can be accurately described, at any rate, in terms of the given instantaneous structures. These instantaneous values can, of course, be measures on both traits and states, for both, as we have just said, are needed to describe the individual at an instant. For example, if factor analysis demonstrates the existence of two distinct general abilities in growing children, namely, fluid general intelligence and crystallized general intelligence, then the intellectual growth process in a given child can be described more accurately in terms of this analysis than if we had no precise way of saying what his intellectual level might be at some given calendar point. A difference, on source trait and state measurements, is thus a way of describing at least the beginning and the end of a process accurately and thus assigning quantitative values to the process change, whether it be gained through psychotherapy or maturational or accidental environmentally determined development.

But this mere difference score is not enough, since it does not provide a means of recognizing how many distinct processes have intervened, in a functional sense, to account for a given change. Processes presumably have their natural forms, in the sense that each has its natural *sequence* of values on states and traits, which can be recognized by this sequential pattern repeating itself, as in dawn or sunset, harvesting, adolescence, or the adjustment process in a successful marriage. Here, again, the multivariate model can provide a firm framework. Any process can be described as a pathway in a multidimensional space, as illustrated in three dimensions in Diagram 1, provided we have first established the dimensions through our source trait and state analysis procedures above. That is, the process is describable as a particular succession in source trait and state measures (these states and traits having been rendered objectively measurable) as indicated in the basic data relation matrix in the upper part of Diagram 1. To discover this pattern it is necessary to study a number of such sequences in different patients and in normal individuals to establish whether there is a highly characteristic sequence, i.e., a "type" now in terms of state sequences. A methodology for handling this exists, but it is a complex one and the reader must be referred elsewhere for an account of it (Cattell, 1966a, 1966b). No experiment of any magnitude has yet been accomplished with this new methodology, so it

Diagram 1. Factor Analysis to Obtain Process Dimensions, and the Representation of a Particular Process

(A) DIRECTLY ON VARIABLES AS SCORE SEQUENCE

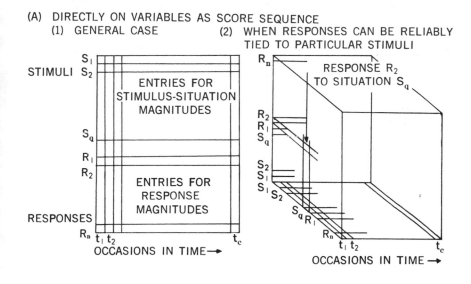

(1) GENERAL CASE

(2) WHEN RESPONSES CAN BE RELIABLY TIED TO PARTICULAR STIMULI

(B) IN FEWER DIMENSIONS, FROM FACTORING VARIABLES, AND EXPRESSED (FOR TWO DIMENSIONS) GRAPHICALLY

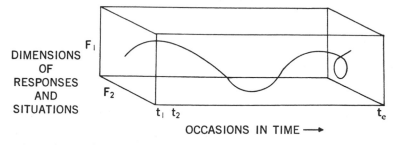

is not yet possible to illustrate the model by clearly demonstrated instances, as is so easily possible in the case of source traits and states.

TYPE

Describing types is a very ancient human amusement, much repeated in our own day by such writers as Jung (1923), Kretschmer (1925), Sheldon and Stevens (1942), and, for that matter, every club gossip. The trouble is that most of the time these writers are not really describing types, but only the imaginary individuals who stand at the opposite ends of some single source trait dimension, be it at the first-order or second-order source trait. Thus, extroversion-introversion is undoubtedly a second-order dimension in the personality domain and it is very simple to speak of an individual at one pole as an extrovert and of the person at the other pole as an introvert. The difficulty is that no one actually stands right at the extreme poles. If this were so, we would be able to designate only two people as "in" the types or, alternatively,

Diagram 2. **Spatial Representation of Species Types**

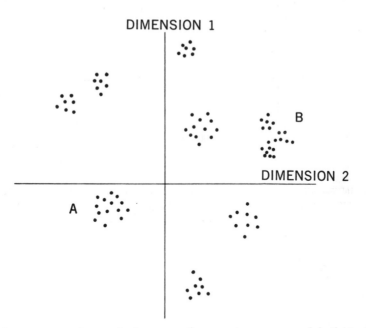

Species types, e.g. syndrome clusters, are discovered as groups of individuals close together, as at A, according to the pattern similarity coefficient r_p. They may group again, loosely, in a genus, as at B. This diagram shows that there can be many more species than dimensions and that distribution on dimensions can remain normal.

would have to choose some quite arbitrary limit at which to cut off as we approach the mean. Obviously it would be much simpler to substitute for any use of "type" in this sense the simple assignment of a score on a single dimension.

But there is another and nonredundant use of "type" in which the speaker means that the individual belongs to some distinct species, in the sense that any biologist uses "species." Such species can be recognized, located, and measured as modal collections of people in multidimensional space, as shown in Diagram 2. If such a diagram were built up by biological measurements on a large collection of animals, for example, then these groups which we call species would show themselves as globular groupings, which would cluster again in terms of genera, and so on through a philogenetic classification system. There has been little real evidence presented that such types exist in human beings, and it is certainly true that, as regards the major source traits, e.g., intelligence, we can demonstrate a normal distribution, with absolutely no modal clustering except the usual mounting up toward the median mid-point. But the lack of recognition of need for such type concepts is partly due to lack of research with adequate methodology. Almost certainly, such true species type groupings would be found in terms of, for example, occupational interest measurements, subcultures such as social class and religious subcultures, various biological constitutional patterns such as Down's syndrome, and, of course, the behavioral symptom syndromes which psychiatrists recognize in the field of pathology.

There is no doubt that, from a prediction point of view, it would be very advantageous to know about the existence of such "clumpings" in psychological trait space. As Meehl (1954) and others have rightly stressed, there are many cases where the simple linear prediction from source traits, as in our above specification equation, does not tightly fit the known facts. Curvilinear relationships and a species typology structure are natural associates in any statistical treatment and belong to the same modification of the model from simple source traits and linear relations. They are not identical, or absolutely necessary concomitants—one can have nonlinearity without actual species type crystallizations. But where we have a type, the combination of trait scores which contributes to a certain end result is different from that which occurs in the general space, i.e., for individuals who are not in types but between types. In other words, the behavior in question becomes a function of the total pattern in a way which is different from the function applied to the source trait scores of an individual when distinct types are not involved. Before types and type methods can be used and involved in prediction and calculations, however, it is necessary to recognize and catalog the psychological types which definitely exist.

The history of attempts to locate types is not a very edifying one. There are serious flaws in such approaches as Q-sort and Q-technique, for example, though what has more recently been called Q-technique (Cattell, 1966b) offers a way out of the difficulties. Indeed, practicable computer programs have now been constructed, e.g., the Taxonome program, into which data can be fed and information returned regarding the groupings. Parenthetically, what is called the multiple discriminant function technique is *not* a means of finding types. It is only a means of using measurements to *separate* types more cleanly once one has spotted by other means, such as Taxonome, what the *natural* main type groupings are. That something badly needs to be done to improve the psychiatrist's technical and conceptual treatment of types is evident from the periodic phases of disillusionment with classificatory schemes which sweep over the psychiatric world. Every mental hospital case conference, for example, is in danger of generating personal disputes from failures to agree on the assignment of a particular individual to a diagnostic category, and, at the national conference level, one periodically sees complete failure to agree even on the nature of the categories into which patients might be placed. Nevertheless, we now have means for attacking this in a more objective and less arbitrary way, namely, by applying the pattern-similarity coefficient to large numbers of mental hospital patients measured on 20 or 30 of the above common source trait scales. It will need much organization and careful statistical work to handle this, but the principles, though complex (Cattell, 1966a, 1966b; Lingoes, 1967; Sokal and Sneath, 1963), undoubtedly now exist to carry out a comprehensive job in this realm.

When we know more about the number of species types which exist and the general "texture" of type distributions in this field, it will be time to begin refining our general specification equation of source traits for predicting pathological behavior into a family of specification equations modified for each particular type and subtype. Meanwhile, we must recognize that the type concept and the accompanying model are an important supplement to the handling of descriptions by source trait scores.

Surface and Source Trait: Psychometric Depth Analysis

The four "ideal forms" which have been briefly operationally designated in the paragraphs above constitute an exhaustive view of the measurement concept resources available to us at the present moment. Indeed, it is difficult to see how any measurement or description can be developed in psychology which will not fall into one of the above four categories. One might be inclined to raise the question whether, for example, an individual's use of defense mechanisms, or the nature of his dynamic conflict, or the character of his ethical and general value system are comprehended by measurements in terms of the above models. The work of Wenig (1962), of Hundleby, Pawlik, and Cattell (1965), and of others shows that defense mechanism reaction tendencies behave like any other source traits and can be so located and measured. The work of Sweney (1966), Williams (1959), and others (see Cattell, 1957) shows that the degree and nature of dynamic conflicts can be expressed both as patterns of positive and negative, integrated and unintegrated scores on dynamic traits and as measures on source-trait-like tension and conflict dimensions. As for value systems, these show as unique source trait patterns within the self-sentiment and the superego factors found either in questionnaire attitude tests or in objective motivation measures of attitudes.

In short, there seems no cogent argument for rejecting the conclusion that the above four models are sufficient for and, indeed, exhaustive of the descriptive devices which any psychiatric diagnostic system may seek to employ. Nevertheless, as stated, they have quite unequal degrees of useful applicability at the present time, because insufficient research has been done to give us, for example, an experimentally well-based equipment of diagnostic types and still less has been done toward recognizing a taxonomy of processes, which are indeed a necessary part of the description of any individual for diagnostic and prognostic purposes.

With this survey of the essentials of possible models briefly concluded, it is appropriate to return to some special developments within the trait model, to which the remainder of this section will be devoted.

When the trait notion is examined more closely, it exhibits a duality, as noted in our introductory section, namely, that psychologists have inveterately used the word *trait* for a correlation cluster or *surface* trait as well as for a simple structure factor or *source* trait. When one designates a conversion hysteric, for example, by indicating such variables as unstable emotionality, a superficiality of social relationship, the presence of apparently physical disabilities which are not truly neurological, and a certain *belle indifférence* of mood, one is strictly speaking of a surface trait, i.e., a pattern of behavior in which these four variables are, as an empirical fact, observed to go together (and which, incidentally, we have reason to believe go together in a lesser degree down the range of deviation, including the average, normal person). In short, if we were to estimate people on these traits and correlate the scores, we would discover a correlation cluster of four variables, the correlations between pairs of which are positive and high in all of the six combinations among the four variables. However, there is every reason to believe, from present evidence, that several distinct factors or influences contribute to this cluster being strongly developed in a particular person, so it is not a single source trait. In fact, if we indicate correlations by cosines among vectors (according to the regular geometric convention for correlations) as in Diagram 3, then four or five correlation clusters can be represented as shown, whereas factors are independent of them, constituting the coordinate system in this case of two distinct source traits.

Incidentally, these models are not peculiar to psychology; we use the surface trait kind of description in many realms of life, where,

Diagram 3. Distinction of Surface and Source Traits: Spatial Representation

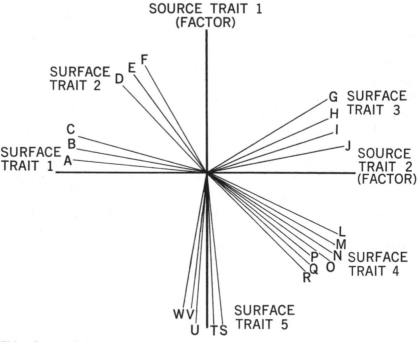

This diagram follows the convention that a correlation between two symptoms (variables) is represented as a cosine. Thus, r of l and g is +0.9. The source traits are uncorrelated. The symptoms bunch in five distinct surface traits which, however, apart from specifics, can be accounted for by only two source traits. (See relation of MMPI to 16 PF Scales in Table 1.) One cluster (Surface Trait 5) happens to coincide with a source trait (Source Trait 1).

again, it is distinct from source trait description. For example, one might say, "This is a wintry day," meaning thereby that the temperature is low, that there is snow or sleet in the air, that people are in overcoats, that the trees are bare of leaves, and that perhaps there is a wind from the north. This is a group of things which tend to go together for a variety of reasons which we could analyze into temperature level, the adaptation process of vegetation, and the economic level which makes overcoats (among many other things) possible, etc. It is these factors which correspond to our source traits while the complex outcome of "wintriness" is the surface trait which we commonly see and recognize.

A prominent source of confusion and indefiniteness in many research results over the past half century in psychology has been a simple failure to distinguish between the surface trait and the source trait concept. The latter is precisely determinant and measurable. The former is apt to "wobble" a little in its definition with local circumstances (a wintry day in Chicago and London are somewhat different patterns). Whereas there may be as few as two source traits at work in a given domain (as in Diagram 3), they can generate, say, a half a dozen different surface trait manifestations. Conversely, a single surface trait may be resolvable into several different factors.

Certain psychological tests, e.g., achievement tests, certain MMPI scales, and some scales in the CPI (California Psychological Inventory), are deliberately put together as surface traits. That is to say, the constructor has been concerned only to demonstrate that his items mutually intercorrelate well, i.e., have high test homogeneity, and he is little concerned as to the factor structure or whether the items are factor-homogeneous as well as test-homogeneous (Cattell and Warburton, 1967). Unfortunately, it is always possible for any psychologist to "create" surface traits in tests simply by making up a lot of items that are almost repetitive and thus intercorrelate highly. Granted that one avoids this artificial game of shaping the world according to one's prejudices, the surface trait concept and the measurement of it should not be disparaged. Provided any instrument is aimed at the centroid of a demonstrably natural surface trait, it will have its usefulness. This is obvious in the pathological realm, where species types almost certainly exist whose elements can often also be considered as a correlation cluster.

Of the more frequently used instruments, the MMPI comes closest to this, with a dozen or so scales, each of which, in principle, is a surface trait measurement. (This needs a little qualification, because the homogeneity of the items is not high, and the way in which they were put together is, in fact, something like a hybrid between orientation to a surface trait and orientation to a type concept. That is to say, items have been put together, without benefit of the multiple discriminant function [but with the general *idea* of the multiple discriminant function], to find bunches which are answered more frequently by syndrome group A than by syndrome group B, C, or D. These items have then been put into a single scale. In doing this, the statistical probability is that one will generate correlation clusters, when correlations are carried out in a general mixed population of clinical types.) Thus, although a few of these scales are neither the one thing nor the other, the best general description of MMPI scales is to designate them as surface trait measurements.

Furthermore, recent research (Cattell and Specht, 1969) confirms that the MMPI scales contain only five or six factors, and that these factors are already in the 16 factors dimensionality of the 16 PF. Consequently, MMPI surface trait scores can be appreciably predicted from 16 PF source trait measurements.* In view of this, a logically minded practitioner might at first come to the practical conclusion that one or the other of these scales is redundant. But this would be missing a more subtle possibility, namely, that additional diagnostic insight could be gained by simultaneously knowing, on the one hand, the patient's scores on his surface trait manifestations and, on the other hand, the profile of his underlying source trait endowments. Tables 1 and 2 show the general nature of the relationships between MMPI and 16 PF scale scores.

In general, by the very nature of the surface-source trait model, any given, exactly specified endowment on a particular source trait is likely to be resolvable into a fair range of possible profiles of endowment on underlying source traits. This statistical statement corresponds to the clinical truth that exactly the same general syndrome

---

*Parenthetically, and for the sake of completeness of the purely formal view of structure and models, it should be noted that surface traits (correlation clusters) exist as entities also in the longitudinal, time-dimensionalized space of P- and dR-technique, i.e., as describers of states and moods. For example, a particular combination of, say, depression, irritability, and anxiety may occur with more than the chance frequency of combination to be expected for these variables and indicate a tendency for the distinct, functionally separable and measurable UI 24 and UI 33 factors, to produce a special surface trait combination. Thus, surface traits are, as it were, particular conglomerates of source traits, which arise through various environmental or other circumstances. They justify being recognized and measured in themselves, and in every case need to be analyzed in terms of the underlying source trait endowments which combine to produce them in the given individual.

Table 1. Correlations between MMPI and 16 PF Scales (Corrected for attenuation on both)

	A	B	C	E	F	G	H	I	L	M	N	O	Q_1	Q_2	Q_3	Q_4
Anx	-13	-26	-40	17	10	-31	-26	06	20	10	-35	63	-18	04	-52	62
Lie	-07	01	29	-25	-02	14	01	-20	-21	03	19	-22	-06	-03	19	-13
F	-07	-38	-41	21	-15	-68	-10	03	23	19	-49	32	20	20	-62	39
K	-04	11	42	-27	02	26	09	-23	-36	-13	35	-43	-02	-06	46	-36
Hs	01	-33	-45	13	-04	-46	-09	-01	24	29	-39	52	-10	12	-48	48
D	-13	-10	-23	-33	-27	-15	-25	00	12	16	-07	20	-20	21	-18	24
Hy	01	30	20	-29	-04	01	03	-05	-13	23	11	-14	-07	-07	08	-05
Pd	-07	-12	-14	-02	01	-37	-05	-08	16	27	-04	24	-11	07	-30	36
Mf	05	10	08	-33	-14	11	-05	14	-26	17	05	-10	03	03	22	-06
Pa	-08	-24	-15	-08	-11	-33	-01	-05	08	20	-18	12	01	-04	-33	21
Pt	-12	-37	-64	02	-15	-47	-29	10	45	25	-29	68	-20	09	-74	71
Sc	-01	-47	-53	16	-09	-59	-13	12	35	23	-51	54	02	10	-72	56
Ma	-01	-15	19	15	20	-25	13	-11	14	11	14	-09	08	-12	-14	12
Si	-33	-10	-17	-49	-42	-09	-44	-13	04	07	-04	26	-10	43	-14	24

Table 2. Predictions (Multiple Correlations) of MMPI Surface Trait Scales from 16 PF Source Trait Scales (With various attenuation corrections)

	Corrected for MMPI Scale Unreliabilities Only	Corrected for 16 PF Scale Unreliabilities Only	Corrected to Ideal Scales for Both	Uncorrected
Anxiety scale	49	64	68	58
Lie L scale	27	35	40	32
Validity F scale	46	58	73	51
Correction K scale	37	49	55	43
Hypochondriasis scale	42	55	62	49
Depression scale	32	36	47	32
Hysteria scale	28	29	43	26
Psychopathic scale	32	32	48	29
Masc.-fem. scale	25	33	38	29
Paranoia	30	36	48	32
Psychasthenia	55	70	78	63
Schizophrenia	48	66	75	58
Hypomania	33	35	48	32
Social introversion	47	52	64	47

category and a given severity on an array of symptoms, can be produced in different patients by fairly different, alternative causes and configurations of source traits. The surface trait tells us what the condition is: the source trait measures tell us what combinations of weaknesses brought it about. This basic nosological truth is respected in quantitative approaches to diagnosis by what has been called *psychometric depth analysis* (Cattell, 1967a). By psychometric depth analysis, we mean an arrangement whereby every patient is given a test score simultaneously for the severity of his syndrome manifestation (on such a test as the MMPI or by psychiatric rating) and for the strengths of his underlying general personality source traits, normal and pathological (by the questionnaire or objective test measures of personality source traits). For example, in fairly typical cases in our files, two individuals were at about the 90th percentile on the conversion-hysteria syndrome, but one of them showed on the 16 PF decidedly lower ego strength, whereas the other showed higher guilt proneness and ergic tension. These source traits are known to be "equivalents" in a number of pathological products. For an enriched diagnosis—in the sense of getting guidance for therapy and of making a reasonably accurate prognosis—it was very important to know that these were the different causative personality structures in the two cases.

In *depth psychometry* functional psychometrics thus opens up to the psychiatrist and general practitioner a new world of information and understanding, made available from contrasting and comparing the results from quantitative analyses at these two levels. Doubtless, the practitioners who follow this up will find a considerable art developing in this area as their experience of examining such data broadens. Admittedly, of course, both of the instruments need improving. We need better and better measures of surface traits, notably those of clinical and sociological importance, and we need to extend the basis of source trait measurements from the dozen or so with which we are now concerned probably to about 25 or 30 if the specific pathological factors are to be included. Moreover, we have to recognize that at the present moment in psychological history there is a tremendous discrepancy between what we know about personality structure purely as structure, through multivariate experimental approaches, and what we know about the further predictive value of these measurements. What we are pleased to call the laws of psychology have so far been founded very much on qualitative types of observation or, if on quantitative types of observation, have been confined to highly specific bits of behavior of humans, or rats, in the laboratory. The whole area of development of psychological laws about the total personality, in terms of its source traits, surface traits, states, etc., still lies before us. What we have described above as the "utility coefficient" of a test (expressed with more precision elsewhere) (Cattell and Warburton, 1967) needs to be continuously raised by research on the source or surface traits which it is designed to measure.

What Is the Utility of Species Type Syndrome Classifications?

The discussion above has pointed out that, in historical fact, psychiatrists have had a good deal of trouble trying to agree on any more than the basic outlines of the classification according to the model of a typology. This has puzzled many psychiatrists, since the notion of discrete disease entities has worked well in more familiar fields covered by their brother physicians. This comparative lack of success, as suggested above, could be tied up with the question of how far mental disorder is a functional imbalance of dimensions normally possessed by everyone, and how far it is a distinct disease entity. The psychologist has reached a position where he can by his measurements contribute an answer, which must be an empirical one, to the question, "Do the varieties of mental disorder actually constitute distinct varieties or do they blend continuously one into another and into the general population?"

In any acceptable philosophy of taxonomy, the description by attributes, e.g., source traits, and the description by types, e.g., pathological syndrome categories, must, nevertheless, in terms of a model, be considered face and obverse of the *same* descriptive system. Any object whatever can be defined either by listing measurements for it on a set of attributes or by sequestering it to a particular named type category. Descriptively both approaches achieve the same end, and it is only when we come to prediction of criterion variables that the two systems may show relative advantages and disadvantages. In the description of the physical world, e.g., by physical scientists, the distinction between the two approaches is a very old one, and the words "Galilean" and "Aristotelian" have been attached to them. The Aristotelian system, so nicely tailored to the use of syllogisms, asks, "Is this a dog? Dogs bite. This is a dog. Therefore, this creature will bite." The Galilean system will try to predict biting from correlation with other attributes, such as the sharpness of the teeth and measures of the formation of the jaw. What the statistician has to recognize, as we have pointed out above, is that the correlation of biting with pointedness of teeth will have a considerably different value within the species dog or the various species of carnivore than when we go across genera and compare dogs with cows. As pointed out above, this changing correlation with species is another way of looking at the intrusion of curvilinear into linear regression methods.

The Aristotelian, species type approach, has perhaps four drawbacks. (1) The physician has to keep a very large number of types in mind. (2) There have been difficulties in separating the pure abstract type concepts themselves from one another. (3) There is generally some difficulty in reliably allocating a particular individual to a type. (4) There is the risk that the busy practitioner may be content with just putting the individual into the type, without proceeding further to recognize the individual's particular attribute deviations *within* the type itself. Nevertheless, it would be foolish to throw away the advantages of being able to pigeonhole a person in a type, for that pigeonhole commonly contains a rich record of experience with the particular disorder, its etiology, and its prognosis, and these are instructively different from those of any other.

Until recent years, the unaided memory and perception of the more gifted clinicians have been the means of furnishing textbooks with a proper recognition of diseases and types. But nowadays we stand on the brink of a new era of precision of type resolution through the use of formulas and computers. Since we have probably been for a generation at the end of our intellectual tether as far as clinician recognition of firmly acceptable psychiatric syndrome types is concerned, the present section will try to show what the new and more formal statistical procedures can do. The first approach in this area was by Q-technique, which correlates people instead of test measurements. From the Q correlation matrix it proceeds to factor analyze people instead of factor analyzing attributes, as in the usual R-technique. Unfortunately, it was a complete, though widespread, mistake to suppose that factors are the same as type groupings. Actually, the factors obtained from correlating people by Q-technique turn out, with suitable transformations, to be the *same* factors as obtained by correlating attributes! That is to say, they are pure *dimensions,* whereas we are looking for *groupings* of people as indicated in Diagram 2 above, *not* dimensions.

The correct procedure for locating types is called a $\bar{Q}$-technique which, like Q-technique, starts out with what we might call a Q-matrix, i.e., a square matrix in the cells of which all possible relations among the given set of people are marked out. However, $\bar{Q}$-technique does not proceed to factor analysis, but has as its goal simply grouping the people in their correlation clusters, precisely as we group traits in clusters to obtain surface traits. There is one other important difference from Q-technique, namely, that we need to use as a measure of resemblance, to insert in the cells, a different index from the correlation coefficient. The latter is defective for this purpose since it loses information. For example, the r formula overlooks the differences in *level* between two people on a profile of traits. To remedy this, I proposed some fifteen years ago the pattern similarity coefficient, r_p, which takes account both of the degree of similarity of shape and the similarity of level of people on a given profile of measurements. Various developments have since taken place in r_p, such as the development of a significance test for it, and research experience has shown it to work well in a variety of areas, from psychiatric types to culture patterns, in obtaining a sound objective classification of objects in groups. Diagram 4 illustrates the coefficient and its method of calculation.

The recent and rapid technical development in $\bar{Q}$-technique is very important for diagnostic research but cannot appropriately be taken up in more detail in a survey article. A few of the key issues can, however, be mentioned. First, it is most desirable to use factor scores, i.e., source trait scores, as the elements of the profile rather than just a set of variables. The reason for this is that variables are often highly correlated, and the formula requires elements to be orthogonal. More important, ordinary variables tend to represent different domains very unevenly if we just take those that first interest us. For example, one might take five cognitive variables, all from the area of intelligence, and only one from the area of cyclothymia-schizothymia. The similarity calculated on these six would give a very biased index of the similarity of two people. By the use of factors, however, we represent each

Diagram 4. Calculation of the Pattern Similarity Coefficient, r_p, from Two Given Profiles

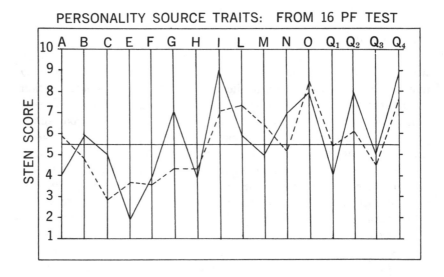

PERSONALITY SOURCE TRAITS: FROM 16 PF TEST

solid line = personality profile of given patient

broken line = personality profile of typical anxiety neurotic (from Cattell and Scheier, 1961)

d   = difference in normalized standard scores (stens) on each factor of patient from diagnostic profile

d =	+1.9	−1.1	−2.1	+1.7	−.4	−2.7	+.3	−1.9
	+1.4	+1.4	−1.8	+.5	+1.4	−1.9	−.5	−1.2
d^2 =	3.61	1.21	4.41	2.89	.16	7.29	.09	3.61
	1.96	1.96	3.24	.25	1.96	3.61	.25	1.44

$\Sigma d^2 = $ 37.94

$$r_p = \frac{122.72 - \Sigma d^2}{122.72 + \Sigma d^2} = \frac{122.72 - 37.94}{122.72 + 37.94} = .53$$

significant r_p at p = .01 for 16 elements is .45

Conclusion: Patient has significant affiliation to anxiety reaction neurotic.

psychological domain by just one element in the profile. An explicit technique for sampling domains is very important here, for otherwise we finish in such absurdities as some of Carl Rogers's followers have made out of his Q-sort proposals. (Actually, since even source trait measures can be somewhat correlated, a more extended formula than that just given above has to be used for all accurate work.)

Finally, one must recognize that when one has the Q-matrix among patients, showing their interrelationships in all possible pairings by the correct r_p indices, it is still necessary to have a systematic and nonsubjective way of "combing" this matrix to find the clusters. These problems have been discussed elsewhere (Cattell, 1967b), and a program called Taxonome (Cattell and Coulter, 1966) has been set up for scanning such a matrix and extracting the more or less independent groupings. "More or less" is an important qualifier here, for the fact is that in a great deal of natural data the true structure is no clearer than that of the cloud masses in a stormy sky, and demands concepts of overlapping categories. If that is the nature of things, the best we can do is to stipulate more exactly what the character of the overlap is. In biological data the Taxonome program gives relatively clear-cut results, because species are apt to overlap regularly within a well-defined genus, and this again in some family, and order in a clearly phyletic model.

Anyone immersed in the technical methodological requirements of a scientific taxonomic system is likely to admire the American Psychiatric Association's classificatory scheme mostly for its success in receiving more social agreement than earlier schemes, which caused endless dispute. But the consensus of opinion is not always truth, and rests precariously upon a social atmosphere of temporary agreement. There is no substitute for getting to work with *measured* source traits in empirical studies using proper statistical techniques for objectively finding the main syndrome clusters.

Such an undertaking will have to be on a proper scale and with considerable support. But meanwhile, on a shoestring and merely at a demonstration level, Karl Delhees, Donald Tatro, and other of my co-workers have explored the objective typological possibilities both with the primary source traits as measured by questionnaires and by objective tests. It can be shown, for example, that, as far as the neuroses are concerned, the psychiatrically accepted syndrome categories of anxiety neurotics, conversion hysterics, psychosomatics, and other presently recognized syndrome groupings appear as very distinctive 16 PF profile patterns (Cattell and Scheier, 1961; Cattell, Tatro, and Komlos, 1964). Furthermore, the work of Delhees shows (Cattell,

1967a) that psychotics measured on twenty source traits measured by objective personality tests will group themselves according to pattern similarity coefficients in a fairly definitely recognizable way. In the main, the statistical approach supports the clinical approach, though it does present some interesting divergences, such as the fact that the patients classified as schizo-affectives do not lie midway between the schizophrenics and affectives, when definite profile measurement is applied, but lie out in a uniquely new direction of divergence.

Granted that advances are successfully made to overcome the first two shortcomings, by (1) finding an objective system for taxonomic classification of types and (2) setting up suitable catalogs of behaviors for describing the central tendency of each type, then only the two last difficulties remain to be overcome. These are (3) setting up diagnostic machinery for assigning a particular patient to a category and (4) expressing an individual's peculiarity by dimensional measures within the type.

An individual's index of belonging to a type can be worked out simply enough by finding the pattern similarity coefficient, r_p, between the profile for the particular individual and the central, defining profile for the type which has been discovered, i.e., the profile obtained by averaging all the people admitted to the type. It is now readily possible very rapidly to handle this by setting up a computer service which would allocate a considerable number of patients (granted their profiles are available on the chief source traits) into their appropriate categories. The next step—that of using the regressions within the type—that is to say, the relations of prognosis, required therapy, etc., to the individual's deviations within the type itself, must follow from the same principles as have been set out above for general source trait prediction in any setting. The important difference is that we now deal with source traits established *within* the category, not the source traits across the whole population, which may differ in number and somewhat in nature.

For example, deviation on a factor of "tendency to have hallucinations" (and associated pathology) has reasonable applicability and precision of meaning only within the schizophrenic and certain other groups, not within the *totality* of mental hospital or normal populations. Most of the discovery of factors specific to syndrome groups and the obtaining of regressions of these upon criteria *within* types still remains to be achieved. In any case, a proper appreciation of the taxonomic model requires that one realize the difference between *intertype* (general population) source traits and *intratype* source traits, if the best combination of typological diagnosis and source trait analysis and prediction is to be achieved in practice.

Incidentally, as a small statistical point, it should be mentioned that although, as we have argued above, the pattern similarity coefficient is best used wherever possible upon a profile of *continuous source trait measurements,* it can also be used with *dichotomous* or *qualitative* (two-set) classifications on each element in the profile. This has been done a good deal in physical medicine, where computer diagnostic procedures, which are essentially centered on the type concept of diagnosis, are already successfully in operation (Overall and Williams, 1961).

Heightening the Effectiveness of a System by Implementation through Textbook and Computer

The advantages of the diagnostic system here proposed are initially at the purely conceptual level, namely, in that operational definition can be given for each of the concepts which are invoked. Source and surface trait, type, state, and process have the character of exact models into which data can be resolved by statistical procedures. From this theoretical advantage, however, there follows almost immediately a bonus at the practical level, namely, that all kinds of uses of the concepts can be aided by calculation and handled with great facility in the modern computer age.

Before looking closely at the computer possibilities, let us pause and make a summary of what has been stated about the model properties as such. Our arguments are:

1. That even what looks like a qualitative evaluation in any diagnosis can always be reexpressed in a quantitative form, and that, therefore, regardless of whether one does or does not use actual psychological tests, a quantitative basis of observation is implicit in all diagnosis and all research on diagnosis.

2. That there is a quite limited number of mathematical models which can be invoked in diagnostic or taxonomic description, centering on four main notions, namely, those of traits, states, processes, and types. It would be difficult to find any verbally meaningful diagnostic system which is not reducible to these four.

3. That although these models can be invoked if necessary to give substance to quite a priori subjective concepts, their special virtue is that they can be related to statistical treatment of data, and that any system of diagnosis which is to be effective and constantly useful will orient its measurement to natural structures in the data expressed in these models. That is to say, psychometric scales, batteries, etc., have their most potent use if built around source traits, types, states, and processes previously found by experimental, statistical treatment of

data. In several other chapters in this volume, many of the tangible outcomes of such research, especially in terms of source traits, have been given substance and illustration, in such psychological concepts as ego strength, surgency, superego strength, etc.

Granted that diagnostic measurement has been organized around these structures demonstrable by multivariate experimental research, a considerable bonus becomes available. One can bring to bear upon prediction all the knowledge which accumulates around these structures. This relating of measurement to "natural history" is what we mean in our heading by "implementation through the textbook." Indeed, unless this development is made, by psychology and psychiatry as pure and applied sciences, the use of quantitative measures will be purely actuarial. It will remain nothing more than much psychometric scale construction has always been: a species of "psychological accountancy." Modern psychology, as distinct from that which perhaps prevailed thirty years ago, increasingly builds up its laws and theories around measurable, psychometrically demonstrable entities. The prospect of using the source trait and type concepts in an effective quantitative fashion is constantly improving through their use in various research studies and the growth of general personality theory. For example, just in the last decade many theories have been proposed for specific source trait factors and we have come to know a good deal, for instance, about the normal life-course age changes of various personality factors.

Although the psychologist likes to emphasize that there is all the difference in the world between a mechanical use of measures and an informed use by a psychologist or psychiatrist educated in personality theory, yet we must not deny the obvious fact that fairly good predictions can indeed be made at the actuarial level. As Goldberg and Werts (1966) have recently shown, if one has a certain amount of psychological measurement data, an immediate prediction, i.e., correlation or regression on a criterion, can be obtained almost equally well, regardless of whether one analyzes that item data into meaningful source traits, or subjectively constructed scales, or the surface trait type of scoring, and so on. This conclusion might almost be said to follow a priori from, for instance, rotational principles in factor analysis, where one rotation of the data is as good as another for any immediate prediction.

However, a substantial difference between psychologically meaningless, actuarial prediction, on the one hand, and the use of functionally unitary traits, types, etc., on the other, can be expected when one tries to predict *outside* the immediate sample of data, and to other times and conditions. And this, after all, is what differentiates a diagnosis offering wise and astute prognosis and guidance of therapy from a therapy using a diagnosis which is merely a classificatory exercise. For example, if one had the intelligence test results on a ten-year-old child and attempted to say something about what his expected performance would be four years later without any knowlege of the natural history of intelligence laws, of the constancy of the IQ, etc., the purely statistical prediction would be a relatively poor one. If, additionally, we know that some brain injury has occurred, or that the child's education is going to be in such and such circumstances, the prediction and understanding in the psychologist's estimate begin decidedly to exceed anything that an examiner working with a computer alone could achieve.

Our reference of measurement to "the textbook," therefore, implies that the diagnostic system here advocated, using measures oriented to natural psychological structures, will give an appreciable potential advantage—as represented by the difference in value between the utility coefficient and the validity coefficient (Cattell and Warburton, 1967)—over an operation with scales and scores on arbitrary scales. In turning next to the second main theme in the title of this section, namely, the use of the computer, we shall still keep this emphasis on functional psychological testing in mind. For when we argue that there are today immense new possibilities for the practitioner from the use of the computer, we emphatically do not mean that merely mechanical, uniform use which operates at a purely actuarial level. In fact, we suppose that a considerable array of further, psychologically meaningful calculations such as "the textbook" makes possible, will be built upon the data first made available as scores on source traits, profiles, states, types, etc. For example, the psychologist will proceed to calculations for different aspects of the prognostic outcome, made according to the specification equation. Then there will be calculations concerning the efficacy of various alternative possible kinds of treatment with the particular case, based on equations from past experience with these kinds of therapy applied to similar personality traits. And, as suggested above, there will be for records and for communication with colleagues, teachers, social workers, etc., clear narrative-style print-outs of various conclusions from the computer, initially expressed in quantitative terms, but reexpressed by the computer programs in verbal summaries arranged by Eber (1966) and others.

Elsewhere (Cattell, 1957) there has been discussion of the *two-file system* in industrial and vocational guidance psychology, which describes how one file is built up by research to organize specification

equation weights discovered for a goodly range of occupations, while
the other alphabetizes the ability, personality, and motivation factor
profiles of the population of clients concerned. By systematically relating
the values in one file to those in the other, literally in the paired
products of the specification equation, it would be possible with a
computer to try out in a matter of a few seconds or minutes the
probable success of a large range of individuals across a large range
of occupations. A print-out could instantly be obtained of the best
possible utilization of the given resources of talent in the given
array of available jobs. A development along the lines illustrated by
this more simple example, but with exploration of many alternative avenues, is indicated for the general clinical use here envisaged.
That is to say, there would be machine storage of a large number of
specification equations, profiles, therapeutic values, etc., from past
clinical research, and, on the other hand, a variety of measurements in
terms of source trait, state, process, and profile values for the various
clients concerned. These could be brought together in a considerable
variety of combinations to answer a considerable variety of questions
regarding the diagnosis, the prognosis, the best tactical steps in treatment, etc.

As a social and professional group, psychiatrists are becoming
increasingly accustomed to the possibilities, through computer aids,
of better social organization of treatment and the better recording of
data for interaction with other institutions and agencies. It is proposed
here that there could be a natural extension of such aids to the clinical
decision process itself *if the measurements fed in were properly organized around a diagnostic system based on the above models and
theoretical concepts.* Furthermore, the day may not be far when
such complex procedures as P-technique, "process analyses" of individuals, will be transmitted through "on line" computer units in the
doctor's office to central computers in which analyses can be almost
instantly carried out, the results rapidly compared with a large library
of stored information on such cases, and the results reported back
while the patient is still in the consulting room. To those who have
vague fears that service to the individual patient will somehow be lost
in this increasing efficiency, one must point out that at present the
demand for mental health services so far exceeds the supply—and
indeed the supply that may ever be economically possible with present
uneconomical use of time—that some better way must be found
of spreading the influence of our limited resources of top-level professional training. There is much now being done by the psychiatrist and
the psychotherapist, e.g., the writing out of long case reports, the

diagnosis by time-consuming consulting room methods which testing by technicians could more reliably handle, etc., which the introduction of a fully informed psychometric diagnostic system, computer-linked, could take over. If we are correct in our expectations of what basic personality research by multivariate methods is now capable of doing, with the introduction of functional psychological measurement, the future holds fascinating possibilities. But it will need social as well as textbook organization, if computer services, complete with computer libraries of psychological specification equation data, are to be efficiently provided for the psychiatric practioner.

Some of the proposals here are checks drawn on the bank of the future—but hopefully the not too distant future. Meanwhile, the individual practitioner can begin to utilize the source trait profile of the client on such batteries, for example, as the 16 PF, MMPI, and O-A, for good "type classification" through the pattern similarity coefficient, and there are beginning to be available research-based specification equations for the necessary variety of prognostic and therapeutic guidance decisions.

REFERENCES

Blalock, H. M. *Causal inference in non-experimental research.* Chapel Hill, N. C.: University of North Carolina Press, 1964.

Cattell, R. B. *Personality, a systematic theoretical and factual study.* New York: McGraw-Hill, 1950.

Cattell, R. B. *Factor analysis.* New York: Harper, 1952.

Cattell, R. B. *Personality and motivation structure and measurement.* New York: World Book, 1957.

Cattell, R. B. *The scientific analysis of personality.* Chicago: Aldine, 1965.

Cattell, R. B. The personality factors, objectively measured, which distinguish psychotics from normals. *Behav. Res. Ther.*, 1966a, **4**, 39–51.

Cattell, R. B. (Ed.) *Handbook of multivariate experimental psychology.* Chicago: Rand McNally, 1966b.

Cattell, R. B. Personality theory and the dynamic calculus, from quantitative experimental methods. In A. M. Freedman and H. I. Kaplan (Eds.), *Comprehensive textbook of psychiatry.* Baltimore, Md.: Williams & Wilkins, 1967a.

Cattell, R. B. Taxonomic principles for locating and using types (and the desired taxonome computer program). Presented at the Conference on Typology, Pittsburgh, Pa., April 1967b.

Cattell, R. B., and Bjerstedt, A. The structure of depression, by factoring Q-data, in relation to general personality source traits in normal and pathological subjects. Bull. No. 16, Malmo, Sweden: Department of Educational and Psychological Research, School of Education, 1966.

Cattell, R. B., and Coulter, M. A. Principles of behavioral taxonomy and the mathematical basis of the taxonome computer program. *Brit. J. math. stat. Psychol.*, 1966, **19** (No. 2), 237–69.

Cattell, R. B., Delhees, K. H., Tatro, D. F., and Nesselroade, J. R. Personality structure in primary objective test factors appearing in a mixed normal and psychotic sample. (In preparation.)

Cattell, R. B., and Scheier, I. H. *The meaning and measurement of neuroticism and anxiety.* New York: Ronald Press, 1961.

Cattell, R. B., and Specht, L. L. What pathological dimensions lie beyond the normal dimensions of the 16 PF? A comparison of MMPI and 16 PF factor domains. *J. Consult. clin. Psychol.*, 1969, **33** (No. 1), 18–29.

Cattell, R. B., Tatro, D. F., and Komlos, E. The diagnosis and inferred structure of paranoid and non-paranoid schizophrenia, from the 16 PF profile. *Indian Psychol. Rev.*, 1964, **1**, 52–61.

Cattell, R. B., Tatsuoka, M., and Eber, H. W. The Sixteen Personality Factor Questionnaire. Champaign, Ill.: Institute for Personality and Ability Testing, 1957.

Cattell, R. B., Wagner, A., and Cattell, M. D. Adolescent personality structure, in Q-data, checked in the High School Personality Questionnaire. *Brit. J. Psychol.* (In press, 1970.)

Cattell, R. B., and Warburton, F. *Objective personality and motivation tests: a theoretical introduction and practical compendium.* Champaign, Ill.: University of Illinois Press, 1967.

Dubin, S. S. A factorial analysis of personality traits in 100 psychopathological subjects. Unpublished Ph.D. thesis. University of Illinois, 1950.

Dubin, S. S., Cattell, R. B., and Saunders, D. B. Personality structure in psychotics by factorization of objective clinical tests. *J. ment. Sci.*, 1954, **100**, 158–76.

Eber, H. W. Recent improvement in 16 PF computer analysis and narrative reporting services. *IPAT News,* No. 20A. Champaign, Ill.: Institute for Personality and Ability Testing, 1966.

Eber, H. W., and Cattell, R. B. Estimating the criterion specification equation from the profile of a criterion group. (In preparation.)

Eysenck, H. J. *The dynamics of anxiety and hysteria.* London: Routledge and Kegan Paul, 1957.

Fruchter, B. *Introduction to factor analysis.* New York: Van Nostrand, 1954.

Goldberg, L. R., and Werts, C. E. The reliability of clinicians' judgments: A multitrait-multimethod approach. *J. consult. Psychol.*, 1966, **30**, (No. 3), 199–206.

Guilford, J. P. *Personality.* New York: McGraw-Hill, 1960.

Harman, H. H. *Modern factor analysis.* Chicago: University of Chicago Press, 1960.

Harris, C. W., *Problems in measuring change.* Madison, Wis.: University of Wisconsin Press, 1963.

Hathaway, S. R., and McKinley, J. C. Minnesota multiphasic personality inventory. New York: Psychological Corporation, 1951.

Henrysson, S. *Applicability of factor analysis in the behavioral sciences.* Stockholm: Almquist and Wiksell. 1960.

Horn, J. L. Fluid and crystallized intelligence: a factor analytic study of the structure among primary mental abilities. Unpublished Ph.D. thesis. University of Illinois, 1966.

Hundleby, J. D., Pawlik, K., and Cattell, R. B. *Personality factors in objective test devices.* San Diego, Calif.: R. R. Knapp, 1965.

Jung, C. G. *Psychologcial types.* London: Kegan Paul, 1923.

Karvonen, M. J., and Kannas, M. Factor analysis of haematological changes in heavy manual work. *Acta Physiol. Scandin.,* 1953, **29**, 220–31.

Kretschmer, E. *Physique and character.* New York: Harcourt, Brace, and World, 1925.

Lingoes, J. C. An IBM 360/67 program for Guttman-Lingoes conjoint analysis. *Behav. Sci.,* 1968, **13**, 421–22.

McQuitty, L. L. Rank order typal analysis. *Educ. psychol. Measmt.,* 1963, **23**, 55–61.

Meehl, P. E. *Clinical vs. statistical prediction.* Minneapolis, Minn.: University of Minnesota Press, 1954.

Nesselroade, J. R. A comparison of cross product and differential-R factoring regarding cross study stability of change patterns. Unpublished Ph.D. thesis. University of Illinois, 1967.

Norman, W. T. Toward an adequate taxonomy of personality attributes: Replicated factor structure in peer-nomination personality ratings. *J. abnorm. soc. Psychol.,* 1963, **66**, 574–83.

Norman, W. T., and Harshbarger, T. R. Matching components of self-report and peer-nomination personality measures. *Psychometrika,* 1965, **30** (No. 4), 481–90.

Overall, J. E., and Williams, C. M. Models for medical diagnosis. *Behav. Sci.,* 1961, **6**, 134–42.

Porter, R., and Schaie, K. W. The child personality questionnaire. Champaign, Ill.: Institute for Personality and Ability Testing, 1969.

Rickels, K., and Cattell, R. B. The clinical factor validity and trueness of the IPAT verbal and objective batteries for anxiety and regression. *J. clin. Psychol.,* 1965, **21**, 257–64.

Schaie, K. W. Equivalence or chaos: a hypothesis testing factor analytic study of behavior rating questionnaire and instrument factors in personality structure research. Annual Meeting, Society of Multivariate Experimental Psychology, Boulder, Colo., 1963.

Scheier, I. H., Cattell, R. B., and Sullivan, W. P. Predicting anxiety from clinical symptoms of anxiety. *Psychiatric Quart. Suppl.,* 1961, **35,** 114–26.

Sheldon, W. H., and Stevens, S. S. *The varieties of temperament.* New York: Harper, 1942.

Sokal, R. R., and Sneath, P. H. A. *Principles of numerical taxonomy.* New York: Freeman, 1963.

Sweney, A. B. Studies of motivation. *International Psychiatry Clinics,* 1966, **3,** 265–88. Boston: Little, Brown.

Sweney, A. B., and Cattell, R. B. Components measurable in manifestations of mental conflicts. *J. abnorm. soc. Psychol.,* 1964, **68,** 479–90.

Uhr, L., and Miller, J. G. *Drugs and behavior.* New York: Wiley, 1961.

Van Egeren, L. F. Experimental determination by P-technique of functional utilities of depression and other psychological states. Unpublished M.A. thesis. University of Illinois, 1963.

Wenig, P. The relative roles of naive, artistic, cognitive and press, compatibility and ego defense operations in tests of misperception. Unpublished M.A. thesis. University of Illinois, 1962.

Wessman, A. E., and Ricks, D. F. *Mood and personality.* New York: Holt, Rinehart and Winston, 1966.

Williams, J. R. A test of the validity of P-technique in the measurement of internal conflict. *J. Pers.,* 1959, **27,** 418–37.

A FACTOR ANALYTIC SYSTEM FOR THE
INDIVIDUAL PATIENT

Applying Cattellian factor analysis to the individual patient, Horn and Sweney assert that complete diagnosis requires assessment of what they define as traits, states, processes, and types. Behavior is assessed in terms of temperament or style (which refers to the particular quality of the behavior), ability (how well behavior accomplishes given purposes), and motivation, the latter being the focus of the present chapter. Motivation is assessed by workable instruments measuring self-report, performance in miniature-situation tests, and naturally occurring behavior. Horn and Sweney survey sixty-eight principles which assess motivation by creating conditions of disruption or deprivation of homeostasis, or by reminding the patient of such a condition. By determining patternings of relationship and variabilities, six or seven component dimensions are extracted from the sixty-eight. Since the original universe of data fed into the factor analytic machinery was of a familiar psychoanalytic nature, it is no great surprise that of the seven component motivational dimensions which emerged, four remained uninterpreted and the balance consisted of (1) an affective free expression of uncontrolled, primitive undifferentiated motivational impulses (i.e., id), (2) a channeling of id impulses in accordance with reality to achieve satisfaction over time (i.e., ego), and (3) a control over impulse by the dominant external culture (i.e., superego).

This personality classification system includes a set of drives which may fluctuate with time and varying situations. These include: security-fear, mating, assertiveness, protectiveness, sensuality, curiosity, gregariousness, pugnacity, appeal, construction, narcissism, self-sentiment, superego sentiment, religious sentiment, career sentiment, and sweetheart sentiment.

Horn and Sweney are saying, in effect, that if we take a good sample of the current diagnostic writings and research and submit it to factor analytic methodology, then it will be clear that we are using a psychoanalytic model of id, ego, and superego forces, plus an array of "drives." The package constitutes the comprehensive lowest denominator of our working psychodiagnostic approach. Interestingly, this approach to motivation and drives ignores the traditional psychiatric Kraepelinian concepts of normality-abnormality and illness-disease.

The Cattell-Horn-Sweney challenge is that their approach is what the more or less standard psychiatric psychodiagnostic system looks like when subjected to factor analytic rigor and systemization. Opposing contributors protest that the initial pool of raw data fed into the collective computer is too disorganized and is taken from too many different personality and psychodiagnostic approaches. The Cattell-Horn-Sweney methodological approach would increase the order and internal structural consistency of *one* psychodiagnostic system, but the final outcome has a different meaning when any and all psychodiagnostic approaches are tossed into the collective data pot. Nevertheless, the Cattellian invitation holds: here is the factor-analyzed general diagnostic system, reflecting considerable research, derived from the published works of clinicians and researchers, incorporating a liberal package of good assessment devices and instruments, modified to apply to the individual, and accounting for the role of the dynamic situation.

2

THE DYNAMIC CALCULUS MODEL FOR MOTIVATION AND ITS USE IN UNDERSTANDING THE INDIVIDUAL CASE

JOHN L. HORN   ARTHUR B. SWENEY

General Orientation

In the chapter by Cattell it was pointed out that a complete system for understanding the individual case will contain four distinct classes of concepts and corresponding measurement procedures—namely, for traits, for states, for processes, and for types. It was further recognized that these classes crosscut others pertaining to qualities of behavior— namely, ability, motivation, and temperament or style concepts. And it was suggested that with respect to any of these kinds of concepts it is useful to keep track of the source of information upon which inference is based—whether from probes aimed at allowing the individual to report on himself (Q-data), from physical-physiological recordings and the individual's attempt to perform in accordance with the instructions for a miniature-situation test (T-data); or from observations of the individual's naturally occurring behavior (L-data). With respect to this broad framework the focus of the present chapter is on a class of motivation concepts obtained primarily from T-data observations and on these as they pertain to mapping trait and state phenomena.

Motivation, like many other important concepts in psychology (and other fields), has a wide variety of meanings and connotations. It is desirable, therefore, to be as clear as possible about the meanings and connotations which are and are not intended in any particular treatment. One purpose of the present chapter is to outline a particular theory about human motivation. This theory has grown, as it were, out of empirical multivariate research. Although complex in several ways, important terms in the theory nevertheless can be pinned down to objective and reasonably accurate measurement operations. A second purpose of this chapter is to indicate the utility and potential of this theory in clinical and counseling settings.

The Model

A RESPONSE TO PROBLEMS OF DEFINING
MOTIVE CONCEPTS UNIQUELY

Almost all measurement in clinical and counseling settings must be regarded as in the nature of what Torgerson (1960) has aptly described as subject-centered (as distinct from stimulus-centered). This is true both in the measurement of traits, viewed as more or less enduring characteristics which distinguish one individual from another despite variation in circumstances, and in the measurement of states, characteristics in which variation within persons over occasions is the principal concern (cf. Horn, 1963a, 1963b, 1966a, 1966b; Horn and Little, 1966). That is to say, when stimuli (e.g., items) are presented to subjects, the principal assumption is that different responses to the same stimuli will occur and will indicate differences between subjects (in a trait-centered approach) or between a given subject on one occasion and that same subject on another occasion (when state is the principal concern). With respect to this variation, the behavioral scientist asks the question: "Can the observed differences in response to a stimulus be attributed primarily to differences in motivation, to differences in ability, or to differences in temperament or style?" Worded otherwise the question is: "To what extent can the observed differences in response be partitioned into differences indicating primarily motive, primarily ability, and primarily temperament and style?" Much research on human personality has floundered on questions of this kind. It is to this kind of question, primarily, that Cattell and his co-workers have directed their efforts in development of the concepts of the dynamic calculus (Cattell, 1944, 1947, 1957; Cattell and Horn, 1963; Cattell, Horn, and Butcher, 1962; Cattell, Horn, Radcliffe, and Sweney, 1964; Cattell, Radcliffe, and Sweney, 1963; Cattell and Sweney, 1964a, 1964b; Cattell, Sweney, and Radcliffe, 1960; Horn, 1961, 1966a, 1966b; Horn and Cattell, 1965; Sweney, 1961, 1962, 1966, 1967; Sweney and Cattell, 1962, 1964, 1967; Sweney and May, 1964).

Viewed in terms of its general and historic use in psychology, motive is a dispositional concept invoked to help explain how an organism comes to behave at all and how it comes to direct its behavior along some lines in lieu of others. That is, a concept of motive is used in distinction from a concept of ability, which aims to explain *how well* behavior accomplishes a given purpose, and in distinction from concepts like temperament and style (cf. Messick, 1961), which seek to explain a particular quality of behavior different from both the direction-oriented (i.e., motive) quality and the adequacy-appropriateness (i.e., ability) quality. Thus, a collection of school boys on a playground may be said to possess different degrees of motivation to leap a high-jump bar; independent of their motives they may be said to possess different abilities to leap the bar; and given two individuals with the same degree of motivation and the same ability (i.e., both clear the same height), one may leap with a vigorous back-roll jump and another with a relaxed forward barrel-roll, thus evincing different styles and temperamental qualities.

It is recognized that this tripartite breakdown of a behavioral unit into distinct elements is to some extent artificial and purely theo-retical, just as it is recognized that to break salt into parts of sodium and chloride is to some extent artificial and purely theoretical. How well a person can perform must be related empirically to his style of performance and to his motivation. Yet the operating assumption is that this conceptualization is useful and that empirically the "how well" is not perfectly determined by style or motive or any combination of the two—and vice versa. Motive, ability, and such concepts as tem-perament and style are regarded as logically independent and somewhat independent in an empirical-measurement sense.

But while this kind of distinction has existed quite generally in psychology for a number of years, it remains true that a measurement distinction between attributes of motivation and attributes of the other behavioral modalities generally has not been achieved. This is particularly true in the area where motivation is to be distinguished from other nonability attributes. That is, what are popularly measured as motives, as in inventories for "interests," "values," "attitudes," "opinions," "needs," "hormic dimensions," etc., often are virtually in-distinguishable from "general personality" attributes, as measured in inventories such as the MMPI, 16 PF, CPI, etc. One of the major characteristics of the dynamic calculus is that in it there is an explicit attempt to define motive in a way that makes it logically, psycholog-ically, and operationally distinct from "general personality" attributes.

Viewed in terms of operations of measurement in general psy-chology, motive is a quality of behavior which can be seen most readily when an organism is prevented from experiencing certain kinds of stimulation or when it is presented with an instance of a class of stimuli known as incentives. That is, it is believed that motivation can be measured by manipulating the environment in a way to set up conditions of deprivation or disruption of homeostasis in the subject; if this cannot be achieved, as usually it cannot be in the measurement of existing status which is required in diagnostic and treatment settings, then it is assumed that motivation can be measured by "reminding" the subject of a condition of deprivation or disruption of homeostasis. In research with lower animals the stimuli used to thus "remind" the organism of its deprived state usually can be seen to be rather closely related to the act of satisfying the need-state associated with the motive. Such stimuli can be easily defined as incentives.

In diagnosis of motivation levels in humans, however, the stimuli which provoke the behaviors upon which diagnosis is based may be only remotely related to satiation of the motive and therefore quite ambiguous as concerns their incentive value. To measure the sexual motivation of a disturbed patient, for example, usually it is not possible, nor desirable, actually to manipulate factors which would increase or decrease the motive; rather, the clinician attempts to probe with appropriate questions to obtain responses which will indicate the extent to which the needs implied by this motive are or are not being realized.

In most cases it has been assumed on the basis of inspection (coupled with common sense and a theory, such as Freudian theory) that particular questions are relevant for provoking responses which indicate motive. Yet it can be seen that because of subjective frames of reference, such questions may mean quite different things to different people. There has been little attempt to follow up this a priori approach with operations which would indicate the extent to which the responses given to such classes of stimuli are, in fact, indicative of motive attributes and are largely independent of general personality attributes.

In an attempt to get around some of these difficulties, the approach in the dynamic calculus model has been to go back, as it were, to the definition given in general psychology for a motive: a motive is an attribute which becomes manifest in behavior when incentive is the principal characteristic of the stimulus pattern to which the organism responds. In thus going back, however, the aim has been to keep the concept squarely within the realm of measurement of humans, as these would be met in the hospital, in the clinic, in the school, and in other walks of life.

In specifying incentives, a priori designation has been the first step, as in other attempts to measure motivation. That is, in answer to the question, "How do we know that the principal characteristic of a stimulus pattern is incentive?" the initial answer has been, "By inspection"—i.e., by fiat, to use the rather apt term which Torgerson (1960) suggested for measurement based upon this premise. However, in the dynamic calculus model there has been an attempt to go beyond this intuitive approach in three important ways: (1) by pooling, as it were, the intuitions of many, many psychologists concerning incentives and manifestations of motivation, (2) by looking at response patterns from several vantage points with the purpose of determining whether they indicate motive or nonmotive attributes, and (3) by bringing the measurement of abilities and other general personality attributes into the same arena as the measurement of motives and frequently checking to establish that measurement of motivation is, indeed, both operationally and empirically independent of measurement of other kinds of attributes.

MODES OF MANIFESTING ANY MOTIVE: THE MOTIVATIONAL COMPONENTS

If one surveys research on motivation over the past sixty years he will find that a large number of behavioral characteristics have been taken to indicate the presence of, or increase in, particular motivations. For example, many psychologists have accepted the subject's own statement of preference as indicating the presence and magnitude of motivation. If, in describing himself, an individual volunteers statements of the kind: "I spend a great deal of time thinking about sexual matters," then it might well be assumed that here is evidence of a high degree of sexual motivation. In making this assumption we are indicating acceptance of a *preference* principle as somewhat valid for determining motivation. That is, we are indicating that in a general way we are willing to accept the argument that persons will often describe their motives in statements which may be taken more or less at face value (i.e., with respect to their *referential* meaning, as Brown [1958] defines this). Certainly, if use is any indication of acceptance, this principle is very widely accepted by those who attempt to understand the individual case, for this is the principle upon which most inventory and interview measurements of motivation are based.

While many psychologists readily embrace this principle in practice, most will, nevertheless, recognize that measurement based upon this principle alone can provide a glimpse of only one facet of a complex motive structure. According to Freudian theory, for example, (as well as theory developed before and since Freud's time), very high motivation of a particular kind may actually prevent one from providing, or subscribing to, statements the referential meaning of which would indicate this motivation. A person bothered by very high sexual motivation may defend against expressing this in explicit terms and manifest it only in the latent meaning of his statements. He might, for example, subscribe to statements of the kind: "Most individuals in our society spend a great deal of time thinking about sexual matters," thereby taking the onus for sexual motivation off himself and laying it on others. This illustrates a principle of naïve projection. Although somewhat less widely employed than the preference principle, naïve projection has been widely accepted in clinical practice as a valid basis for inferring motivation.

Thus illustrated are two principles—but only two from among many. For it is widely accepted, also, that an individual who is not able to subscribe to preference statements indicating sexual motivation may nevertheless indicate his preferences by displaying a great deal of fantasy about sexual matters, by showing a great deal of defensive fluency on matters in this area, by overreacting physiologically to stimuli of a sexual nature, etc. That is, many behavioral outcomes have been recognized as indicative of a state of heightened motivation. A selection of principles based upon these observed outcomes is provided for illustrative purposes in Table 1.

Table 1. Some Principles of Motivation Measurement Which Have Been Applied in Device Construction

(After Cattell, 1957; Cattell and Horn, 1963; Cattell, Radcliffe, and Sweney, 1963; Horn, 1966a)

With increase in interest in course of action expect increase in:

1. Preferences. Readiness to admit preference for course of action.
2. Autism. Misperception. Distorted perception of objects, noises, etc. in accordance with interest (e.g., Bruner coin perception study).
3. Autism. Misbelief. Distorted belief that facts favor course of action.
4. Reasoning distortion. Means-ends. Readiness to argue that doubtfully effective means to goal are really effective.
5. Reasoning distortion. Ends-means. Readiness to argue that ends will be easily reached by inapt means.
6. Reasoning distortion. Inductive.
7. Reasoning distortion. Deductive.
8. Reasoning distortion. Education of relations in perception (e.g., analogies).
9. Utilities choice. Readiness to use land, labor, and capital for interest.
10. Machiavellianism. Willingness to use reprehensible means to achieve ends favoring interest.

11. Fantasy choice. Readiness to choose interest-related topic to read about, write about, or explain.
12. Fantasy ruminations. Time spent ruminating on interest-related material.
13. Fantasy identification. Preference to be like individuals who favor course of action.
14. Defensive reticence. Low fluency in listing bad consequences of course of action.
15. Defensive fluency. Fluency in listing good consequences of course of action.
16. Defensive fluency. Fluency in listing justifications for actions.
17. Rationalization. Readiness to interpret information in a way to make interest appear more respectable than it is.
18. Naïve projection. Misperception of others as having one's own interests.
19. True projection. Misperception of others as exhibiting one's own reprehensible behavior in connection with pursuit of interest.
20. Id projection. Misperception of others as having one's own primitive desire relating to interest.
21. Superego projection. Misperception of others as having one's own righteous beliefs relating to interest.
22. Guilt sensitivity. Expression of guilt feelings for nonparticipation in interest-related activities.
23. Conflict involvement: Time spent making decision under approach-approach conflict (both alternatives favor interest).
24. Conflict involvement. Time spent making decision under avoidance-avoidance conflict (both alternatives oppose interest).
25. Threat reactivity. Psychogalvanic resistance drop when interest threatened.
26. Threat reactivity. Increased cardiovascular output when interest threatened.
27. Physiological involvement. Increased cardiovascular output when interest aroused (threatened or not).
28. Physiological involvement. Finger temperature rise when interest aroused.
29. Physiological involvement. Increased muscle tension when interest aroused.
30. Perceptual integration. Organization of unstructured material in accordance with interest.
31. Perceptual closure. Ability to see incomplete drawings as complete when material is related to interest.
32. Selective perception. Ease of finding interest-related material imbedded in complex field.
33. Sensory acuity. Tendency to sense lights as brighter, sounds as louder, etc., when interest is aroused.
34. Attentivity. Resistance to distraction (lights, sounds, etc.) when attending to interest-related material.

Table 1. Some Principles of Motivation Measurement Which Have Been Applied in Device Construction (continued)

35. Spontaneous attention. Involuntary movements with respect to interest-related stimuli (e.g., eye movements).
36. Involvement. Apparent speed with which time passes when occupied with interest.
37. Persistence. Continuation in work for interest in face of difficulty.
38. Perseveration. Maladaptive continuation with behavior related to interest.
39. Distractibility. Inability to maintain attention when interest-related stimuli interfere.
40. Retroactive inhibition when interest-related task intervenes.
41. Proactive inhibition by interest-related task.
42. Eagerness. Effort. Anticipation of expending much effort for course of action.
43. Eagerness. Money. Anticipation of spending much money for course of action.
44. Activity. Time. Time spent on course of action.
45. Activity. Money. Money spent on course of action.
46. Eagerness. Exploration. Readiness to undertake exploration to achieve interest-related ends.
47. Impulsiveness. Decisions. Speed of decisions in favor of interest (low conflict).
48. Impulsiveness. Agreements. Speed of agreeing with opinions favorable to interest.
49. Decision strength. Extremeness of certainty for position favoring course action.
50. Warm-up speed. Learning. Speed warming-up to learning task related to interest.
51. Learning. Speed learning interest-related material.
52. Motor skills. Apt performance to effect interest.
53. Information. Knowledge influencing and related to course of action.
54. Resistance to extinction of responses related to interest.
55. Control. Ability to coordinate activities in pursuit of interest.
56. Availability. Fluency. Fluency in writing on cues related to course of action.
57. Availability. Free association. Readiness to associate to interest-related material when not oriented by cue.
58. Availability. Speed of free association. Number of associations when interest aroused.
59. Availability. Oriented association. Readiness to associate interest-related material with given cue.
60. Availability. Memory. Free recall of interest-related material.
61. Memory for rewards. Immediate recall of rewards associated with interest.

62. Reminiscence. Ward-Hovland effect. Increased recall over short interval of interest-related material.
63. Reminiscence. Ballard-Williams effect. Increased recall over long intervals of interest-related material.
64. Zeigarnik recall. Tendency to recall incompleted tasks associated with interest.
65. Zeigarnik perseveration. Readiness to return to incompleted task associated with interest.
66. Defensive forgetfulness. Inability to recall interest-related material if goal not achievable.
67. Reflex facilitation. Ease with which certain reflexes are evoked when interest aroused.
68. Reflex inhibition. Difficulty in evoking certain reflexes when interest aroused.

While most of the principles of Table 1 will be accepted by a substantial number of psychologists as valid for the measurement of motivation, still the prospect of having to consider each and every one of these in the assessment of a particular motive is bewildering, to say the least. Surely, the practicing psychologist reasons, there must be a way of simplifying this prospect. Yet in theory it can be argued that each manifestation should be considered, for if a diagnosis is based upon observations obtained through use of only one of these principles, or on the basis of only a few principles, there exists a distinct possibility that the diagnosis will be seriously in error because in the particular individual under consideration motivation is expressed primarily in ways indicated by principles that have not been considered. In the dynamic calculus there is an attempt to recognize both the need to simplify the measurement problem implied by the great diversity of principles indicated in Table 1 and the need to retain as much as possible of this diversity in measurements of motive manifestations.

One way of simplifying the measurement problem is to classify the principles a priori and then measure through one principle in each of the resulting classes. Thus, projective principles might be distinguished from learning principles and both be distinguished from physiological principles, after which one might select a projective, a learning, and a physiological device to measure, say, sexual motivation. A difficulty with this approach is that it still permits one to leave out important manifestations of motive—and without fully realizing it! Moreover, this approach contains few provisions for learning about different ways in which motivation is manifested or organized within persons, and yet the questions implied here are of considerable interest. For example, some theory in psychology suggests that patterns of expression of any motive may indicate choices of defense mechanisms, such as rationalization or fantasy (cf. Erickson, 1960), and such patterns might be resident in measurements based upon the principles of Table 1. Thus, an alternative to the a priori approach suggested above is to determine the extent and patterns of relationships among manifestations of a motive and then, using this information, construct a set of measurement operations in which the maximum variability possible through each principle can be accounted for, using a small subset of all principles. This is the approach developed in the dynamic calculus model.

In the research upon which this part of the model is founded, devices based upon the principles expressed in Table 1 have been developed to measure particular, rather narrow segments of motives. A "segment of motive" in this context is an attitude such as might be represented by the preference statement of the kind: "I want to enjoy greater sexual satisfaction." It must be emphasized that the preference statement is not literally the attitude; it merely represents it. The attitude itself is a complex structure expressed in the various ways indicated by the principles in Table 1. In a typical study 30 or 40 devices (based upon as many principles) have been developed to measure a single attitude.

In most studies device measurements have been obtained in ways that make them ipsative (cf. Cattell, 1944; Clemans, 1956, 1965; Horn, 1963b; Horn and Cattell, 1965). That is, it has been recognized that the behavior manifested through a particular device may involve not only motivation variance but also variance attributable to various ability and nonmotive attributes. Therefore, procedures have been employed to remove these latter sources of variance in considerations of the interrelationship among device measurements.

In the next step in this research the ipsative measurements obtained with 30 or 40 devices have been intercorrelated (adopting a linear model), and the correlations have been studied with the aim of discovering a parsimonious system for representing the observed behavioral variations. The evidence from this study may be summarized in terms of three major points, as follows:

1. The measurements of a single segment of motivation (by means of the principles in Table 1) often are *positively* correlated. It is going beyond the evidence to assert that *all* correlations between different possible manifestations of a motive are positive, but there is a clear suggestion that if reliabilities were improved, most of the correlations would be positive, although not necessarily large. In practical terms this means that a measurement obtained by use of one principle is likely

to be somewhat predictive of measurements obtained by use of other principles.

2. But to note that the correlations are not necessarily large is to recognize that even with corrections for attenuation due to un-reliability there is considerable independence in measurement through the various devices. Typically, the obtained correlations are in the neighborhood of .2 to .3. With reliabilities of the order of .6 or .7, the implication is that no more than about 50 percent of the variance observed on any two devices is common to the two. Thus an inference about motivation based upon *one* principle alone often would be different from an inference concerning the same motive but based upon another principle. In practice this means, of course, that considerable error must attach to decisions about motivation when they are based upon only one or a few principles.

3. Although there is considerable independence among the different ways of manifesting motivation when considered pair-by-pair, still if all are considered at once, there is much overlap and redundancy of measurement—so much, in fact, that it is probably not correct to argue that there are over 68 independent and reliable modes of expression of motivation, as is implied by Table 1; instead, the research thus far conducted suggests that some 6 or 7 linearly independent dimensions are sufficient to account for most of the reliable variation obtained in measurements based upon principles. These dimensions are referred to in the dynamic calculus model as *motivational components*.

The nature of the motivational components is suggested by the summary of results given in Table 2. In this table the columns (labeled

Table 2. Summary of Primary Motivational Components Results to 1965

	Alpha	Beta	Gamma	Delta	Epsilon	Zeta	Etc.
Preferences	43		49				
Autism	37		30				
Reasoning distortion:							
means-ends, ends-means	49						
Fantasy: choice to explain							
and read	45		30				
Identification preference	51						
Defensive reticence	31						
Defensive fluency	27						
Naïve projection	37						
Guilt sensitivity	32						
Utilities choice	45						

Table 2. Summary of Primary Motivational Components Results to 1965 (continued)

	Alpha	Beta	Gamma	Delta	Epsilon	Zeta	Etc.
Persistence: motor activity	32						
Id projection	38						
Perceptual closure	37						
Attention: auditory distraction	41	40					
Information		26					
Learning		37					
Memory for rewards		35					
Warm-up in learning		31					
Fantasy: time ruminating		39					
Control		21					
Availability: unoriented association	31		47				
Availability: oriented association			51				
Reasoning distortion: analogies			38				
Selective perception			38				
Expectancy: effort to be expended			23				
Perseveration: low perceptual integration			32				
Fantasy: sentence completion			38				
Superego projection			38				
Threat reactivity: cardiovascular				43			
Threat reactivity: psychogalvanic				51			
Conflict involvement: slow decisions				42			
Reminiscence					54		
Defense against recall					40		
Availability: speed association					35		
Impulsiveness: decision speed						38	
Impulsiveness: agreement speed						48	
Decision strength						52	
Fluency on cues							33
Persistence: perceptual task							43

alpha, beta, and so on) correspond to the components. The numbers in the body of the table are average (over several studies) factor coefficients—roughly the correlations between the components and the devices listed along the left in the table. Absence of a number indicates that the average factor coefficient is nearly zero.

How are these results to be interpreted? One thing is certain: detailed interpretation of each component is *not* a prerequisite for their use. It is a general characteristic of science that newly observed regularities are used before they are fully understood. Early sailors observed a relationship between onset of scurvy and absence of fruits in the diet and then used this knowledge to prevent the scurvy long before the observed relationship was correctly interpreted. Similarly, astronomers, using carefully recorded observations of perturbations, were able to make quite accurate predictions about orbits of planets before they could correctly interpret the observed regularities. Indeed, it seems that we must often get on with the business of using empirical findings if we are to gain an understanding of them. And so it would seem with the motivational components. Although the first four of these were identified over ten years ago (Cattell and Baggeley, 1956) and tentative interpretations were provided at that time, the principal insights into the meaning of the components has come in very recent years from attempts to use this form of measurement in clinical and counseling diagnosis. There is still much that needs to be learned if we are to provide adequate explanations for these observed regularities. However, from the experiences of those who have used the motivation components model in diagnosis, as well as from research conducted in the clinical setting, some rather general descriptions of the motivational component results have been derived.

Contrary to what might have been hoped, the components are not readily interpreted in terms of the defense mechanisms which Anna Freud so clearly described. However, there is a sense in which they represent concepts that are somewhat similar to the defense mechanisms. For example, the alpha component represents fantasy to a large extent and the beta component has some of the quality of intellectualization or rationalization. However, these ties are tenuous at best, and, in fact, most of the evidence from clinical use suggests that some of the components, at least, are better interpreted in terms of Sigmund Freud's concepts of id, ego, and superego.

The alpha component appears to represent an *affective* expression of motive. That is, through this expression there seems to be an absence of control over the impulse; the need is not intellectualized or otherwise rationalized; instead, there is ingenuous, free expression in the immediate present, as if one were letting his unencumbered feelings speak, as it were. The concept implied here is thus not unlike that which Freud discussed as the id impulse.

The beta component, on the other hand, appears to represent primarily a long-circuited *instrumental* (cf. Peak, 1965) expression of motive. That is, in this case the manifestations indicate the extent to which the motive impulses have been, and are being, channeled to achieve satisfaction over relatively long periods of time and in accordance with those realities which dictate that not all needs can be perfectly satisfied and the satisfaction of one must sometimes preclude the satisfaction of another. The concept implied is rather similar to that which Freud discussed as ego.

The gamma component may complete the Freudian triad of id, ego, and superego. That is, it is possible that the expressions of this component involve control over the impulse by the values of the dominant culture, as these are incorporated into personality structure through affect-laden teachings of early childhood. Perhaps through this component the motive is expressed as the superego dictates that it should be expressed. The subjunctive mood is used here because the evidence of experiment and clinical use neither rules out this interpretation, nor provides consistent support for it. In Tapp's (1958) inquiry into the matter, for example, several of the devices which were constructed to represent aspects of the superego concept did not correlate uniformly with the gamma component. On the other hand, as can be seen in Table 2, superego projection appears in the factor. Similarly, in the clinical work of the authors and others with whom they have talked, it has been noted that the person who is "bound in," as if by superego constraints to behave "properly," often expresses somewhat reprehensible impulses through the gamma component.

The last four components indicated in Table 2 are even less well understood than the first three. The delta component is defined primarily by physiological measurements and thus appears to represent the fact of some independence between internal bodily reactions in motivation and overt behavorial reactions. The epsilon is a riddle for which there is, as yet, little understanding. Cattell (1957) has speculated that it represents the effect of unconscious memories on the expressions of motive, a hypothesis similar to that implied in Jung's discussion of unconscious complexes. Zeta appears to be a factor of urgency and impulsiveness in expression of a motive. Eta would seem to indicate the extent to which the motive sustains activity in an immediate situation in which there are distractive influences.

When the interrelations among the seven motivational components are examined by factor analytic procedures, it is found (Cattell and

Baggeley, 1956; Cattell, Radcliffe, and Sweney, 1963) that the beta, gamma, and eta components fall together into one broad dimension, labeled I, while the alpha, delta, epsilon, and zeta components define another broad dimension, labeled U. Thus it would appear that the U-dimension represents mainly undifferentiated expressions, bound neither by reality-oriented learning nor by the learning implicit in superego structure: this is thus referred to as the *unintegrated* dimension of expression. The I-dimension, on the other hand, seems to embody both the integration achieved through ego function and that imposed through superego function; therefore, it is referred to as the *integrated* dimension of expression of motivation.

From a practical point of view these findings suggest that a major portion of variability in expression of a motive can be adequately represented in terms of a relatively small number of concepts and corresponding measurements. It is not necessary to use all of the principles listed in Table 1, provided that devices are selected in such a way as to give valid measurements on each of the seven components of motivation. Indeed, it may be that in many uses it will be sufficient to sample for only the two second-order dimensions of expression. In any case, some unique components of expression will be omitted, and it is theoretically possible that one or more of these could have some value in diagnosis. But until well-formulated hypotheses dictate otherwise, it is probably best to utilize the more parsimonious models.

MAJOR MOTIVES OF MAN: THE DYNAMIC STRUCTURE FACTORS

The evidence on components deals with the question: "How is any motive expressed?" But there is the other question: "What motives?" On this question there has been speculation over the ages. Indeed, a large part of man's culture, as in his literature and art, in his philosophy and religion, as well as in his science, is concerned with describing and explaining the motives which drive men. Numerous writers, philosophers, theologians, psychiatrists, psychologists and others have compounded all manner of catalog and theory about supposed motives. Perhaps the most that can be said about such attempts is that among the lists and descriptions actually provided there has been sufficient overlap to suggest that some motives, such as hunger and thirst, are well established by naturalistic observation, and some others are either well established or indicate misconceptions shared by many. However, this still leaves many supposed motives which appear in only one or a very few lists. And it still leaves unanswered the question: "What motives are prominent in man?" Also, while insightful theorists have noted that man is driven by such motives as assertiveness and that concerned with maintaining and enhancing the self (the self-sentiment), this observation is not enough to provide the measurements which are needed if we are to establish, for use in detailed clinical analysis, the normal and abnormal ranges of motive levels, the patterns of such levels which indicate problems, and, in general, the information which is needed to understand an abnormality associated with motivational dysfunction. Research representing a second major emphasis in the dynamic calculus model has been directed at answering this question "What motives?" and thus has aimed at providing a basis for measurement of motives for use in diagnosis and clinical research.

In discussion of the motivational components research we referred to *attitude* as a unit of observation of a "segment of motivation." Now we must consider a hypothetical universe of such attitudes and imagine that we are sampling from this universe. That is, in order to talk intelligently about "What motives" we must have some idea about a domain of elementary units of behavior which represent a motive of one sort or another.

In the area of study of abilities, the elementary sampling unit of the domain is represented in the idea of a *complexity* with which a subject must cope; each elementary instance of coping is a behavioral unit exemplifying an ability. In the motive domain, the comparable unit would seem to be represented in the idea of an *incentive* to which the subject reacts; each instance of thus reacting is the behavioral unit. In the ability domain, a complexity is embodied in what is called the *problem,* several instances of which are provided in a typical ability test. In the motive domain, an incentive is embodied in what is called the *attitude,* and several items are constructed to represent this in a typical attitude test. In ability measurements a problem is stated in several ways, or through several facets, to use the terminology favored by such writers as Guttman (1965) and Humphreys (1962). For example, analogies problems may be couched in purely verbal terms, in numbers, in geometric forms, in pictures, etc. Similarly, in line with the evidence on motivational components, an attitude may be stated in several ways—i.e., be measured through several device-tests of the kind listed in Table 1. Finally, just as the problems to be studied to gain an understanding of the abilities of man should deal with many things (not to mention cabbages and kings), so the sampling of attitudes to study the motives of men should involve considerable variety and be as comprehensive as possible.

On purely logical grounds one must object that this rational scheme for sampling within a domain is inadequate simply because the bounds for the domain are difficult to comprehend and therefore arbitrary. The problem in this regard is not unlike that which the astronomer meets when he attempts to propound a generalization about the physical universe (e.g., is it expanding?). The practical counter to this argument is that a domain must first be defined by examples and later comprehended by empirical study based upon use of these examples. From this study, rules are developed for producing, or looking for, instances of elements in the domain. In this way the domain itself may come to be more adequately comprehended. Today, relative to sixty years ago, there are many more ways of illustrating what is meant by phrases like "the domain of ability problems" or "the universe of physical objects," but this would not be true if empirical investigation of these domains had had to await a logically adequate specification of their boundaries. And so it would seem that the business of answering the question "What motives of man?" must get on with the task of sampling from the domain of attitudes, however shadowy the boundaries for this domain may now be.

To date, over 200 attitudes have been tried out in the research upon which the dynamic calculus model is based. Preliminary statements of attitudes were obtained from many sources, including the writings of anthropologists, sociologists, philosophers, and novelists, as well as the work of psychiatrists and psychologists. To get these preliminary statements in a form such that they could be compared and to make as explicit as possible the incentive quality, the course of action, and the object of the attitude, the statements were rephrased in the format: "I want so much to do this with that" (cf. Cattell, 1957). Using this preference statement as a guide, items were constructed to measure an attitude through each of several devices of the kind indicated in discussion of motivational components. Thus, an attitude of the form: "I want to make love with an attractive person of the opposite sex" might be measured through fantasy time ruminating, autistic misbelief, superego projection, and conflict involvement, for example. In a typical study 40 or 50 attitudes would be measured with 6 to 20 items in each of 2 to 10 devices. In most studies the device subscores for a particular attitude were converted to standard score form and added (i.e., over devices) to give the attitude measurement. That is, the score on the above-mentioned attitude would be obtained by adding standard scores on fantasy time ruminating, autistic misbelief, etc. In some studies attitudes were analyzed within each device separately. In either case the correlations between different attitudes were obtained and studied by factor analytic and other means. Some of the results from this research are shown in Table 3.

The factors in the table are named and numbered in the leftmost

Table 3. Summary Descriptions of Dynamic Structure Factors that Have Been Replicated in Two or More Studies with Adults and/or Children

Erg or Sentiment	Major Attitudes. Begin Each with "I want"	Average Loadings Adult	Children
1. Security-Fear Erg	More protection from nuclear weapons	48	
	To reduce accidents and diseases	33	22
	To stop powers that threaten our nation	38	
	To go to mother when things go wrong		43
	To be at home safe		38
	To grow up normally		31
2. Mating (Sex) Erg	To love a person I find attractive	52	
	To see movies, TV shows, etc. with love interest	34	
	To satisfy mating needs	52	
	To enjoy fine foods, desserts, drinks	37	
	To spend time with opposite sex		38
	To dress to impress opposite sex		38
	To go to parties where couples are invited		32
3. Assertiveness Erg	To increase salary and status	36	
	To excel fellows in chosen pursuits	40	
	To dress smartly and command respect	40	
	To maintain good reputation	33	20
	To read more comics		34
	To see that my team wins		39
4. Protectiveness Erg	Proud of parents and help satisfy their needs	47	
	To ensure that children get good education	40	
	To help distressed adults and children	40	
	To help spouse avoid drudgeries	33	
	To take care of pet		38
	Siblings to mind me		38
5. Sensuality Erg (also called Narcism or Narcissism)	To enjoy drinking and smoking	38	
	To enjoy fine foods, desserts, delicacies	41	
	To sleep late, take it easy	31	
	To enjoy own company	37	

	To eat well		32
	To have more holidays		41
6. Curiosity Erg	To listen to music	37	
	To know more science	29	37
	To enjoy graphic arts and theatre	40	
	To make my pictures beautiful		29
7. Gregariousness Erg	To participate actively in sports	50	
(Sports Sentiment)	To follow team and be a rooter	48	
	To spend time in companionship with others	23	28
	To play games with friends		36
	To go to parties where couples are invited		38
8. Pugnacity Erg	To destroy powers that threaten our nation	42	37
	To see violence in movies and TV shows	20	
	To get even with others		37
9. Appeal Erg	Turn to parents for affection	60	
(also called	To heed parents and turn to		
Parental Sentiment)	them in need	39	
	To feel in touch with God or similar principle	55	
	Proud of parents and help satisfy their needs	47	
	Influence of religion to increase	60	
10. Construction Erg	Take things apart, see how they work		38
	To make projects in school		33
11. Narcissism Erg	To have attractive face and figure		32
	Nice clothes to wear		31
12. Self-Sentiment	To control impulses and mental processes	40	32
	Never to damage self-respect	35	27
	To excel in my line of work	38	
	To maintain good reputation	37	34
	Never to become insane	39	
	To be responsible, in charge of things	31	
	To know about science, art, literature	31	
	To know more about myself	33	
	To grow up normally		28
13. Superego Sentiment	To satisfy sense of duty to church, parents, etc.	41	

Table 3. Summary Descriptions of Dynamic Structure Factors that Have Been Replicated in Two or More Studies with Adults and/or Children (continued)

Erg or Sentiment	Major Attitudes. Begin Each with "I want"	Average Loadings Adult	Children
	Never to be selfish in my acts	41	
	To avoid sinful expression of sex needs	33	
	To avoid drinking, gambling — i.e., "vice"	21	
	To maintain good self-control	28	31
	To admire and respect father		28
14. Religious Sentiment	To worship God		34
	To go to church		33
15. Career Sentiment	To learn skills required for job	34	
	To continue with present career plans	33	
	To increase salary and status	27	
16. Sweetheart Sentiment	To bring gifts to sweetheart	51	
	To spend time with sweetheart	41	

column. The phrases in the middle of the table represent attitudes. That is, these are the verbal paradigms which were used to guide construction of items in each of the particular devices through which the attitude was measured. The numbers along the right represent, roughly, the correlation between the attitude (as measured in several devices) and a factor: the numbers are literally average (over several studies) factor coefficients. In this table absence of a number in one of the two columns at the right means that the attitude was not used. For example, the attitude "I want to go to mother when things go wrong" was not used in studies with adults (however appropriate it might be for work in marriage counseling).

The concepts represented by the factors of Table 3 are labeled *ergs* and *sentiments*. If one does not care for these terms, he might substitute something like "primary drive" and "secondary drive," respectively, realizing, however, that in the present context the concepts are not those derived from armchair speculation and naturalistic observation, as is true of most listings of drives, but instead represent regularities observed under the above-mentioned conditions of investigation. Cattell has proposed that a new terminology be used to refer to patterns identified with the new methodology outlined above.

The term *erg* (from the Greek *ergon,* meaning work, as in the unit of work in physics) is used to "tag" a factor which seems to represent an innate disposition to become attentive to a particular class of incentives, to experience a particular quality of emotion in respect to this reaction, and to initiate certain patterns of behavior which can be seen to be directed toward preserving the individual or his species as a biological entity. For example, hunger and thirst are factors of this kind, although they were not identified in the studies upon which Table 3 is based.* In these cases the patterns of behavior which lead to satisfaction are directed at preserving the individual per se and the species only secondarily. Other ergs are less clearly related to survival of the individual, but pertain more directly to survival of the species. The mating and protective ergs, and perhaps the gregariousness and curiosity ergs, fall into this category. These examples illustrate, also, that in some cases it may be desirable to do more refined analyses to identify narrow patterns within patterns, as in research directed at identifying specific hungers.

It must be realized, of course, that in discussing innate patterns in this way it is not contended, as is sometimes supposed, that the complex behaviors actually observed in such a pattern just suddenly appear, as does the nest building of the wren, or that they inevitably grow in a culturally invariant form, as does the pubic hair of a Caucasian male. Much learning is implicit in the patterns which appear and this gives a particular culture-bound quality to the operationally defined ergs. Thus, the hunger erg identified in Asian cultures will involve more refinements on attitudes relating to rice than will the same erg identified in contemporary U.S.A. But such cultural and sub-cultural (for there will be these too) variations do not by any means deny the fact that an innate disposition is responsible for the observed patterns and they do not preclude the possibility that this disposition can be inferred from the evidence of somewhat different patterns in different cultures, although, of course, such variations do introduce very real difficulties in interpretation.

The concept of sentiment in this context derives from McDougall's

---

*The ingenuously curious might ask, "Why haven't hunger and thirst patterns been identified in this research?" The answer seems to be: (1) these two patterns are already well-established by the evidence from other studies, (2) they are rather easily identified by conventional means, (3) they have not been re-garded as particularly interesting for understanding between-person (i.e., trait) differences in motivation, and, thus, (4) few attitudes were samples which would provide variation from these sources.

Actually, in a more ingenuously inspired study by Horn and Bramble (yet to be published) attitudes representing hunger and thirst were devised. Measurements of these were obtained on ten separate occasions over a period of a week and newly developed procedures for distinguishing between trait and state patterns (see Horn, 1963a, 1966a, 1966b; Horn and Little, 1966) were used to identify hunger and thirst factors of the form of those shown in Table 3.

theory (e.g., McDougall, 1932) in which drivelike patterns involving several innate drives were distinguished from the drives themselves. This basic idea was made popular under the heading of "functional autonomy" in Gordon Allport's writings and appears also in the concept of secondary drive, as developed by learning theorists. The essential notion is that through learning the energies, the emotional qualities, etc., of ergs become associated with and, in the individual's perception, controlled by a particular object or institution. In Cattell's development of the concept several ergs become thus involved through what he refers to as *confluent learning*. That is, he recognizes that an individual in real life (perhaps in contrast to a laboratory situation) does not simply satisfy this or that need; he attains some satisfaction and frustration of several needs. Probably there is a sense in which the individual works to maximize his total satisfaction of all needs. In any case, satisfactions and frustrations associated with different ergs frequently can flow together, as it were. When a particular object or institution regularly is instrumental in bringing about such confluence (as when a mother controls the satisfaction and frustration of many of her child's needs) or regularly is associated in a classical conditioning sense (as the self is thus necessarily associated), then that object or institution can assume some of the qualities of the incentives which more primitively arouse the ergs involved.

The self, for example, is a very complex compound of many emotions associated with the satisfaction and frustration of many needs. That object which is perceived as the self has been perceived as instrumental in bringing about some of these end states and, even when not so perceived, it has been perceived as the agent in which the confluence occurred. To recognize that an individual may desire to preserve or destroy himself (i.e., his self) is to observe that he may wish to continue or end the satisfaction and frustration of the many needs associated with this object. Such desires to preserve or destroy make up the total structure which is labeled the sentiment to self, or self-sentiment.

Whether or not these erg-sentiment theories are accepted as useful, the covariational patterns among attitudes represent empirical generalizations which need to be given some consideration in a comprehensive account of human personality. To avoid begging the question in deciding on the merits of the erg-sentiment theories, we may refer to the patterns as simply *dynamic structure* factors, to distinguish them from the *motivational component* factors identified in the same general program of research and discussed in the previous section. These two systems of factors constitute the basic referents of the dynamic calculus model. The combinations of these in the definition of other concepts, such as conflict and integration, and the combinations used in diagnosis and prediction indicate the operations of the *calculus* in the dynamic calculus model.

DYNAMICS WITHIN THE MODEL

At this point the reader might well ask: "But where, other than in the name, do *dynamics* come into the model?" In considering this question we must move along several rather distinct pathways, for the ideas posed by the concept of dynamics cover a wide range and have quite different implications for research and diagnosis.

A great deal of theory in psychology has eschewed the concept of trait, as defined earlier in this chapter and in the chapter by Cattell, and has emphasized instead concepts which characterize the *situations* which provoke patterns of behavior and point to *change* within individuals. For example, in many sociologically oriented theories the principal concern is to describe situations which produce behaviors indicating assumption of a role. Often the implicit notion is that individual differences indicating traits either do not exist or are not important. When such a theory is used to conceptualize behavioral pathology an argument is developed to show how circumstances can conspire to place an individual in situations wherein he must assume roles that are maladaptive (cf. Newcomb, 1954). In considering therapy, then, it is argued that new situations must be arranged to allow (or require) the individual to assume new roles that are not maladaptive. Similarly, in learning-theory explanations of behavioral abnormalities it is assumed that the focus must be on describing a series of situations—learning experiences—which produce maladaptive behavior in any person who passes through them. Such descriptions as these are what some psychologists and psychiatrists mean when they refer to the dynamics of behavior.

In the dynamic calculus model, however, the term *dynamic* refers to more than this. That is, it includes consideration of these matters, but it also recognizes that any time an individual meets with a set of stimuli characterizing a situation, there follows an interaction which involves not only these stimuli but also the unique trait characteristics of the individual insofar as these are developed up to the particular time. The resulting behavior does not characterize the situation alone or the individual alone, but some meeting of the two. This does not deny the fact that certain kinds of situations will for most, or even all, individuals produce a change of behavior in a given direction. For example, it is acknowledged in the dynamic calculus model that almost any individual exposed to severe electric shock will learn to fear such shock. But what is emphasized in the dynamic calculus model is that the intensity of the fear acquired in this kind of situation is partly a function of the fear level already developed in the individual prior to the shock and is partly a function of the existing level of other drives in this individual. The practical, research-relevant implication of this emphasis is that it forces us to create new study designs for gathering and analyzing data.

The principal research methodology associated with theories wherein the aim is to describe situations has been one involving uni-variate comparisons of statistics of central tendency for groups. In the simplest case, a number of individuals are exposed to a set of stimuli characterizing the situation of interest, a number of individuals are prevented from reacting to these stimuli, measurements of behavior are obtained on both sets of individuals, and the difference between the means on these measures for the two groups is examined to determine whether or not it is too large to be regarded as a chance difference; if it is too large, then it is concluded that the situation is responsible for the observed difference in average of the single dependent variable—i.e., the behavioral measurements. Typically, the differences found in this way correspond to correlations of about .2 or .3 between the situation variable and the outcome variable. This implies that about 4 to 10 percent of the variance of behavioral measurements is accounted for by the situation. In other words, the implication is that there are notable individual differences in reactivity to situations, as these are typically studied. The aim in the general dynamic calculus model is to more nearly account for this variability.

One approach to this problem has been through multivariate study of the individual case, and we may point to three studies exemplifying this approach in the area of dynamic calculus measurements (Cattell and Cross, 1952; Shotwell, Hurley, and Cattell, 1961; Williams, 1958, 1959).

Some of the results from the Cattell-Cross study are presented for illustrative purposes in Figure 1. The curves in this rather complex diagram are for measurements of several dynamic structure factors obtained on each of the 80 occasions (days) recorded along the abscissa. The measurements were obtained on a single individual and are expressed relative to his mean score over all occasions. Thus, when the curve is high in the diagram it means that the individual's dynamic structure score is large relative to his "typical" score on that factor.

It will be noted that in general the curves indicate gradual changes and trends, rather than frequent fluctuations. The suggestion is that the individual doesn't change overnight, so to speak, but instead changes gradually and systematically in a particular direction. The individual involved here was a student, then experiencing problems related to the fact that he was wanting to study drama and his parents had wanted him to study science. He was seeking some help with this problem through the student counseling center of the university he was attending. Along the abscissa are recorded various events which occurred as gathering of the data proceeded. It will be noted that these events relate to the rise and fall of various dynamic structure factors. Thus, for example, there is rise in both the fatigue and the narcissism factors during the period in which the individual performs in a three-act play and there is a steady rise in the parental sentiment

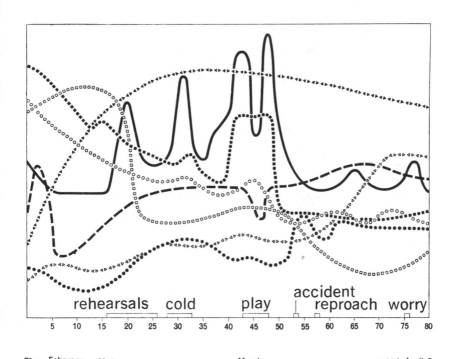

Figure 1. Dynamic Structure Measurements over 80 Occasions
(From Cattell, 1957)

(protective erg) and corresponding steady fall in the fear erg (fear for oneself) from the point at which his father was injured in an automobile accident. Findings such as these illustrate that the dynamic structure factors are sensitive to changes in ongoing day-to-day motivation: this kind of change is one aspect of a concept of dynamics in motivation. Such results illustrate, also, dynamic interaction in the expression of different motives.

Cattell and Cross (1952) intercorrelated the attitude measurements of which the above-mentioned dynamic structure scores were comprised and performed a factor analysis on the resulting correlation matrix. That is, they performed a P-technique factor analysis on the variation from time to time *within* a person. The results from this analysis illustrated that the factors found in day-to-day variations in attitudes within a particular individual represent some of the same functions as are indicated in R-technique studies of variation *between* persons in the expression of attitude on a single occasion. In other words, this evidence suggests that the dynamic structure factors represent *functional unities:* not only are they characteristics by which one individual can be distinguished from another, as a man with a large heart may be distinguished from a man with a small heart, but they are also characteristics indicating a function within the individual, like the function of the valves and muscles of the heart in pumping blood. This is another important aspect of the concept of dynamics in motivation.

Often, in using the term *dynamics* in general psychology, we have reference to development and to particular kinds of confrontations of a motivated individual with the vicars of society or with the raw physical environment. Thus, a conflict can be seen to be the resultant of dynamics in which an individual, driven by elementary impulses, acquires both an affection and a hatred for a complex entity such as his mother. Dynamics in this sense are represented in the model by algorisms in which motive measurements are combined to provide operational definitions of such concepts as conflict, repression, and confluence.

The studies of Williams (1958, 1959) are interesting not only because they illustrate this meaning of dynamics in the model, but also because they exemplify an approach to diagnosis which may become increasingly more common as computers get better and cheaper and more clinicians become aware of, and able to utilize, the potential of the computer.

If we consider a particular expression of attitude within the model, there is the implication that in this are embodied the expressions of several ergs and sentiments. At a crude level this may be represented with the idea of a linear partitioning of the variance of an attitude into variance associated with each of several dynamic structure factors. That is, the score of person i for attitude j can be written:

$$(1) \quad A_{ji} = b_{ji}E_{ij} + \ldots + b_{jm}E_{mi} + s_{ji}S_{ij} + \ldots + s_{jp}S_{pi}$$

where the E and S terms correspond to erg and sentiment factor scores respectively and the b and s weights represent the extent and direction of relationship between expression of the attitude, A, and satisfaction of the erg or sentiment drive. If all of these weights are positive it implies that satisfaction for all ergs and sentiments is realized through expression of the attitude in question. Confluence is then optimal as far as this attitude is concerned. If, on the other hand, some of the signs are negative, it implies that satisfaction of one erg or sentiment is attained only at the expense of dissatisfaction of another erg or sentiment. If such opposition in signs is found in analyses within an individual, as in P-technique analysis, then it can be taken as one kind of operational definition of conflict. The Williams studies were designed to explore this concept of conflict.

In his major analyses Williams performed P-technique factorings separately for each of ten persons. Five of these persons were mental hospital patients characterized in terms of various clinical assessments as having experienced and developed various forms of severe conflict. Five of the persons were "normals" matched with the patients on several demographic variables (age, social class, etc.) and were believed to have suffered and developed only moderate amounts of conflict. A measure of conflict was defined in terms of the number of negative signs for the factor coefficients obtained on each individual. As thus defined, conflict was significantly higher for the patients than for the normals and it was significantly correlated with clinical evaluations of the degree of conflict. Moreover, for each patient (and for the "normals," too, for that matter) Williams was able to break down the degree of conflict in terms of the particular ergs and sentiments that were principally involved. For one patient conflict could be seen to be particularly potent in the area of sexual expressions and superego prohibitions, whereas for another patient the principal contribution to conflict could be seen to involve pugnacity and the self-sentiment. It is this kind of analysis which may become more common as the potential of the computer is more fully utilized in our practice.

Conflict is also given operational definition in terms of the second-order motivational components. It will be recalled that the alpha, delta, epsilon, and zeta components correlated in such a way as to indicate a U, *unintegrated,* dimension of expression of motivation, whereas other components went into a broad dimension labeled I, to stand for integrated expressions of motivation. Interpreted more fully, the former can be seen to represent undifferentiated, primitive, idlike impulses, whereas the latter represent learned attempts at control of impulse in accordance with superego demands and long-circuited programs aimed at enhancing and preserving the self. On this basis, conflict in a particular erg or sentiment, as well as conflict over several dynamic structure factors, can be defined in terms of a discrepancy between integrated and unintegrated expressions. Measurements based upon this kind of definition have been used both in research (e.g., Cattell and Sweney, 1962) and in description of the individual case.

This approach to the measurement of conflict may be brought from the second order down to the primary order to illustrate a more intricate meaning of the term *dynamic* in the dynamic calculus model. We have noted that the motivational components are positively correlated, but that the intercorrelations are small. This means that quite different patterns of expression can occur for any motive. To oversimplify the matter by supposing that measurements in each of the components are dichotomized at the median to provide "high" and "low" categories, thus:

Alpha	Beta	Gamma	Delta	Epsilon	Zeta	Eta
a_1	b_1	c_1	d_1	e_1	f_1	g_1
a_2	b_2	c_2	d_2	e_2	f_2	g_2

a pattern in the present context is defined as a particular combination of the *a, b, c, d, e, f, g* categories.* We can see that with seven components, each dichotomized in the manner indicated, there are 2^7 (i.e., 128) possible patterns, although if measurements in one component are correlated with measurements in another component, some of these possible patterns will not appear—or will not appear with sufficient frequency to warrant generalization. In general, within a particular dynamic structure factor, such as the mating erg, all possible patterns will not appear. Those which do appear, however, represent particular qualities of expression of a motive and it is reasonable to suppose that these will relate to various pathways and crossroads in the dynamics of development (cf. Cattell, 1950). For example, in the expression of sexual motivation a pattern of low alpha, high beta, low gamma, and high zeta and eta would seem to represent a

---

*Pattern in this sense is a subspecies of the concept which Cattell defined as *type* in his chapter of this book.

pattern of dynamics such as McDougall's theory would advocate as producing the "truly civilized man," whereas a pattern of low alpha, low beta, high gamma, low zeta, and high eta would appear to represent the dynamics recommended by application of a Protestant ethic in child-rearing. These are just speculations, of course, but they illustrate one important meaning of the term *dynamics* as it is applied to help conceptualize the motivations of an individual.

There are yet other nuances of meaning of the concept of dynamics as it is used in the model (see Cattell, 1950, and Horn, 1966a, for example), but these examples should be sufficient to illustrate some of the major connotations and to point the way toward consideration of the applications of the dynamic calculus model in attempts to comprehend the individual case.

Some Applications

The concepts of the dynamic calculus model should be given consideration quite apart from consideration of attempts to apply these concepts to the problems of diagnosis, evaluation, etc., as met in a clinical practice. For there are some long steps to be made in going from research and theory-development to a particular technology, and these steps may be improperly made, and the technology quite inadequate, even when theory and the research upon which it is based are quite sound. Indeed, if a model is at all complex, as we might suppose it should be if it is to represent phenomena as complex as the motivations of man, then we might expect that it would need to be nurtured rather carefully, perhaps over an extended series of false starts, before it would yield its fruit of truly valid technical applications. In any case, although the proof of the recipe is in the eating of the pudding, we should recognize that this is a one-way "proof."

DEVELOPMENT OF PRACTICAL MEASURING INSTRUMENTS

Although the dynamic calculus model has been under development over a period of about twenty years and is based upon a considerable body of research, only in recent years have there been attempts to put the basic concepts of the model into the form of measurement devices for use in applied settings. The reasons for this apparent lag in going from the theoretical to the applied are difficult to specify, but no doubt one reason has to do with the sheer complexity of the model. The general theory implies that each of several motives of man should be measured in terms of several elementary units, termed attitudes, each of which should be assessed through several devices representing several components of motivation. More than this, although the matter was not given extensive treatment in previous sections (but see Horn and Cattell, 1965), the model implies that scores and subscores should be ipsative, so as to allow for control for the possible influences of several vehicles. The technical problems involved in achieving ipsatization are enough in themselves to generate a very extensive literature (e.g., the reference list in the above-mentioned article), and it cannot be claimed, even now, that the questions in this area have been properly asked, much less solved. Small wonder that practical tests based upon the dynamic calculus model did not suddenly appear as soon as some of the major concepts had been explicated! However, noteworthy progress has been made on many of the problems in this area; several instruments for use in applied settings have been designed; and although the ideal has not been attained, some workable scales have been developed.

In the overall design for construction of tests based upon the dynamic calculus model, consideration was given to possible applications in vocational and educational settings, as well as in clinical diagnosis and evaluation, and some thought was given to use with problems of development. A design for a kernel set of three tests was conceived. One of these tests, the Motivational Analysis Test (MAT), was to include dynamic factors and components of major relevance for clinical diagnosis and evaluation with older teen-agers and adults. A second test, the Vocational Interest Measure (VIM), was to be such that it could be a useful supplement to the MAT in some clinical applications, but would be comprised primarily of sentiments having particular relevance for vocational counseling, selection, and placement. This, too, would be for use with older teen-agers and adults. The third test, the School Motivation Analysis Test (SMAT), was to include some of the factors of both the MAT and the VIM, and thus mesh with them, but to be developed for use with an age level just below that for which the MAT and VIM were intended. In the overall plan the aim was to develop tests for use with progressively younger children as research at these lower age levels showed the way.

At the time of this writing a MAT (Cattell, Horn, Radcliffe, and Sweney, 1964) has been published, a SMAT (Cattell and Sweney, 1964b) is available for limited use, and a VIM (Sweney and Cattell, 1964) is available for use in research but probably will not be released in publication for several years. The major work in applied settings has been done with the MAT, so in what follows primary attention will be given to it.

The MAT consists of four major subtests strategically chosen to allow for group administration and yet represent both the primary motivational components and the second-order U (unintegrated) and I (integrated) factors among these. As shown in Table 4, it allows for measurement of 10 dynamic structure factors, each assessed through at least two attitudes; the self and superego sentiments are assessed through 6 and 4 attitudes, respectively. In all, then, there are 28 attitudes, each measured in each of 4 motivational component devices and with several items in each device.

In obtaining scores for a particular dynamic structure factor, the subscores obtained within a motivational component device either are, or can be, ipsatized to remove variance associated with the device, per se. In two of the devices (uses and associations) what is called the "self-ipsatization procedure" is employed and is built into the test in a way that does not allow the user readily to circumvent it; in the other two devices (estimates and information) analytic ipsatization procedures exist as options. The subscores for the two devices of the I component can be combined to provide an estimate of the integrated component in each dynamic structure factor and, similarly, two sub-scores for each factor can be summed to provide a U, unintegrated, measure. Total motivation in a particular erg or sentiment is obtained as a sum of these scores. A conflict score (deriving from the second concept of conflict discussed above) may be obtained for each dynamic factor separately by taking the U-I difference, and these separate con-tributions to conflict may be summed to provide an estimate of overall conflict. Procedures for obtaining several other derived scores are outlined in the test manual.

The measurements obtained with the MAT are objective in two senses of this term:

1. In the sense that subjective evaluations of the scores are not required, or permitted, in the scoring. As in the MMPI, for example, the score is obtained by use of an objective key, so that, barring minor clerical errors, the score obtained by one scorer will agree perfectly with the score obtained by another scorer. In this respect the MAT may be contrasted with TAT measurements of achievement and affilia-tion motivation (McClelland, Atkinson, Clark, and Lowell, 1953).

2. In the sense that subjective evaluations (by the respondent) of the purposes and intent of the measurement are, if not eliminated, then much reduced relative to what they might be. This is a very subtle point, but in general the idea is that a score is obtained in such a way that the respondent is not made aware of the attribute being assessed and thus is not allowed to distort his responses systematically in a way to produce a desired outcome. In this respect MAT measure-

Table 4. Attitudes Covered by the Ergs and Sentiments
Assessed by the MAT

(The attitudes subsidiary to a given erg or sentiment are indented under the erg or sentiment concerned. Each attitude is measured in four devices: autism, means-end knowledge, end-for-means [projection], and ready association. The wording which describes the attitudes below is not the actual wording of any question or questions on the test, but is simply a brief statement designed to represent the content and meaning of the attitude.)

A. ERGS
   1. Mating
      (a) I want to fall in love with a beautiful woman-handsome man.
      (b) I want to satisfy my sexual needs.
   2. Assertiveness
      (a) I want to be smartly dressed with an appearance that commands admiration.
      (b) I want to increase my salary and social status.
   3. Fear
      (a) I want my home better protected against the terror of an atomic bomb attack.
      (b) I want to see the danger of death from disease and accidents reduced.
   4. Narcissism-comfort
      (a) I want to lie in bed in the mornings and have a very easy time in life.
      (b) I want to enjoy fine foods, fine drinks, candies, and delicacies.
   5. Pugnacity-sadism
      (a) I want my country to go all out to destroy the enemy.
      (b) I want to see movies or plays showing gangster fights and violence, where many people are injured or slain.

B. SENTIMENTS
   6. Sentiment to self-concept
      (a) The social reputation component of the self
         (1) I want to maintain a good reputation and command respect in my community.
         (2) I want a normal, socially approved relation to a person of the opposite sex.
         (3) I want to look after my family so that it reaches proper social standards.
         (4) I want to be proficient in my career.
      (b) Control and understanding of self, per se
         (1) I want to keep my impulses under sufficient and proper control.
         (2) I want never to damage my sense of self-respect.
         (3) I want never to lose my mind (become insane).

(4) I want to know myself better (to be wise about myself).
7. The superego sentiment to socio-parental sanctions (the moral-ethical "ideal self")
   (a) I want to satisfy a sense of duty to my community, my country, and my God.
   (b) I want to see an end to gambling, idleness, excessive drinking, prostitution, and all other forms of vice.
   (c) I want to be unselfish in my acts.
   (d) I want to avoid sinful, improper occasions of sexual expression.
8. Career-profession
   (a) I want to learn more about the technical skills in my job or job-to-be.
   (b) I want to stick with my job or chosen career.
9. Sweetheart-spouse
   (a) I want to spend time with my sweetheart, enjoying our common interests.
   (b) I want to bring gifts to my sweetheart, to share in his or her delight in them.
10. Home-parental
   (a) I am proud of my parents and want them to be proud of me.
   (b) I want to turn to my parents for affection, comradeship, and guidance.

ments are similar to those obtained with the TAT and different from those obtained with questionnaires such as the MMPI.

This last point may be made clearer by considering a particular item from one of the devices of the MAT. To measure fear in the estimates device, the subject is asked to respond to a stimulus of the form: "Modern life has increased the incidence of heart disease by . . . (a) 0 percent, (b) 7 percent, (c) 15 percent, (d) 25 percent." Now, granted that the item is quite ambiguous when considered from a purely logical point of view, still the evidence of research shows that it does provide valid variance on an attitude of concern for health which, in turn, is an element of the fear erg. The principle upon which the item is scored is that of autism: that is, a person perceives things not necessarily as they are, but in accordance with his needs. In the present example, if one is fearful about his health, he perceives things as consonant with his fear—i.e., he sees the incidence of heart disease as on the upswing. The subject is not required to evaluate his own fears; he is asked to make an estimate about "how things are out there." And until one is told the fact, it is by no means obvious, even to a psychologist, that the item is used to measure fear motivation. It is in this sense that response to the item can be objective relative to the respondent's subjective evaluations of the purposes, etc., of the measurement.

Norms for the MAT were established on a sample of 2100 teenagers and adults drawn from various walks of life. The various subscores, as well as the total scores and derived scores, are expressed as normalized standard scores (stens) relative to these norms.

The VIM and SMAT involve different dynamic structure factors and different motivational component devices than are contained in the MAT, but in terms of general design, format, scoring, etc., they are similar to it.

MAT PROFILES AND RELATED INFORMATION ON RELEVANCY

Although the term *validity* is well established in psychometric parlance as an important criterion for evaluation of tests, it is a bit misleading. A test obviously is not simply valid or invalid; it may be valid for one purpose but quite invalid for another. Perhaps, therefore, at least initially, it is better to talk not about a test's validity, but about its relevancy with respect to various kinds of jobs which such a test might be called upon to do. At any rate, this is the approach taken here.

The MAT has been used rather extensively in diagnosis and evaluation of sociopathic conditions. Typical of results obtained in this area are those of House (1967). These are summarized in Figure 2. In this diagram the U and I sten* scores for each dynamic structure factor are plotted in the upper section and the total and conflict scores are plotted in the lower section. It will be noted that overall conflict is high and is particularly high in the areas of superego, self-, and sweetheart-spouse sentiment development and in the fear and mating ergs. If these conflicts are broken down analytically in terms of the I and U sten scores, it can be seen that whereas the fear conflict stems from a particularly high unintegrated expression, the conflict in the other areas stems primarily from particularly low integrated development. Thus, it appears that the delinquent's dimly felt needs for sexual gratification are not particularly different from those of others, but his organization of these into effective means for gratification are somewhat defective. Particularly lacking is integrated development of the self-sentiment. This, in itself, is partly indicative only of youth, but when it persists with age and when it is accompanied by low total self-sentiment development, it usually indicates difficulties of a kind where acting out is a notable symptom. The particularly high unintegrated fear is also quite

*A sten of	1	2	3	4	5	6	7	8	9	10
is obtained by about	.023	.044	.092	.15	.19	.19	.15	.092	.044	.023

of the persons represented by a standardization.

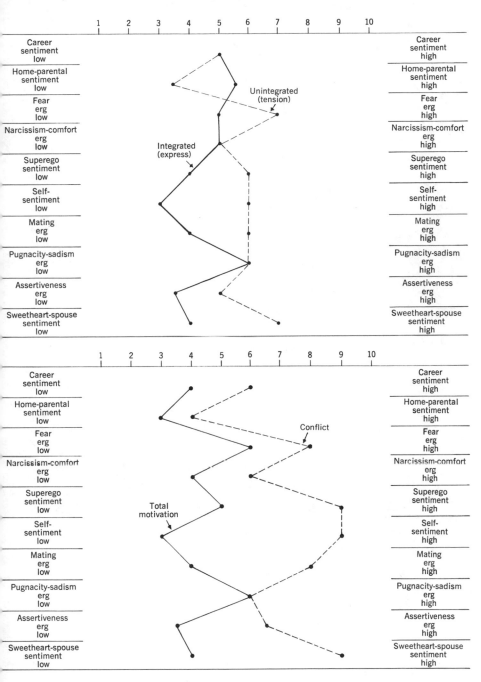

Figure 2. Motivational Patterns of Juvenile Delinquents
(House, 1967) *N* = 126 Males

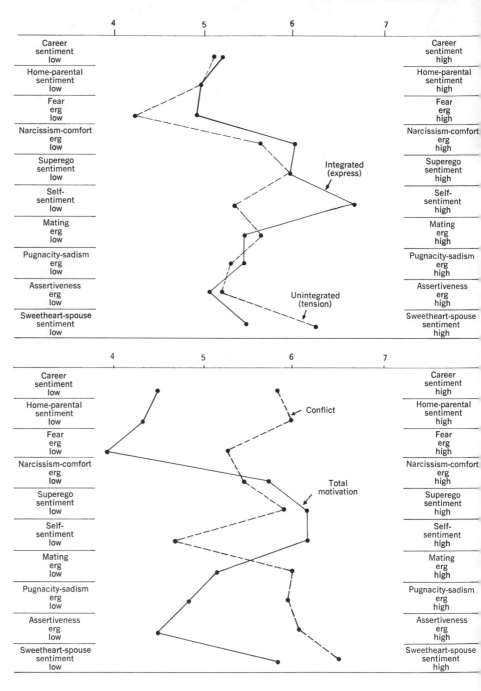

Figure 3. Motivational Patterns of Seminary Students
(Davis, 1966) $N = 267$ Males

characteristic of this group, for, contrary to what their aggressive demeanor may suggest, delinquents often are fearful.

Seminary students constitute a kind of logical opposite of delinquents. It is, therefore, of some interest to note that the MAT profiles for this group are in several respects opposite to those for delinquents. This may be seen by considering data provided by Davis, as summarized in Figure 3. In contrast to the comparable scores for delinquents, the integrated and total self-sentiment scores are particularly high for seminary students. Superego development is high, as would be expected. Fear, both unintegrated and integrated, is low. However, in the area of sex motivation (in the sweetheart-spouse sentiment and mating erg), seminary students are not unlike delinquents, although they show somewhat higher integrated development; the conflict scores in this area are high for both delinquents and seminary students.

Also notable in the profiles for seminary students are the particularly low total investments in career and assertiveness and the relatively high conflict in this latter area. Apparently, even in these days, entering a seminary is not represented as career investment and since this latter represents a socially acceptable means for harnessing the self-assertion motive, it is perhaps not surprising that seminary students should show heightened conflict in this area.

In Figure 4 are shown the profiles for a small sample of chronically unemployed males. In gathering the data upon which these profiles are based Lawlis defined "chronically unemployed" as: "Having held at least six different positions in one year, not one of them for more than two weeks, and having quit or having been fired before the contracted term of employment had been completed." In other words, "chronically unemployed" in this context refers to individuals who can get a job but who cannot seem to hold one. A question being asked in many circles these days is "Why are some individuals like this?" The profiles of Figure 4 suggest that part of the answer to this question is to be understood in terms of particularly low assertiveness coupled with high unintegrated but low integrated investments in career and superego sentiments, the result being that conflict is particularly high in these areas. Notable, also, is the high conflict in the self-sentiment. With respect to conflict in the self- and superego sentiments the chronically unemployed are similar to delinquents, but in other respects the profiles for these two groups are different. In other words, although there is overlap of what we label as "chronically unemployed" and "delinquent," the suggestion here is that the dynamics for the two are different.

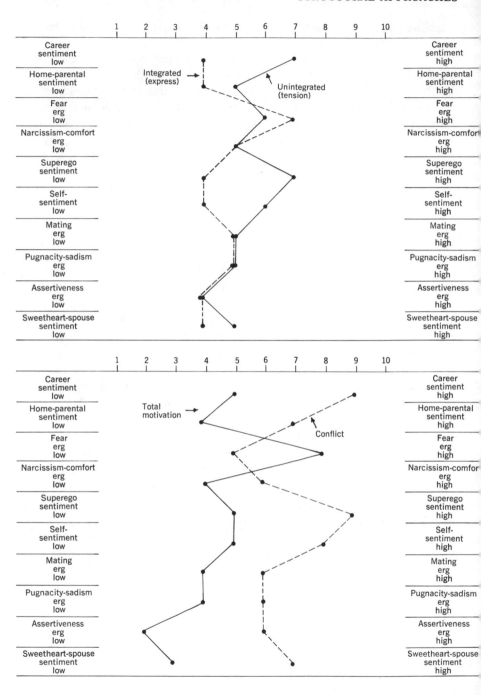

Figure 4. Motivation Scores of the Chronically Unemployed
(Lawlis, 1967)   *N* = 28 Males

Some Emerging Developments

In any field, progress in solution of a set of problems invariably raises new questions. So it is that work with the dynamic calculus model, both in pure research and in applications, has provoked quite new developments of a rather diverse kind. In the space remaining we can only hope to suggest the flavor of these developments, not outline them fully.

The question of what happens to the defense mechanisms within the dynamic calculus model is one that has provoked considerable interest. Cattell and Sweney (1964a) and Sweney and May (1967) have attempted to get this question into perspective by constructing devices to represent facets of each of the defense mechanisms, as these are defined in general clinical theory. The results from this line of research show that the defense mechanisms, as classically conceived, simply are not separate and distinct functional unities in the behaviors of people. However, separate measures can be obtained to represent several of these, and Sweney and May have made scales for these in what they call the Defense Mechanisms Index (DMI). This would seem to have considerable promise for analyzing conflict associated with mode of expression of motivation.

In using the MAT in marital and premarital counseling, as well as in work with delinquents and young people generally, it has become apparent that the major conflicts and deficiencies adumbrated by the test results often have to do with motivational investments involving the members of the family of origin and the family of procreation. Accordingly, Cattell and Sweney (1962) have begun to focus research on specific questions in this area. They have asked about the relationships among motive patterns for child-father, child-mother and mother-father pairings. Their early results present a picture that is too complex to summarize here. Suffice it to say that this line of research points to several places where it may be necessary to modify the dynamic structure model.

Summary

The dynamic calculus model represents an attempt to define human motive concepts objectively rather than subjectively, to define them in accordance with general theory in psychology (dealing with motives of organisms other than the human), and to define them in a way that clearly distinguishes them from other kinds of attributes, such as abilities or "general personality traits."

Any particular motive can be manifested in any one of a large number of ways. This presents a very bewildering prospect for those who would measure the strength of a motive. However, the many ways of expressing a motive are found to be dependent one upon the other. Roughly six or seven modes of manifestation account for a major portion of the observed variability. These "modes" are referred to as motivational components. Although some unique qualities of expression may be lost, the strength of a motive is well represented by six or seven measurements through these components. At a general level these represent both an unintegrated and an integrated expression of motive.

The particular motives of man are no doubt numerous, but several rather broad behavioral patterns can be seen to represent fundamental biologically based and socially based functions. These are roughly equivalent to the drives and secondary drives discussed in other contexts, but they derive directly from behavioral measurements on humans and from analyses with these measurements. They are referred to as ergs and as sentiments or merely as dynamic structure factors. Research completed to this date, including analyses on variations within persons as well as analyses of variation between persons, indicates 16 of these structures.

Dynamics are defined in terms of short-period changes within a person, in terms of pathways of development, and in terms of interactions among and between environmental factors and personal characteristics, such as motives. These concepts of dynamics are recognized in several ways within the dynamic calculus model.

Several attempts have been made to construct general purpose, practical tests to represent the major concepts of the dynamic calculus model. The Motivational Analysis Test (MAT) is the most fully developed example of the results of these efforts. It provides for measurement of 10 dynamic structure factors, each through 4 motivational component devices and over at least 2 attitudes.

The MAT has some relevance for understanding the dynamics of both normal and disturbed persons.

Research is still under way with the dynamic calculus model. Recent indications are that it will be expanded to include more detailed recognition of defense mechanisms and to provide for a more analytic description of the motivations in familial interactions.*

*We thank Mr. J. Sandoval for helpful comments he made on a draft of this chapter.

REFERENCES

Brown, R. *Words and things.* Glencoe, Ill.: Free Press, 1958.

Cattell, R. B. Psychological measurement: normative, ipsative, interactive. *Psychol. Rev.,* 1944, **51**, 292–303.

Cattell, R. B. The ergic theory of attitude and sentiment measurement. *Educ. psychol. Measmt.,* 1947, **7**, 221–46.

Cattell, R. B. The discovery of ergic structure in man in terms of common attitudes. *J. abnorm. soc. Psychol.,* 1950, **45**, 598–618.

Cattell, R. B. *Personality and motivation structure and measurement.* New York: World Book, 1957.

Cattell, R. B., and Baggeley, A. R. The objective measurement of attitude motivation. *J. Pers.,* 1956, **24**, 401–23.

Cattell, R. B., and Baggeley, A. R. A confirmation of ergic and engram structure in attitudes objectively measured. *Austral. J. Psychol.,* 1958, **10**, 287–318.

Cattell, R. B., and Cross, K. Comparison of the ergic and self-sentiment structures found in dynamic traits by R- and P-techniques. *J. Pers.,* 1952, **21**, 250–71.

Cattell, R. B., and Horn, J. An integrating study of the factor structure of adult attitude interests. *Genet. Psychol. Monogr.,* 1963, **67**, 89–149.

Cattell, R. B., Horn, J., and Butcher, J. The dynamic structure of attitudes in adults. *Brit. J. Psychol.,* 1962, **53**, 57–69.

Cattell, R. B., Horn, J., Radcliffe, J. A., and Sweney, A. B. *The motivational analysis test, MAT.* Champaign, Ill. Institute for Personality and Ability Testing, 1964.

Cattell, R. B., Radcliffe, J. A., and Sweney, A. B. The nature and measurement of components of motivation. *Genet. Psychol. Monogr.,* 1963, **68**, 49–211.

Cattell, R. B., and Sweney, A. B. Components measurable in manifestations of mental conflict. *J. abnorm. soc. Psychol.,* 1964a, **68**, 479–90.

Cattell, R. B., and Sweney, A. B. *The school motivation analysis test, SMAT.* Champaign, Ill.: Institute for Personality and Ability Testing, 1964b.

Cattell, R. B., and Sweney, A. B. Objective measurements of motivational investments in interfamilial relationships. Unpublished factor analysis. 1962.

Cattell, R. B., Sweney, A. B., and Radcliffe, J. A. The objective measurement of motivation structure in children. *J. clin. Psychol.,* 1960, **16**, 227–32.

Clemans, W. V. *An analytic and experimental examination of some properties of ipsative measures.* Ph.D. thesis. University of Washington, 1956; Psychometric Monogr. No. 14, 1965.

Davis, C., and Sweney, A. B. Motivational patterns in seminary students. Manuscript. 1967.

Erickson, C. W. Individual differences in "choice" of defense mechanisms. Lecture given at the University of Illinois. 1960.

Guttman, L. A faceted definition of intelligence. *Scripta Hierosolymitava,* 1965.

Horn, J. L. *Structure among measures of the self-sentiment, superego and ego concepts.* Unpublished A.M. thesis. University of Illinois, 1961.

Horn, J. L. The discovery of personality traits. *J. Educ. Res.,* 1963a, **56,** 460–65.

Horn, J. L. Equations representing combinations of components in scoring psychological variables. *Acta Psychol.,* 1963b, **21,** 184–217.

Horn, J. L. Motivation and dynamic calculus concepts from multivariate experiment. Ch. 20 in R. B. Cattell (Ed.), *Handbook of multivariate experimental psychology.* Chicago: Rand McNally, 1966a.

Horn, J. L. *Short period fluctuations in intelligence.* Denver, Colo.: Denver Research Institute Report No. DRI-614, 1966b.

Horn, J. L., and Cattell, R. B. Vehicles, ipsatization and the multiple-method measurement of motivation. *Canad. J. Psychol.,* 1965, **19,** 265–79.

Horn, J. L., and Little, K. B. Isolating change and invariance in patterns of behavior. *Multivar. Behav. Res.,* 1966, **1,** 219–29.

House, A. M. Prediction of juvenile delinquent offenses from personality measures. In symposium: Research toward isolating a "losers syndrome" with objective personality tests. Southwestern Psychological Association. Houston, Tex., 1967.

Humphreys, L. G. The organization of human abilities. *Amer. Psychologist,* 1962, **17,** 475–83.

Lawlis, Frank. The dynamics of the chronically unemployed. In symposium: Research toward isolating a "losers syndrome" with objective personality tests. Southwestern Psychological Association. Houston, Tex., 1967.

McClelland, D. C., Atkinson, J. W., Clark, R. A., and Lowell, E. L. *The achievement motive.* New York: Appleton-Century-Crofts, 1953.

McDougall, W. *Energies of men.* London: Methuen, 1932.

Messick, S. Personality structure. *Annu. Rev. Psychol.,* 1961, **12,** 93–129.

Newcomb, T. M. Role behaviors in the study of individual personality and of groups. In H. Brand (Ed.), *The study of personality.* New York: Wiley, 1954, 331–45.

Peak, H. Attitude and motivation. In M. R. Jones (Ed.), *Nebraska symposium on motivation.* Lincoln: University of Nebraska Press, 1965.

Shotwell, A. M., Hurley, J. R., and Cattell, R. B. Motivational structure of a hospital mental defective. *J. abnorm. soc. Psychol.,* 1961, **62,** 422–26.

Sweney, A. B. Faktoranalytische methoden in der motivationsforschung Cattell, *Z. esp. angew. Psychol.,* 1961, **8,** 136–48.

Sweney, A. B. *Fear anxiety profile: an analytic test of areas of threat.* Lubbock, Tex.: Psychometric Research Bureau, 1962.

Sweney, A. B. Studies of Motivation, *International Psychiatry Clinics,* 1966, **3**, 265–88. Boston: Little, Brown.

Sweney, A. B. In Symposium: Research toward isolating a "losers syndrome" with objective personality tests. Southwestern Psychological Association. Houston, Tex., 1967.

Sweney, A. B., and Cattell, R. B. Relationship between integrated and unintegrated motivation structure examined by objective tests. *J. soc. Psychol.,* 1962, **57**, 217–26.

Sweney, A. B., and Cattell, R. B. *Vocational interest measure* (research edition). Champaign, Ill.: Institute of Personality and Ability Testing, 1964.

Sweney, A. B., and Cattell, R. B. Objective test measurements of vocational interest and motivation. *Psychol. Rep.* (in press).

Sweney, A. B., and May, M. J. *Defense mechanism inventory.* Lubbock, Tex.: Psychometric Research Bureau, 1964, 1967.

Tapp, J. *An examination of hypotheses concerning the motivational components of attitude strength.* Unpublished M. A. thesis. University of Illinois, 1958.

Torgerson, W. S. *Theory and methods of scaling.* New York: Wiley, 1960.

Williams, J. R. *The definition and measurement of conflict in terms of P-technique.* Unpublished Ph.D. thesis. University of Illinois, 1958.

Williams, J. R. A test of the validity of the P-technique in the measurement of internal conflict. *J. Pers.,* 1959, **27**, 418–37.

FACTOR ANALYSIS, NATURAL TYPES, AND HOSPITALIZED PSYCHOTICS

Lorr's aim is to develop a meaningful structure for representing the psychotic disorders, a structure which is specifically derived from and applicable to hospitalized men and women diagnosed as functional psychotics. The psychodiagnostic data are observed symptoms-complaints. Lorr defines a symptom-complaint as an observable behavior, posture, attitude, or subject report which a skilled observer judges to be an indicator of a behavior disturbance. These symptoms-complaints fall into groups or complexes which tend naturally to occur with high frequency—i.e., syndromes. These natural syndromes of psychosis include: excitement, hostile belligerence, paranoid projection, grandiose expansiveness, perceptual distortions, anxious intropunitiveness, retardation and apathy, disorientation, motor disturbances, and conceptual disorganization.

These syndromes or factors provide the basis for grouping or sorting persons into homogeneous, mutually exclusive subsets with common sets of characteristics. Lorr's typology is offered in place of the standard subcategories of psychoses or as a more precise analysis with respect to symptomatology. The acute psychotic types include: excited, excited-hostile, hostile paranoid, hallucinated paranoid, grandiose paranoid, anxious-depressed, retarded with motor disturbances, disoriented, anxious-disorganized, excited-disorganized, and retarded-disorganized.

Lorr finds his factor-analytically derived types roughly comparable with the standard psychiatric classification into kinds and categories of psychosis. Lorr's findings lend research corroboration to the standard subcategories of psychosis—with minor refinements here and there. But more important, his methods constitute an attractively systematic approach to grouping persons into types on the basis of observable clinical behavior and symptomatology.

3

A TYPOLOGICAL CONCEPTION OF THE
BEHAVIOR DISORDERS

MAURICE LORR

Introduction

Numerous criticisms have been directed against conventional psychiatric diagnosis. There appears to be agreement that the system is unreliable, that it is lacking in validity for most ordinary users, and that it is inapplicable to a high proportion of cases. Additionally, it is mistakenly conceptualized on the medical model of disease (Szasz, 1960). The intent here is not to suggest an alternative scheme to replace psychiatric diagnosis. My purpose is limited to the presentation of arguments in favor of a typological research approach to representation of the psychotic disorders. This viewpoint will be illustrated by a computer-derived set of mutually exclusive classes for acute psychotics based on interview behavior.

Since the presentation is concerned with the concepts of symptom, syndrome, and type some definitions and distinctions are needed. As ordinarily defined, a *symptom* refers to a sign of any change occurring during disease and serving to point out its nature and location. The term will not be used to refer to signs of disease. As used here a symptom will mean any observable behavior, posture, attitude, or subject report which a skilled observer judges to be an indicant of a behavior disturbance. Ordinarily, the subject will be unaware of the significance of these signs. A *complaint* will refer to what a subject reports as distressful to him. Examples of symptoms are bizarre postures or beliefs that others conspire against him, as well as interpersonal behaviors such as defiance of authority. Examples of complaints are reports of shyness with strangers, feeling tired, or fear of high places.

Traits are often distinguished from symptoms and complaints by characterizing the former as universally present, as ego-syntonic, and as relatively enduring (Foulds, 1965). Symptoms and complaints are presumably present only in a portion of the population, distressful to the person or his associates, and relatively transient. To some extent this distinction is meaningful, but a more careful scrutiny of the concept of behavior disorders reveals difficulties. To the extent that "problems in living" and "problems in getting along with others" are germane to the concept, the distinction fails. Recognized trait dimensions such as anxiety, submission, conscientiousness, hostility, and dependency must also be included as definers of behavioral disorder.

The term *syndrome* will refer to a group or complex of symptoms and complaints that tend to occur together with high frequency. A syndrome is thus a dimension or factor that contributes to the definition of the domain of behavior disorders. An example of a syndrome is psychomotor retardation, a tendency for a person to respond slowly or not at all.

A *type*, on the other hand, is a group of persons who are distinguished by a common set of characteristics that set members apart from others. A type is a multivariate concept; all members are characterized by a specific range of scores on the various dimensions of individual variation employed to describe them. Analogously, a psychotic type consists of a group of individuals distinguished by a range of scores on the syndromes that define the psychotic disorder. Examples of clinical types are hysterics, psychopaths, and anxious depressives.

Advantages of a Typology

With symptom and complaint, syndrome and type defined, discussion can turn to the merits and uses of a typology. It is perhaps obvious that types facilitate communication. The unique pattern of characteristics make members of a type easily recognized, remembered, understood, and differentiated from nonmembers in a given domain. To label a person a psychopath, an anxious depressive, or a schizoid is to suggest immediately a broad pattern of traits and expected behavior. A depressed patient will be dejected in mood, self-reproachful in attitude, and a candidate for electroshock. Types thus provide predictive gains immediately upon recognition of belonging to a type. Inference can be made to a wide range of information generally lacking in single attribute measurement.

By maintaining the identity and integrity of the individual in the analysis it is possible to show how the entire profile of scores, considered simultaneously, is more than the sum of its parts. Improvement in predictive accuracy takes place through the operation of higher order dependencies and existing interactions. Interactive joint effects are ignored in ordinary linear regression. The possibilities of configural relations have been demonstrated by Meehl (1950), Horst (1954), and Lubin and Osburn (1957). Thus, a second advantage is that type membership may provide enhanced predictions to outside criteria, particularly if relations among variates are strongly nonlinear. Also, a sample of persons, identical or homogeneous in profile, will tend to be more homogeneous as to criterion-relevant behavior than a mixed sample (Toops, 1948).

When discrete, qualitatively distinct subtypes can be demonstrated, this knowledge, in and of itself, reflects an increased understanding of a domain. The taxonomy can facilitate the discovery of laws not observable within mixed samples. Indeed, the subtypes may suggest hypotheses and experiments relative to common structure, common processes, and common antecedents associated with each. In this way types lend themselves to theory development.

At this point it is necessary to distinguish between "natural" and special-purpose types. Natural types are those subgroups that emerge from a typological analysis of a psychological data matrix without resort to an external criterion. The analysis proceeds without recourse to any a priori information as to the number of subgroups or their nature. Special-purpose types are those established through the prediction of specific criteria such as response to chlorpromazine or length of hospitalization. Such criterion-related subgroups are typically useful only for the purpose designed. Characteristics predictive of response to an antipsychotic drug will have no necessary value for predicting response to an antidepressant drug. It follows that each new decision calls for yet another validation of a special-purpose class. It also means that individuals psychologically very different are grouped together simply because they possess attributes predictive of a particular criterion. Suppose, for example, response to aspirin defined a class. Included in this class would be persons suffering from arthritis, toothache, fever, and headache. It is clear that such subgroups would have very little generality. It follows from this that an important claim for natural types is that they are multipurpose. In general, it seems likely that more scientific propositions can be stated about such subgroups than for decision-related classes.

Typological Analysis

Typological analysis is a procedure for determining whether a specified sample is homogeneous or whether it represents a mixture coming from several populations. If the sample represents a mixture, then the analyisis is designed to recover and to identify the "clusters" or subgroups of persons present. Ordinarily, neither the number of groups nor their nature are known in advance, although informed guesses can be made. Nor is it known which individuals come from which populations.

The typing process involves sorting persons into homogeneous, mutually exclusive subsets on the basis of similar attributes or measures. The complementary task of sorting measures so as to define dimensions is performed by some variant of factor analysis. Unfortunately, through usage, both typological analysis and factor analysis have been called "cluster analysis." In order to avoid this confusion, the numerical procedures for isolating types, if they exist, will be called typological analysis here.

The first stage in a typing analysis is to choose and measure a set of characteristics on which all individuals will be compared. All major sources of behavior variation in the domain of similarity should be represented among the measures. Otherwise, important profile dimensions will be missing from the data matrix utilized in determining the degree of resemblance between individuals. Suppose, for instance, that measures of depression were omitted from a set of tests designed to compare psychotics. It would not be possible to identify existing depressive subtypes.

The next step in the typing process is to select some appropriate index of similarity and to compare each individual with every other one. The resulting N by N matrix then forms the basis for the typological analysis. Cronbach and Gleser (1953), in their review of most available indices, discuss the relative advantages of distance measures and related coefficients.

Numerous computerized procedures are available for conducting the typological analysis (McQuitty, 1961; Saunders and Schucman, 1962; Ball and Hall, 1965; Lingoes, 1966; Lorr and Radhakrishnan, 1967). The main precaution to be taken is to select a search procedure appropriate to the body of data. The process should determine rather than impose structure on data. Natural types reflect the data while arbitrary classes are those created by the arbitrary chopping up, or partitioning of individuals into "efficient" subgroups (Forgy, 1965).

Once the subgroups present in a sample have been distinguished, the problem is to establish rules for best assigning new cases to one of the classes distinguished. Discriminant function, multiple cutting scores, and similar procedures may be developed and applied to new cases.

A Typology for Psychotics

AIMS

The overriding goal has been to develop a fruitful and meaningful structure for representing the psychotic disorders. A first essential step was the construction and successive definition, by means of factor analysis, of a set of measures of the main dimensions of psychotic behavior. These measures hopefully define many of the constructs basic to subsequent research. The second step involved the exploration of the behavior domain in order to discover and identify any existing homogeneous subtypes. Much of this has been reported in *Explorations in Typing Psychotics* (Lorr, 1966). The third goal, yet to be achieved, is to collect validity data in support of the set of classes determined by typological analysis.

The exposition that follows will first describe the measures which provided the criteria for the typing procedures that followed. Next, some of the findings from a study of acute psychotics will be presented.

THE MEASURES

The attribute domain consisted of currently observable behaviors and self-reports ratable in a 30- to 45-minute interview of the patient. While social history data and other available information could be used to structure the interview, such data were not to form the basis for the ratings. Other media such as questionnaires and objective tests were considered but were rejected for a number of reasons. It is difficult to obtain reliable and valid performances or self-reports from a high proportion of psychotics. Many are resistive, disturbed, or inaccessible to routine testings. Furthermore, validated measures of psychopathology are simply not available. In fact, the very lack of such measures of specified dimensions of disorder suggested the need for a set of criteria against which more objective devices could be validated. Behavior ratings, on the other hand, can be highly reliable and stable. Insofar as competent judges agree, the ratings are direct measures of individual variations on the dimensions observed and need no further "validation" at most other media (ward or home), and observers (nurses, relatives) can be utilized to demonstrate consistency across these conditions.

Details of the construction, development, and refinement of the Inpatient Multidimensional Psychiatric Scale (IMPS) have been reported elsewhere (Lorr, Klett, and McNair, 1963; Lorr and Klett, 1966). Perhaps it would suffice to say that the major sources of individual variation were established by means of repeated factor analyses. Large samples of untreated newly hospitalized psychotics interviewed and rated independently by two raters provided the basic data. The 75 items of the standard IMPS consist of 45 nine-point intensity items, 13 five-point frequency items, and 17 dichotomous items.

Each syndrome (factor) is regarded as a relatively unitary dimension of behavior. Low scores represent a mild degree of disturbance while high scores represent a severe degree of disturbance. The names given the syndromes are intended to describe the underlying response pattern. For convenience in referral, each syndrome is also identified by three letters. The ten syndromes may be characterized as follows:

Excitement (EXC): The patient's speech is hurried, loud, and difficult to stop. His mood level and self-esteem are elevated and his emotional expression tends to be unrestrained or histrionic. He is also likely to exhibit controlling or dominant behavior.

Hostile Belligerence (HOS): The patient's attitude toward others is one of disdain and moroseness. He is likely to manifest much hostility, resentment, and a complaining bitterness. His difficulties and failures tend to be blamed on others.

Paranoid Projection (PAR): The patient gives evidence of fixed beliefs that attribute a hostile, persecuting, and controlling intent to others around him.

Grandiose Expansiveness (GRN): The patient's attitude toward others is one of superiority. He exhibits fixed beliefs that he possesses unusual powers. He reports divine missions and may identify himself with well-known or historical personalities.

Perceptual Distortions (PCP): The patient reports hallucinations (voices and visions) that threaten, accuse, or demand.

Anxious Intropunitiveness (INP): The patient reports vague apprehension as well as specific anxieties. His attitudes toward himself are disparaging. He is also prone to report feelings of guilt and remorse for real and imagined faults. The underlying mood is typically dysphoric.

Retardation and Apathy (RTD): The patient's speech, ideation, and motor activity are delayed, slowed, or blocked. In addition, he is likely to manifest apathy and disinterest in the future.

Disorientation (DIS): The patient's orientation with respect to time, place, and season is defective. He may show failure to recognize others around him.

Motor Disturbances (MTR): The patient assumes and maintains bizarre postures and he makes repetitive facial and body movements.

Conceptual Disorganization (CNP): Disturbances in the patient's stream of thought are manifested in irrelevant, incoherent, and rambling speech. Repetition of stereotyped phrases and coining of new words are also common.

RELIABILITY AND VALIDITY OF IMPS

Evidence of the reliability and validity of the syndrome measures can only be summarized here. Interviewer-observer agreement was generally assessed by means of the intraclass correlation coefficient. These coefficients computed form various sample ranges from .80 to .96. Even the individual items have a median of .77 and a range from .61 to .92.

As was indicated earlier, IMPS syndromes have been shown to be invariant factorially across five large samples. The ten hypothesized syndromes emerge in each analysis as predicted. There is also evidence of the equivalence of the syndromes across rating media (Lorr and Cave, 1966). Eight of the ten IMPS syndromes were found to be equivalent to comparable measures obtained on the hospital ward from ratings made by nurses and psychiatric aides. The Psychotic Reaction Profile (Lorr, O'Connor, and Stafford, 1960) provided the ward measures.

The syndromes measured by IMPS have also been found to be the same in both men and women (Lorr and Klett, 1965). Of twelve factors postulated, ten were the same as those previously isolated and were equivalent for men and women.

The IMPS has been successfully used as a criterion of change in studies of the effects of various psychopharmacological agents. It has been found to be sensitive to change and to differential change (Caffey et al., 1964; Cole et al., 1964; Lasky et al., 1962). Finally, it can be used to predict response to drugs and find the "right way for the right patient" (Klett and Moseley, 1965; Goldberg et al., 1967).

METHOD OF ANALYSIS

The procedures for finding existing subgroups within a sample and then matching across samples has been fully reported elsewhere (Lorr, 1966). Therefore, only an abbreviated description need be presented here. The ten syndrome scores are first converted to standard score form in order to be comparable in metric. Each patient's ten syndrome scores or profile are fed into a computer and compared with the profiles of all other patients in the sample of 150 cases the computer can process. The computer then sorts together into subsets all profiles judged to be mutually "similar" by virtue of exceeding a specified value of the index of similarity. The two indices of similarity used were the correlation coefficient and the congruency coefficients. Allied analyses have shown that application of independent typological procedures yield essentially the same results (Lorr and Radhakrishnan, 1967). Saunders and Schucman's procedure (1962) involves use of squared distances between profiles and seeks to isolate all nonoverlapping subsets which are mutually closest to each other. Application of the Saunders algorism to the same profile yielded essentially the same number and variety of subtypes. Approximately 60 percent of the sample analyzed could be categorized rigorously into one of the nine subtypes found. Another 20 percent could be assigned to the various subgroups when criteria of admission were relaxed.

THE ACUTE PSYCHOTIC TYPES

The patient sample in which the acute psychotic types were identified was drawn from sixteen state and university hospitals and clinics. The 374 men and 448 women had been diagnosed functional psychotics and their hospitalization was for either the first or the second time. Each case was interviewed and rated by the interviewer and an independent observer within ten days of admission. All patients were examined prior to treatment or while on a minimum drug dosage schedule.

Each psychotic type may, of course, be characterized by its mean syndrome score profile. However, such a characterization is likely to be deceptive as, typically, there are individuals who score below and above the general mean. Instead, each class will be described in terms of those syndromes on which nearly all members score either above or below the general mean on the standard score scale. Now, high scores are indicative of behavior deviation from the norm. Thus, most distinguishing syndromes are those on which all members score above the general mean. Syndromes on which all members score low are also important since they imply a relative absence of pathology. In contrast, syndromes on which members of a type score equally often above and below the general sample mean are simply undifferentiating and may be ignored.

Nine male types were evaluated in at least two separate samples. Of these, seven essentially similar subgroups were found in the sample of women. For details on matching and related technical procedures

Table 1.

Mean Syndrome Scores of 9 Psychotic Types among Male Patients

	Syndrome									
Type	EXC	HOS	PAR	GRN	PCP	INP	RTD	DIS	MTR	CNP
Excited	1.29	−.65	−.80	−.32	−.53	−.68	−.48	−.28	−.03	.47
Excited-Hostile	1.42	1.39	.33	.05	−.51	−.75	−.74	−.46	−.29	.34
Hostile Paranoid	−.52	.80	.17	−.42	−.55	−.43	−.55	−.24	−.40	−.61
Hallucinated Paranoid	−.53	.04	1.24	−.23	1.32	−.05	−.24	.22	−.52	−.12
Grandiose Paranoid	.12	−.41	.20	2.02	.51	−.46	−.45	−.14	−.61	−.13
Anxious-Depressed	−.46	−.63	−.80	−.54	−.43	1.15	−.45	−.45	−.44	−.62
Retarded-Motor Disturbed*	−.70	−.83	−.68	−.56	−.55	−.30	1.43	.06	.52	−.26
Disoriented*	−.43	−.84	−.93	−.60	−.38	−.88	.87	3.29	.39	.18
Anxious-Disorganized	−.50	.10	1.28	−.44	2.20	1.19	1.61	.62	1.18	.48

Mean Syndrome Scores of 2 Female Psychotic Types

Excited-Disorganized	2.13	.54	1.40	2.28	1.16	−.04	.13	−.20	1.51	1.81
Retarded-Disorganized	−.73	−.92	−.83	−.51	−.41	−.25	1.50	1.13	.38	−.19

*Unique to male patients.

the reader is referred to the full report (Lorr, 1966). The male types are described briefly below. Table 1 presents the mean syndrome score profiles of each subgroup.

Excited: The members of this type are characterized mainly by elevated Excitement scores. While high scores on Conceptual Disorganization are frequent, not all are above the mean. Some patients in the group also manifest above-average scores on Motor Disturbances and Grandiosity. Twenty-two percent of the excited type are diagnosed as Manic.

Excited-Hostile: The scores of all members are above the mean with respect to Excitement and Hostility. Scores on Paranoid Projection are also above the mean. Roughly two-thirds of the type were diagnosed as Paranoid. It is thus likely that the class represents one variety of paranoid disturbance.

Hostile Paranoid: Most patients in this class have scores elevated both on Hostile Belligerence and Paranoid Projection. However, some members exhibit elevated scores only on Hostile Belligerence or only on Paranoid Projection. Excitement scores tend to be conspicuously low. Approximately 64 percent of the type are diagnosed Paranoid type.

Hallucinated Paranoid: The class has as members patients scoring well up on Paranoid Projection and Perceptual Distortion. This means that in addition to delusional misinterpretation of the action of others as persecutory or conspiratory, the type members also hear voices that accuse, threaten, or order. Diagnostically, 71 percent of the group are categorized as Paranoid type.

Grandiose Paranoid: All type members have extremely high scores on Grandiose Expansiveness. Most members, but not all, have, in addition, elevated scores on Paranoid Projection and Perceptual Distortion. In brief, members exhibit attitudes of self-importance and superiority, and report the possession of unusual gifts and powers. At times they identify with well-known personalities or claim special divine missions. Approximately 78 percent are diagnosed Paranoid type.

Anxious-Depressed: The members of this class are all distinguished by above-average Anxious Intropunitiveness. A few patients also receive mildly elevated scores on Retardation. Fifty-five percent of the group are diagnosed as Depressed (Psychotic or Involutional) while the remainder are classed as Schizo-Affective, Acute Undifferentiated, or Paranoid. The Anxious-Depressives are the most frequent of the types identified.

Retarded with Motor Disturbances: Members of this type all have scores elevated on Retardation and Apathy. They are seen as slowed in speech and movement; they may also whisper, block, or fail to answer at all. Many of the class members also manifest high Motor Disturbances scores. This means they may posture, manifest bizarre or manneristic movements, talk to themselves, and show muscular tension. The diagnoses for this group vary widely, the most common being Acute Undifferentiated (37 percent).

Disoriented: Members of this patient type all have extreme Disorientation scores. In addition, some members have high scores on Retardation, Motor Disturbances, and Conceptual Disorganization. The most frequent psychiatric diagnosis is Schizophrenia, Simple type (36 percent).

Anxious-Disorganized: All members of this type show elevated scores simultaneously on Anxious Intropunitiveness, Perceptual Distortion, and Retardation. Many members also receive high scores on Paranoid Projection. Members are typically diagnosed as Paranoid or as Acute Undifferentiated. The presence of anxiety in conjunction with behavior disorganization suggests that the type represent a subvariety of schizophrenics.

As was stated earlier, seven of the male types are equivalent to those found among women. The subgroups that appear to be unique to women may be described as follows:

Excited-Disorganized: All members of this class have elevated scores on Excitement, Paranoid Projection, Grandiosity, and Conceptual Disorganization. In addition, many score high on Hostile Belligerence, Perceptual Distortion (Hallucinations), and Motor Disturbances. However, none of the group are disoriented. Evidently the Excited-Disorganized represent an acutely disturbed group. Members are most likely to be diagnosed as Manic or as Schizophrenic, Acute Undifferentiated type. Perhaps the type is transitional and metamorphoses into another subtype.

Retarded-Disorganized: Among men, the Disoriented type was differentiable from the Retarded-Motor Disturbed. Such a separation was not possible among women. Members of the Retarded-Disorganized type have strongly elevated scores on Retardation. In addition about two-thirds of the group also manifest high scores on Disorientation and Motor Disturbances. Members tend to be diagnosed either as Depressed or as Catatonic.

An examination of the subgroups suggests the presence of four kinds of patients. There appear to be four Paranoid types (Excited-Hostile, Hostile, Grandiose, and Hallucinated) and one Excited class. An Anxious-Depressed group represents the depressive disorders. The behaviorally disorganized subgroups include the Disoriented, the Retarded-Motor Disturbed, and an Anxious-Disorganized class. The Excited-Disorganized among women and the Anxious-Disorganized may represent transitional states, but research is needed to verify this conjecture.

TYPE AND DIAGNOSTIC CLASS COMPARISONS

One approach to the understanding of the statistically derived subtypes is to compare them with clinically derived diagnostic classes. Tables 2 and 3 show the degree of correspondence for those cases that could be classified into one of the computer-derived subtypes. It should be noted that the category called Depressed includes manic-depressive, depressive type; psychotic depressive reactions; and involutional psychotic reactions (APA, 1952). The diagnoses represent the combined judgment of the two observers.

The schizophrenic classes will be examined first. Those categorized as paranoid subtype evidently do not have the same profile. Patients subdivide mainly into Excited-Hostile, Hostile, Grandiose, and Hallucinated. The breakdown is essentially the same for men and women.

Table 2. Distribution of Initial Diagnoses of the 9 Patient Male Types

			Initial Diagnosis					
Type	Manic	Par.	Schizo-Aff.	Acute Undiff.	Depr.	Simple	Cata.	Chronic Undiff.
Excited	4	5	3	2	1	1	0	2
Excited-Hostile	5	26	3	2	1	1	0	1
Hostile Paranoid	0	18	1	1	4	2	0	1
Grandiose Paranoid	1	15	0	1	1	0	1	2
Hallucinated Paranoid	0	7	0	0	0	0	2	0
Anxious-Disorganized	0	8	0	7	1	0	1	2
Anxious-Depressed	1	2	7	6	28	3	1	3
Retarded-Motor Disturbed	0	3	2	11	4	1	4	5
Disoriented	0	1	0	1	0	4	2	2
N	11	85	16	31	40	12	11	18

Table 3. Distribution of Initial Diagnoses of the 9 Patient Female Types

			Initial Diagnosis					
Type	Manic	Par.	Schizo-Aff.	Acute Undiff.	Depr.	Simple	Cata.	Chronic Undiff.
Excited-Disorganized	4	1	1	3	1	0	0	1
Excited	6	0	4	4	2	0	1	2
Excited-Hostile	9	18	5	3	2	0	0	0
Hostile Paranoid	0	27	0	0	0	2	0	5
Grandiose Paranoid	0	15	0	2	0	0	0	0
Hallucinated Paranoid	0	11	0	0	0	0	1	0
Anxious-Disorganized	0	5	0	9	6	0	3	1
Anxious-Depressed	0	7	9	8	32	3	1	3
Retarded-Disorganized	0	2	1	11	15	2	16	6
N	19	86	20	40	58	7	22	18

The schizo-affectives of both sexes are categorized either as Anxious-Depressed or as Excited and Excited-Hostile. This class thus includes two very different kinds of patients that should not be grouped together.

The acute undifferentiated tend to be allocated by computer to the

Retarded-Motor Disturbed and to the two anxious subtypes (Anxious-Depressed and Anxious-Disorganized). The female acute undifferentiated sort into Retarded-Disorganized and two anxious subtypes. Again, the diagnostic category is so defined as to include two polar opposite symptom profiles.

The simple subtype males are few in number and thus generalization is hazardous. However, they tend to be assigned by computer to the Disoriented or to the Anxious-Depressed. Female patients are allocated similarly.

The catatonics are allocated principally to the Retarded-Motor Disturbed. The female catatonics tend to be classified as Retarded-Disorganized, the equivalent of the male Retarded-Motor Disturbed. Here the conventional psychiatric category and the statistical class are nearly equivalent. As may be seen from inspection of the last column in Tables 2 and 3, the chronic undifferentiated indeed exhibit "a mixed symptomatology."

If attention is now turned to the nonschizophrenics it is seen that the manic subtype among males sorts into the Excited and the Excited-Hostile. The female manics are additionally categorized as Excited-Disorganized. The presence of paranoid delusions, hallucinations, grandiosity, and conceptual disorganization as definers of the Excited-Disorganized suggests that patients so classified were probably misdiagnosed.

Patients diagnosed as depressed are categorized by computer mainly as Anxious-Depressed. However, those in whom psychomotor retardation is more evident tend to be allocated into the Retarded-Motor Disturbed when male, and into the Retarded-Disorganized when female.

The cross-comparisons clearly indicate that there is substantial agreement between the categories of the two systems. Indeed, it would be most surprising if there were little or no correspondence. However, the computer-derived scheme provides a much more precise breakdown with respect to symptomatology. It should be remembered that the definitions of the official nomenclature utilize other criteria besides current behavior and symptoms. In addition to symptoms, criteria such as premorbid personality, duration and course of illness, type of onset, age, and precipitating events are introduced as qualifying conditions for membership in a diagnostic class. IMPS ratings are restricted to currently observable behaviors, attitudes, and reported feelings. For this reason alone, one should not anticipate a close correspondence between the two approaches.

The typological comparisons confirm what clinicians already

know: patients called "schizophrenic" are behaviorally an extremely diverse lot. A large fraction are paranoid while the remainder may be characterized as excited, anxious, or "withdrawn." The contrast between the paranoid and the "withdrawn" deserves some comment. The withdrawn group is typically defined as those who are retarded, motor disturbed, conceptually disorganized, and disoriented. Venables (1954) and his associates have developed rating measures of Withdrawal and Paranoid Schizophrenia. Johannsen (1963) and his associates have reviewed available experimental data on the paranoid versus withdrawn distinction. In addition, there is substantial recent evidence in support of this separation. The computer-derived subtypes can, of course, facilitate further experimental work in this area.

Summary

This paper was primarily concerned with a presentation of the merits of a typological approach to the psychotic disorders. Concepts of symptom and complaint, syndrome and type were redefined. The advantages of a typology over a purely dimensional structure for representing psychotic behavior was briefly argued. The nature of typological analysis and the steps essential to a meaningful analysis were sketched.

Findings from a typological analysis of interview data were next described. The ten dimensions that served as measures of behavior deviation were summarized along with evidence of reliability and validity. Finally, the acute psychotic subtypes evolved were characterized and compared with conventional psychiatric classes.

It would appear that additional research should be pushed in two directions. Evidence in support of the practical or scientific value of the psychotic subtypes is needed. Follow-up studies of a cohort of newly hospitalized patients would make possible an evaluation of the predictive value of the categories. Do they predict length of stay, duration out of the hospital, or likelihood of readmission? The subtypes should also be contrasted relative to response on common antipsychotic or antidepressant drugs. Correlation with social history data similarly might be revealing of differences.

The symptom patterns that characterize each subtype represent the major targets of therapeutic intervention. However, little is known of the stimulus side. There is need to study the patient's deviant behavior in *relationship* to varying environmental conditions. The social stimuli that reinforce and maintain problem behavior also call for detailed analysis. It would be useful to know the dimensions of interpersonal stimuli correlative to the dimensions of behavior disturbance or disorganization.

REFERENCES

American Psychiatric Association Mental Hospital Service. *Mental disorders. Diagnostic and statistical manual.* Washington: Author, 1952.

Ball, G. H., and Hall, D. J. *Isodata, a novel method of data analysis and pattern classification.* Standard Research Institute, Menlo Park, Calif. April 1965.

Caffey, E. M., Jr., Diamond, L. S., Frank, T. V., Grasberger, J. C., Herman, L., Klett, C. J., and Rothstein, C. Discontinuation or reduction of chemotherapy in chronic schizophrenics. *J. chron. Dis.*, 1964, **17**, 347–58.

Cole, J. O., Klerman, G. L., and Goldberg, S. C. Phenothiazine treatment in acute schizophrenia. *Arch. gen. Psychiat.*, 1964, **10**, 246–61.

Cronbach, J. L., and Gleser, Goldine C. Assessing similarity between profiles. *Psychol. Bull.*, 1953, **50**, 456–73.

Forgy, E. W. Cluster analysis of multivariate data: efficiency versus interpretability of classifications. American Association for Advancement of Science, Biometric Society Meetings. Riverside, Calif., June 22, 1965.

Foulds, G. A. *Personality and personal illness.* London: Tavistock Publications, 1965.

Goldberg, S. C., Klerman, G. L., and Cole, J. O. Changes in schizophrenic psychopathology and ward behavior as a function of phenothiazine treatment. *Brit. J. Psychiat.*, 1965, **3**, 120–33.

Goldberg, S. C., Mattsson, N., Cole, J. O., and Klerman, G. L. Prediction of improvement in schizophrenia under four phenothiazines. *Arch. Gen. Psychiat.*, 1967, **16**, 107–17.

Horst, P. Pattern analysis and configural scoring. *J. clin. Psychol.*, 1954, **10**, 3–11.

Johannsen, W. J., Friedman, S. H., Leitschuh, T. H., and Ammons, H. A study of certain schizophrenic dimensions and their relationship to double alternation learning. *J. consult. Psychol.*, 1963, **27**, 375–82.

Klett, C. J., and Moseley, E. C. The right drug for the right patient. *J. consult. Psychol.*, 1965, **29**, 546–51.

Lasky, J. J., Klett, C. J., Caffey, E. M., Jr., Bennett, J. L., Rosenblum, M. P., and Hollister, L. E. Drug treatment of schizophrenic patients: a comparative evaluation of chlorpromazine, chlorprothixene, fluphenazine, reserpine, thioridazine, and triflupromazine. *Dis. nerv. Syst.*, 1962, **23**, 698–706.

Lingoes, J. C. An IBM 7090 program for Guttman Lingoes smallest space analysis. *Behavioral Sci.*, 1966, **11**, 75–76.

Lorr, M. (Ed.). *Explorations in typing psychotics.* London: Pergamon, 1966.

Lorr, M., and Cave, R. The equivalence of psychotic syndromes across two media. *Multivariate Behav. Res.*, 1966, **1**, 189–95.

Lorr, M., and Klett, C. J. Constancy of psychotic syndromes in men and women. *J. consult. Psychol.*, 1965, **29**, 309–13.

Lorr, M., and Klett, C. J. *Inpatient multidimensional psychiatric scale.* Revised manual. Palo Alto, Calif.: Consulting Psychologists Press, 1966.

Lorr, M., Klett, C. J., and McNair, D. M. *Syndromes of psychosis.* Oxford: Pergamon Press, 1963.

Lorr, M., Klett, C. J., McNair, D. M., and Lasky, J. J. *Inpatient multidimensional psychiatric scale.* Manual. Palo Alto, Calif.: Consulting Psychologists Press, 1963.

Lorr, M., O'Connor, J. P., and Stafford, J. W. The psychotic reaction profile. *J. clin. Psychol.*, 1960, **16**, 241–45.

Lorr, M., and Radhakrishnan, B. K. A comparison of two methods of cluster analysis. *Educ. psychol. Measmt.*, 1967, **27**, 47–53.

Lubin, A., and Osburn, H. G. A theory of pattern analysis for the prediction of a quantitative criterion. *Psychometrika*, 1957, **22**, 63–73.

McQuitty, L. L. Typal analysis. *Educ. psychol. Measmt.*, 1961, **21**, 677–96.

Meehl, P. E. Configural scoring. *J. consult. Psychol.*, 1950, **14**, 165–71.

Saunders, D. R., and Schucman, H. Syndrome analysis: an efficient procedure for isolating meaningful subgroups in a nonrandom sample of a population. Paper read at 3d Annual Psychonomic Society Meeting. St. Louis, Mo., September 1962.

Szasz, T. S. *The myth of mental illness.* New York: Hoeber-Harper, 1960.

Toops, H. A. The use of addends in experimental control, social census, and managerial research. *Psychol. Bull.*, 1948, **45**, 41–74.

Venables, P. H. A short scale for rating activity withdrawal in schizophrenics. *J. ment. Sci.*, 1954, **103**, 197–99.

FUNCTIONAL APPROACHES TO
PERSONALITY CLASSIFICATION

What we called structural approaches aim at organizing underlying concepts and making them internally more consistent. To those with a job to do, however, a defined task to accomplish, or some practical function to carry out, preoccupation with clarification is only a preliminary. What they need is a classification system which is useful and functionally oriented. Their aim is to put a classification system to work. There seems no reason why both approaches cannot be combined, so that a classification system may be put to work on some defined function, tightened up conceptually, put back to work, tightened up, and so on.

The two functional approaches in this section demonstrate how a classification system may be modified so as to be useful in psychotherapy. Reuben Fine proposes that therapeutic accessibility is the major guideline for a functional classification of candidates for psychoanalytic therapy. Molly Harrower proposes a set of categories for the classification of mental health potential in terms of likelihood of success or failure in psychotherapy.

A DIAGNOSTIC DIMENSION FOR THE
PSYCHOANALYST

Fine levels three criticisms against the standard psychiatric system:
(1) Emotional disturbances are unrelated to neurophysiological variables, and cannot be classified on the basis of a medical model of
physical organic illness. (2) A mere living adjustment to society is not
evidence of psychological normality or health. (3) The standard psychiatric categories are virtually useless as predictors and even more
useless with regard to treatment. Having dispensed with three pillars
of the Kraepelinian psychiatric system, Fine offers his own psychological
psychoanalytic platform: (1) Emotional disturbances are fully understandable in terms of psychosocial variables. (2) The undertaking of
psychological psychoanalytic treatment is a positive action designed to
achieve happiness for the patient. (3) Therapeutic accessibility serves
as the guideline for a classificatory schema.

Therapeutic accessibility depends upon the patient's degree of
openness to his own inner life, the likelihood of improvement, and the
ability of the patient to establish a relationship with a therapist. These
variables form the basis of a psychoanalytic diagnostic approach to
therapeutic accessibility, but Fine adds two more central considerations.
First, there are organic conditions; only nonorganic conditions are
treatable. Second, normality, neurosis, and psychosis are considered
to be stages along a continuum; thus, they are all potentially treatable
if the condition is not demonstrably organic.

For Fine, Kraepelinian-psychiatric categories contribute little to
the functional purpose of assessing therapeutic accessibility and, there-

119

fore, other variables are assessed. However, the measurement of therapeutic accessibility is limited to patient variables, whereas other contributors would supplement these with therapist variables and patient-therapist interactive variables.

Although one could complain that therapeutic accessibility truncates and attenuates the uniqueness of the individual, we must keep in mind that the task-oriented requirements of such a functional system supervene over such considerations. Nevertheless, it is clear that an adequate dimension of therapeutic accessibility requires further work, isolation of useful variables, research inquiry, and establishment of methods of assessment. A central problem involves a head-on confrontation with neurophysiological variables which appear to be theoretically dismissed but clinically present as entangling variables. Fine severs psychoanalysis from its neurophysiological theoretical foundation only to reinstitute organic variables in his psychodiagnostic approach.

The Kraepelinian-psychiatric psychodiagnostic system would insist that therapeutic accessibility is high with neurotics, low with psychotics, and so on. Why propose a new approach when the present one can do the job? It is on this issue that Fine's psychoanalytic theory must confront both the Kraepelinian-psychiatric theory and other psychoanalytic theories.

4

THERAPEUTIC ACCESSIBILITY AS A
BASIS FOR DIAGNOSIS

REUBEN FINE

By now it has become a truism that the prevailing systems of diagnosis are of little value, either clinically or theoretically. This applies to the revised nomenclature of the American Psychiatric Association as well as to the old Kraepelinian approach. Before another system is set up, it would be wise to subject the underlying thinking of the past to a searching examination to see what its philosophical assumptions were and, if possible, to avoid the mistakes previously made.

"Diagnosis" is a concept which derives from medicine. For a long time a strictly medical way of thinking was in control. What the physician had to determine was the immediate symptomatology, the broader complex of symptoms (the true diagnosis), the presumed course of the illness, and the prognosis at the time.

Furthermore, this medical way of thinking was based on a specific hypothesis, that the bizarre manifestations of the psychotic (and to a lesser extent the neurotic as well) were due to brain pathology. Sooner or later research would uncover this brain pathology, and medical science would then decide whether it was curable or incurable. The discovery of the syphilitic origin of paresis and of the abnormal EEG in epilepsy were taken as encouraging signs that research was proceeding in the right direction. For the practicing psychiatrist there was nothing to do in the meantime but make the patient as comfortable as possible—and wait.

Historically, the management of mental illness by medicine was due to the urgent need to rescue these unfortunates from the clergy,

121

who had for several centuries been calling them witches or possessed by demons and had been torturing and killing them, sometimes in huge numbers. The switch came at about the time of the French Revolution, which spread its humanitarian ideals in many directions, even though in this case it was inspired only by the horrors that it saw, and not any specific scientific discovery (Alexander and Selesnick, 1966; Menninger et al., 1964; Zilboorg, 1941).

Furthermore, mental illness, like any other, was seen as an isolated affliction. Like pneumonia or diphtheria, it could strike anybody. It had no more to do with the personality structure of the patient than any other illness. For their own good and for the good of society, the best thing to do was to isolate the mentally ill in hospitals, until research could catch up with the problem.

After almost two centuries, it can fairly be said that the medical hypothesis, if not completely refuted, has virtually no evidence to confirm it. On the contrary, the overwhelming mass of evidence is that mental illness, even in its most severe forms, is a psychosocial disorder essentially unrelated to organic illness (cf. Redlich and Freedman, 1966).

I

Therapy has served to highlight the fact that in traditional diagnosis four vital aspects of the individual were ignored: intelligence, socioeconomic status, age, and sex. These are all incidental in any standard medical diagnosis and, consequently, it was assumed that they were also incidental in mental disorders. Everything now suggests that they are vital to the understanding of the patient.

Intelligence is by now quite well explored. It has been possible to break it down into subelements, to develop tests which measure the component parts as well as the whole, and to correlate it with other areas of psychological functioning.

A comparison of intelligence measurement with personality "diagnosis" is most fruitful. Nobody would dream of calling a person "stupid," "normal," or "smart" and letting it go at that in any serious investigation. It is well known that a person can function well in certain areas and poorly in others, and that any global rating is apt to be misleading shorthand.

It is also known that intelligence and other psychological functions are intimately interrelated. It is absurd to think that a schizophrenic episode in a man with an IQ of 140 is identical with that in IQ 70; such a position is maintained only because of the medical analogy. In less critical instances, it could easily be shown that the structure of the personality differs considerably at different IQ levels. Modern psychoanalytic theory, which stresses the role of the ego, part of which consists of intellectual functioning, can readily explain such findings.

Socioeconomic status is another variable which is strongly involved in personality functioning. Marked differences are found from one society to another; what is "normal" in one country is bizarre in another, and vice versa. Within our society the personality of any individual is intimately interwoven with the milieu in which he lives.

Further relevant evidence along these lines is offered by the extensive research of the past twenty-five years which has shown the close connections of all organisms with the environment in which they live. Instinctual behavior has to be looked upon as an interaction between innate forces and external factors which impinge on these forces. In man the primary component of the external environment is other human beings. The manifestations of personality depend to a considerable extent on the particular persons with whom the individual is interacting at the moment (cf. Leighton et al., 1957).

The significance of age in personality structure has been voluminously documented; clinically no one would think of describing a person without knowing how old he was. A schizophrenic episode in a 50-year-old man is radically different from that in a 5-year-old boy. The misconception that there is one kind of illness, like typhoid fever, which can appear at any age, has stymied progress in many ways. For example, the promise of family therapy, which deals mainly with the child, could not be appreciated until this misconception was overcome.

Finally, personality manifestations in the two sexes are markedly dissimilar. Men and women, as Reik once put it, speak different languages. Even some common disturbance such as depression has a dynamic meaning for one sex which may be entirely lacking in the other.

In any thoroughgoing revision of the diagnostic system, all of these factors must be given due weight. Mere patchwork, such as the hodgepodge nomenclature issued by the APA in 1952, will not do.

The enormous progress made in knowledge of and ability to measure intelligence has several causes. Extensive empirical research is one. But empirical research, if it is not guided by some clear-cut conceptual framework, is often worse than useless. Intelligence testing has been guided by the idea that it is basically a measure of learning ability, and this notion has acted as a beacon light which anyone could see when he was shipwrecked, and thus could prevent him from slipping too far away from shore.

In the field of personality no such beacon light has been visible. The guiding principle implicit in the old Kraepelinian system was the ability to function in society. If a person could get along, he was "sane"; if he could not, he was psychotic. This, however, was only roughly true, since it could be argued by traditional psychiatrists (and has been argued to the bone) whether a suicidal patient is "psychotic" or not. That somehow this carries the implication that self-destruction is more "normal" than hallucinating mother's voice has more or less been ignored.

At any rate, it needs little to convince the present-day clinician that functioning in society is far from being an adequate proof of mental health. If anything else were needed, the Mid-Manhattan Study by T. A. C. Rennie and his co-workers concluded that four-fifths of those living in Manhattan in the area studied suffer from some demonstrable form of emotional disability, while one-fourth could be classified as seriously disturbed, even though they were not hospitalized. In an earlier day, Freud's findings were pooh-poohed because they allegedly were based on his experience with Viennese Jews; later research has established that for the most part his subjects were not Jews, and many of them were not even Viennese. No doubt the Mid-Manhattan Study will be discounted because everybody knows how wacky New Yorkers are, unlike the healthy denizens of Chicago or Des Moines. But enough of this. The evidence is clear.

II

Diagnosis has two purposes: to classify and to predict. The more closely these two functions dovetail into one another, the more successful will the diagnostic system be. Dissatisfaction with the present system, as has been indicated, comes about because so few useful predictions can be made on the basis of the available classificatory systems.

Now, the experiences which have had the most profound effect on clinicians in the present century have been those in psychotherapy. Decried as unscientific, demonstrated to Eysenck's satisfaction as futile, deplored by physicians as antimedical (any drug is worth a thousand words, especially if it shuts the patient up), dismissed by behavioristic psychologists as a form of magic or at best suggestion, psychotherapy has nevertheless gone its merry way, growing, developing, and enveloping more and more of the psychological domain. I propose, then, that in spite of the deficiencies in our present knowledge, we take *therapeutic accessibility* as the guideline for any classificatory approach to personality.

It is necessary first to summarize in unavoidably brief and dogmatic form what is known about therapeutic accessibility. The main basis of our knowledge is still the classic analytical procedure and its offshoots, which by now has been carried out in substantially the same form on hundreds of thousands of patients, of all ages and sexes, in all countries and climates. Actually, more than any other procedure known to scientific psychology, classic analysis comes closest to being a well-controlled experiment. Both the analyst and the patient are constrained to behave within certain well-defined limits; if they exceed those limits the analysis ends. And what the psychoanalytic experiment lacks in strict scientific rigor, it makes up in relevance to the human enterprise.

In summary, the following conclusions emerge from the therapeutic experiment:

1. No essential difference is found between those who come to therapy and those who do not. Freud always insisted that no clear line could be drawn between the normal and the abnormal (Fine, 1962). Sullivan once remarked that the difference between those who are in therapy and those who are not is that those who are in are in, while those who are not are not. In a recent study, Hendin, Gaylin, and Carr (1965) attempted to apply a research method based on psychoanalytic theory, using nurses as subjects. They called them nonpatients (some had been in therapy and stopped, but they were chosen essentially at random from the nursing staff of a large hospital). Even on this superficial basis they displayed many problems which called for therapy.

Therapy, in other words, is a form of self-study applicable to everybody. It is not a cure of the sick in the statistical sense, but only in the ideal sense (cf. Fine, 1967). It thus resembles religion, which calls upon mankind to seek salvation, or education, which offers to teach anyone who can benefit from the teaching, much more than it resembles conventional medicine, with its emphasis on illness and treatment. (It should be noted, however, that therapy does not differ so radically from medicine in the broader humanistic sense which seeks to prevent illness as well as to cure it when it arises.)

The implication of this finding can scarcely be overestimated. Above all, it means that *therapy should be looked upon as a positive action designed to reach happiness rather than a negative one meant to alleviate illness.*

In a great many cases a subtle change takes place in the attitude of the analytic patient toward his illness. At first he comes to treatment in a state of despair (as most people still do on the contemporary scene), convinced that he is far "sicker" than those around him. Gradually, as he discusses his family, friends, acquaintances, colleagues, superiors and inferiors at work, and people at large, this attitude changes. Then his initial attitude undergoes a radical reversal. Instead of feeling sicker than others he becomes acutely aware of the illness which is hidden behind their façade, and begins to feel superior because at least he has done something about his illness and is doing more. The "sick" are healthy because they are doing something about their illness, while the "healthy" are sick because they stagnate in their defensive rituals.

In a recent paper, Saul and Wenar (1965) put it very well:

The inevitable and simple conclusion is that if all children were properly reared, we would have a world of emotionally mature men and women. What we see instead is not human nature but a variety of characterological disorders which are so nearly universal that we mistake them for human nature.

2. Most people who seriously engage in therapy derive benefit in terms of improved self-understanding, functioning, and well-being. Some benefit more than others. Some feel their lives totally transformed; others experience lesser changes. But the great majority are helped, in ways that will be defined more precisely later.

3. For successful analysis a certain openness to the inner life is an indispensable prerequisite. Those who do not have this openness are: (a) people with a low IQ; (b) many people with low socio-economic status; (c) those with excessive hostility; (d) the conventional "psychopath"; (e) the paranoid; (f) the excessively rigid (e.g., many among the devoutly religious or the politically fanatic); (g) those with too little real-life hope (e.g., the hopelessly ill or the older person who is dying).

4. For many who are not amenable to the classic procedure (e.g., children, schizophrenics) certain modifications prove therapeutically beneficial.

5. The goal is not cure but improvement. Therapy is thus in every respect a learning procedure.

6. Understandably dissatisfied with the conventional criteria for the good life, psychoanalysis has developed its own philosophy of living. Briefly, this has been stated as ability to love, ability to work, and freedom from symptomatology. In more detail, the following criteria can be set up (Fine, 1967): (a) Acceptance of a therapeutic

attitude as part of life. This involves the willingness to face whatever comes to mind, and to communicate on a meaningful basis with other people. (b) A pleasure-oriented attitude. (c) A rich feeling-life. (d) Acceptance of sexual gratification as an essential part of life. (e) Love as the basis for warm interpersonal relationships. (f) Capacity to work. (g) Release of creative potential. (h) A satisfactory role in the family. (i) A good sense of identity that serves as a base for a satisfactory social role. (j) Reduction of hostility and other negative emotions. (k) Freedom from symptoms.

7. The goal in psychotherapy, child-rearing (intrafamilial), and education (extrafamilial) then becomes one of helping the person fulfill these criteria as closely as possible.

8. A parallel with intelligence can be noted here: the root concept in therapeutic accessibility is the capacity to learn about oneself from another human being.

III

In the light of the above findings in psychotherapy, what value can still be attached to conventional diagnoses? Involved are such concepts as self-understanding, functioning, well-being, openness to the inner life, a more progressive philosophy of living. How can these variables seriously be compressed into some new diagnostic system?

As an example of the confusion engendered by the notion of diagnosis, and the real issues at stake, I would like to cite a recent instance from my practice. A patient who had been in psychotherapy for some time left, against the wishes of the therapist. Several years later he decided to marry a Catholic girl (the patient himself was not a practicing Catholic). The church requires that in such instances the patient must submit a note from the psychiatrist (or therapist) stating that, to his knowledge, the patient is capable of understanding the responsibilities of marriage. Accordingly, the patient wrote requesting such a note.

Innocent though such a request may be on the surface, upon reflection it can be seen to cover up a whole host of searching questions. Why should it be assumed that a patient who has been in psychotherapy is less likely to understand the responsibilities of marriage than one who has not? Obviously, this derives from the notion that whoever goes for treatment is "sick," while the one who does not is well, an erroneous notion which has already been discarded.

Still another, deeper issue is involved. The Catholic church takes a view of life in general, and of marriage in particular, which is in a number of respects sharply at variance with the analytic ideal. It is dubious of pleasure, seriously (and needlessly) delimits sexual gratification, has nothing to say about the release of creative potential, encourages a number of social roles (e.g. monks, nuns, priestly celibacy) which are inimical to the good life, and has a view of love which differs in many essential respects from the analytical view. Even with regard to symptoms it places a higher premium on saintliness than on freedom from symptoms, so that, for example, hearing the voice of God is "good" even though it may be accompanied by a total deterioration of the personality.

In other words, the analyst would have to maintain that the Catholic view of life fosters unhappy marriages. The whole question of the patient's acceptance of the responsibilities of marriage is thus seen to be completely absurd. In effect, the analyst is being asked to testify that the patient is ready to do himself harm.

The clash of values encountered in this situation, as in so many others that could be cited, can only be resolved first by empirical investigation (what are the realities of a Catholic marriage as contrasted with a non-Catholic) and then by an affirmation of whatever the individual chooses to believe. In either case, the church's request is senseless. If it wishes to screen applicants for marriage, it should set up its own criteria, not refer to a discipline which is such a sharp critic of its way of life.

If taken seriously, the psychotherapeutic point of view has a profound effect on every religious undertaking, since it poses the insistent question of the effect of any religious doctrine or practice on the psychology of the believer. In recent years, the need to keep the clergy celibate has been widely debated. Even more startling is a report from Mexico that the abbot of a monastery requires that all the postulants be psychoanalyzed before they are permitted permanent residence in a monastery. If a man is to become a monk, he argues, he must do so on conscious rather than unconscious grounds (cf. Pfister, 1948). Understandably, the church has censured the monk (*New York Times,* May 28, 1967).

In none of these discussions does the question of diagnosis play any significant role. Numerous others could be cited, where diagnosis is equally irrelevant.

The diagnostic system of the American Psychiatric Association has been revised about every ten years since 1917 (Brill, 1965). If a theoretical concept leads to such contradictions in practice, it is necessary to reexamine the concept. The history of science is replete with notions which looked good at the time but because of persistent frustrations eventually had to be abandoned. Phlogiston in chemistry, the ether in physics, and vitalism in biology are all good examples.

Diagnosis will, we predict, go the same way. It derives from the by now exploded assumption that emotional disturbances can be classified in the same way as physical illnesses. It obfuscates so many basic philosophical issues that it eventuates in a host of pretentious jargon. The prevalence of diagnostic reasoning was one reason for Sullivan's remark a quarter of a century ago that psychiatry is neither science nor art but sheer confusion. Instead of shuffling and reshuffling labels, it is best to discard the concept entirely and to approach the problems from a fresh point of view.

IV

A theory must account for the knowledge that exists at the present time. Accordingly, attention must first be directed toward an evaluation of the diagnostic system currently in vogue.

Every astute clinician knows that, in practice, the traditional distinctions are virtually useless. In the psychoses Kraepelin's four classic varieties of hebephrenic, paranoid, simple, and catatonic cannot be differentiated in any meaningful way. The basic differences between schizophrenia and manic-depressive psychosis vanished with World War II. Even the existence of manic-depressive psychosis as some definable entity is questionable, since there are many depressives who never become manic, and many manics as well as hypomanics who rarely show signs of depression. The category of schizo-affective psychosis, listed in the 1952 classification, is so contradictory that it was bitterly fought by the old guard; nevertheless, the clinical observation stands, that some psychotics combine schizophrenic and affective features. Essentially, as Jones, Menninger, and others have insisted, there is only one "disease," with many variations.

"Psychosis," "neurosis," and "normality" are viewed as stages on a continuum, rather than illnesses qualitatively different from one another. Freud put it as follows in his 1937 paper *Analysis Terminable and Interminable:*

Every normal person, in fact, is only normal on the average. His ego approximates to that of the psychotic in some part or other and to a greater or lesser extent; and the degree of its remoteness from one end of the series and of its proximity to the other will furnish us with a provisional measure of what we have so indefinitely termed an "alteration of the ego."

Because of this structure of the ego, and the consequent variability found in the clinical picture, the concepts of "latent psychosis" or "underlying schizophrenia" become virtually meaningless. A diagnostic category such as that of "pseudoneurotic schizophrenia" proposed by some psychiatrists is sheer nonsense. Patients do experience an exacerbation or alteration of symptoms; in fact, symptom substitution is the rule rather than the exception. But to jump from this fact, true of most people, to diagnostic categories merely obscures the real problems.

An example will serve to make the issues clearer. A patient who suffers from anxiety, somatic symptoms, insomnia, and irascibility is admitted to a hospital. Later he develops clear-cut delusions and hallucinations. For the earlier stage we are now asked to use the diagnosis of "pseudoneurotic schizophrenia." Actually, the character structure of this patient was always extremely repressed. He had little pleasure, few sexual contacts, no love relationships, was filled with hatred and bitterness. The treatment he was given (drugs, reassurance therapy) was extremely poor. His despair about ever getting anything out of life continually deepened. Sensible therapeutic intervention at almost any point could have stopped or reversed the deepening despair. Instead, he was saddled with a label of "pseudoneurotic schizophrenia" and became progressively worse.

Just why one patient of this kind develops delusions or hallucinations, while another does not, remains a puzzle. But it can only be solved by empirical investigation, not by artificial labels.

The current division of the neuroses into hysteria and obsessional neurosis stems from Freud. His classification has largely replaced all the other diagnostic categories proposed during the last two centuries. But Freud himself recognized that in the great majority of cases mixed neuroses are encountered. Furthermore his classification antedates his ego psychology. If a full description of the ego structure were given, as is usual nowadays, these diagnoses also lose their meaning.

In the misguided attempt to combine psychoanalytic and psychiatric notions it is often stated that neurosis involves an inner conflict between the ego and the id, while other disturbances, such as character disorder, do not. Upon closer examination, this boils down to the question of whether anxiety is conscious (ego-dystonic) or unconscious (ego-syntonic). To call one "neurotic" and the other not is totally misleading. Because of the discovery of unconscious anxiety, its genesis, and the defenses against it, the whole concept of neurosis requires rethinking. Present knowledge again indicates that neurosis is some point or range on a continuum, and how it is determined depends on a variety of factors, including the values of the investigator.

When the definition of normality is considered, it becomes clear that the traditional narrow psychiatric approach is far wide of the mark. Actually, Kraepelin never gave the matter of normality much thought, and his followers have continued in his footsteps. The image of normality presented in this paper is an ideal, based on psychoanalytic theory and practice (cf. Offer and Sabshin, 1966). This view again reinforces the continuum approach to personality structure and emotional disturbance.

It is important to note that the increasing search for a physiological basis for emotional disturbance has yielded nothing of any consequence. In a recent review Kety (1965) once more finds that nothing of any conclusive nature has been established about biochemical factors in schizophrenia. As for the milder conditions, it has long been recognized that physiological explanations are pure speculation. Our thinking today rests squarely on the search for the dynamic-familial factors in personality.

In the functional-dynamic framework suggested here, psychiatric symptoms are only one of eleven items to be considered in evaluating an individual. One major reason for this is that, in any consideration of psychiatric symptomatology, what proves to be decisive is precisely the other factors, rather than the traditional diagnosis. For example, in the conventional treatment of the schizophrenic, the major prognostic factor, regardless of the treatment modality, is always the "premorbid personality." Looked at more carefully, this means that the closer the patient came to the analytic ideal the more hopeful the outlook is for a recovery from the severe despair in which he now finds himself. Thus the question of diagnosis is again misleading, while what is significant is the functional dynamic approach to the patient and his troubles.

In addition to being confusing, adherence to conventional diagnosis has led to a considerable amount of psychiatrogenic disorder. Once a patient is labeled a schizophrenic, the psychiatrist becomes pessimistic about the prognosis. This pessimism turns into an inadequate therapeutic approach; for example, the therapist will be afraid to give "dynamic" interpretations because the patient with a fragile ego will then crack up. In most cases this procedure frightens the patient, and leads to a breakdown more quickly than any other.

The weakest aspect of the traditional diagnostic system is its application to therapy. By and large, it is assumed that certain diagnostic entities have a poor therapeutic prognosis. Historically, this poor prognosis has been related to a variety of postulated physiological factors, and research has been directed towards uncovering these factors. As already mentioned, all this research has yielded no tangible results.

In the meantime, Freud's functional-dynamic approach led to great strides forward in the area of therapy. It was shown that many conditions hitherto considered inaccessible could respond to therapy. And the therapeutic results could be firmly grounded in a satisfactory theory of psychoanalytic psychology, a fact of immense importance which is too often overlooked in discussions of this topic.

Many psychoanalysts (cf. Stone, 1954) generally have the feeling, which this writer shares, that virtually all the psychopathological conditions known to man which are not demonstrably organic are accessible to psychotherapy, provided that suitable modifications in the classical procedure are introduced. Again, this brings psychotherapy closer to education: all men are educable, and all men are treatable. Barriers to educability are found for many reasons: age, physical illness, lack of capacity, prior indoctrination, lack of motivation, excessive transference, either positive or negative, and so on. Similar barriers to treatability can be enumerated. In all these barriers, however, the conventional diagnoses play a subordinate role.

Historically, psychiatrists have been most impressed by the apparent untreatability of the psychotic. But while this clinical observation is roughly true, it must be qualified in many different ways. Mere hospitalization produces a remission of symptoms in about 25 percent of schizophrenics (Bellak, 1958). In certain kinds of patients (e.g., catatonics) this percentage goes up to 50 percent.

Furthermore, many kinds of intervention tend to produce dramatic results. The introduction of moral treatment in the first half of the nineteenth century led to a sharp rise in discharges. When this was replaced by the organic psychiatrist's attempt to focalize brain pathology the therapeutic results dropped noticeably (Alexander, 1966). Sullivan reported discharge rates of 70 to 80 percent on first admissions; others who have approached the schizophrenic therapeutically have had similar experiences. In a recent paper, Bryce Boyer reports on satisfactory office treatment of schizophrenics (Boyer and Giovacchini, 1967).

Two main problems arise in the psychotherapy of schizophrenics: one is the approach used, the other is the point at which intervention takes place. In traditional psychiatry the approach used was a purely rational one; it failed completely. This led to a feeling of hopelessness about the condition which surely made it worse. Boisen in his classic *Exploration of the Inner World* (1962) relates that in a hospital stay of several months he spent only fifteen minutes talking to a psychiatrist. When he recovered spontaneously, no one believed him.

With regard to the second problem, concerning the point at which intervention takes place, it is now crystal clear that schizophrenia is the end product of a long process of personality deterioration. It is the despair that follows a long series of unsuccessful attempts to make contacts with people, analogous in many ways to the exhaustion stage of the General Adaptation Syndrome which Selye (1956) describes. So much harm has been done by this time that it becomes understandable why the problem is so enormously difficult. Furthermore, the more severe the disturbance, the greater the demands on the therapist. Nevertheless, dedicated individuals have repeatedly reported successes in the most seemingly hopeless cases (cf. Sechehaye, 1951).

Instead of the demonological approach to mental illness embodied in the traditional diagnosis, a functional-dynamic analysis of the therapeutic process leads to an entirely fresh orientation. Therapy can be divided into four stages: (1) establishing the relationship; (2) clarifying the dynamics; (3) working through the dynamics; (4) termination (Fine, 1962; Wolberg 1954). Severe emotional disturbance generally involves a regression to the oral stage. In this oral regression the patient creates the greatest difficulties about establishing a relationship. His demands are so excessive, his behavior so infantile, and his language so bizarre that only specially trained individuals can cope with him. Then, even under the best of circumstances he may break off therapy because he does not like the other person.

Thus, *untreatability is in most cases the inability to establish a relationship*. This proposition gives a dynamic cast to the problem of therapy. If the problem is one of being unable to establish a relationship, efforts should be directed towards that problem. The schizophrenic may well demand inordinate amounts of time; few therapists are willing to spend eight years with a patient day in and day out, under the most trying conditions. But, then, it should be said that the effort required to help a patient is not available, rather than hide behind the myth that the patient is untreatable.

A parallel is available in the famous case of Helen Keller. The devotion which her nurse-teacher brought to her charge literally made her a miracle worker. Thousands of other children, often afflicted with less severe handicaps, never reach anything remotely resembling a comparable stage in development because they cannot find an equally devoted teacher.

Another instance in which the two approaches can profitably be compared is that of homosexuality. It has required exhaustive research to demonstrate the obvious fact that homosexuality is basically a fear of the opposite sex (Bieber et al., 1962). But first the various diagnostic approaches had to be taken care of: homosexuality is a defense against schizophrenia, a constitutional anomaly, a normal social deviation, and so on. Careful study of any homosexual reveals the severely disturbed conditions under which he is brought up.

Bieber and his group found that about 30 percent of their patient population were able to move on to heterosexuality (50 percent of those who were bisexual at the beginning). As with schizophrenia, this could be seen as the reversal from an extremely low point; intervention at prior stages could be expected to yield a much higher percentage of change. And in the broader area of the total range of homosexuals, it still remains true that the great majority refuse to go for treatment, that is, establish a relationship with a therapist. Here, too, public education could be expected to lead to better therapeutic results, since it would highlight the unwillingness of so many regressed individuals to make contact with their fellowmen.

V

The purpose of this paper is to offer some clarification of the problems surrounding diagnosis, to suggest an alternative framework to the one currently in vogue, and to propose a research program. In this final section I would like to make some comments on the research aspect of the functional-dynamic approach described here.

Scientific methodology in psychoanalytic psychology has always rested heavily on the integration of material from divers sources of investigation. For example, the similarity of productions of children, schizophrenics, primitives, and dreamers has been one of the most potent sources of the conviction of the essential unity of all mankind.

In the field under discussion here, a vast amount of material is available from many different sources. All of this can be integrated with the help of the analytic ideal as a conceptual framework.

There are studies on pleasure (Szasz, 1957), sexuality (Fine, 1965), love (Hunt, 1959), creativity (Barron, 1963), and all the other topics covered. These have to be integrated under the general heading of the interrelationship between family structure and personality.

Nevertheless, our information is still manifestly inadequate. New research should be directed toward systematically exploring all the problems involved in the ideal structure of personality. Interrelationships among the various categories must be studied systematically. Eventually we may come up with a smaller number of concepts than the ones suggested here, but this is a matter of relatively little significance. Much of past research must be discarded, especially that based on traditional diagnostic classification, but much can be retained.

The approach suggested here is based on the intuitive kind of factor analysis that emerges from the researches of psychoanalysis. These are the basic concepts that have to be explored further to make psychology fully scientific.

That intuition plays a vital role in science is underscored in a recent paper by the mathematician R. L. Wilder (1967). He writes:

> The role of intuition in research is to provide the "educated guess," which may prove to be true or false; but in either case progress cannot be made without it and even a false guess may lead to progress. Thus intuition also plays a major role in the evolution of mathematical concepts.

Over the past few years F. C. Thorne has been developing a series of scales not too dissimilar from those suggested here (Thorne, 1965). He lists an integration-level test series, which includes a personal health survey, sex inventory, personal development study, ideological survey, social status survey, life style analysis, and existential analysis.

While diagnosis can be discarded, some system of classification will always be useful. What will emerge from this kind of research based on an intuitive approach to what is important in human life is hard to say. Certainly, though, it will resemble a series of measures of different aspects of the personality, rather than one oversimplified total summary. And it will always be guided by the dynamic question of the treatability or therapeutic accessibility of the individual.

REFERENCES

Alexander, F., and Selesnick, S. *The history of psychiatry.* New York: Harper and Row, 1966.

Barron, F. *Creativity and psychological health.* Princeton, N. J.: Van Nostrand, 1963.

Bellak, L. *Schizophrenia.* New York: Logos Press, 1958.

Bieber, I., Dain, H. J., et al. *Homosexuality.* New York: Basic Books, 1962.

Boisen, A. *The exploration of the inner world.* New York: Harper, 1962.

Boyer, L. B., and Giovacchini, P. L. *Psychoanalytic treatment of characterological and schizophrenic disorders.* New York: Science House, 1967.

Brill, H. In B. Wolman, *Handbook of clinical psychology*. New York: McGraw-Hill, 1965. Ch. 24.

Fine, R. *Freud: A critical reevaluation of his theories*. New York: David McKay, 1962.

Fine, R. The goals of psychoanalysis. In A. Mahrer, *The goals of psychotherapy*. New York: Appleton-Century-Crofts, 1967.

Fine, R. Psychoanalytic Theory of Sexuality. In R. Slovenko, *Sexual behavior and the law*. Springfield, Ill.: Charles C Thomas, 1965.

Fine, R. The basic technique of psychotherapy. (In press.)

Freud, S. *Analysis terminable and interminable*. London: Hogarth, 1937.

Hendin, H., Gaylin, W., and Carr, A. *Psychoanalysis and social research*. New York: Doubleday, 1965.

Hunt, M. *The natural history of love*. New York: Knopf, 1959.

Jones, E. *Papers on psychoanalysis*. 5th ed. London: Bailliere, Tindall & Cox, 1948.

Kety, S. Biochemical theories in schizophrenia. *Int. J. Psychiat.*, 1965, **1**, 409–46.

Leighton, A., Clausen, J. A., and Wilson, R. N. *Explorations in social psychiatry*. New York: Basic Books, 1957.

Menninger, K., Mayman, M., and Pruyser, P. *The vital balance*. New York: Viking, 1964.

Offer, David, and Sabshin, M. *Normality*. New York: Basic Books, 1966.

Pfister, O. *Christianity and fear*. London: Allen & Unwin, 1948.

Redlich, F., and Freedman, D. *The theory and practice of psychiatry*. New York: Basic Books, 1966.

Saul, L., and Wenar, S. Early influence on development and disorders of personality. *Psychoanal. Quart.*, 1965, **34**, 327–79.

Sechehaye, M. *Symbolic realization*. New York: International Universities Press, 1951.

Selye, H. *The stress of life*. New York: McGraw-Hill, 1956.

Srole, L., Langner, T. S., Michael, S. T., Opler, M. K., and Rennie, T. A. C. *Mental health in the metropolis*. New York: McGraw-Hill, 1962.

Stone, L. The widening scope of indications for psychoanalysis. *J. Amer. Psychoanal. Ass.*, 1954, **2**, 567–94.

Szasz, T. *Pain and pleasure*. New York: Basic Books, 1957.

Thorne, F. *The integration level test series*. Brandon, Vt.: Clinical Psychol. Pub. Co., 1965.

Wilder, R. The role of intuition. *Science*, 1967, **156** (No. 3775), 605–10.

Wolberg, L. *The technique of psychotherapy*. New York: Grune & Stratton, 1954.

Zilboorg, G. *A history of medical psychology*. New York: Norton, 1941.

Zilboorg, G. Freud in the cloisters. In *Atlas*, January 1967, pp. 33–37.

Zilboorg, G. Priest in Mexico censured for psychoanalyzing monks. *New York Times*, May 28, 1967.

THE SCALING OF MENTAL HEALTH POTENTIAL

Projective tests provide a rich set of clinical inferences which are lost when included under a single loose category such as "hysteric." Furthermore, Harrower says, the present diagnostic categories reflect morbid psychopathology; there are no categories for the healthy positive side of personality. If patients are understood in terms of the projective realm, why not derive a category system in the same realm? These are the kinds of considerations which led Harrower to abandon the standard psychodiagnostic system and to create a set of scales for the assessment of mental health potential.

The battery consists of five projective techniques. Two major scales emerge, one to assess heterogeneity and one to assess homogeneity of performance. The homogeneous scale refers to individuals whose performance on the five tests was approximately equal, either high or low. This scale ranges from very superior, superior, within normal limits plus, within normal limits, within normal limits minus, to impoverished. For example, the first three positions reflect above-average personality endowment, a balance of acceptable personality assets, warmth and outgoingness, psychological fitness, intellectual control, and inner resources. The heterogeneity scale includes gifted, with problems; high potential, with problems; gifted, but disturbed; potential, but disturbed; disturbed, but with potential; disturbed; and very disturbed. The projective scales of mental health potential are described within the context of a long-term research study which related response to psychotherapy with position on the scales.

137

An implicit intent of the proposed scales is to describe persons in general terms of mental health potential. Harrower's scales are thereby potentially applicable to persons in general, rather than restricted to the clinical population considered as having mental disorders under the present psychiatric nomenclature. Thus, the concept of mental health potential provides a basis for a more comprehensive range of applicability.

5

PROJECTIVE CLASSIFICATION

MOLLY HARROWER

A noted French mathematician once remarked that if triangles were to envisage a God they would see him as having three sides. Thus, when a psychodiagnostician envisages a classification system it stands to reason he would want to build his diagnostic types from the raw material of a battery of projective techniques!

No one, however, embarks on an attempt to construct a new classification system, regardless of its kind, without strong motivation. Let me begin, therefore, by enumerating the principal factors which virtually forced me into five years of research—years which culminated in the formulation of some projective types or test "look-alikes."

The first of these was a feeling of increased frustration at having to epitomize the diversity of findings from a detailed psychodiagnostic examination, into the straitjacket of existing psychiatric labels. This frustration arose from the realization that I was constantly doing violence to the raw material of the tests and doing the patient an injustice in my final summaries.

As anyone who has handled the projective techniques knows, he is frequently forced to attach, let us say, the label of "hysteric" to widely diverse projective test productions. One patient so labeled may, for example, show imaginative potential, artistic ability, and ego strength within the tests, while another, also so labeled, will show a much more poverty-stricken, impulsive, and crude production. Yet, confronted with that multiple-choice assortment of schizophrenic, obsessive compulsive, manic-depressive, psychopathic personality, and the like, in both cases the label of "hysteric" would have done least violence to the test findings.

A second frustration arose from the fact that there exists no classification for normal, healthy persons or for persons with a predominant amount of mental health potential. Brammer and Shostrom (1960) have pointed this out and I have constantly reiterated it (1965). As things now stand, if any label is to be given as a summation of the test record, even one that shows enormous potential or brilliance, it must have a somewhat psychopathological flavor, for the best we can do is to modify the existing psychiatric labels in the hope of toning down their impact.

Yet, why must we assume that everyone tested inevitably needs description along psychopathological lines? Why are there no labels, say, to differentiate between several outstanding candidates for some important position, who show no psychopathology, but who severally show a healthy, but different, pattern on the projective battery.

Another annoyance or frustration inherent in the present system can best be described by comparison with the way in which intelligence tests are handled. Any intelligence test gives its answer on a scale pertinent to that test, and to that test alone. For example, the testee scores high or low as compared with others who have taken the same test. On the projectives, however, there is no scale where one can "place" an individual or whereby the answer given is in terms of the extent of mental health potential.

It is like counting apples and then giving answers as to the number of bananas. A projective record based on the Rorschach, figure drawing, TAT, sentence completion, and the like *should,* just as an intelligence test, be classified in terms of achievement within the projective realm.

Of course, it is easy to see how this state of affairs arose. Intelligence tests existed long before clinical psychologists were called into the mental health field. If an IQ was requested, it was tested for, and the answer given as *a position on the scale of intelligence.* But when Rorschach, a psychiatrist, first formulated his findings, he sought to bring his test into the realm of existing psychiatric categories in an understandable effort to make it more generally acceptable to *his* colleagues.

Psychologists have struggled ever since to follow along this unrewarding line of thought. Interestingly enough, however, one must not forget that Rorschach originally formulated classifications of his own. By this I mean his description of Rorschach records in terms of their being coarted, coartive, extratensive, introversial, and ambiequal. When he made such observations he was a true scientist observing the material itself. But unfortunately these classifications fell by the wayside and were not sufficiently meaningful to enough people.

One way of describing my new projective classification system, therefore, is to go back to Rorschach and take his descriptions more seriously, adding to the inkblots other projective tests which, from their own individual angles, contribute more detailed assessment of the individual's mental health potential.

These strong feelings of dissatisfaction concerning psychodiagnostic deficiencies might not in themselves have proved potent enough to make me dedicate myself to the formulation of a classification system. There was another important factor which I should call a feeling of obligation, for in the course of fifteen years in practice as a psychodiagnostician, 2131 patients were referred to me for psychodiagnostic evaluation, prior to entering into some form of psychotherapeutic endeavor, be it long-term or short-term therapy. The referents were 276 therapists, utilizing various methods, and trained in various ways. Thus, I decided to start on an ambitious follow-up program to attempt to discover what had happened to these patients. I was interested in knowing how the pretherapy test profile related to the outcome of therapy as judged by the therapist. I was interested in knowing to what extent the patient reported as improved by his therapist would indicate that improvement if retested psychodiagnostically. I was interested, among many other things, in discovering how many patients had actually been treated by full-term analysis, psychotherapy, counseling, or various forms of short-term treatment.

I argued to myself something like this: If I could achieve a follow-up study to discover what had happened to these patients, and if at the same time I could find a way to classify their pretherapy test findings in some meaningful projective system, it might be possible to discover what "type" of projective person, as envisaged in the tests, did well or poorly in various forms of therapy. At the same time, it seemed to me that if I could get follow-up data from my therapists, I would be able to validate any new classification system that I developed. If I came up with a *scale* of mental health potential, for instance, I could ask, "Is it true that a greater mental health potential as reflected in the pretreatment tests results in a better chance of improvement in therapy?" Or put it this way, "What is the relationship between mental health endowment as reflected in the projectives and the capacity to respond to the therapeutic situation as assessed by the therapist?"

I do not need to go into the details of some of the initial stages of this research. Suffice it to say, questionnaires were sent out concerning 1600 patients to approximately 200 of the 276 therapists.

The questionnaire for each patient dealt with the following questions: How long has this patient been in treatment? What type of therapy was employed? On a four-point scale, would the patient be rated as having shown "Good Improvement," "Moderate Improvement," "Slight Improvement," or "No Improvement" at all?

Half a page was left for additional material concerning the patient's progress, to be supplied by the therapist. After a period of three years, 1493 questionnaires had been returned, a startlingly high percentage.

From these 1493 returned questionnaires, 622 case records (each containing a battery of six projective tests) were selected for intensive study on the basis of the fact that the information given by the therapist in these cases was sufficiently detailed and indicated that the patient had been followed for at least four years subsequent to termination of treatment.

It is easy to see, I think, that before any meaningful correlations could be sought between test findings and results of psychotherapy, long-term or brief, the standardized psychological or projective categories of which I have been speaking had to be determined.

To this end, the 622 records were studied and, again, to cut a long story short, there finally emerged two scales of what we may call nonintellectual or personality endowment, as reflected by scores on a battery of five projective techniques. One of these scales, which we have called the "Homogeneous Scale," showed individuals whose performance on the five tests was approximately equal. They could have excellent performance on all tests or, conversely (at the bottom of the seven-point scale), extremely poor performance on all tests. But such persons appeared to function homogeneously, and one level of performance could be utilized to describe the totality of their tests.

Such a classification took care of 358 test records, but there remained 264 which somehow could not be fitted into the scale. Finally, a second scale, which reflected the inhomogeneity, or the heterogeneity, of the individual's test performance was formed. Here, two factors were combined: positive assets, running side by side with varying degrees of disorganizing or disruptive and frankly pathological material. This scale again ran the gamut from the "Gifted" individual with one area of minor problems, to the "Very Disturbed" individual whose pathology had, so to speak, eaten up or colored the entire psychological output.

Let me discuss the steps in these two scales in greater detail, giving you an overall picture. First they may be listed under the names which were selected to describe the various groups of look-alike test records.

Homogeneous Endowment	Heterogeneous Endowment
Very Superior	Gifted, with Problems
Superior	High Potential, with Problems
Within Normal Limits (+)	Gifted, but Disturbed
Within Normal Limits	Potential, but Disturbed
Within Normal Limits (−)	Disturbed, but with Potential
Mediocre	Disturbed
Impoverished	Very Disturbed

THE HOMOGENEOUS SCALE

Very Superior, Superior, Within Normal Limits Plus. The first three positions on the Homogeneous Scale can be spoken of together in that each, in varying degrees, indicates above average personality endowment in all measurable test areas. Persons whose total test performance can be categorized under any of these three headings will have shown themselves to be above average in endowment or will have displayed above-average ability in all the tests contained in the personality battery.

Essentially, the persons in these three groups have shown a balanced and uniform performance, leading one to postulate a balance of acceptable personality assets. For example, they are to a more than average degree warm and outgoing toward others. They combine adequate intellectual control with freedom and spontaneity. They possess inner resources, depth, and intuitive sympathy for others. Such persons will show both creativity and a capacity for routine work. They are the psychologically fit, showing no constitutional weaknesses in the psychological framework.

On this analogy with physical fitness, one can say that though individuals in these test groups may at times become somewhat disturbed psychologically—even the basically physically healthy person can catch the grippe—they will not become chronically ill because of inherent psychological weaknesses.

Within Normal Limits. The persons so categorized are the psychologically average citizens, those with no outstanding defects or difficulties, but with no great psychological potential. They performed all the tests well enough to get by satisfactorily. The Within Normal Limits test scores are, so to speak, a base line above which we may look for various degrees of additional richness in the personality and below which we may expect some problems to arise simply because the individual lacks substance or richness.

Within Normal Limits Minus, Mediocre, Impoverished. We can speak of these three positions on the scale together in that, again in varying degrees, the persons who fall into them have reflected below-average endowment in all the seven tests given in the battery. The uniformity we have spoken of before is found in these below-average subgroups. As the name implies, the Impoverished group reflects a bare minimum of those measurable qualities listed previously. Persons in this group show little emotional warmth, a complete lack of imagination or creativity, an inhibition of all spontaneity and flexibility. Interestingly enough, such persons are frequently of the highest intelligence, an important fact showing that intellectual endowment does not necessarily go hand in hand with the facets of the well-rounded personality that our scale attempts to measure.

THE HETEROGENEOUS SCALE

So much, then, for the three key positions on a scale of personality endowment that reflects an essentially uniform performance throughout the variety of tests.

The need to construct a second scale of personality endowment—which we have called a Heterogeneous Scale—comes from the fact that many persons cannot be classified as possessing Above Average, Average, or Below Average personality endowment because the various component parts making up that endowment are not all of a kind. Some persons, for example, show giftedness, richness, or great potential in some areas and at the same time clearly exhibit disturbed functioning or acute problems in others.

On the second scale it is possible to distinguish two rather than three major divisions. There are those persons whose giftedness (or high potential) runs parallel to what we have called problems, as opposed to those who—as measured by some tests—have equal giftedness or high potential but show profound disturbance or serious pathology as measured by other tests.

Gifted-Problems, High Potential-Problems. Concerning the first two positions in this scale—the Gifted with Problems and the High Potential with Problems—the emphasis is on the positive component. These two positions are comparable to the above-average categories on the Homogeneous Scale. Many of the qualities we mentioned when describing persons in the Very Superior, Superior, and Within Normal Limits Plus groups may also be found here. However, a person in the Gifted with Problems or High Potential with Problems categories will show in one or two areas that a consistently high level has not been achieved. It may be, for example, that an overabundance of creative imagination leads to withdrawal into fantasy rather than into constructive, outgoing activity. In such individuals, the important balance factor —namely, the need for warm relationships with others—may be absent,

Regardless of what the "flaw" is, the poor showing on one or two aspects of the tests will stand out in sharp contrast to the giftedness or the potential shown in the rest.

Our prediction for the persons whose test scores place them in either of these categories is a favorable one, provided that circumstances do not trigger the particular problem to an excessive degree.

Gifted-Disturbed, Potential-Disturbed, Disturbed-Potential, Disturbed, Very Disturbed. As soon as our classification has to include the word "disturbance"—be it combined with giftedness or with potential—our predictions for success in therapy or in other fields must be hedged with "ifs" and "provided such and such does not occur."

In varying degrees, those persons whose test findings must be classified as including a disruptive or disturbing element are subject to internal sabotage. Their brilliance, their giftedness, their energy, their creativeness may be undermined from within.

Finally, when the disturbing elements obscure all but a fragment of the personality as at the lower end of the Heterogeneous Scale, our prognosis must be a somewhat pessimistic one, unless some form of therapeutic intervention can be guaranteed.

Now that we are, as psychodiagnosticians, equipped with some measurable categories, so that we do not need to rely on psychiatric pigeonholing in the description of our test data, we may go back again to the results of the questionnaire.

Their therapists rated 622 cases in the following way: 134 were described as showing "Good Results"; 212—"Moderate Improvement"; 129—"Slight Improvement"; 147—"No Improvement" at all.

And what relationship did our descriptive categories bear to the outcome of therapy? A significant one. Namely, the greater the psychological endowment, that is, the higher scores obtained on the projectives, the fewer failures in psychotherapy were found. Table 1 shows these relationships for both scales, and when a biserial coefficient of correlation was calculated, using success and failure as criteria, the coefficient was found to be .438 significant beyond the .01 level of confidence. Thus, we are entitled to say that the chances of failure to respond to therapy increase as the position on the scale worsens.

So far so good. The new classifications seem meaningful in terms of what it takes to respond successfully to therapy. They also proved meaningful and helpful in predicting success in a chosen field. A study

Table 1.

Homogeneous Scale		
Descriptive Evaluation of Total Performance	*No. in Group*	*% of Cases Failing to Respond to Any Type of Therapy*
Very Superior	5	0
Superior	17	0
Within Normal Limits +	71	10
Within Normal Limits	73	14
Within Normal Limits −	83	21
Mediocre	74	27
Impoverished	35	54
Total	358	

Heterogeneous Scale		
Descriptive Evaluation of Total Performance	*No. in Group*	*% of Cases Failing to Respond to Any Type of Therapy*
Gifted-Problems	45	13
Potential-Problems	67	19
Gifted-Disturbed	13	31
Potential-Disturbed	51	31
Disturbed-Potential	46	30
Disturbed } Very Disturbed }	42	50
Total	264	

of several hundred ministers has been reported elsewhere (Harrower, 1964, 1965) and reveals that at least one of the contributing factors to outstanding performance in a field is positive mental health potential as measured by the projectives.

The real value of any classification system, however, is the extent to which it can be used by many investigators and can attain a certain amount of universality. Can any psychologist with good projective training use it? We believe that they can, and with reliability.

In this section I shall try to demonstrate how the process of classification takes place. I am assuming that the reader's main interest is not so much with a theoretical system, as with the possible usefulness of this method to classify projective records of his own.

Thus, I am concerned primarily with making the concept of the graded scale, or scales, of mental health potential, understandable and usable. I will do this by illustrating three positions on the Homogeneous Scale, the Very Superior, Within Normal Limits, and Impoverished, that is, the top, the midpoint, and the bottom, and by illustrating three key positions on the Heterogeneous Scale, the Gifted-Problems, Gifted-Disturbed, and Very Disturbed.

Obviously, in such a short presentation as this, not all of the positions on the scales, not all thirteen projective types, can be dealt with in detail. The original publication (Harrower, 1965) must be consulted in order that the scores which differentiate each group are fully understood.

Let us begin by looking at two actual cases, and start with the consideration of their Rorschach records, which we will place side by side for comparison. Are these records alike? If not, in what way do they differ?

Card 1

Halloween mask.
Trolls climbing a hill.
Mannequin.
Woman's body, waist down, weighing.
Face of a screeching cat.
Two women chatting.
Stuffed bison head.
Map of southern Maine coast outline.
Ice-cream cone falling out of a child's
    hand.
Sherlock Holmes espying something.
A phoenix.
Profile of a man.

Some kind of animal with wings.

Card 2

Two people at costume ball dancing.
Two bears doing circus tricks.
A white top spinning.
A dead blackbird lying on a road.
A colorful moth.
A Shakespearean jester with a gargoyle
    on his headpiece.
A muddy river bottom.
A vulva.
A piece of op-art.

Two bears sticking together.

Card 3

2 gentlemen bowing a greeting.   Animals or people, but not
2 chicks imitating them.   people.
2 lions doing acrobatics.
A pointing hand.
Pelvic bone structure.
A fish swimming away from a net.
A wide water bottle.
A toy poodle with big collar strutting
  in a dog show.
Two Ubangis' heads.
Pair of lips.

Card 4

Pelt of wild game.   I have no idea.
Seedpod of poppy.
Huge boot.
Woman acrobatic dancer almost bent
  double.
Profile of an old man.
Woman in clown outfit.
Two ancient men telling sagas to one
  another.
An ass hole.
Dark clouds.

Card 5

A magnificently robed ballerina on   Some insect.
  points.
Head of moustached man.
A woman's calf.
An English bobby.
Pelican.
Child's legs.
Profile of boyar with fur hat.
A giraffe walking in a forest.

Card 6

Indian chief.   Some kind of lion rug.
Totem.
Bearskin rug.

Muslim women gossiping.
2 kidneys.
A tank rumbling along rough terrain.
Its reflection in a swamp.
An "elephant man" pontificating.
Female genital lips.
Head of a chicken.

Card 7

Two puppies playing.   Elephants.
A woman's legs spread wide from
   thigh up.
Parrot.
Head of court jester.
Dam and hydroelectric generator.
Profile of Snow White.
Skull of cow lying in desert.
Lamp on a table.

Card 8

A heraldic emblem.   Gophers.
2 lambs heads—sleeping.
2 rodents climbing rocks.
Head of a grumpy oaf.
Frogmen swimming.
Head of a furry kitten.
Mountain and glacier.
Egyptian statue.

Card 9

2 devils spouting fire.   Can't find anything.
2 green ceramic pitchers in shape of
   female head.
Ku Klux Klanner on the march.
Appendix.
Head of a mountain goat chewing its
   cud.
Profile of thoughtful man.
Leering babboon.
Cello.
Hippopotamus just coming out of
   brackish water.

Card 10

Modern painting.   Crabs, snake.
Spider.
Maple seed floating in air.
Locust blossom.
2 show dogs.
2 caterpillars.
Rabbit's head.
2 girls sucking from a contraption.
Peach pit.
2 turkeys' heads.
Sweet potato.
A rocky coastal path.
Grasshopper.
An arbor trellis in a garden.

Just by reading the responses, or taking the material at its face value, it is clear that these are the products of profoundly different experiences. Otherwise expressed, they represent profoundly different psychological worlds constructed out of the inkblots' meaninglessness. In the record on the left-hand side of the page, which is one taken from those classified as Very Superior, the "world" that has been constructed is many-faceted, well-populated, filled with a variety of projections. The record on the right (chosen from the Impoverished group) is barren, limited, and meager in the extreme.

Now, if we become more technical and consider the summarized scores we find that the record on the left has 17 M's and on the right none, that the color representation in the left-hand record is unusually rich (FC 10, CF 3), whereas the color is absent on the other. We see that the F percent is at the optimal level in the Very Superior record, neither over- nor underemphasized, whereas the 78 percent F, in the Impoverished record, again reflects the barrenness and rigidity.

	Very Superior					Impoverished			
R	W%	D%	d%	DdS%	R	W%	D%	d%	DdS%
96	12	52	14	22	9	56	44		
M	17	F	33	FC' 3+1	M		F	7	FC'
FM	13	F−		FC 10	FM	1	F−		FC
m	6+1	F%	34	CF 3	m		F%	78	CF
k		Fc	11+1	C	k		Fc	1	C
K		c		Csym	K		c		Csym
FK					FK				

What do these records have in common? Only the absence of F minus responses, an important common denominator as it turns out, because it places them both, even if at opposite ends, in the Homogeneous Scale.

Let us now consider and contrast the drawings of these two persons. As we might expect, they reflect an equally different concept of the human being. They are executed in contrasting manners. The first shows not only a realistic portrayal of a human being, but one in action. The second portrays a tiny, pathetic person.

How about material from the TAT? Again, diversity and richness are contrasted with a bare minimum of a response to the picture.

Very Superior	*Impoverished*
"The man has just arisen from the sweet embraces of his beloved. The hour has come when he must leave this world of warmth and tenderness and go out into the business world. His account books are on the table before him. They contain the names of those who are delinquent in the payment of their bank notes and his day's task is to pressure these people until they make a payment. He knows that in some of these homes there is sickness and unemployment and trouble of one kind or another. He does not like his role. He will go out, however; he will make the nasty phone calls; he will write threatening letters. But when the day is done he will return to the warm arms and sweet-smelling hair of his love. She doesn't want him to leave. Playfully she clutches at his leg to prevent his departure, but he will go and he will return and she will be waiting for him. This is the only time when he feels himself to be truly alive and she knows it."	"A man returned home to find his wife dead. He is grieving."

If we consider the subtest scores on the Verbal Bellevue Wechsler for these two individuals we are in for an interesting surprise. They are almost identical, both falling in the Very Superior group of the total population.

Weighted Scores	Info.	Comp.	Digit	Arith.	Sim.	Info.	Comp.	Digit	Arith.	Sim.
	18	17	17	16	17	17	18	17	18	18

Impoverished

Very Superior

In other words, high intellectual assets can accompany the Impoverished personality as well as the individual who reflects himself as Very Superior through the medium of the projectives.

The contrast between these two records, between the Very Superior and the Impoverished, now that it is pointed out in this way, may seem obvious. It is always true that the end positions on the scale are the easiest to discuss or clarify but, naturally, not all records fall as simply into position as this. In our original study we found that only 5 persons out of 622 went into the Very Superior group, 35 fell into that of the Impoverished, but a much larger percentage of the patients are classified as Within Normal Limits.

What does our midline or average position on the scale look like? One such case is given in detail.

Within Normal Limits: Rorschach Record

Card 1

1. A bat.
2. A bird.
3. A violin.

Card 2

1. Two dancers.
2. Two Indian children's faces.
3. Two sheep.

Card 3

1. A bow tie.
2. Two smoking pipes.
3. Two waiters in an Alphonse and Gaston act over a bowl of stew or soup (i.e., "After you Gaston," etc.).

Card 4

1. A pair of boots.
2. An eskimo dog's (husky's) head looking down from above.

Card 5

1. A bat.
2. Two bearded men's faces.
3. A wishbone or a pair of tweezers.

Card 6

1. A duster.
2. A crab.
3. Part of a mink coat.
4. Face of a king with a crown on his head.

Card 7

1. Statues of two winged imps.
2. Two rabbits' feet.
3. A topographical map of a stretch of coastline (including a harbor).

Card 8

1. Two rodents.
2. A person's shoulders (covered by a shirt).
3. The vertebrae of a fish or bird.

Card 9

1. Reindeer antlers.
2. Oriental dragon likenesses.
3. Two elephants' heads.
4. Start of a volcano or geyser eruption.

Card 10

1. Two many-footed insects.
2. Two cleavers or lobster claws.
3. Two boxing gloves.
4. Two birds.
5. A bow tie.

At face value, then, it seems that in terms of variety, richness, and productivity this production would fall about halfway between the two other samples.

The summarized scoring shows that both M and color responses are represented, but in modest amounts.

Within Normal Limits

R	W%	D%	d%	DdS%	
33	24	55	15	6	

M	2	F	17	FC′	
FM	4	F−		FC	2
m	+1	F%	52	CF	
k		Fc	6	C	
K	1	c		Csym	
FK					

The drawing reflects an average attempt at portraying a realistic human being.

It seems fair to say that the Within Normal Limits tests are at a higher level, or are "richer," than those shown by the individual classified as Impoverished. On the other hand, they are not as well

Within Normal Limits

rounded or rich as those reflected by a member of the Very Superior group.

As we said before, we cannot spell out all the positions on the Homogeneous Scale. However, the Rorschach scores, and drawings from persons classified as Within Normal Limits Plus and Within Normal Limits Minus are given here to suggest the intermediate stages. It should be noted that the Within Normal Limits Minus record has some color responses, but no human movement. On the other hand, the Within Normal Limits Plus score reflects four human movement responses (as opposed to the two that constitute the maximum permitted in the Within Normal Limits group). In this score, well-balanced color responses are also reflected.

The drawing for the case which we have chosen here in the Within Normal Limits Minus group, is poorer, less adequate than that in the position on the scale immediately above it, namely, that from

Within Normal Limits Plus					Within Normal Limits Minus				
R	W%	D%	d%	DdS%	R	W%	D%	d%	DdS%
19	26	53	11	11	20	20	60	5	15
M	4	F	3	FC′	M		F	11	FC′
FM	3+1	F−		FC 3+1	FM	5	F−		FC 2
m		F%	16	CF 1	m	1	F%	55	CF 1
k		Fc	2	C	k		Fc		C
K	1	c	1	Csym	FK		c		Csym
FK	1								

Within Normal Limits Plus

Within Normal Limits Minus

Within Normal Limits. In the same way, the drawing from the case of the Within Normal Limits Plus is slightly superior.

However, it is important, in the processes of seeking to classify any given record, to realize that it is not necessary for every test in the total battery to be richer or "better" than those in the immediately lower group. Even one clearly superior test can upgrade a record. One inferior test can downgrade it.

As far as the Homogeneous Scale is concerned, then, the concept of the graded scale of mental health potential seems a meaningful one. Test scores based on the Rorschach, the Figure Drawing, and the TAT can be arranged linearly so that the fuller and more developed personality can be seen to emerge. The gap between the Very Superior production and that given by the Impoverished individual can be filled in by as many as three intermediate steps. Naturally, the more steps we introduce, the harder it will be to differentiate one from the other, but it seems quite clear that the scale calls for a midpoint (Within Normal Limits) and points halfway between this "average" midpoint and the respective ends of the scale.

As stated above, the scale with five intermediate steps includes the stage of Superior between Very Superior and Within Normal Limits Plus and the stage of Mediocre between Within Normal Limits Minus and Impoverished.

We do not have quite the same kind of graded performance when we are considering those records which we have placed, for want of a better arrangement, in the so-called Heterogeneous Scale. Here we seem to be dealing with four distinct variables. On the positive side, we have spoken of assets as Giftedness and Potential. On the negative side, we have differentiated between Problems and Disturbances.

By *Giftedness* we mean those outstanding qualities in a record (originality, productivity) which, other things being equal, would have placed the individual in the Very Superior group of the Homogeneous Scale.

By *Potential* we mean those less outstanding but nonetheless positive features found at the level of Within Normal Limits Plus or Within Normal Limits on the Homogeneous Scale.

By *Problems* we have chosen to indicate the absence of certain important test ingredients in a total record. One particularly striking absence, for example, is the nonexistence of any color reponses in an otherwise brilliant and original Rorschach record.

The use of the term *Disturbances,* on the other hand, we have reserved for responses which have a flagrantly pathological quality. For instance: a striking disregard of reality showing up in a high F minus percent; bizarre thinking as reflected in strange, atypical answers on the Similarities; bizarre concepts as found in the Rorschach or Most Unpleasant Concept test; crude and primitive expression of ideas in the TAT; drawings which disregard the usual properties of the human figure; unmodified use of pure color.

It is more accurate to say, then, that we have two short Heterogeneous Scales, rather than one. In the first we have Giftedness combined with Problems, and Potential combined with Problems. These two classifications, or categories, might be thought of as a link between the Homogeneous and Heterogeneous Scales. That is, there *is* a discrepancy between the level of two parts of the test record, but that discrepancy does not include blatantly pathological material.

When we deal with records in which Disturbance highlights part of the raw material (that is, where the negative aspects must be thought of as more serious than problems), we have the possibility of five different constellations, as follows. Giftedness in one part of the tests combined with Disturbance in another (Gifted-Disturbed). Potential in some aspect of the material combined with Disturbance (Potential-Disturbed). Then there is the type of record where Disturbance predominates, and seems to gain the upper hand and where the potential for mental health remains only as a modifying factor (Disturbed-Potential). Finally, we move into areas where the record shows practically nothing but the disrupting and disorganizing features (Disturbed, and Very Disturbed).

We can now set up our scales in the following way:

Very Superior		
(Superior)	Gifted-Problems	Gifted-Disturbed
Within Normal Limits Plus		Potential-Disturbed
Within Normal Limits	Potential-Problems	Disturbed-Potential
Within Normal Limits Minus		Disturbed
(Mediocre)		Very Disturbed
Impoverished		

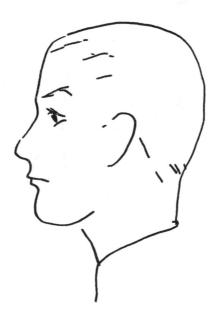

Gifted-Problems

For illustrative material from the Heterogeneous Scales we have chosen the Rorschach score and drawing from a record classified as Gifted-Problems, and the full Rorschach record, scores, and drawings from records of samples from the Gifted-Disturbed and Very Disturbed groups.

The trademark of records classified as Gifted-Problems is the large number of M responses in the Rorschach, and the absence or virtual absence of color responses. Very frequently it is found that the

Gifted-Disturbed   Very Disturbed

drawings of a human figure are of the "head only" type, and show a faraway expression in the eyes. An illustration is given here.

Gifted-Problems

R	W%	D%	d%	DdS%
34	38	62		9

M	13	F	10	FC'	
FM	5	F−		FC	1
m	1	F%	29	CF	+1
k		Fc	3	C	
K	+1	c	1	Csym	
FK					

We reproduce here material from the Gifted-Disturbed and Very Disturbed categories. As will be readily seen, the Rorschach record of the individual classified as Gifted-Disturbed is characterized by great productivity and originality, but also by bizarre content and poor form responses. There is much explosive and disruptive color. Although not given here, the scattergram shows a sharp drop in the Comprehension and Similarities on the Wechsler.

The Rorschach record of the Very Disturbed individual shows only disorganizing elements.

Sample drawings are also included.

Rorschach Record

Gifted-Disturbed | Very Disturbed

Card 1

Two winged Santa Clauses hanging onto either side of a large beetle.
Woman's lips and legs.
Immature claws of a crab.
One of the puffball mushrooms.
Woman's head.
Gnarled, pointing finger.
Undeveloped fetus.
Brace of dead birds hanging from hunter's belt.

A human being split in two.

Card 2

Two bears lying face down, having left bloody trail behind and with

Blood.
The form of a triangle.

each having one wounded and
bleeding forepaw.

Coral growths.

Two bears, facing away with wounded
rear paws, and headless, raise their
deformed forepaws in a gesture of
victory.

External vaginal organs.

Two old women shouting at each
other.

Skate or manta.

Swimming eels.

Broad-beamed woman of 1850s standing on tiptoe, wearing red striped
hose.

Outstretched arms, the drive
to be superior.

Fresh blood.

A human sacrifice.

Card 3

Pair of prim, prissy old men holding
bowling balls.

Stomach and gullet dissected from
anemic cadaver.

Female genitals.

Lungs connected by sternum.

Thyroid gland.

Opening to deep hole, with middle section partly covered over.

Testicles and ducts.

Pelvic bone.

Cross section of vertebra.

Section through skull, just above first
vertebra.

Eccentrically made human
beings.

Card 4

Animal-skin rug.

Female genitals.

Anus with hemorrhoids.

Goose hanging neck over an edge of
something.

Protozoan.

Priest reading breviary.

Mouth and feelers of crab.

The dead in shrouds.

Feet.

Unreal, nothing, exceedingly
wild, disgusting, I dislike
this intensely.

Card 5

Bat.
Butterfly.
Head of penis.

Meaningless.

Card 6

Female genitals.
Woodchucks talking to each other.
Penis.
Ermine skins.
King Farouk's buttocks (per the
   Droodle).

A face . . . outstretched arms,
   ugly.
A bedspread.
A surrealistic human being.

Card 7

Two Negro women with backs to each
   other, turn their heads for one last
   remark.
Female genitals.
Upswept hairdo.
Fetus.
Lips smeared with lipstick.
Dog's head. (Pekingese.)
Two people standing alone on desert.
Trained dancing dogs.
Cross section of vertebra.

Something sexual.

Card 8

Animal (coon?), crawling up the face
   of a cave.
Coral formations.
Spinal column.
Female genitals.
Tissue masses.
Agate.
The dead in shrouds.
Sex symbol.

Feeling of fear, something
   tearing it apart.

Card 9

Two jolly dragons.
The inevitable female genitals!
Feces (wrong color).
Heads of Scotty dogs.

Unnatural, disagreeable.
Blood.
Makes me fear something.

Card 10

Two parakeets, with long topknots, angry.

Female genitals.

Pleasant little beings blowing kisses.

Angry marine animals.

Cancer cell.

Caterpillars eating the eyes of a rabbit or grasshopper.

Head of bull.

Ovaries and tubes.

Baby, nursing bottle.

Crazy, disgusting, animals tearing around.

	Gifted-Disturbed			
R	W%	D%	d%	DdS%
71	18	52	8	22

M	11 (3 −)	F	25	FC′
FM	9	F−	8	FC 2
m	2 + 1	F%	47	CF 5 (1 −)
k		Fc	8 + 2	C
K		c		Csym
FK	1			

	Very Disturbed			
R	W%	D%	d%	DdS%
12	50	34	8	8

M	1 −	F	1	FC′
FM		F−	7	FC
m		F%	67	CF 2
k		Fc		C 1
K		c		Csym
FK				

REFERENCES

Brammer, Lawrence M., and Shostrom, Everett L. *Therapeutic psychology, fundamentals of counseling and psychotherapy.* Englewood Cliffs, N. J.: Prentice-Hall, 1960.

Harrower, Molly. Psychological tests in the Unitarian Universalist ministry. *J. Religion Hlth.,* 1963, **2** (No. 2).

Harrower, Molly. Mental health potential and success in the ministry. *J. Religion Hlth.,* 1964, **4** (No. 1).

Harrower, Molly. *Psychodiagnostic testing: an empirical approach.* Springfield, Ill.: Charles C Thomas, 1965.

COMPREHENSIVE APPROACHES TO
PERSONALITY CLASSIFICATION

Structural approaches to psychodiagnosis, classification, and personality definition retain a parent conceptual framework while seeking to increase internal systematization and consistency; they tighten up the internal workings of the larger theoretical framework. In contrast, comprehensive approaches propose wholesale conceptual systems, personality theories, and psychodiagnostic frameworks; everything is revised from top to bottom; there is a different model of man, of human behavior, and of personality. Functional approaches have their eye on a particular task or job, and put a working diagnostic approach to use on that task or job. In contrast, comprehensive approaches offer general classification systems for understanding personality, and these are available for a broader spectrum of purposes.

Employing a behavioral modification theory, Hans J. Eysenck proposes a set of dimensions for personality classification. Timothy Leary operates within an existential-transactional theory, and proposes sets of variables for the psychologist's assessment of a subject's internal experience and external behavior. Frederick C. Thorne also utilizes an existential approach; he proposes sets of assessing-categorizing variables related to psychological states, integration, and existential situations. A need-goal theoretical framework is the basis for Mahrer's proposal of major motivational needs, assessed through an evaluation of historical themes and clinical behaviors. Steve Pratt and Jay Tooley provide an overall transactional-contractual model of man for purposes of the taxonomy of personality.

A BEHAVIOR MODIFICATION APPROACH

Eysenck's criticisms of existing psychodiagnostic systems appear to be of two kinds. The first is that they do not lend themselves nicely to experimentation. Empirical data are not adequately accounted for. Hypotheses are neither clearly stated nor are they experimentally testable. Methods of measurement are at best unreliable and nebulous. His second criticism is that existing systems fail to educe and to describe the etiology of the various diseases and plausible related avenues of treatment.

The core of Eysenck's approach is the set of variables and factors relating to conditionability. Basic to conditionability is a neurophysiological-anatomical locus of inherited structures related to the ascending reticular activating system, the cortex, and the visceral brain. Certain personality variables are related to the ease or difficulty of conditionability. For example, introverts condition more speedily and strongly; extraverts condition less well. A neurotic disorder may therefore be understood in terms of the formation of conditioned autonomic responses to normally neutral stimuli, and the motor movements made in response to them. Psychopathic disorders are accounted for by the absence of those conditioned responses which comprise "conscience."

The actual categories of the standard diagnostic system are to be replaced with personality dimensions. For example, psychosis, although not qualitatively differing from normality, is related to normality along a quantitative dimension. Neurosis is likewise a dimension, separate from psychosis, with several subdivisions. The task of psychodiagnosis

167

is essentially to ascertain the ease or difficulty of the formation of conditioned responses in various fields, each patient constituting a fundamentally different experimental problem.

Eysenck's approach differs from the present standard psychiatric nomenclature. Concepts of normality, neurosis, and psychosis are retained, but the meaning and theoretical interrelationships among these concepts are altered drastically. The Kraepelinian neurobiological underpinnings are also retained, but Eysenck has utilized altogether different neurophysiological-anatomical linkages to his major personality dimensions. Traditional concepts such as normality, neurosis, psychosis, hysteria, extraversion, and introversion gain their meaning from the nature of their interconnections with the ease or difficulty of conditionability. The old terms are retained, but the old psychodiagnostic system is gone.

His system promises to develop its own categories based almost exclusively on direct relationships to ease or difficulty of conditionability in various fields. The approach is not yet completed, but is moving toward the development of a set of general personality dimensions of demonstrated utility and a specific classification system appropriately suited to an understanding of the individual patient in terms of behavior modification.

6

A DIMENSIONAL SYSTEM OF PSYCHODIAGNOSTICS

H. J. EYSENCK

Introduction

It is well known that existing systems of psychodiagnostics are inadequate in many ways, but it may be useful to list briefly the reasons for this inadequacy in order to see in what ways a better system would differ from present-day ones. (1) In the first place, then, the present system is not based on any knowledge of *etiology;* we do not know the causes of such alleged "diseases" as hysteria, schizophrenia, psychopathy, anxiety state, or manic-depressive illness. There are admittedly many theories about these causes, but their very number proves that none of them has sufficient support to make it more plausible than any other. (2) In the second place, the present system, while descriptive, is so in such a poorly coordinated and codified manner that inter-rater reliability is too low for any worthwhile agreement to be achieved. In extreme and "typical" cases there is agreement, particularly among psychiatrists trained in the same school, but over the whole range of psychiatric cases there is no agreement, with the possible exception of contrasting psychotic patients as a whole with neurotic patients as a whole; within these great groups reliability coefficients slump to near-zero values (Eysenck, 1967b). (3) As a consequence, possibly, of these two causes, there is little connection between diagnosis and treatment (Bannister et al., 1964). Medically, the only raison d'être of diagnosis is to ensure proper treatment; the absence of any strong relation between the two is completely damning for the present system.

(4) A fourth source of weakness is the absence of any concern with empirical testing of hypotheses relating to diagnostic problems.

169

Systems are advocated without any regard to experimental evidence, and in conformity with these systems general statements are made which go counter to much of the evidence. Consider the following statement, which appears in Wolman's *Handbook of Clinical Psychology* (1965, p. 1134): "The difference between neurosis, character neurosis, and psychosis is a matter of degree." This is presented as fact, although the evidence, which will be reviewed below, strongly points to the opposite conclusion; Wolman may be right, but it can surely not be right that questions of basic importance in the field of diagnostics are settled without any discussion of, or appeal to, the empirical evidence. It is not unlikely that the present weakness of diagnostic theory and procedures is related to this quite general disregard for empirical data, and this equally prominent stress on inspired, suprarational systems which have no close touch with reality and present purely semantic solutions to very factual problems.

(5) Closely allied to this problem is another one, namely,· the failure of most authors to state the fundamental hypotheses underlying their particular system in such a form as to make it empirically testable. Wolman, in the quotation given above, presumably has in mind some sort of dimensional system in which normality, neurosis, and psychosis lie along one single axis, but this psychoanalytic hypothesis is stated in such a vague manner that no deductions can be made from it. Loevinger (1955) has taken the present writer to task for testing this one-dimensional theory of mental illness (Eysenck, 1955a) because in her interpretation of the Sybilline Books, consequences flowed from the theory different from those deduced by the writer; clearly Loevinger and Wolman disagree in their reading of Freud, but neither they nor he puts the theory in such a form that it can be falsified by experiment —surely the very beginning of a scientific approach to any subject.

(6) The vague and nonempirical, nonexperimental character of present systems of diagnosis has encouraged, and may even be said to demand, the use of equally unreliable, nebulous, and invalid methods of testing. Eysenck (1952b), Zubin, Eron, and Schumer (1965), and many others have pointed out the failings of so-called "projective" techniques, and there is now a large body of well-controlled data which show that the usual claims of protagonists of these methods are quite unfounded; nevertheless these tests are still used as widely as ever, demonstrating clearly that to those concerned with psychodiagnostics scientific considerations of evidence and proof are quite secondary to faith and belief.

(7) This faith and these beliefs are also strongly in evidence when we consider methods of treatment, which ideally should be linked in a

rational manner with diagnosis. For most if not all neurotic disorders, and for many psychotic ones as well, psychotherapy is recommended quite uncritically, and the unwarranted assumption is made that (a) psychotherapy produces amelioration of mental illness to a greater extent than does spontaneous remission, and (b) that cures, once achieved, are permanent and not subject to relapse. Eysenck (1965a) has given up-to-date review of the evidence on the former point, and Cremerius (1962) has shown that many different methods of psychotherapy, including psychoanalysis, have relapse rates, over a ten-year follow-up period, of between 50 and 75 percent. It is important to mention here the failure of psychotherapy to produce lasting cures in neurotic disorders, because to many psychodiagnosticians the (imaginary) success of the treatment is taken to argue for, and validate the diagnostic procedures used; conversely, failure of the treatment argues strongly against the value of the diagnostic procedures used.

We thus arrive at a rather dismal picture in which unreliable, invalid, and largely arbitrary tests are used to arrive at unreliable, invalid, and largely arbitrary diagnoses which are irrelevant to the methods of treatment to be used, methods which in turn are quite ineffective! The picture is not made any more cheerful by the almost religious fervor with which these false beliefs are held by practitioners, by their refusal even to state their underlying hypotheses in such a form as to make them testable, and their distaste for, and neglect of, such empirical evidence as may be available and contradict these beliefs. What is required, clearly, is something which on every single point is opposite to the present pattern. We must be concerned with fundamental problems; we must state our hypotheses in testable form; we must use empirical and experimental methods of verification or falsification; we must hold our hypotheses in a tentative manner, rather than embrace them with loving enthusiasm; we must relate our diagnostic system to some form of etiological theory, and through it to some forms of treatment which, when subjected to empirical test, show a performance which is in excess of that put up by spontaneous remission. In addition to all this, we should be able to relate our results to general psychological theory, particularly to learning theory, and we should deduce from our general system predictions as to the possible diagnostic usefulness of objective, reliable, and valid laboratory tests which would aid us in our diagnostic and treatment procedures. It is the purpose of this chapter to suggest a system which, with all its imperfections, has attempted to go a little way in this direction, and to discuss some of its features. Fortunately, many of its details have been discussed in other publications, to which reference will be made; otherwise the task of compressing all of this material into such small space would prove impossible.

Fundamental Problems

CATEGORICAL OR DIMENSIONAL?

The present system of psychodiagnostics is categorical, thus imitating the usual medical type of nosology. A patient, by being diagnosed, is put into a category; he is a hysteric, or a psychopath, or a schizophrenic, or a compulsive, or an anxiety state, or an obsessional. The artificiality of these categories and their failure to accord with reality, is often admitted by the system of multiple diagnosis; thus a patient may be declared to be an anxious hysteric with schizophrenic undertones, or a depressive obsessive-compulsive individual with psychopathic tendencies. The question is seldom asked of whether this slavish following of medical practice in a new and possibly entirely different field is reasonable and rational, and many psychiatrists and clinical psychologists seem unaware even of the very existence of a problem here. Nevertheless the problem is of course a very ancient one, and there is much evidence concerning it. When Galen wrote about his "four temperaments" in the second century A.D., and when Immanuel Kant translated these types into descriptive German in his *Anthropologie* fifteen hundred years later, it was explicitly assumed that a person fell into one or the other of these four categories (sanguine, choleric, melancholic, or phlegmatic) but that no mixtures or admixtures were permissible. Wundt (1903) was the first to change this categorical system into a dimensional one by grouping together the emotional types (melancholic and choleric) as opposed to the unemotional ones (phlegmatic and sanguine), thus creating a dimension of *emotionality;* similarly he grouped together the changeable (extraverted) types (choleric and sanguine) as opposed to the unchangeable (introverted) types (melancholic and phlegmatic), thus creating a second, independent dimension, as shown in Figure 1, which also contains in the quadrants the personality descriptions given by Kant and Galen.

Modern research has borne out the importance and the reality of these two dimensions (Eysenck and Eysenck, 1969), as well as the implicit distribution of individuals along these dimensions in the form of a normal bivariate surface; in the personality field, dimensionality, rather than categorical "type" grouping, has been uniformly accepted as nearer reality. (It is curious that textbook writers, in making this point, seldom give credit to Wundt for his pioneering work; they also

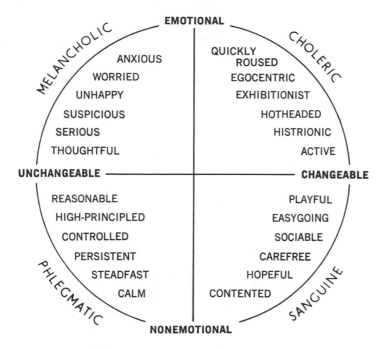

Figure 1. Galen-Wundt theory of personality structure.

usually misrepresent Jung and Kretschmer as holding the older, categorical "type" point of view when both are quite explicit in their espousal of the dimensional point of view [Eysenck, 1960a]. They, and the writer, use the term "type" not as implying a categorical sorting of people and discontinuities between them, but as a supraordinate concept implying empirical correlations between traits, which are the subordinate concepts. Figure 2 illustrates this hierarchical conception with respect to the extraverted "type.")

We thus have a marked contrast between the psychologist's *dimensional* picture of human personality, and the psychiatrist's *categorical* picture of neurotic and psychotic patients. It is of course possible that what is true of the normal person is not true of the patient, that psychiatric dysfunctions may indeed be separate illnesses which produce categorical divisions in the dimensional system. Szasz (1961) has argued against this view of neurotic disorders as "diseases," and the notion is in fact so alien to current psychiatric thinking that it need hardly be taken very seriously. The reasons for this rejection are not far to seek; there is a complete absence of the specificity which is characteristic of physical illness, there is no separate etiology, and there are no obviously different types of treatment. (Aristotle already suggested the *quantitative* nature of the division between mental normality and mental abnormality.) Nevertheless, we must not decide so important a question by appeals of this nature; clearly, a more experimental course of inquiry is called for.

No standard method is available to solve problems of this type, and the writer has designed the method of *criterion analysis* (Eysenck, 1950) for use to decide questions of qualitative and quantitative differences between groups. This method relies on the administration of sets of objective tests to two criterion groups (e.g., normal and psychotic); a criterion column sets out the biserial correlation of the tests with the criterion, i.e., the ability of the tests to differentiate the two groups. The next step consists in the calculation of two matrices of correlations, one for each of the groups, between all the tests; these are then separately factor analyzed. If the two groups are distinguished quantitatively, then the within-group covariances should be similar, and give rise to identical factors; if the two groups are distinguished qualitatively, then no such similarity should exist. Furthermore, the two factors should be proportional to the criterion column if, and only if, the group differences are quantitative. This method was applied to normal and psychotic groups, 100 Ss in each; 20 tests were administered and used

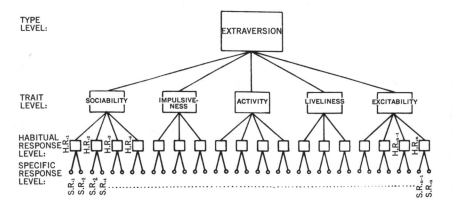

Figure 2. Hierarchical model of type and trait concepts.
(From Eysenck, 1947)

in the analysis. The psychotic group consisted of 50 schizophrenics and 50 manic-depressives. The between-groups comparison of covariances showed them to be very similar, and the respective correlations of the factors extracted from the normal and psychotic groups with the criterion column were .90 and .95. The results indicate very strongly that psychoticism is a dimensional variable, not a categorical one, and that psychotics are not distinguished qualitatively from normals (Eysenck, 1952a). Similar results have been reported when normals and neurotics were compared (Eysenck, 1950), showing that neurosis, too, gives rise to a dimensional, not a categorical variable, and that neurotics are not distinguished qualitatively from normals.

Provisionally, then, we may conclude that the evidence supports the dimensional framework, and fails to support the categorical framework. Unfortunately, the problem does not seem to have attracted as much attention as it would seem to deserve, and the studies mentioned are the only relevant ones which have come to the writer's notice. It will be clear that they do not suffice to establish such an important conclusion in any unequivocal manner. Neither the number of patients used, nor the number and selection of tests employed, can be said to have been sufficient to make any definitive conclusion feasible; at best we have a suggestion as to the more likely direction in which a conclusion may be found. Nor is the method itself such as to guarantee success; it seems quite likely that more powerful methods will be suggested by others more competent in mathematical statistics. Nevertheless, the striking nature of the findings may be interpreted as indicating some interesting and possibly important regularity within nature which deserves to be followed up.

ONE DIMENSION OR TWO?

We have already mentioned the hypothesis that neurotic and psychotic disorders lie along one continuum, such that the psychotic symptoms are indicative of a more deep-seated and severe disorder than the neurotic ones, but also such that with an increase in stress the latter can turn into the former. Opposed to this Freudian theory is the orthodox psychiatric theory according to which neuroses and psychoses are located along different and independent dimensions. These two theories may be shown in diagrammatic form: the one-dimensional one in Figure 3a, the two-dimensional one in Figure 3b. (From Eysenck, 1955b.) This, clearly, is a problem of fundamental importance. What statistical methods are open to us for its solution?

The writer has suggested the use of discriminant function analysis for this purpose; a brief and relatively nontechnical account of this

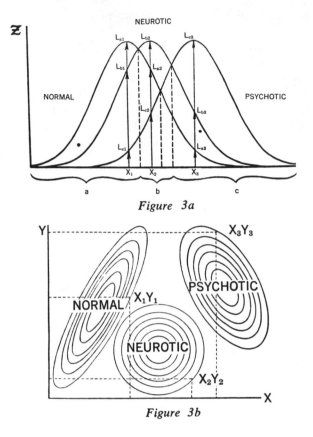

Figure 3a. One-dimensional model of relation between normal, neurotic, and psychotic subjects.

Figure 3b. Two-dimensional model of relation between normal, neurotic, and psychotic subjects. (From Eysenck, 1955b)

procedure will be found in Slater's chapter in Eysenck (1960b). In this method, n groups are tested or measured by means of m tests or measurements, and the analysis discloses the number of significant latent roots, which cannot exceed $n-1$ or $m-1$, whichever is the smaller, but which may not reach either value. Thus if a neurotic, a psychotic, and a normal group are tested by means of at least three tests, the method may result in two, one, or no significant latent roots; this would correspond to a statement that the results require two or one dimensions (or, of course, when none of the latent roots are significant, that the groups cannot be distinguished by means of the tests chosen). This method is preferable in many ways to factor analysis, as fewer assumptions are made and more acceptable tests of significance are available; interesting comparisons between the two methods, used on the same set of data, are presented by Slater in another chapter in Eysenck (1960b), and yet another comparison by Eysenck and Claridge (1962).

A programmatic study by Lubin (1951) has been discussed in some detail in Eysenck (1952b). Four dexterity tests from the General Aptitude Battery of the U.S. Employment Service were applied to 50 normal, 50 psychotic, and 50 neurotic Ss, and the results analyzed by means of discriminant function analysis. Two significant latent roots were found, and the means of the three groups were found to lie in the two-dimensional space thus generated as shown in Figure 4. The two variates jointly correlated with the criterion to the extent of .78; 71.3 percent of the Ss were correctly identified by these extremely simple and objective tests. The execution of the experiment was less well controlled than might have been desired, and made its repetition with a better choice of tests desirable. Two such repetitions are in fact available.

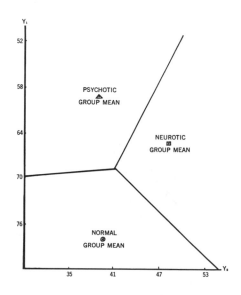

Figure 4. Discriminant function analysis of performance on four tests of psychotics, neurotics, and normals. (From Eysenck, 1952b)

S. B. G. Eysenck (1956) used 123 normals, 53 neurotics, and 51 psychotics; all of them were administered 6 objective tests, and a discriminant function analysis was performed. Two significant latent roots were again discovered, and Figure 5 shows the distribution of scores on the two axes corresponding to these two variables. Again it was found that 71 percent of the Ss could be correctly identified on the basis of these tests; it was also suggested that the amount of mis-classification shown in the study was due in large measure to faults in the criterion, rather than in the tests and their combination. Devada-san (1964) has replicated Eysenck's study on an Indian population with very similar results.

Eysenck (1955a) published a similar but smaller study, in which 20 normals, 20 neurotics, and 20 psychotics were tested on 4 tests. Again two significant latent roots were found, and the results are shown in detail in Figure 6. The number of correct classifications was 65 percent, using one criterion, and 75 percent using another; again we find much the same proportion of cases misclassified as in the two studies mentioned above. Two cases, marked A and B in the figure, had been classified as "neurotic" by the psychiatrists; their scores fell

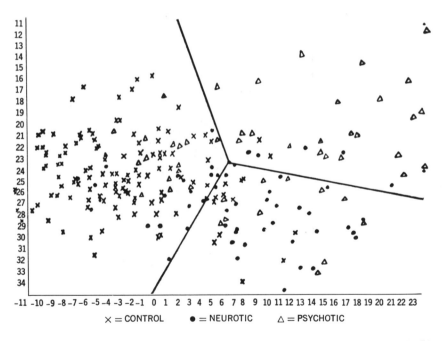

$\times$ = CONTROL $\bullet$ = NEUROTIC $\triangle$ = PSYCHOTIC

Figure 5. Distribution of scores of 123 normals, 53 neurotics, and 51 psychotics on two canonical variates. (From S. B. G. Eysenck, 1956)

right into the psychotic cluster. They, therefore, count as misclassifications. Yet when they were readmitted to the hospital later on, the revised diagnosis was "psychotic." Here again, therefore, it may be suspected that much of the unreliability in the diagnosis is in fact due to unreliability in the criterion.

Factor analysis has given similar results, too, in the sense of requiring two rather than one dimension to accommodate neurotic and psychotic symptoms. Trouton and Maxwell (1956) used 45 rated items on a random sample of 819 patients at the Maudsley and Bethlehem Royal Hospitals, intercorrelated these items, and factor analyzed the resulting matrix. Two clear-cut factors of neuroticism and psychoticism emerged; their nature can best be seen from Figure 7, which is taken from Eysenck (1960c). (A third factor opposes schizophrenic to manic-depressive symptoms, while a fourth factor is labeled "inactivity-withdrawal," and may be related to introversion.) Factor scores were calculated for the members of various diagnostic groups, and their means plotted (Figure 8). The oblique line running across the diagram gives a complete separation of the psychotic from the neurotic diagnoses. Patients with psychotic diagnoses tend to have elevated neurotic factor scores; patients with neurotic diagnoses are all below any of the psychotic groups on psychotic factor scores.

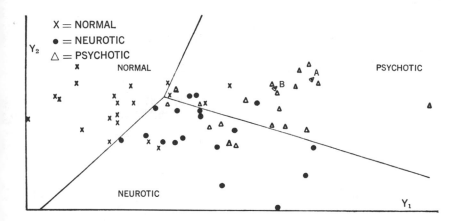

Figure 6. Distribution of scores of 20 normals, 20 neurotics, and 20 psychotics on two canonical variates. (From Eysenck, 1955a)

Table 1 and Figure 9 give the individual scores of 70 neurotic patients, 30 psychotics, and 20 normals, in order to show that the effects noted above are not artifacts produced by diagnostic grouping. There is one psychotic patient, marked B, whose score falls well into the neurotic group; on readmission he was rediagnosed "neurotic." There are two neurotics, labeled A in the diagram, whose scores fell well into the psychotic group; on readmission to the hospital these were rediagnosed as psychotic. The possibilities of dimensional description, using these four factors, are illustrated in Figure 10, which plots the standard scores of three patients (one anxiety neurosis, one agitated

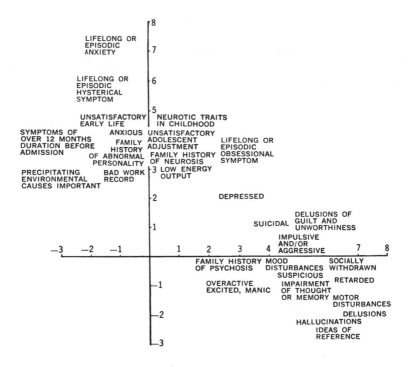

Figure 7. Factor analysis of 45 rated items on a random sample of 819 patients. (From Trouton and Maxwell, 1956)

depression, one schizophrenia); the patterns are quite distinct and probably more informative than any diagnostic label could hope to be, as well as having the advantage of being quantitative.

Cattell's work agrees well with the main conclusion to be drawn from the above-mentioned studies; he concludes his survey of his own studies by saying that "psychoticism is a direction of abnormality distinct from neuroticism and anxiety. As a result, neurotic-contributory factors are not psychotic-contributory, that is, the neurotic-contributory factors discriminate between neurotics and normals, and between neurotics and psychotics, but they do not discriminate between psychotics and normals." Figure 11 shows the profiles of neurotics and psychotics, as compared with normals, on the 16 questionnaire factors which Cattell recognizes; the marked differences will be obvious. Cattell adds in a footnote to this figure: "The objective test evidence . . . confirms that psychotics are not significantly different from normals

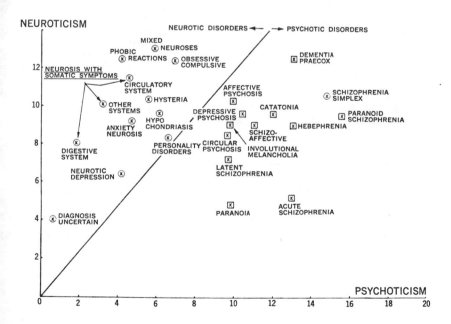

Figure 8. Means of factor scores for various diagnostic groups.
(From Eysenck, 1960c)

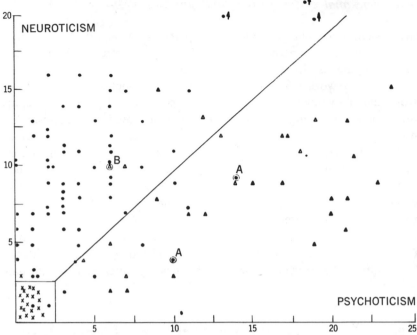

Figure 9. Individual scores of 70 neurotics, 30 psychotics, and 20 normals. Normals are designated by crosses, neurotics by circles, and psychotics by triangles. (From Eysenck, 1960c)

Table 1. Individual scores of normal and patient subjects as analyzed by symptom pattern score, showing amount of misclassification. (From Eysenck, 1960c)

DIAGNOSIS	NORMAL	NEUROTIC	PSYCHOTIC	TOTAL
NORMAL (×)	19	1	0	20
NEUROTIC (•)	2	60	8	70
PSYCHOTIC (△)	0	4	26	30
	21	65	34	120

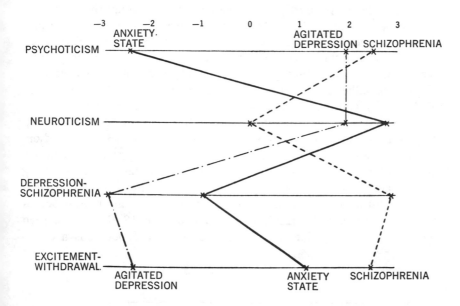

Figure 10. Dimensional description of three patients on four factors.
(From Eysenck, 1960c)

on factor M, Non-Conformity, F(Q)II, Anxiety, and F(Q)I, Introversion." Cattell's work is far too extensive to allow of summary here, but the agreement with our own studies is reassuring (Cattell and Scheier, 1961, p. 112).

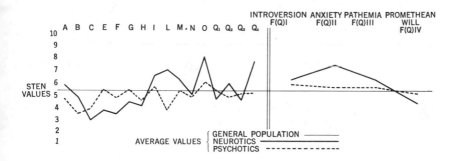

Figure 11. Scores of neurotics and psychotics, respectively, on Cattell's factors. (From Cattell and Scheier, 1961)

Even studies purporting to prove the unidimensional theory reveal, when properly analyzed, the clear-cut existence of two factors. Consider the case of the Bühler, Bühler, and Lefever (1949) "Basic Rorschach Score." These authors recognize four levels of personality integration, ranging from normal through neurotic and psychopathic to psychotic. Proceeding rather in the manner familiar from the construction of the MMPI, they constructed a compound measure of Rorschach indices which would give optimal differentiation between various clinical and diagnostic groups; this measure had a reliabilty of .83. The authors claim that clinical groups characterized by increasing severity of illness do in fact have increasingly higher scores on this test, thus validating a single-continuum type of theory. The present writer has plotted eight of the constituent scores of the Basic Rorschach against level scores (Eysenck, 1960a); the result is shown in Figure 12. It will be seen that, far from being linearly related, the observed function is a curvi-

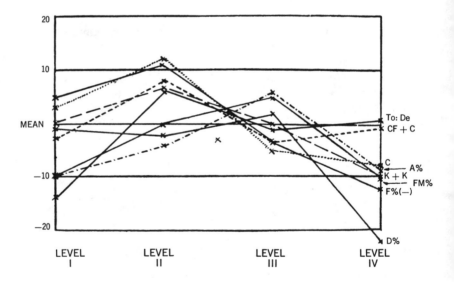

Figure 12. Curvilinear relation between "basic Rorschach score" and
normal—neurotic—psychopathic—psychotic dimension.
(From Eysenck, 1960a)

linear one between score and level; on these indices level-two patients (neurotics) have higher scores than do level-four patients (psychotics); indeed, on some of these, psychotics actually have lower scores than normals! It is apparent that Bühler et al. have thrown together in one "score," indices having quite different regressions on neurotic and psychotic disorders, which is statistically impermissible and psychologically misleading; some indices show neurotics to have high scores, but not psychotics, while on others psychotics have high scores, but not neurotics. These data support, rather than contradict, those of the other studies cited.

Perhaps even more convincing than statistical studies are genetic observations and experiments, such as those reported by Cowie (1961) from the Institute of Psychiatry at the Maudsley Hospital. She argued that if it is true that psychotic and neurotic disorders are orthogonal to each other, then we would expect that the children of psychotic parents should not show any greater degree of neuroticism than would the children of normal parents. Conversely, the unidimensional theory would have clear implications genetically regarding the higher degree of neuroticism to be expected in the children of psychotic parents. In actual fact the children were found, if anything, to be less neurotic than the children of normal parents—a finding which supports the two-dimensional hypothesis, and which may also serve as a warning to those who would overstress the importance of environment in giving rise to neurotic disorders—it is difficult to imagine a more severe stress to a child than having a psychotic parent. Her results are thus particularly important in that they give support to the two-dimensional theory from a direction quite different from those discussed thus far. Provisionally, at least, we must conclude that the unidimensional theory, in spite of its widespread and almost axiomatic acceptance by psychoanalysts, finds no support in the experimental or statistical literature; all serious studies in the field contradict the assumptions on which this theory is built.

The possibility might of course have to be considered that the unidimensional theory might be rephrased so as to fit the facts. It might be suggested, for instance, that the relation between the two major types of mental disorder was unidimensional but nonlinear. Unless the actual relation were more precisely specified, however, such a view could not be said to have much value, as it could obviously not be verified or falsified. In any case, it would still not account for the results obtained by Cowie. Nor is there any indication that such a restyled version of his theory would be acceptable to Freud. As the evidence stands at present, it clearly contradicts any form of unidimensional theory actually held by past or present writers.

SUBDIVISIONS OF NEUROSIS

Neurotic disorders are obviously not all alike, and the problem arises of differential diagnosis. Following Janet's division of neurotic disorders into two great groups, Jung suggested that introverts were more prone to psychasthenic disorders, extraverts to hysteric disorders; Eysenck's original factor analytic studies of 700 neurotic patients seemed to support such a division (Eysenck, 1947). Figure 13 shows the results; a factor of neuroticism loads on all the notations, and a bipolar factor divides the "dysthymic" from the "hysteric" disorders. No independent measure of extraversion-introversion was used at the time, but later studies demonstrated that while Jung was right in thinking of hysterics as being more extraverted than dysthymics, nevertheless the hysterics were not on the whole more extraverted than selected normal groups

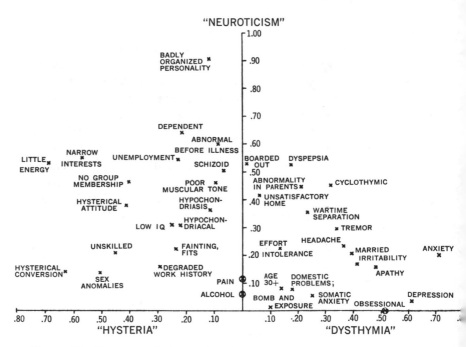

Figure 13. Factor analytic study of 700 neurotic patients, showing the division of neurotic disorders into hysterical (extraverted) and dysthymic (introverted) symptoms. (From Eysenck, 1947)

(Eysenck and Eysenck, 1969). Later studies showed that psychopaths and criminals occupied in fact the position of high E (extraversion), high N (neuroticism) which Jung had allocated to the hysterics (Eysenck, 1965c). There seems to be some doubt even about the homogeneity of the diagnosis of "hysteria"; conversion hysterics and hysterical personalities appear to differ in their scores on N and E (Ingham and Robinson, 1964).

A factor analytic study by Hildebrand (1953, 1958) gave results which are fairly representative; he used normal Ss as well as groups diagnosed as anxiety state, obsessional neurosis, reactive depression, conversion hysteria, psychopathic state, and mixed neurosis. There are certain experimental and statistical complexities to this study which cannot be discussed here for reasons of space; Slater (1960) has given a clear account and reanalysis of Hildebrand's data. Figure 14 shows the relative positions of the various diagnostic groups; plotted are the means of their factor scores for the various tests administered them.

A similar study, comparing factor scores of 16 normals, 16

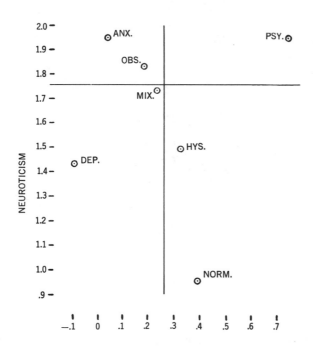

Figure 14. Mean factor scores of psychopathic, hysterical, mixed, obsessional, anxious, and depressed groups, as compared to normals, in two-factor solution. (From Slater, 1960)

hysterics, and 16 dysthymics, was carried out by Eysenck and Claridge (1962), using a battery of six tests. The results are shown in Figure 15. All the subjects taking part in the experiment have had their factor scores plotted, and the means for the three groups form the corners of the triangle drawn in. Factor 1 may be identified as intro-version-extraversion, factor 2 as neuroticism-stability. Most of the hysterics are found in the high N—high E quadrant, most dysthymics in the high N—low E quadrant.

Cattell has published data which also show a similar bifurcation, with dysthymic disorders toward the high N, low E extreme, and psychopaths and sociopaths toward the high N, high E extreme. Figure 16 shows his results; it should be noted that in his terminology "anxiety" is used where the writer uses "neuroticism," and vice versa; this is confusing, but is a purely verbal difference which does not affect the factual similarity between the two sets of data. (Cattell and Scheier, 1961).

Other factor analyses have been discussed in Eysenck (1960a);

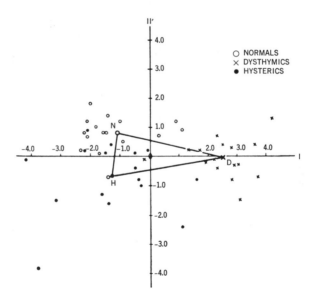

Figure 15. Distribution of 16 normals, 16 hysterics, and 16 dysthymics in two-factor space. (Triangle connects mean scores of three groups.)
(From Eysenck and Claridge, 1962)

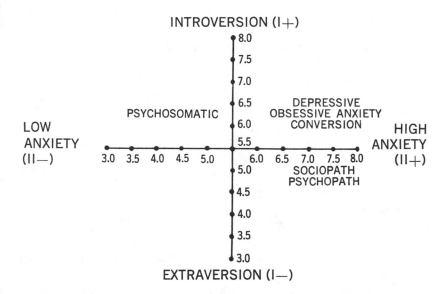

Figure 16. Positions of different neurotic groups in Cattell's system of classification. (From Cattell and Scheier, 1961)

it will here be of more interest to turn to the application of discriminant function analysis to data of this kind. An early study by Rao and Slater (1949) gave results shown in Figure 17; obsessionals and anxiety state patients are opposed to hysterics and psychopaths in the

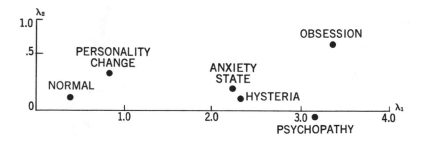

Figure 17. Positions of different neurotic groups on two canonical variates. (From Rao and Slater, 1949)

second dimension, which, however, failed to reach a satisfactory level of significance, possibly because of the poor choice of tests.

Discriminant function analyses have also been undertaken of the Hildebrand study and the Eysenck and Claridge experiment. The former was reanalyzed by Slater (1960) in an important paper which throws much light on the theoretical assumptions of factor analysis and discriminant function analysis, and illustrates their similarities and differences. He finds that three dimensions are required to accommodate the scores on the tests of the various group; Figure 18 shows the positions of the groups in relation to the first and second vectors. He then went on to consider the problem of the projection of a D-space on an f-space, reports (Figure 19) the scatter of the groups in the plane defined by the first two principal components of the dispersion within groups. It will be seen that, as he puts it, "the expectation deduced from the hypothesis this experiment was designed to test are supported admirably in every respect by the evidence shown in this picture."

If this were all, we might count this study as giving complete confirmation to our hypothesis. The picture is clouded, however, by the existence of a third dimension which may or may not be identical

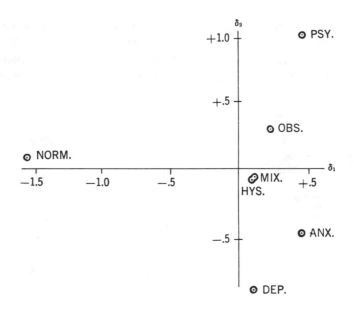

Figure 18. Discriminant function analysis of data analyzed by factor analysis in Figure 14. (From Slater, 1960)

with psychoticism; the experiment was not designed to reveal such a factor, and cannot be interpreted with any confidence. It is not implausible that psychopaths and obsessionals might have higher scores on psychoticism than hysterics and anxiety states, but the evidence does not permit us to say so with confidence. Further work is clearly required to sort out this particular complication.

The results of the Eysenck-Claridge experiment, when scores were submitted to discriminant function analysis, show a very clear-cut picture. Figure 20 shows the main results; it will be noted that there is no overlap at all between hysterics and dysthymics on the first discriminant function, and little overlap between normals and neurotics on the second. The results are a good deal clearer than the results from the factor analysis carried out on the same data, and shown in Figure 15. This is not surprising; canonical analysis of discrimination was specially developed as a statistical tool for maximizing discriminance, while factor analysis was designed for a different purpose. As Slater (1960) puts it: "In a limited sense the canonical analysis is an optimal procedure, and extracts all the information obtainable from the data

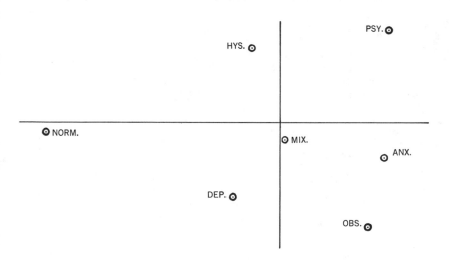

Figure 19. Scatter of groups analyzed in preceding diagram in the plane defined by the first two principal components of the dispersion within groups. (From Slater, 1960)

about the differences between the groups," whereas "accuracy is lost inevitably at two stages in the course of a factor analysis." When it is a question of testing specific hypotheses about the mutual relations between psychiatric groups, then discriminant function analysis is the preferred procedure.

We may close this section by showing in summary form some results from administering the Maudsley Personality Inventory to various groups whose position in the two-dimensional framework of our theory follows from our assumptions. Figure 21 shows the results of a number of studies, and it will be agreed that on the whole the data support the results so far reported. The extent to which data of this kind throw light on the dimensional and categorical systems of diagnosis, repectively, is a point which will be discussed in detail later on.

SUBDIVISIONS OF PSYCHOSIS

Kraepelin, Bleuler, and Kretschmer divided psychotic disorders into two main groups, schizophrenics and manic-depressives, and the last-named suggested that a major personality dimension, analogous to extraversion-introversion, could be constructed by going from one extreme through schizoids and dystonics to syntonics and cycloids (Fig-

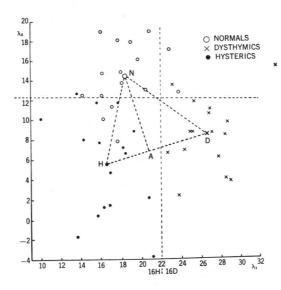

Figure 20. Discriminant function analysis of data analyzed by factor analysis in Figure 15. (From Eysenck and Claridge, 1962)

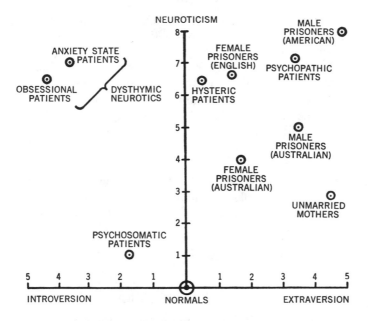

Figure 21. Positions of various groups in relation to questionnaire measures of neuroticism—emotionality and extraversion. (From Eysenck, 1965c)

ure 22). This suggestion runs counter to the genetic evidence, which suggests that quite specific genes are reponsible for the occurrence of the major psychotic disorders (Shields and Slater, 1960). Eysenck (1952a), in an article already mentioned, applied the technique of criterion analysis to this problem; the outcome was an unqualified negative. Psychoticism as a whole had shown itself to be a quantitative

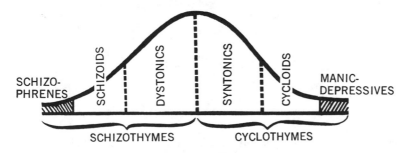

Figure 22. Personality description advocated by Kretschmer.
(From Eysenck, 1960a)

variable, ranging all the way from normal to extreme abnormality; no dimension corresponding to schizophrenia vs. manic-depressive insanity could be discovered. This agreement of the statistical procedure of criterion analysis with the genetic work already mentioned suggests that Kretschmer may have been working along the wrong lines.

Nevertheless, there are suggestions which may be held to point in the opposite direction. Consider for example the work of Shagass and his colleagues on the sedation threshold (Shagass and Kerenyi, 1958). They have shown in a whole series of studies that, as expected by the present writer's theory, extraverts have low sedation (and sleep) thresholds, introverts high ones. Patients suffering from neurotic depressions have high thresholds; patients suffering from psychotic depressions should, according to Kretschmer, be extraverted and have low

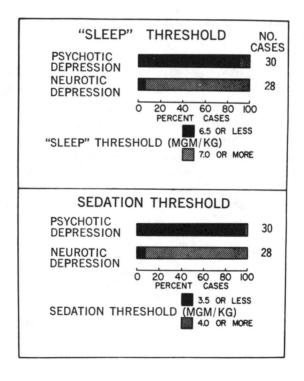

Figure 23. Sleep and sedation thresholds of patients suffering from psychotic and neurotic depression, respectively.
(From Shagass and Kerenyi, 1958)

thresholds. As Figure 23 shows, this is actually so; the differences between the groups are quite large. (A more thorough review of the evidence on sedation thresholds is given in Eysenck, 1967a.)

In another type of experiment, Palmai and Blackwell (1965) showed that psychotic depressives have a pattern of salivary flow which is different from that of normals; patients show maximum flow in the afternoon, normals in the morning. This is relevant because Colquhoun and Corcoran (1964) have shown that on simple, repetitive tasks introverts perform better in the morning, extraverts in the afternoon. This would lead one to assume that neurotic depressives would show a salivary pattern exactly the opposite to that of the psychotic depressives, and in some unpublished studies Palmai has shown just that. Figure 24 gives some of his data. The agreement with predictions from a Kretschmer-like theory, identifying introversion and schizothymia, on the one hand, and extraversion and cyclothymia on the other, is striking. This is not the place to review the whole literature, but it will be clear that the last word has not been said on this controversy.

There has been much work on the factor analytic study of ratings

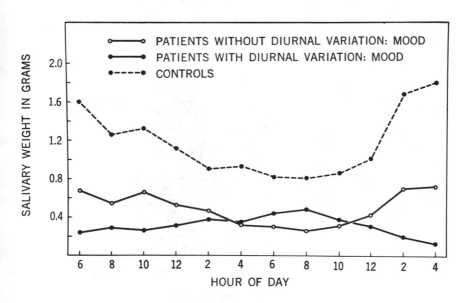

Figure 24. Salivary flow of psychotic depressives (patients with diurnal variation in mood) and neurotic depressives (patients without diurnal variation in mood), as compared with controls.
(From unpublished study by G. Palmai)

of behavior in psychotics; summaries of this work are available else-where (Eysenck, 1960a; Lorr et al., 1962; Lorr, 1966). As a chapter by Lorr is included in this book, discussing his own work, there is little point in discussing it here also; in a later section we shall return to a consideration of certain methodological issues raised by him. On the factual side, let us merely note that his analysis leads him to the postulation of ten primary factors in psychotic behavior, of which eight fit reasonably well together in the form of a circle (Figure 25): "The correlations of any specified variable with its neighbors decrease monotonically in size as a function of their sequential separation. Half-way through the sequence, the correlations increase in size monotonically until the main diagonal is reached on the other side."

When submitted to discriminant function analysis, the ten primary factors give rise to three main dimensions; Figure 26 shows the positions of six of Lorr's types in this three-dimensional framework. These three dimensions correspond in part, but only in part, to higher-order factors calculated by him from the intercorrelations between the ten primary factors. It is notable that many of his primary factors have also appeared in one form or another in factor analytic studies reported

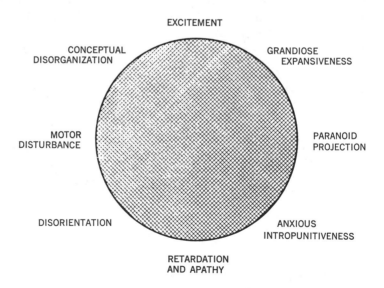

Figure 25. Two-dimensional descriptive system of psychotic behavior.
(From Lorr, 1966)

by earlier writers; there clearly is some degree of orderly reliability in this confused field.

Causal Factors in Dimensional Systems

Dimensional systems, like other taxonomic devices, have a certain aura of arbitrariness (Sokal and Sneath, 1963). The writer has always insisted that in order to obtain a rational, scientific system of diagnosis, the results of statistical analysis, whether factor analysis, discriminant function analysis, or even the implicit types of analysis performed by

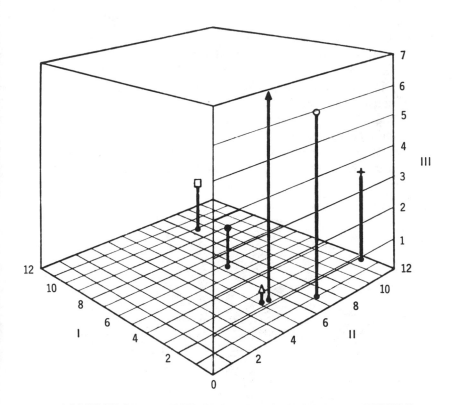

LOCATION OF PATIENTS OF SIX TYPES IN THREE DIMENSIONS
DETERMINED BY THREE CANONICAL VARIATES
+ EXCITED-GRANDIOSE, ○ EXCITED-HOSTILE, ▲ PARANOID,
△ INTROPUNITIVE, ● RETARDED, □ DISORGANIZED.

Figure 26. (From Lorr, 1966)

psychiatrists in their formation of subjective judgments, should be linked with causal theories of a psychological or physiological nature, which in turn should generate testable hypotheses of a behavioral character. Some attempts to do so have been undertaken in relation to extraversion and neuroticism (Eysenck, 1967a); as regards psychoticism efforts to find such hypotheses have been rather less far-reaching and less successful (Eysenck, 1961; Payne and Hewlett, 1960). We may perhaps use the former theories as an example of the kind of model which we are looking for.

The theory is based on certain facts which will not be documented here; full discussion of the evidence is given in Eysenck (1967a). (1) Individual differences in extraversion-introversion have a strong hereditary basis. (2) Individual differences in neuroticism-stability have a strong hereditary basis. (3) Individual differences in extraversion-introversion are basically related to differences in the excitation-inhibition balance of the individual (Eysenck, 1957). (4) Individual differences in neuroticism are basically related to differences in thresholds of emotional activation. These fundamental facts suggest the search for a neurological-physiological-anatomical locus for the inherited structures which must be presumed to underlie function; it is a well-established principle in biology that only structure can be inherited, not function.

The results of this search are illustrated in Figure 27. It is argued

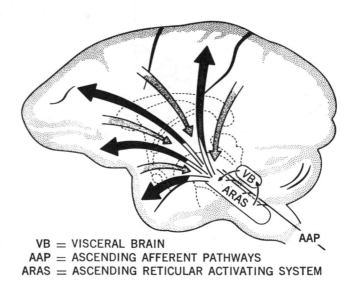

VB = VISCERAL BRAIN
AAP = ASCENDING AFFERENT PATHWAYS
ARAS = ASCENDING RETICULAR ACTIVATING SYSTEM

Figure 27. Diagrammatic representation of brain stem arousal system and limbic system as determinants of two main dimensions of personality. (From Eysenck, 1967a)

that the excitation-inhibition balance for any given individual is determined by the low or high thresholds of his ascending reticular activating system, which is known to determine the state of arousal of the cortex, and which also possesses a synchronizing portion which causes cortical inhibition when stimulated. It is further argued that the emotional lability for any given individual is determined by the low or high thresholds of his visceral brain, which is known to determine the rate of autonomic reactivity to incoming stimuli. There are, of course, complex relations (1) between reticular formation and visceral brain, and (2) between reticular formation and cortex; it is impossible to enter into these at this place, and the reader must be referred to *The Biological Basis of Personality* (Eysenck, 1967a). Both physiological and psychological deductions are possible from a theory of this nature. Thus, the greater state of arousal of the introvert postulated by this theory is borne out by EEG studies showing introverts to have lower alpha amplitude and higher alpha frequency, on the physiological side, and by their having lower sensory thresholds, greater responsiveness to stimulation, and fewer "blocks," on the psychological side.

Such causal theories must, of course, be related to the phenomena which form the basis of the descriptive, dimensional system. They should be able to explain, if they are to be of any use, why it is introverts who are more prone to dysthymic disorders, while extraverts suffer more from psychopathic and criminal tendencies. How can the theory explain the symptomatology of hysterics in terms of such concepts as arousal and inhibition? And even if such links could be forged, would it be possible to show the relevance of diagnosis and explanation, as so conceived, to treatment? It is these questions which will be dealt with in the closing pages of this chapter.

One of the crucial deductions to be made from the theory outlined above relates to the postulation of greater ease of conditioning in introverts under certain circumstances, as compared with extraverts. Pavlov already showed that cortical arousal (excitation) facilitated conditioning, while cortical inhibition impeded the formation of strong and lasting conditioned responses, and Magoun (1964) has shown that modern electrophysiological experiments give much support to Pavlov's generalizations. Eysenck (1965d) has summarized the evidence on the relationship between conditioning and extraversion in humans, and has shown that under suitable conditions (which themselves can of course be deduced from the theory) introverts do indeed form conditioned responses more speedily and more strongly. In a later study, Eysenck and Levey (1967) have compared eyeblink conditioned responses of introverts, extraverts, and ambiverts under all combinations of variation of three parameters: CS—UCS duration, long vs. short; UCS strength, strong vs. weak; and reinforcement, partial or complete. It was predicted that short CS—UCS interval, weak UCS, and partial reinforcement would favor conditioning in introverted Ss, long CS—UCS interval, strong UCS, and complete reinforcement conditioning in extraverts. Results agree well with prediction (Eysenck, 1967a).

These results should be seen in the context of the writer's theory of neurotic and criminal behavior. Again there is no space here to go into details; these are furnished in *The Causes and Cures of Neurosis* (Eysenck and Rachman, 1965), and in *Crime and Personality* (Eysenck 1965c). Essentially, however, we may regard *dysthymic* disorder as being due to the formation of conditioned autonomic responses to normally neutral stimuli; these conditioned responses and the motor movements made in response to them constitute the neurotic disorder. *Psychopathic* disorders, and many types of criminal behavior, are due to the absence of those conditioned responses which are thought to be the basis of socialized, moral, ethical conduct, and which are often referred to simply as "conscience." Under identical external conditions we would expect introverts, who condition better, to be predisposed to develop dysthymic disorders, and extraverts, who condition less well, to develop psychopathic disorders, or, to put it slightly differently, to fail to develop a "conscience," and thus to behave in immoral and antisocial ways. This brief outline is of course incapable of accommodating any of the numerous theoretical details, experimental confirmations, or additional hypotheses which alone can make the picture convincing; for these the reader must be referred to the sources cited above. It may, however, be of some interest to consider in some slight detail the "conversion" reactions of the hysteric.

In terms of our theory, hysterics are relatively extraverted, and hence should not condition easily, except under conditions of strong UCS, and other conditions favoring extraverts. Why should strong stimuli favor extraverts disproportionately? The answer may lie in Pavlov's law of transmarginal inhibition; there is some evidence that introverts, as expected, show transmarginal inhibition at lower levels of stimulation than do extraverts (Eysenck, 1967a). However that may be, hysterical reactions are usually reported under conditions of strong stimulation, e.g., during wars and revolutions, or in connection with sexual misadventures. Again, extraverts have lower thresholds for cortical inhibition, and as Pavlov already suggested, some types of mental illness are likely to be related to abnormal functioning of the internal inhibition mechanism; Magoun (1964) points out that "it is now possible to identify a thalamo-cortical mechanism for internal inhibition, capable of modifying activity of the brain partially or globally, so that its sensory, motor and higher functions become reduced and cease." In addition to certain conditioned responses, it is of course such inhibitions (paralysis, functional blindness and deafness, failure of memory) which are characteristic of the hysteric, who is supposed to "convert" his emotional disturbances into physical symptoms. In the terms of this theory, there is no "conversion," but rather a strong excitation of the thalamocortical portions of the reticular formation which mediate inhibition. There is direct evidence of such a connection between motor inhibition and extraversion, when the subject is in a state of high autonomic activation (Eysenck, 1967a), and this theory is more parsimonious than the Freudian, as well as having both psychological and physiological support.

These theories are of course directly linked with therapy, and the numerous volumes and papers dealing with behavior therapy (Eysenck, 1960d, 1965b; Eysenck and Rachman, 1965) may be consulted regarding details. What is of interest here is the relevance of diagnostic tests to behavior therapy. Unfortunately there has been relatively little attempt to conduct experimental or clinical research in this area to any significant degree, but it is possible to suggest certain likely relationships, and to point out ways in which direct links could be forged. Consider, for instance, the process of desensitization; according to J. Wolpe this process implied a conditioning of parasympathetic responses to the CS which in the past has become conditioned to sympathetic responses. If we take this (grossly oversimplified) paradigm seriously then we would expect that patients who condition easily would be more likely to respond to this counter-conditioning treatment than would patients who condition only poorly. An unpublished study in the Maudsley Laboratories has shown that this prediction can indeed be verified at an acceptable level of statistical significance, thus not only linking eyeblink conditioning as a diagnostic technique with prediction of success in therapy, but also affording experimental support to the theory proposed by Wolpe. In view of the importance attributed to the formation of conditioned responses in our system, it would seem desirable to ascertain the ease or difficulty of formation of such responses *in more than one field* in all patients coming in for treatment.

The same argument may apply to questionnaire measurement of E and N; routine administrations of such measures as the Eysenck Personality Inventory (EPI) (Eysenck and Eysenck, 1965) may give important clues with respect to treatment. To give just one (unpublished) example, two adolescents were admitted to the Children's Unit because of extreme reading difficulties; one was extremely extraverted, the other extremely introverted. The hypothesis was put forward that the extravert had failed to benefit from lessons because of strong reactive inhibition to long continued monotonous teaching; a comparison of the reactions of the two patients to long and short training sessions, respectively, did in fact show that the extravert benefited only from short sessions, and not at all from long ones. The introvert, per contra, benefited most from long sessions. Many other (anecdotal) examples could be given of single applications of the system of thinking and diagnostics expounded here; the difficulty is of course that here, as with all clinical work, applications tend to be unique, in the sense that the particular pattern of circumstances which gave rise to the set of symptoms presented by the patient is not likely to recur in precisely that form.

In the absence of experimental studies, it may be useful to turn to certain problems in behavior therapy which would seem to demand some answer in terms of diagnostic investigations. Why is it that some patients appear to benefit from desensitization in which hierarchies of anxiety-producing situations are imagined, while others have to be confronted with real-life examples of such situations and objects? Fortunately the latter group is in a minority, but it does exist, and should be capable of being distinguished in terms of some measures of strength of imagery, perhaps. (Strength of imagery itself has been shown to correlate with introversion.) Why is it that some patients fail to generalize the benefits of desensitization in the clinic to objects and situations outside, when most patients find no such difficulty? Could laboratory studies of a diagnostic kind, involving generalization gradients, be of use in this connection? Many such diagnostic problems are thrown up by the actual practice of behavior therapy, and should ideally find an answer in terms of the system under consideration; in due course much useful experimental work will no doubt be devoted to questions such as these.

E is of course not the only variable which is of relevance to behavior therapy; N too can be of the utmost importance. Aversion therapy, for instance, appears to be far more successful when patients are not too high on N; when they are high on N the therapy often makes them worse rather than better. A good example of this is given in Eysenck (1960d); treatment of writer's cramp by shocking deviant movements was successful in low-N Ss, but exacerbated the deviant reactions in high-N Ss. It would be of considerable interest to know whether this generalization could be shown to hold with other types of aversion therapy, and in other types of disorder. Autonomic recording in conjunction with behavior therapy is often used to prevent excessive anxiety developing in the course of treatment; similar methods of recording, used as a diagnostic device, might be useful in forecasting the speed with which hierarchies could be worked through, and the size of the just noticeable differences (j.n.d.s.) which might be tolerated by the patient.

In this connection, reference may be made to the recent demonstration by P. Lang (unpublished) that behavior therapy can be committed to tape and administered by computer, and that this method of treatment, which holds out considerable promise, is not inferior to personal treatment on the whole. It may be predicted that different types of personality will react quite differently to this rather unusual situation, and in view of the high value which extraverts place on personal interaction, it seems reasonable to predict that the more extraverted patients will prefer, and possibly benefit more by, personal treatment, while the more introverted patients will prefer, and possibly benefit more by, computerized impersonal treatment. There is some evidence that in more orthodox machine learning situations extraverts do much less well than do introverts (Eysenck, 1967a), and the extrapolation of this finding to the therapeutic situation does not seem to fanciful.

The conclusion to be drawn from this discussion must surely be that there are many rational links between behavior therapy and the diagnostic system outlined in this paper, but that hitherto relatively little work has been done in this connection. Consequently, all we can offer at this stage are suggestions for experimental work and for clinical use; there is no well-established body of knowledge which we might draw on. This is not really surprising, of course, in view of the youth of behavior therapy; it is less than ten years since it became a usable and proven technique of therapy, and in this time most energy has naturally been devoted to improving the technique and establishing its effectiveness. It may be hoped that in the next few years advances will also be made in respect of the diagnostic side; it is the writer's firm belief that treatment could be much improved and shortened, and many disappointments and wrong choices avoided, if more attention were paid to the diagnostic side of this general body of theory.

One important outcome of our discussion, however, relates to rather a different conception of diagnostic testing, one which stresses the unusual and unique features of each special patient, rather than the general and nonspecific ones which many patients have in common. If we stress the relevance of conditioning and autonomic lability, as

inherited, constitutional personality parameters, to the development of
neurotic disorders, then we must of course also recognize the relevance
of specific traumatic events and accidental environmental influences
which act through the mechanisms of learning and conditioning. This
means, in effect, that we must regard each patient as fundamentally
a separate experimental problem, to be solved, like all experimental
problems, by the postulation of likely hypotheses and by the design
and execution of appropriate experimental procedures. This line of
approach has been specially developed by Shapiro (1951, 1957, 1961),
and it complements the approach outlined in the last few pages. A
decision has to be made in each case as to whether it is the common
or the specific elements which predominate, and in accordance with
that decision the line of diagnostic testing will have to be chosen.
But in all cases, of course, the main stress must be on the application
of psychological knowledge, gained in the laboratory, to the solution
of essentially psychological problems; the idea that recourse to traditional psychiatric nosology or more modern psychoanalytic mythology
can help in deciding choice of treatment for the patient has been
thoroughly exploded.

REFERENCES

Bannister, D., Salman, P., and Lieberman, D. M. Diagnosis-treatment rela-
    tionships in psychiatry—a statistical analysis. *Brit. J. Psychiat.*, 1964,
    110, 726–32.
Bühler, C., Bühler, K., and Lefever, D. W. Development of the Basic
    Rorschach Score. California: Copyright 1949. Quoted from H. J.
    Eysenck, 1960a.
Cattell, R. B., and Scheier, I. N. *The meaning and measurement of neurot-
    icism and anxiety.* New York: Ronald Press, 1961.
Colquhoun, W. P., and Corcoran, D. V. J. The effects of time of day and
    social isolation on the relationship between temperament and perform-
    ance. *Brit. J. soc. clin. Psychol.*, 1964, **3**, 226–31.
Cowie, V. The incidence of neurosis in the children of psychotics. *Acta
    Psychiat. Scand.*, 1961, **37**, 37–87.
Cremerius, J. *Die Beurteilung des Behandlungserfolges in der Psycho-
    therapie.* Berlin: Springer, 1962.
Devadasan, K. Cross-cultural validity of twelve clinical diagnostic tests.
    J. Indian Acad. appl. Psychol., 1964, **1**, 55–57.

Eysenck, H. J. *The dimensions of personality.* London: Routledge & Kegan Paul, 1947.

Eysenck, H. J. Criterion analysis: an application of the hypothetico-deductive method to factor analysis. *Psychol. Rev.,* 1950, **57**, 38–53.

Eysenck, H. J. Schizothymia-cyclothymia as a dimensional personality. *J. Pers.,* 1952a, **20**, 345–84.

Eysenck, H. J. *The scientific study of personality.* London: Routledge & Kegan Paul, 1952b.

Eysenck, H. J. Psychiatric diagnosis as a psychological and statistical problem. *Psychol. Rep.* 1955a, **1**, 3–17.

Eysenck, H. J. *Psychology and the foundations of psychiatry.* London: H. K. Lewis, 1955b.

Eysenck, H. J. *The dynamics of anxiety and hysteria.* London: Routledge & Kegan Paul, 1957.

Eysenck, H. J. *The structure of human personality.* London: Routledge & Kegan Paul, 1960a.

Eysenck, H. J. (Ed.). *Experiments in personality.* 2 vols. London: Routledge & Kegan Paul, 1960b.

Eysenck, H. J. Classification and the problem of diagnosis. In H. J. Eysenck (Ed.), *Handbook of abnormal psychology.* London: Pitman, 1960c.

Eysenck, H. J. (Ed.). *Behaviour therapy and the neuroses.* New York: Pergamon Press, 1960d.

Eysenck, H. J. Psychosis, drive and inhibition: a theoretical and experimental account. *Amer. J. Psychol.,* 1961, **118**, 198–204.

Eysenck, H. J. Principles and methods of personality description, classification and diagnosis. *Brit. J. Psychol.,* 1964, **55**, 284–94.

Eysenck, H. J. The effects of psychotherapy. *Int. J. Psychiat.,* 1965a, **1**, 97–178.

Eysenck, H. J. *Experiments in behaviour therapy.* New York: Pergamon Press, 1965b.

Eysenck, H. J. *Crime and personality.* New York: Houghton Mifflin, 1965c.

Eysenck, H. J. Extraversion and the acquisition of eyeblink and G.S.R. conditioned responses. *Psychol. Bull.,* 1965d, **63**, 258–70.

Eysenck, H. J. *The biological basis of personality.* Springfield, Ill.: C. C Thomas, 1967a.

Eysenck, H. J. The contribution of clinical psychology to psychiatry. In J. G. Howells (Ed.), *Modern perspective in world psychiatry.* London: Oliver & Boyd, 1967b.

Eysenck, H. J., and Claridge, G. The position of hysterics and dysthymics in a two-dimensional framework of personality description. *J. abnorm. soc. Psychol.,* 1962, **64**, 46–55.

Eysenck, H. J., and Eysenck, S. B. G. The Eysenck Personality Inventory. San Diego, Calif.: Indust. & Educ. Testing Service, 1965.

Eysenck, H. J., and Eysenck, S. B. G. *Personality structure and measure-*

ment. London: Routledge & Kegan Paul, 1969. San Diego, Calif.: R. R. Knapp, 1967.

Eysenck, H. J., and Levey, A. Konditionierung, Introversion-Extraversion und die Stärke des Nervensystems. *Z. für Psychol.,* 1967, **174**, 96–106.

Eysenck, H. J., and Rachman, S. *The causes and cures of neurosis.* San Diego, Calif.: R. R. Knapp, 1965.

Eysenck, S. B. G. Neurosis and psychosis: an experimental analysis. *J. ment. Sci.,* 1956, **102**, 517–29.

Hildebrand, H. P. A factorial study of introversion-extraversion by means of objective tests. Unpublished Ph.D. thesis. London, 1953.

Hildebrand, H. P. A factorial study of introversion-extraversion. *Brit. J. Psychol.,* 1958, **49**, 1–12.

Ingham, N., and Robinson, J. O. Personality in the diagnosis of hysteria. *Brit. J. Psychol.,* 1964, **55**, 276–84.

Loevinger, J. Diagnosis and measurement: a reply to Eysenck. *Psychol. Rep.,* 1955, **1**, 277–78.

Lorr, M. (Ed.) *Exploration in typing psychotics.* London: Pergamon Press, 1966.

Lorr, M., Klett, C. J., and McNair, D. M. *Syndromes of psychosis.* London: Pergamon Press, 1962.

Lubin, A. Some contributions to the testing of psychological hypotheses by means of statistical multivariate analysis. Unpublished Ph.D. thesis. London, 1951.

Magoun, H. W. *The waking brain.* Springfield, Ill.: C. C Thomas, 1964.

Palmai, G., and Blackwell, B. The diurnal pattern of salivary flow in normal and depressed patients. *Brit. J. Psychiat.,* 1965, **111**, 334–38.

Payne, R. V., and Hewlett, J. H. G. Thought disorder in psychotic patients. In H. J. Eysenck (Ed.), *Experiments in personality.* Vol. 2. London: Routledge & Kegan Paul, 1960.

Rao, C. R., and Slater, P. Multivariate analysis applied to differences between neurotic groups. *Brit. J. stat. Psychol.,* 1949, **2**, 17–29.

Shagass, C., and Kerenyi, A. The "sleep" threshold. A simple form of the sedation threshold for clinical use. *Canad. Psychiat. J.,* 1958, **1**, 101–9.

Shapiro, M. B. An experimental approach to diagnostic psychological testing. *J. ment. Sci.,* 1951, **97**, 748–64.

Shapiro, M. B. Experimental method in the psychological description of the individual psychiatric patient. *Int. J. soc. Psychiat.,* 1957, **3**, 89–102.

Shapiro, M. B. A method of measuring psychological drugs specific to the individual psychiatric patient. *Brit. J. med. Psychol.,* 1961, **34**, 151–55.

Shields, J., and Slater, E. Heredity and psychological abnormality. In H. J. Eysenck (Ed.), *Handbook of abnormal psychology.* London: Pitman, 1960.

Slater, P. Experiments in psychometrics. I. Factor analysis and some allied procedures. II. Canonical analysis of discriminance. III. A re-examination of some data collected by H. P. Hildebrand. In H. J. Eysenck

(Ed.), *Experiments in personality.* Vol. 2. London: Routledge & Kegan Paul, 1960b.

Sokal, R. R., and Sneath, P. H. A. *Principles of numerical taxonomy.* London: W. N. Freeman, 1963.

Szasz, T. S. *The myth of mental illness.* New York: Hoeber-Harper, 1961.

Trouton, D. S., and Maxwell, A. E. The relation between neurosis and psychosis. *J. ment. Sci.,* 1956, **102**, 1–21.

Wolman, B. J. Mental health and mental disorders. In B. J. Wolman (Ed.), *Handbook of clinical psychology.* New York: McGraw-Hill, 1965. Pp. 1119–39.

Wundt, W. *Grundzüge der physiologischen Psychologie.* 5th ed., Vol. 3. Leipzig: W. Engelmann, 1903.

Zubin, J., Eron, L. D., and Schumer, F. *An experimental approach to projected techniques.* New York: Wiley, 1965.

EXISTENTIAL-TRANSACTIONAL PREFACE TO A CLASSIFICATION SYSTEM

An existential psychology, says Leary, understands the individual in terms of ongoing, here-and-now moments. A transactional psychology requires an open collaborative relationship between the psychologist and the person studied. For classification purposes, the existential approach suggests the collection of natural records and the study of natural events in a natural field. Instead of imposing prefabricated variables on the situation, the psychologist is to use a conceptual language arising out of the natural data. The existential approach especially emphasizes a distinction between an inner life of consciousness, internal reality, experiential truth, and, on the other hand, an outer life of behavior, the observer's factual subject matter. Maps, models, and measures for describing inner experience must be developed and related to maps, models, and measures for describing external behavior.

The transactional approach allows and encourages the patient himself to define the variables and the subject matter to be studied. In fact, the patient is to help plan, design, and construct the record-collecting devices. The atmosphere is such that the patient is willing to expose himself; this is accomplished by treating the "patient" as a person, a human being, and by not keeping secrets from him.

Out of these existential-transactional considerations arises a bifurcated procedure. We measure the patient's intimacy, commitment, involvement. This is accomplished by a space-time classification of his behavior—where and how he spends his time, how much time is shared. We also localize the level of consciousness at which he is functioning.

Seven levels of consciousness are posited, and the diagnostician and patient must be at the same level of consciousness.

Such an approach calls for a conceptual language to describe the inner world of existential events and the outer world of external behavior. This conceptual language, it appears, must go beyond literary humanist descriptions to provide working maps of an existential-experiential, transactional-interpersonal personality structure. The direction is toward a psychological system for understanding, taxonomizing persons on the basis of an existential-transactional conceptual language.

7

THE DIAGNOSIS OF BEHAVIOR AND THE DIAGNOSIS OF EXPERIENCE

TIMOTHY LEARY

Existential-Transactional Diagnosis

Modern dynamic psychology claims to study the internal and external aspects of human nature—the indirect and the direct, the covert and the overt, the said and the unsaid, the done and the undone, the experienced and the expressed. This relatively new intellectual position has made a flashy contribution to our conceptions of human nature. The impact of dynamic theory upon every aspect of intellectual life (and I want to stress *intellectual* as opposed to practical) is currently so evident that I need not pause to elaborate or demonstrate.

And now this said, I shall proceed to a critical examination of the practical applications of this broad field, in particular, psychodiagnosis.

Current theories of personality, our methods of assessment, and our techniques of treatment have not yet succeeded in helping man and his society to solve the pressing problems which he faces. I would suggest that the reasons for this disappointing performance are philosophic. Dynamic psychology is based on scientific philosophies which are outdated, ineffective, one-sided, and in terms of human values—dangerous. The outmoded philosophies to which I refer are the impersonal, abstract, static, externalized, control-oriented conceptions of nineteenth-century physics which led men to classify the elements and processes of a depersonalized subject matter and to determine the general laws which governed these elements and processes.

I am convinced of the need for a science of psychology which is existential and transactional. By *existential* I mean a concentration on flexible concepts and methods which grow out of the unique changing situation. By *transactional* I refer to an open collaborative attitude between the psychologist and the person studied.

Now at this point you have every right to ask about the meaning of these two terms—existential and transactional. Certainly any reasonable contract between author and reader would call for specifications of these terms, would call for operational definitions spelling out exactly how human ingenuity can be applied to human problems. How can we use our brains to do good and to do good well and to do good measurably well? May I summarize some of the specific ways in which we might make our endeavors more existential, i.e., more in tune with the specific reality:

1. Why not study natural data, events as they occur, rather than artificial situations which *we* arrange in our offices (e.g., tests, experiments)?

2. Why not use a conceptual language which arises from the data rather than imposing our own favorite, prefabricated variables upon the situation? Here I suggest we should be more flexible and eclectic in selecting concepts, recognizing the semantic flimsiness of verbal abstractions.

3. Since behavioral transactions are not static but continually changing why not continue to collect natural records throughout the term of the transaction being studied? Why not expect our techniques and our concepts to change throughout the term of inquiry, as our subject matter changes?

4. Since behavioral transactions are not standardized, but always unique and then repeatable, why do we routinely rely on our own SLANT (Standardized Language for the Analysis of Transactions, e.g., tests)? Why not let the natural transaction produce its own records which we can SCORE* and measure and interrelate? If and when the need for standardized tests grows collaboratively out of this natural situation, why not construct, revise, or design a measuring instrument for this unique situation?

5. Why do personality and clinical psychologists ignore or blur the difference between consciousness and behavior? Why not develop maps, models, and measures for describing inner events and relate these with separate models and measures for describing external behavior?

You will see that I am suggesting in these five points that we *not* impose our favorite standard variables, tests, experiments, concepts, symbols on the situation. I see this as a form of intellectual narcissism which Western science has held up as the ideal, and I am implying

---

* SCORE is shorthand for Schema for the Classification Of Recorded Events.

rather a collaborative surrender to the unique data, a yielding to the data, a calculated and sensitive passivity to the idiosyncratic facts of the unique reality we are studying. I suggest that we attempt to select from the enormous storehouse of verbal abstractions available to us those which seem to fit the human situation we deal with. Let the situation determine the variables.

Next let me list some specific ways in which we can make our endeavor transactional, i.e., emotionally realistic. Here I refer to methods by means of which we can accept and adjust to this following reality: that when we study our fellowman we must treat him as what he is, a *human being,* and not as an object to be dissected, manipulated, controlled, predicted by scientists or clinicians.

1. The problem we study should not grow out of our intellectual needs or our practical concerns, or out of our professional inertia or our personal preoccupations, but should rather be a collaborative decision on the part of the subject and ourselves. The patient helps define the variables.

2. When feasible and relevant, the subject or patient should help design and construct the record-collecting devices or test forms.

3. The patient or subject should be seen and treated not as a passive thing to be done to but as the equal of the psychologist in the collaborative research. The patient, after all, is the world's leading authority on the issue at hand—his own life and the transactions in which he is involved. Here I am urging *phenomenological equality.* Always get the viewpoint of the patient on every issue, question, and decision, and treat this viewpoint as equal to your own.

4. I now come to the inevitable and unmistakable criterion of unreality and depersonalization on the part of the psychologist: *secrecy.* Although psychologists regularly claim to hold no secrets, although we are committed to the open society, although we say that the patient must help himself and work out his own solutions—in reality, we act as though there are secrets. Most of our psychometric, clinical, and institutional machinery is set up on the basis of secrecy. Our professional identity is tied to the mysterious, based on the practice of keeping information from the subject. But let us look at this secrecy in the cold light of the following reality. We are, after all, dealing with human beings. We cannot treat human beings objectively, i.e., as objects, without eliciting exactly the same reactions. If we depersonalize patients, rest assured they will depersonalize us back. If we keep secrets from them, rest assured they will keep secrets from us.

5. Next, I want to speak directly to the topic of this book: psychodiagnosis. The notion of one person observing, measuring, and then

forecasting the behavior of another grows out of the philosophy and methodology of nineteenth-century physics. I hold it to be dehumanizing and insulting, and, what is worse, ineffective. Note how diagnosis is based on secrecy. If we collaborate with the subject, plan and think with him then diagnosis in the classic sense is impossible. The design is corrupted. Note too that diagnosis is based on highly subjective symbol selection on the part of the scientist who decides what to measure. The collaborative sort of research which I am endorsing accepts a different notion of diagnosis and prediction. The subject and the therapist (i.e., the collaborators in the joint research) agree as to which natural records they wish to change. They set up criteria as goals and then they both work to meet the forecasted standards.

Clinical psychology, psychiatry, and psychotherapy are involved to a much greater degree than our professional pride would like us to admit in a complex, fascinating game of secrets with our clients. This game is entertaining. It is much more complex than chess, demanding knowledge of a broad set of vague concepts and repertoire of gamesmanship techniques. It is more important than chess, being played for the highest prizes known to man—profitable fees, life adjustments, and the most prized token of all, man's pride in his inviolacy and individuality.

But what does philosophy have to do with diagnosis? I think it has a lot to do with the topic of our book, for I believe that our philosophic assumptions underlie what men do. What we assume and think and what we do not think clearly underlie the behavior which follows. If we wish to appraise or improve the efficacy of our behavior as diagnostician, we must inquire into our assumptions about the reality which we confront.

In place of or in addition to the complex conceptions of modern dynamic psychology, I should like to suggest a very commonsense notion of human behavior. Men live two lives: an inner life of consciousness and an outer life of behavior. All the behavioral sciences, and all of their applications—education, social welfare, politics and political science—all these disciplines concern themselves with nothing more than how men experience and how men act. A realistic psychology is one which takes into account the uniqueness of human awareness, the incredible multilevel nature of consciousness—learned, sensory, somatic, cellular—and the relation of inner experience to behavior.

Underlying almost all theories of consciousness, whether they are dynamic, psychedelic, or nondynamic, is the basic premise: what a person does is determined by how he experiences, and what a person experiences is related to what he does. There are many qualifications to this axiom. Certainly we would want to distinguish between consciousness and talking. What a person says is often not what he experiences. Then, too, there are many awarenesses which do not lead to action directly and indeed may inhibit action. Included here would be fear fantasies, consummatory (as opposed to blueprint) fantasies, fantasies about the past, fantasies about supernatural events. All of these are, of course, related indirectly to future action and these relationships hinted at by dynamic psychology can, I believe, be studied quite simply and profitably by a realistic point of view. Let me illustrate. If an under-developed community states that it wants economic growth, but we discover that the consciousness of villagers is concerned with sexual imagery, then we can expect increases in the birth rate and a low economic rate of growth. There are, I recognize, many complications involved in these issues, which space prevents us from discussing.

Consciousness may well be the most misunderstood and overlooked aspect of human psychology. Our dynamic theories have consistently tended to mystify the topic of consciousness, forcing the content of man's awareness onto the procrustean bed of favorite concepts. Our social and moral norms often drive experience underground. Just as the dictator finds it difficult to penetrate the conforming behavioral façade of his subjects and can never tell what they really think, so do we psychologists run into walls (which we may call resistance and denial) when we seek to extract, for our own purposes, the inner content of our subjects.

Consciousness is the blueprint for action. Action is an expression of consciousness. What we rarely are aware of, we rarely do. People will share their inner blueprints with you when it is reasonable, feasible, and relevant *to their interests* to do so. They are eager to collaborate but reluctant to yield.

The Philosophy of the Internal and External

Psychological diagnosis must take into account the difference between internal and external phenomena. Western psychology has never satisfactorily resolved the tension between internal-subjective and external-objective. We have consistently imposed the method, language, and goals of the external upon the internal continuum. *The two can be related only if their logical separation is kept clear.*

ART AND SCIENCE

First, we must distinguish between two different approaches to reality—the scientific and the artistic.

Science is the study of behavior, events external to the experiencing nervous system. Science is the study of recorded movements and the communications of these movements to others for the purpose of changing their symbol systems.

Art is the study of experience, events registered *by* the molecular, cellular, somatic, and sensory communication systems within the body —and the communicating of these experiences to others, for the purpose of sharing, i.e., of "turning others on." Art can be just as precise, disciplined, systematic as the symbol systems of external science.

Existential-transactional diagnosis requires that the psychologist teach the patient how to be a scientist in observing his behavior and an artist in describing his experience.

Failure to make the distinction between external-internal, between the mechanically recorded external and the neurally registered internal, leads to a variety of confusions. It is necessary, first of all, to realize that a different ontology, epistemology, logic, ethic, and politics is required for internal and external events. Our notions about objectivity then become clarified. Only external events (recorded behavior) can become part of a scientific (game) contract. Internal events (sensory, somatic, cellular, molecular experience) require an artistic contract, i.e., an explicit contract between the "one-who-turns-others-on" and the "one-who-is-to-be-turned-on." The patient must become an artist who cares enough about the psychologist to turn-him-on to his experience.

REALITY IS EXPERIENTIAL, SUBJECT MATTER IS OBSERVABLE

Internal ontology concerns *reality*, which is always subjective-experiential. Reality is what is registered by your neurons, your cells, and your recognition molecules. External ontology concerns *subject matter*, which can be contractually defined within the scope of inquiry.

TRUTH IS EXPERIENTIAL, FACT IS OBSERVABLE

Internal epistemology concerns *truth*, which is always subjective-experiential. *Truth* is what is registered by your neurons and cells and molecules. Thus in the internal, nongame world of direct experience there is no difference between truth and reality. External epistemology concerns *fact* which can be contractually legislated within the scope of inquiry. Words always define a subjective or experiential epistemology unless operationally defined.

INTERNAL LOGIC IS ASSOCIATION, EXTERNAL LOGIC IS SYMBOL RELATING

Internal logic concerns associations, which are always subjective-experiential, the connections made by your neurons and your molecular receptors. External logic deals with formal systems of *relating* external symbols.

GOOD IS EXPERIENTIAL, RIGHT IS OBSERVABLE

Internal ethics concerns the good which is always subjective-experiential. Good is what feels good to your sensory, somatic, cellular, and molecular receptors. External ethics concerns rules governing behavior, which can be defined only within the scope of contract—the right and wrong of the game.

INTERNAL FREEDOM AND EXTERNAL FREEDOM

Internal politics concerns the freedom to move along the static-ecstatic continuum, freedom and control of consciousness. External politics concerns the freedom and control of behavior.

The philosophy presented above is summarized in Table 1.

Table 1. The Philosophy of Internal and External

Philosophic Issues	Internal	External
which govern your experiencing and your behavior whether you know it or not.	i.e., within the sensory, somatic, cellular and molecular recognition systems—always private and unique to me—but communicable to others by means of art.	outside the nervous system—movements in space-time which can be made part of social contracts with others.
ONTOLOGY What is reality?	REALITY is always "my reality," what is registered by my cellular, neural, and molecular recognition systems.	SUBJECT MATTER There can be no external or consensual reality, only subject matter agreed upon (or confusedly not-agreed-upon) with others.
EPISTEMOLOGY What is truth?	TRUTH is always "my truth," always unique. What I "know," i.e., what my cellular, neural, and molecular systems register, what I sense, experience.	FACT There can be no external truth, only facts consensually agreed upon in explicit game contracts with others (or disastrously implicit and different).

Table 1. The Philosophy of Internal and External (continued)

LOGIC	ASSOCIATIONS	RELATIONSHIPS
What is related to what and how?	The network of connections in my cellular, neural, and molecular systems that links units of "my reality." Always unique to me.	The connections of symbols and sequences of subject matters. Formal systems (grammatical, mathematical, or game) which should be consensually agreed upon explicitly with others.
ETHICS	GOOD AND BAD	RIGHT AND WRONG
What is good?	The attraction - repulsion network of "my unique imprint structure." What moves toward or away from the goals of "my games," biological or personal social.	in terms of external game rules, which should be consensually agreed upon with others, but which, disastrously, are usually implicit.
POLITICS	FREEDOM AND CONTROL	FREEDOM AND CONTROL
Freedom	of my own consciousness, or my own systems, cellular, neural, and molecular, my brain vs. my symbolic mind. Power or slavery of consciousness.	of behavior, the familiar politics of social and personal behavior. Where you place your body and the movements you can make in space-time. External power or slavery.
CREATIVITY	NOVEL EXPERIENCE	NOVEL BEHAVIOR
	beyond symbols. Can be produced by ecstatic or psychedelic experience by molecular intervention.	can be taught or coached.

SYSTEMATIC STUDY AND COMMUNICATION	ART	SCIENCE
	Everyone is an artist (creative or robot) when they communicate about experience.	Everyone is a scientist (accurate or inaccurate) every time they study or communicate about events in space-time.

THE APPLICATION OF THE PHILOSOPHY OF INTERNAL AND EXTERNAL TO PSYCHOLOGICAL RESEARCH

When we set out to study consciousness and such elusive states of consciousness as ecstasy, we must be specially sensitive to the delicate ontological web which we approach. Psychodiagnosis provides excellent illustrations of the effects of confusing these issues.

There is the observer's "subject matter" and there is the subject's "reality," and usually these have no relation. The psychiatrist sees hebephrenic psychosis while the subject may be experiencing molecular ecstasy. The outside observer has an entirely different view from the experiencing person.

There is the observer's "fact" and the subject's "truth." The psychiatrist asserts it is a fact that the subject sat in a catatonic state for two hours, refusing to talk; the subject knows the truth to be that he was spinning far out of space-time into an ecstatic dance of molecules which made words inadequate and irrelevant. Notice, of course, that both are "right." But the conflict in perspective leads the patient to feel misunderstood, makes the patient feel bad, and makes the psychologist feel frustrated. The aim of psychodiagnosis should be to make the patient feel wiser and feel good.

There is the logic which relates external symbols such as words and ritual sequences and there is the internal neurological association network—each cell in the brain connected on the average with 25,000 other cells and the number of associations per second greater than "the number of atoms in the universe." Observer logic and neurologic cannot communicate; so the patient is committed to the mental hospital.

There is the ethic of game rules and there is the molecular, cellular, somatic, sensory "feel-good."

There is the politics of external freedom and control and there is internal freedom, freedom from your own mind, freedom to feel good, freedom to let the cerebral network flash in associations without being limited to game perceptions, freedom to find "truth" within, freedom to contact a cellular or molecular reality beyond game dimensions.

From the standpoint of *science* there is the need for languages and measurement methodologies for external behavior, i.e., movements in space-time. From the standpoint of *art* there is the need for languages and methodologies capable of paying respect to the flowing complexity of the internal, the countless levels of neurological decoding, the countless levels of consciousness. Table 1 summarizes these distinctions and the different perspectives to which they give rise.

The Diagnosis of Behavior

Once the philosophic distinctions between internal and external are clear the definition and the operations of behavioral psychology become straightforward. Indeed they become simplistic to the state of boredom. Pure behaviorism (excluding consciousness) is the measurement and control of robot action. The challenge of psychology is the systematic correlation of behavior and consciousness.

Behavioral science is human engineering. The empty and dull nature of this enterprise is concealed by the tendency to confuse behavior and consciousness. The terms used by psychologists and behavioral scientists tell us how the mind of the scientist works. Psychoanalytic theory, for example, tells us how analysts experience the world.

The languages used by psychologists to describe interpersonal events actually are removed from and unreliable projections onto behavior. Aggression, dominance, dependence do not refer to acts of people. They refer to states of mind. They are terms for describing consciousness.

Let me illustrate from my own studies of interpersonal behavior. In a lengthy series of investigations starting in 1948, I found that almost all the concepts in the English language which refer to interpersonal motives could be arranged in a two-dimensional grid. This circumplex model has been tested out in several subsequent studies by other psychologists (Leary, 1956; Lorr, 1962; Foa, 1961). Minor variations exist in placement around the circular continuum, but the interpersonal circle works. But why does it work? Did an omnipotent psychologist deity decide that interpersonal behavior is circular? To answer these questions you must make the external-internal distinction. The terms used by layman and psychologist to describe interpersonal events (and for that matter almost all events) have to do with implied motivation; they have nothing to do with movements in space-time. These terms refer to states of consciousness. We *experience* the world in terms of mythic images. The terms for our experience fall into a circumplex model because our Western consciousness is egocentric. Copernicus to the contrary, most of us really experience a geocentric universe and an egocentric world.

We naïvely experience the world in terms of radii extending out from us. Power is above us. Submission is south. We are compelled to and away from others in horizontal vectors. Our magnificent cortex is capable of experiencing complexity a thousandfold greater than our verbal language. But our simple conceptual minds cannot grasp more than two or three dimensions. In 1948 my own mind boggled at more than two dimensions for experienced interaction. Thus the circle of experience.

Behavior is movements in space-time, that is all. The ontological issue is single: movements in space-time.

Interpersonal behavior refers to the movements of two or more persons who share the same space-time.

Measurement of behavior is the recording and indexing of movements in space-time. The decision as to which behavior to record and which indices to use is based on subjective choice on the part of the measurer. Transactional theory holds that the movements of any structure in space-time will be better understood if the experiential perspective from within the structure is known. The atomic physicist must "experience" like an atom. In psychodiagnosis the collaboration of the subject should be sought in the selection of what to record and what labels to use.

Psychotherapy is a complex and ontologically confusing game. It combines changes in consciousness (psyche) with a medical abstraction (therapy). Our Harvard research project (Leary, Metzner, and Alpert, 1965) did not use the term psychotherapy. We attempted collaboratively to alter or expand consciousness. We also tried collaboratively to change behavior. We tried to reduce helplessness—internal or external.

In order to develop a science of behavior we require new schemata and new languages for measuring and classifying movements in space-time. Our present schemata are inefficient because they confuse internal-external. They jumble together the observations, interpretations, evaluations of the experiencing scientist, with narrow measurements of the subject's behavior. Another source of inefficiency is the application of cumbersome global terms to broad-ranging sequences of changing movements.

These two confusions are illustrated by the case of the three Parisian Behavioral Diagnosticians. André, age 6, Marcel, age 8, and Pierre, age 10, walking through the Bois de Boulogne ran across an undressed couple making lively movements on the grass. André, age 6, exclaims, "Look, they are fighting." Marcel, a sophisticated 8, replies, "Oh, no, André, they are making love." Pierre, a true Parisian at 10, adds, "Yes, and very badly too."

The empirical studies of the reliability of psychiatric diagnosis suggest a similar difficulty in labeling and evaluating behavior in terms of global experiential terms.

There are two types of schemata for measuring behavior which correspond to the two aspects of my definition—(1) movements, (2) space-time. I should like to present first a model for classifying space-time factors and then proceed to schemata for measuring movements.

CLASSIFICATION OF SPACE-TIME ELEMENTS OF BEHAVIOR

The first step in diagnosing behavior is to determine where the subject spends his time, how long, how frequently, and with whom. Location in space-time is a relatively straightforward task. Recording, measurement, and cartographical representation present certain economic and technical problems involving use of electronic devices, but philosophically the issues seem clear-cut.

The most direct measures of interpersonal behavior would be based on continuous recordings of movements, but for practical diagnostic purposes it is useful to collect samples locating the subject in space-time and clarifying the movements made. Let me illustrate. For a two-week period in 1962 I carried a kitchen timer bell with me throughout the day. At the moment of waking in the morning I would set it to ring in ten minutes and continued to reset it for ten-minute intervals until retiring in the evening. The bell set up an internal discipline of "waking-me-up," in the sense of G. I. Gurdjieff, and allowed a time-sample of my behavior (movements in space-time) during the day. As each shrill jangle interrupted my inner train of consciousness and my outer game sequence I would enter on a sheet: (1) the time, (2) the place, (3) a description of my behavior, (4) my posture, (5) number of others present, (6) behavior of others, (7) a classification of my behavior according to a game-classification. (See Table 2.)

I also entered on the sheet a summary of my consciousness (where my head was at) in terms of a complex system of internal diagnosis (see last section, below).

A tabulation of these seven behavioral categories made it possible to construct summary indices on a daily and weekly basis (see Table 2). Such summary sheets reveal with amazing clarity my ecological and behavioral characteristics during this period. I note that five times more units were spent with daughter than son (oedipal factors?). I note that

Table 2. Sheet for Recording Ten-Minute Samples of Space-Time Locations and the Contents of Consciousness

Time	Place	Movements	Posture	Others Present	Other's Movements	Other's Posture	Movements Indexed According to Game
9:30	Bed	Sleeping	Lying	0			Body maintenance
9:40	Bathroom	Washing	Standing	0			Body maintenance
9:50	Bedroom	Dressing	Standing	0			Body maintenance
10:00	Kitchen	Cooking	Standing	4	Eating	Sitting	Body maintenance
10:10	Kitchen	Cooking	Standing	4	Eating	Sitting	Body maintenance
10:20	Bedroom	Dressing	Standing	0			Body maintenance
10:30	Car	En route to church	Sitting	3	En route to church	Sitting	Religion
10:40	Church	Listening	Sitting	35	Listening	Sitting	Religion
4:00	Son's room	Watching TV	Sitting	1	Watching TV	Sitting	Recreation
4:10	Son's room	Watching TV	Sitting	1	Watching TV	Standing	Recreation
4:20	Daughter's room	Helping with homework	Standing	1	Homework	Sitting	Intellectual

60 percent of my posture involved the barbarous instrument we call a chair (chairman behavior? power motives?). I note that 41 percent of the time was spent alone (introversion? alienation?).

A very powerful diagnostic and therapeutic tool is thus available to the psychologist. Diagnosis involves the subject himself studying his own behavior. This leads directly to the functional corollary: if you want to change your behavior, start by changing your space-time locations. My interpersonal relations could easily be changed by spending more time with my son, more time sitting on the floor looking up at others, and so on. (Changes in consciousness must go along with alterations of behavior to avoid robotization.)

The diagnosis of interpersonal behavior in noncircular form is also facilitated by the space-time location system. Here again we ignore such tempting variables as dominance-submission, hostility-affiliation (which reflect only our Western states of consciousness), and we focus simply on the basic interpersonal question: what space do they share? what time do they share? We thus define a powerful entity (in psychological jargon, a variable) which we might call intimacy, commitment, involvement. We might hazard a behavioral operational definition of *love as the amount of space-time shared*.

Here is the basic interpersonal issue—how much space-time will you share? Your office? Your home? Your bedroom? Your body? What kind of time will you share? Day or night? By appointment only?

The shared-space-time definition of love uplevels the emotional definition. The fact that the husband and wife spend thirty years together day and night is considered much more important than the kind of emotional game they play (fighting, submitting, cooing, dominating).

Table 3 illustrates a matrix for diagnosing interpersonal behavior according to this behavioral scheme. Time is plotted along the horizontal axis—the more formal and briefer duration on the left and the more intensive, informal on the right. The space continuum runs from the most mutual public location (bottom) up to the most intimate (internal body space shared).

My hypothesis is this: all other factors (i.e., kinds of movements) being held constant—the more space-time shared the greater the influence in changing behavior. If you want to change someone's behavior—share space-time with him. Your space-time is the most valuable and potent instrument you have. Following this hypothesis we should expect that the upper right corner of the grid defines the most potent behavior-change relationships and the lower left the least. Thus we see that mother-child relationships (nine months of internal body sharing) and marital relationships (extended duration of internal body sharing) are

Table 3. Illustration of a Simplified Schema for Classifying Space-Time Aspects of Interpersonal Behavior

Space Sharing	Time Sharing		
	Low duration scheduled time —usually occupational	*Medium duration nonscheduled time— usually friendship*	*Extended duration—usually familial or tribal*
Sharing internal body space	Prostitution, transient sexual contacts	Lovers	Mother-child, Husband-wife
Reciprocal home sharing	Mutual entertainment with colleagues, friends	Entertaining friends	Family or tribe
Neutral nonwork locations	Dining and recreational contacts	Dining, drinking, and recreational contacts	Family or tribal outings
His home only	Professor's tea for students		
Reciprocal office	Visits between colleagues		
His office only	Doctor-patient		
Public rooms	College lectures		

the most potent change situations. The college lecture and the doctor-patient interviews are the least potent. This hypothesis suggests that if you can't "mother them" or marry them, the best way to influence behavior is to engage in reciprocal home visits or meet regularly in extra-work locations (bars, restaurants, beaches). The most successful programs for dealing with our most difficult social "problems," Alcoholics Anonymous (Co-Founder, 1957), the Slack-Schwitzgebel street-corner project (Slack, 1960; Schwitzgebel, 1962), Synanon, Halfway Houses, and the student volunteer work with mental patients (Kantor and Greenblatt, 1962), utilize this principle and scrupulously avoid the power-loaded environment of the scheduled interview in the expert's office.

Other space-time grids can be constructed which specify other factors relevant to the inquiry at hand—free vs. paid time, free vs. paid space, day vs. night space, time sharing, and so on. Such schemata spotlight the most basic behavorial issues—where, when, and with whom.

There are many practical applications of such schemata. Often we get so involved with dynamic theories and diagnostic impressions that we forget that the first functional issue in behavior change is presence. Clinicians seem to prefer subjective internal language, so they talk about "motivation for treatment." Will the patient come? Will he continue to come? How can we change him if he won't share space-time with us?

During 1962-1963 our Harvard Psychedelic Project tested these theories in the rehabilitation of prisoners in a Concord, Massachusetts, reformatory. In the prison these space-time factors became dramatically and logically obvious. Consider a young "delinquent." He is sentenced to prison at age 19. Now who is going to shape his behavior? Those with whom he shares most space-time. And who are they? Other prisoners. The older convicts with whom he shares cell, meal table, shop bench, yard time (and very often body space). Old pros in the cops and robbers game. Next to other convicts he will share most time with guards. Many prison officers, like prisoners, share the same belief about the unchangeability of personality. "Cons are all alike, they don't want to change." "Cops are all alike. They'll never give you a fair shake." Onto this scene comes the middle-class professional. He calls the convict into his room in the prison clinic and spends from thirty to forty minutes a week. His well-intentioned interventions according to the space-time formula are pitifully limited. The same situation exists in mental hospitals. Fellow patients, attendants, nurses, and doctors—a descending order of behavior-change potency. A recent book by Kesey (1962) has presented this issue in beautiful detail.

What are the implications of the space-time formula? First—don't send the kid to prison. Keep the disturbed person out of the hospital. Keep them outside, sharing time and space with persons whom you want them to emulate. If incarceration or commitment is necessary then do everything you can to change the movements (talk and action) of the persons with whom the subject shares space-time. In our prison project we spent most of our time with older convicts discussing rehabilitation programs and coaching them to lead groups for other convicts. Convicts act as research technicians, test interpreters, tutors for university graduate students (Leary et al., 1965a). The more responsibility for behavior change assigned to convicts, guards, fellow patients, attendants, the more behavior will change. The role of the professional changes too in the light of the space-time formula. The number of patients or clients with whom we can share even formal occupational office space-time is limited. The professional should share his space-time with those who share intimate space-time with the subjects. They are the effective change agents. The professional becomes collaborative consultant rather than doctor or therapist.

MEASURING MOVEMENTS

Behavior is movements in space-time. The preceding section has discussed a schema, a formula, and some applications of the space-time issue. We shall now consider the measurement of the second part of the definition—*movements*.

Remember our three youthful French diagnosticians? When they leave the Bois de Boulogne and report to the folks back home, what is the epistemological status of their observations? No records exist of the movements they observed. Their report is subjective. What exists is their memory. This points up a basic issue about behavior which is often overlooked. From the scientific point of view we never study behavior—a jumble of observed movements in the grass—we can only study records of behavior. We observe movements. But we measure and index records.

The ontology and epistemology of the behavioral sciences is quite simple. There are only four kinds of records of behavior:

1. Records of muscle movements, physiological or cinematographic.
2. Records of vocal movements (tape recordings).
3. Nonverbal artifactual records of behavior (Greek vases, drawings, things made).
4. Records of verbal behavior (written or spoken).

Since 1955 I have been developing schemata for counting and measuring records of natural behavior (Leary, 1964a; Leary and Gill, 1959): process analysis of the freely expressed. Behavior can be described in terms of indices based on objective counts. A tape recording of verbal behavior during a ten-minute period yields up one hundred indices (counts not ratings) which can be charted as they vary over time. The molecular units are simple counts of movements. How many words spoken? How many references to self? How many references to mother? Interpersonal behavior is described in terms of comparisons of the patterns of indices of the participants sharing the same space-time.

The comparisons of the participants in terms of the simplest counted indices provide exciting and revealing evidence of the interchange. Figure 1 presents an illustrative profile of one type of verbal movements made by a patient and therapist during twelve hours of psychotherapy. The therapy sessions were taped and transcribed. Non-professional technicians counted the number of references to the patient by the patient and by the therapist. The index percent of references to patient (Pt%) is obtained by dividing the number of references to patient by the total number of statements in the interview.

First, we notice that the patient refers to herself only 10 percent of the time during the first session and continues to avoid herself as subject until the ninth session. From this time on, her verbal noises can be scored as referring to herself at least 50 percent of the time. Profiles of

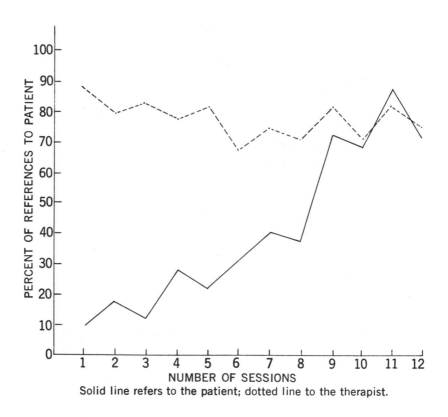

Solid line refers to the patient; dotted line to the therapist.

Figure 1. Percentage of Verbal Movements by Patient and Therapist Referring to Patient as Subject during Twelve Hours of Psychoanalytically Oriented Psychotherapy

indices of behavior varying over time can be irrelevant or vitally useful depending upon the task-goal. In this illustration the reluctance to talk about self in the early sessions could be experienced by and labeled by a clinician as externalization. This one profile tells us some little thing of importance—she starts off not talking about herself.

But when we consider the therapist's profile a more meaningful pattern emerges. We notice the extreme discrepancy. In the first session the therapist is concentrating on little else than the patient (87 percent). Her low indices now take on greater significance. The patient and therapist are clearly not together. She refuses to discuss *his* topic—her. And the therapist is not following her conversational lead.

Indices of the free natural movements of persons sharing space and time are invariably dynamic and revealing. This type of measure is obvious, molecular, simple to convert and index, and loaded with philosophic and social dynamite.

First there is the linguistic reform. A new language develops; a language of objective indices based on molecular events. Pt% means percent of references to the patient. The term $(Pt^1 - Pt^2)$ defines a discrepancy—the references of speaker 1 compared with those of speaker 2. In another publication (Leary et al., 1965a) I have presented a language of over seventy indices which can be combined into thousands of discrepancy terms (comparing the same speaker at different times or different speakers at the same time). This reduces and can even eliminate the need for a verbal, conceptual language. The index language of behavior becomes like that of chemistry: a list of basic indices and an endless list of possible combinations. Chemistry would be slow to advance if it depended on verbal vocabulary—salt, sugar; the situation is no different for a psychology of behavior.*

There is a second philosophic implication underlying profiles of natural records. Notice that we score and index the therapist's behavior as well as that of the patient. A strict behavioral approach is also existential in that the subject-object, doctor-patient relationship is undercut. Figure 1 ruthlessly profiles the movements of both participants without distinction of role or status. The approach is automatically transactional —forcing us to the recognition that all our contexts are interpersonal and that we never study a patient but always the patient-in-his-interpersonal-field.

* Psychology, unlike chemistry, has also to deal with internal events— experience, consciousness. A different set of terms and methods are required for the internal.

In a preceding section I have mentioned Schema for the Classification Of Recorded Events (SCORE). The SCORE technique of recording and indexing movements has two implications of which we must be aware. SCORE does not rely on the verbal concepts and theoretical abstractions upon which we psychologists rely. Perhaps even more radically, it puts the doctor-scientist-expert into the field of inquiry alongside the patient.

The same two issues reappear when we study the interpersonal implications of psychological tests. Psychological tests are paradoxical procedures. They are based on a philosophy which postulates essences or enduring internal traits and which encourages the notion that one group of people (professionals) can study another group (patients or subjects) in terms of the phenomenological abstractions held by the professionals. Most psychologists are democratic by temperament and intellectually committed to field, cultural, and interpersonal assumptions. Yet they routinely rely upon tests and experiments which are manipulative and one-sided, which measure the movements of only one member of the transaction. This is not very democratic.

We have found it more profitable to stick to an interpersonal point of view in our scientific posture as well as our concepts. Whenever it is feasible and reasonable we collect records from all participants—not just in free, natural recordings, but also where tests or standardized structural instruments are used, and even in the doctor-patient situation in diagnosis.

When we use the interpersonal checklist (a standardized form) we ask the patient to rate himself and his therapist. We also ask the therapist to rate himself as well as the patient. Patients, clients, subjects are diagnosing professionals all the time. It is only good sense to include within the scope of inquiry the patient's diagnoses and therapist's responses to tests.

The conventional one-sided, patient-only test does not of course lend itself to interpersonal measures, because these tests are designed to measure internal traits. For interpersonal* measurement, a different type of assessment instrument is required—one which is designed for the specific situation, often constructed by all participants, filled out by all participants, and interpreted by all. The standardized language of the test holds only for the interpersonal group (i.e., the group who share space-time). Such an instrument would have to be modified to fit a

---

* *Interpersonal* is used here as movement of two or more persons sharing the same space-time.

different interpersonal context. Thus we have the Smith Family Mood Questionnaire, the Ace Company Creativity Scale.

The Diagnosis of Consciousness

Consciousness is energy received by structure. Structure is energy in transitional state. There are as many levels of consciousness in the universe as there are forms of energy. Each form of energy creates structures which receive, store, and transform it.

There are as many levels of consciousness available to the human being as there are neurological, sensory, anatomical, cellular, molecular, atomic structures within the human body. The human body is a galaxy of communication systems, i.e., energy patterns being sent and received by structure. When a psychologist sets outs to define the levels of consciousness he usually comes up with mental abstractions which tell us only about his own trip. The classic levels of consciousness are varieties of "game symbols." Thus, Freud defines the conscious as routine, conventional, normal game awareness; the unconscious as unthinkable, naughty (repressed) games, and the superego as consciousness of highly valued good games. Freud is not defining different levels of awareness, he is simply listing symbols of differing social meaning. Such listings differ among psychologists and from culture to culture.

An empirical, existential psychology of consciousness recognizes the energy-structure nature of consciousness, defines the levels of consciousness in terms of observable physical structures, and specifies the chemical-electrical processes which produce the predicted level of consciousness. The topic of human consciousness has vexed psychologists and philosophers for thousands of years. Why? Because of the lack of scientific instrumentation and empirical knowledge about the physiology and biochemistry of the human body and the life process.

The body is the seat and center of consciousness. Our theory of consciousness must come to its senses and resurrect the body. Consciousness is a biochemical process. Our knowledge of consciousness must be based on our understanding of psychochemical process. An empirical science of consciousness had to await the development of instruments for changing consciousness. Before the discovery of the microscope, physiology and medicine were crude sciences based on macroscopic observation. Before the discovery of psychedelic chemicals, psychology and psychiatry were in the same state as physiology and medicine before the microscope. We are now able to define the different levels of consciousness, to produce them, to study them systematically, and to make our observations of consciousness replicable.

At our present level of neurological and biochemical understanding (crude and primitive) it is appropriate to consider seven levels of consciousness:*

1. Sleep
2. Stupor
3. Symbolic
4. Sensory
5. Somatic
6. Cellular
7. Molecular

The order in which these levels of consciousness are listed is based on the age, speed, power, complexity, expansiveness, and planful wisdom of the energy-structure.

Molecular energy, for example, is older, faster, more complex, more pervasive, and "wiser" than the cellular. Molecules plan, design, and manufacture grosser forms of energy structure. Cellular structure is older, more enduring, more complex, more pervasive, and wiser than bodies and somatic organs, etc. The DNA code plays its game in terms of species, classes, and Linnaean kingdoms—animal versus botanical.

Psychological diagnosis (except in the most administrative sense) cannot be carried out unless the diagnostician is aware of the level of consciousness (or combination of levels) of the other. In the words of those born after 1945, the diagnostic question is: "Where is your head at?" The seven levels just listed help you locate your head.

Notice that each of these levels of awareness can be produced or turned off by chemicals—naturally produced by or introduced into the body:

1. *Sleep* is produced by fatigue by-products or opiates, barbiturates, tranquilizers. These chemicals "turn-off" emotions, symbol discrimination, sensory awareness, etc.

2. *Stupor,* including emotional awareness (emotional states are a form of stuporous consciousness contraction), is produced by endocrine processes and by alcohol. These chemicals turn-off symbol discrimination, sensory awareness, somatic sensitivity, etc.

3. *Symbolic awareness* is facilitated by undefined psychoactive humors (serotonin?) and by energizers such as caffeine, coca, pep pills. These chemicals turn-off sensory awareness, somatic sensitivity, cellular memory, etc.

---

* These levels of consciousness are described in greater detail in other publications: Leary, 1962, 1964a, 1964b, 1965a, 1965b, 1965c, 1966a, 1966b, 1967; Leary, Metzner, and Alpert, 1965; Metzner, 1963; Weil, Metzner, and Leary, 1965. The applications of this theory of consciousness to issues of diagnosis, measurement, and psychotherapy are presented in the following publications: Fisher, 1963; Leary, 1965d, 1966b; Leary et al., 1965a.

4. *Sensory awareness* is produced naturally by biochemical-electrical stimulation of the nerve endings of the external sense organs and facilitated by marijuana and mild doses of more powerful psychedelic chemicals (hashish, mescaline, LSD). Powerful sensory stimuli and chemicals like marijuana can focus consciousness away from (i.e., turn-off) emotional, symbolic, somatic, cellular, and molecular awareness or can entangle these latter in hallucinatory combinations.

5. *Somatic awareness* is produced naturally by energy exchanges at the sympathetic and parasympathetic nerve endings of the internal somatic organs and by exercises or chemicals which specifically stimulate somatic organs. Autonomous nervous system activity turns-off emotional, symbolic, sensory, cellular, and molecular consciousness or entangles these latter in hallucinatory combinations.

6. *Cellular awareness* is produced naturally at the intersection points between the neurological and the cellular and can be induced by the more powerful psychedelics—psilocybin, mescaline, LSD. Here we deal with "out-of-the-body" experiences, racial and phylogenetic memories which have been reported throughout human history and which have been substantiated by leading philosophers (some Western, mainly Eastern) and psychologists (including Fechner, Jung, Freud, William James).

7. *Molecular consciousness* is produced by strong doses of LSD, and such newer psychedelics as STP.

The state of consciousness known by that vague, catch-all term *hallucinatory* is explained, in this system, as a double or multiple exposure of two or more levels of consciousness. Hallucinations are real. They are combinations of two or more levels of reality. Imagine looking at your doctor's face—one eye normal, the other eye attached to a microscope. The resulting sensory collage is analogous to a hallucination. From the standpoint of psychiatric diagnosis, it is crucial that the diagnostician understand the various levels of consciousness and be alert to the level of the patient. Logical, symbolic communication is distorted or vitiated when the other-one's consciousness is at a nonsymbolic level. This is often confusing and frustrating to the diagnostician who operates exclusively at the logical-symbolic level.

Imagine the diagnostic or psychometric interaction between a "straight" doctor and a patient at these different levels of awareness:

1. Patient sleeps; he does not respond. He is diagnosed as comatose. He cannot play the symbol game with the doctor.

2. Patient is in a stuporous or intoxicated state. He reacts to the doctor's symbols only in emotional behavior: cries, laughs, snarls, boasts. Patient is diagnosed as psychotic or delirious or drunk. The doc-

tor must change the patient's level of consciousness before engaging in symbolic communication.

3. Patient is at symbolic level of consciousness. Conventional communication results: "How are you?" "I am depressed."

4. Patient is at the sensory level. Doctor talks symbolically. Patient centers on fact that doctor has bad breath (olfactory) or that the light shines eerily off the yellow stain on the doctor's teeth. Communication is impossible but the patient gets blamed for being psychotic. A sensitive diagnostician attempts to "tune-in" on the patient's level of consciousness.

If the patient is caught at the level of sensory awareness you can reach him only through the senses. A good diagnostician, therapist, priest, husband, etc. can "turn-on" to the level of consciousness of the other-one.

5. Patient's consciousness is trapped at somatic level—let us say in the circulatory system. Doctor suggests patient go to the dance tonight. Patient is aware of blood pumping up his arteries, squeezing into the capillary network in his skull. He feels blood dripping in his head. His head feels marshy and soggy. How can he consider going to the dance? The sensitive clinician determines that the patient's consciousness is trapped in his body and knows how to contact and free the patient.

6. The patient's consciousness is flipped out beyond the body into cellular memories. His protein file cards are spinning racial recollections. He sees the doctor as a furry wolf, a thin, long-legged heron, an ominous dark spider. He cringes. The doctor labels the patient psychotic. He could say: "You see me as many things. I am friendly and want to help you."

7. The patient is spun into the molecular level of consciousness. Everything—his body, the outside world—is seen as a shimmering mosaic of vibrations. The psychiatrist is seen as a shuttling pattern on the retinal TV screen. The patient is transfixed in wonder and confusion.

Each of these levels of personality has many sublevels, defined in terms of observable structure. At the symbolic level the game must be defined in terms of the criteria of social games. At the sensory level consciousness can be trapped in the eye, ear, nose, etc. An enormously complex but operationally obvious system for the diagnosis of consciousness is available.

Space-time-game classifications diagnose behavior. Where is the patient's body at? The seven levels of consciousness diagnose where the patient's head is at. Accurate localization of behavior and consciousness is the task of diagnosis. Accurate diagnosis, collaboratively worked out with the patient, is effective therapy for both patient and doctor.

REFERENCES

Co-Founder. *Alcoholics Anonymous comes of age.* New York: Harper, 1957.

Fisher, G. Dosage levels of psychedelic compounds for psychotherapeutic experiences. *Psychedelic Rev.,* 1963, No. 1.

Foa, U. Convergences in the analysis of the structure of interpersonal behavior. *Psychol. Rev.,* 1961, **68** (No. 5), 341–55.

Kantor, D., and Greenblatt, M. Wellmet: a house where students lead mental patients to rehabilitation. *Ment. Hosp.,* March 1962.

Kesey, K. *One flew over the cuckoo's nest.* New York: Viking Press, 1962.

Leary, T. *Interpersonal diagnosis of personality.* New York: Ronald Press, 1956.

Leary, T. How to change behavior. *Proceedings of Fourteenth Congress of Applied Psychology.* Copenhagen: Munksgaard Press, 1962.

Leary, T. The effects of test score feedback on creative performance and of drugs on creative experience. Paper read at 1962 Utah Conference on Creativity. In C. W. Taylor (Ed.), *Widening horizons in creativity.* New York: Wiley, 1964a.

Leary, T. Introduction. In D. Solomon (Ed.), *LSD—the consciousness expanding drug.* New York: Putnam, 1964b.

Leary, T. *Measuring verbal interaction in Freudian and Rogerian psychotherapy.* Millbrook, N.Y.: Unitas Press, 1964c.

Leary, T. The experiential typewriter. *Psychedelic Rev.,* 1965a, No. 7.

Leary, T. Neo-symbolic communication of experience. *Psychedelic Rev.,* 1965b, No. 8.

Leary, T. Programmed communication during the psychedelic session. *Psychedelic Rev.,* 1965c, No. 8.

Leary, T. The religious experience: its production and its interpretation. In G. Weil, R. Metzner, and T. Leary (Eds.), *The psychedelic reader,* New Hyde Park, N.Y.: University Books, 1965d.

Leary, T. Politics and ethics of ecstasy. *Cavalier,* July 1966a.

Leary, T. *Psychedelic prayers after the Tao te Ching.* New Hyde Park, N.Y.: University Books, 1966b.

Leary, T. The politics, ethics and meaning of marijuana. In D. Solomon (Ed.), *Marihuana papers,* New York: Bobbs-Merrill, 1967.

Leary, T., and Clark, W. H. The religious implications of consciousness expanding drugs. *Religious Educ.,* 1963.

Leary, T., and Gill, M. The dimensions and a measure of the process of psychotherapy: a system for the analysis of content of clinical evaluations and patient-therapist interactions. In E. A. Rubenstein and M. B. Parloff (Eds.), *Research in psychotherapy.* Washington, D.C.: American Psychological Association, 1959. Pp. 62–95.

Leary, T., Metzner, R., Presnell, M., Weil, G., Schwitzgebel, R., and Kinne, S. A change program for adult offenders using psilocybin. *Psychother.,* 1965a, **2,** 61–72.

Leary, T., Metzner, R., and Alpert, R. *The psychedelic experience*. New Hyde Park, N.Y.: University Books, 1965b.

Lorr, M. Approaches to interpersonal behavior schema. Paper read at Seventh Annual Research Conference on Chemotherapy Studies in Psychiatry and Broad Research Approaches to Mental Illness. Veterans Administration, Cincinnati, Ohio, March 27, 1962.

Metzner, R. The pharmacology of psychedelic drugs. *Psychedelic Rev.,* 1963, No. 1.

Schwitzgebel, R. Critical analysis and evaluation of the experimenter-subject role relationship in the reduction of known male adolescent crime. Unpublished doctoral dissertation. Harvard University, 1962.

Slack, C. Experimenter-subject psychotherapy: a new method introducing intensive office treatment for unreachable cases. *Ment. Hyg.,* 1960, **44** (No. 2), 238–56.

Weil, G., Metzner, R., and Leary, T. *The psychedelic reader*. New Hyde Park, N.Y.: University Books, 1965.

MOTIVATIONAL NEEDS, HOSPITALIZATION, AND A CLASSIFICATION SYSTEM

Personality is understood in the next two essays in terms of motivational needs which underlie behavior. Clinical behavior is understood to express given motivational needs, to be goal-directed, and to be characterized by striving, directionality, and a "reaching out" tendency. Clinical behaviors related to hospitalization are similarly regarded as motivated by underlying needs and directed toward meaningful psychological goals. Thus, the process of hospitalization is interpreted as a psychodynamic process with psychological significance as a means of expressing or instrumenting needs; that is, hospitalization affords the patient expression of his psychological goals.

The system describes hospitalized males in terms of six major motivational needs, which are the backbone of its psychodiagnostic system: (1) avoidance of threat, subcategorized into avoidance of sexual threat, avoidance of the threat of loss of a significant figure, avoidance of the threat of punishment, and avoidance of the threat of adult manhood; (2) punishment, subcategorized into self-directed and externally directed punishment; (3) acceptance of impulses; (4) structure and control, subcategorized into structure and control of primitive disintegration, of aggressive impulses, and of sexual impulses; (5) dependency, subcategorized into nuturant dependency, induced dependency, and instrumental dependency; and (6) identification. One or more of these motivational needs is proposed as the explanatory key to the patient's personality processes, his recent psychological history of life experiences, and his clinical behaviors (including "symptomatology").

237

The process of psychodiagnosis is an assessment of both the clinical history and the major clinical behaviors to arrive at a diagnosis in terms of one or more of these motivational needs.

Proponents of the standard psychiatric system would ask whether this proposed system is more than a restatement of what is already well known in hospital psychiatry, viz., that there are secondary gains to psychiatric illness. It is perhaps questionable whether the six "motivational needs" are not six of a potentially large number of secondary gains which must be properly understood, but which certainly do not form the basis for a classification system.

It could also be objected that a comprehensive system derived from study of a male population at only a single hospital is inadequately tested, although admitting that a comprehensive system might conceivably be built upon the concept of motivational needs. Other criticisms might be that the proposed system is not shown to be superior to the standard nosology, and could be interpreted merely as a discussion of the psychodynamics surrounding hospitalization, one utilizing a terminology only slightly different from accepted psychiatric nosology, and placing undue explanatory power on a few secondary gains, while failing to account for the major determining forces of the various illnesses and diseases described in the present nosological framework.

8

MOTIVATIONAL THEORY: FOUNDATIONS OF PERSONALITY CLASSIFICATION

ALVIN R. MAHRER

The purpose of the present chapter is to describe the foundations for understanding and classifying persons on the basis of motivational needs. The guiding assumption is that all persons may be described and classified on this basis. But the focus will be specifically directed toward those persons who become patients in "mental" hospitals or in "psychiatric" wards. The aim will be to illustrate how a concept of motivational needs may be used as a foundation for a personality classification of all "hospitalized psychiatric patients" and, by implication, of all persons. The motivational needs presented here are intended to apply to the general class of hospitalized psychiatric patients. Additional motivational needs would have to be posited for a more comprehensive personality classification of persons in general.

Motivational Needs and Recent Life Changes

Prior to an individual's entering a mental or psychiatric hospital, certain changes may be understood as having occurred in their lives. Some of these recent life changes may occur immediately prior to hospitalization, whereas with other patients these changes may have occurred weeks, months, or even years before the actual hospitalization. These recent life changes serve to bring into operation the motivational need or needs which characterize the person upon entering the hospital. At least three kinds of recent life changes may be posited.

239

PATIENT-DETERMINED THREATENING SITUATIONS

Deeper personality processes are responsible for shaping persons' lives so that they are then faced with a situation containing a high degree of threat (Mahrer, 1967a). For example, a husband's personality processes may lead him to induce his wife into adulterous behavior. A woman's personality needs may fashion a situation in which she is deserted by her husband and left with the responsibilities of a broken family. A business-man may sabotage his firm into a point where he is faced with a situation of likely bankruptcy. The personality processes of one son may direct him toward a violent encounter with his father, precipitating long-hidden murderous feelings. Another son may find himself in a threatening situation when he finally goes beyond the limits of the family's tolerance.

Further examples might include: A son may be quite fearful of being the strong male in the family. When his father dies, the son's personality processes invest the situation with threat. For a man with underlying fears of passivity, a situation of becoming too old to remain the aggressive foreman is invested with a high degree of threat. When a wife carries out lesbian behavior, the situation becomes highly threatening for a husband with exacerbated homosexual tendencies. The personality processes of one brother may lead to an interlocking with another brother so that a cruel outburst by one activates the other's hidden sadism. A father's antisocial tendencies may be threateningly acted out when he subtly paves the way for his son to commit a crime.

The individual's own personality processes play a large role in bringing about situations and in investing them with threat. It is understandable how reluctant we are to acknowledge the extent to which an individual serves as the architect of his own threatening situations. Yet in some cases, we create the threatening situation by our own energies. In other cases, we are quite prepared to be terribly threatened by the situations in which we find ourselves. In still other cases, we attach ourselves to significant other persons whose actions place us in the threatening situation. For many potential patients, their own personality processes tend to determine and bring about situations which are invested with threat. Some of these patient-determined threatening situations require a long time for their gradual development, whereas others are brought about quite suddenly (Fenichel, 1954a, p. 58; Freeman, Kalis, and Harris, 1964, p. 414; Mahrer, 1967a).

CHANGES IN THE LIVES OF SIGNIFICANT OTHER FIGURES

Some individuals are extremely bound up with the psychological pushes and pulls of a few significant figures. These bonds were established in early childhood and, for some persons, are so strong that a change in the lives of the significant other figures will act to bring about a change in the person's own life. When an individual is so powerfully linked, since early childhood, to these other significant figures, he is especially vulnerable to changes in the lives of these other figures.

If such strong bonds exist between a mother and her son, then serious changes in her life will tend to effect changes in the motivational needs of her son, throughout both their lives. The adult son will tend to be especially affected by the mother's death or serious illness or divorce or remarriage or any other significant change in her life. The effect will show itself as a change in the son's motivational needs.

The primitive personality. The basic foundations and origins of personality have been attributed either to biological-genetic-constitutional endowments which are a part of the newborn physical infant or to the learning experiences which occur between the developing organism and the external environment. Another approach traces the basic foundations and origins of personality to the psychological field surrounding the infant. This psychological field is composed of the personality processes of the significant interacting individuals encompassing the infant and may be defined as the infant's basic or primitive personality (Mahrer, 1967a). Thus, a mother's motivational needs for being protected and loved and a father's motivational needs for acceptance also constitute the basic foundations of the infant's primitive personality by virtue of their role as components in the primitive field encompassing the infant.

The physical infant, according to this interpretation, is only a part of the larger psychological field which is the personality of the infant. In other words, the primitive personality of the infant includes the personality processes of the significant figures in interaction. It includes motivational needs for being protected and loved (located in the mother) and motivational needs for acceptance (located in the father). This mutuality of shared personality processes makes it understandable that enormous bonds may occur between parent and child, especially as articulated in the writings of Fingarette (1962, p. 151), Mahler (Speers and Lansing, 1965), Haley (1963, pp. 108–9), and Jackson (1957). The motivational needs of some parents and other early significant figures are such that the infant is drawn especially tightly into the personality processes of these significant parental figures. Under these circumstances, the child is welded much too closely to the personality processes of these figures and cannot separate his own personality from theirs. He becomes little more than a vehicle of behavioral expression for the motivational needs of these other figures throughout the balance of his ensuing life (Bateson, 1961; Haley, 1963; Mahrer, 1967a; cf. Tybring, 1962). When meaningful changes occur in the lives of these significant parental figures, there is an especially profound resonance in the personality of the child, even during his own adulthood.

CHANGES IN EXTERNAL NEED-IMPLEMENTERS

A third class of recent life changes affecting motivational needs includes a shift in external implementation and facilitation of a person's motivational needs. These motivational needs require quite explicit external agents, objects, or situations. A dominating individual may require a submissive partner; motivational needs for power call for a certain appropriate situation for their expression. A decline in the availability of adequate and appropriate external agents, objects, or situations constitutes a serious life change which affects the motivational needs.

One person's life may be spent in a series of sanctuaries and retreats, beginning with his particular family, a withdrawn role during his adolescent years, and his choice in adulthood of an isolated rural existence; as changes reduce the availability of the rural retreat, his unchanged needs begin to require a new sanctuary and retreat. Another person may exist in what Davis, Freeman, and Simmons (1957) and Freeman and Simmons (1958a) term a "one-person chronic ward" wherever he is, i.e., not working, cared for by others, moderately bothersome to those about him; only so long as his family and community tolerate and fulfill these needs does he remain outside the hospital. A person may need a relationship with a somewhat punitive, gruffly accepting, highly authoritarian father figure; loss of the father figure leaves this needed role in a state of psychological vacuum. Another person's motivational needs call for a series of parents or parent-surrogates with whom the person relates dependently so that he is able to complain and wail at their failure to understand him, provide for him, help him, or nurture him; loss of these particular parents or parent-surrogates requires other means of implementing the same motivational needs. Accordingly, the decline in availability of adequate motivational need-implementing agents, objects, or situations constitutes a significant life change exerting an impact upon a person's motivational needs.

These three classes of life changes are by no means exhaustive of the ways in which motivational needs are brought into operation. But they represent three major avenues which culminate in hospitalization. Our position is that the beginnings of the road to hospitalization lie in these and other psychological life changes (Darbonne, 1967; Harris, Kalis, and Freeman, 1963; Rogler and Hollingshead, 1965) rather than in concepts of disease processes and the onset of "mental illness." The occurrence of these life changes is accompanied with a change in the individual's major motivating needs, the next step in the sequence culminating in hospitalization.

Motivational Need States

Recent life changes lead to a change in the major motivational needs. This means that the personality processes are now directed toward revised goals congruent with the revised motivational needs. We may now return to the three major classes of life changes and focus on the altered motivational needs and associated new external goals.

MOTIVATIONAL NEED FOR AVOIDING OR EXPERIENCING A THREATENING SITUATION

Once deeper personality processes bring about a threatening situation, the person may either undergo the full experience of the threat or avoid the threat. One motivational need is to experience the threatening situation; the alternative motivational need is to avoid it.

Once the husband is faced with the threat accompanying an adulterous wife, his motivational need may lead him, for example, to experience the threat of inadequacy and homosexuality or, on the other hand, to seek ways of avoiding this particular threat. A woman whose personality processes left her with no husband and a broken home may be under an altered motivational need either to undergo the full painful experience of insecurity or to seek ways of avoiding the threat of ever-increasing insecurity. A businessman whose personality processes brought his firm to bankruptcy may be under the motivational need either to experience the threat of failure and disillusionment or to seek means of avoiding such a threatening situation. A son's personality processes trigger long-hidden murderous impulses toward his father; his motivational need may be to avoid or to be subjected to the experience of strong retaliation and inordinate guilt. Another son may force his family beyond their limits of tolerance; he now may be under the altered motivational need to avoid the threat of, for example, final rejection by the family, or to undergo the experience of being severely rejected.

For some individuals, personality processes tend to bring about situations fraught with threat. There is an altered motivational need, directed toward either the avoidance or the painful experiencing of the given threatening situation.

MOTIVATIONAL NEED TO UNDERGO CHANGES INITIATED BY SIGNIFICANT OTHER FIGURES

When a person is linked with significant parental figures because of especially strong bonds in the primitive personality, changes in the lives of these other figures induce analogous changes in the person's own life. The person may then be described in terms of motivational needs to undergo specified kinds of changes. The death of a mother may bring about a motivational need in the son to undergo some kind of death. The general decline of a father may induce a son to operate on a motivational need to experience some sort of general decline. The deterioration of a parental figure may call forth motivational needs in a daughter to go through some kind of deterioration.

Recent life changes in the lives of these significant other figures tend to bring about changes in the motivational needs of the individuals linked to them. Accordingly, such individuals are now motivated toward the goal of undergoing analogous life changes.

MOTIVATIONAL NEED FOR NEW NEED-IMPLEMENTERS

The decline in availability of adequate external agents, objects, or situations for the implementation of motivational needs creates a heightened state requiring other means of implementation. An individual who can no longer retreat from society in one way is under a motivational need to find some other means of retreating from society; hospitalization, for example, may well serve such motivational needs. The loss of a dependency-providing husband may lead the motivational needs of a wife to turn toward hospitalization as an available means of implementing this particular motivational need. A young man who lost the structure and containment afforded by a controlling family is under a motivational need for new means of implementing the structure and control. Once again, recent life changes are accompanied by changes in the motivational needs, in these instances, for new ways of implementing the motivational needs.

MOTIVATIONAL NEEDS AND BASIC PERSONALITY PROCESSES

Personality structure is conceptualized in terms of basic personality processes and motivational needs. We may describe some individuals in terms of motivational needs for avoiding or experiencing a threatening situation, for undergoing changes initiated by significant other figures, or for new need-implementers. These motivational needs are the critical determinants of the subsequent changes culminating in hospitalization. It is urged that an understanding of hospitalized patients emphasize, first, the significant life changes in patients' lives and, second, the motivational needs flowing out of such significant life changes. More basic personality processes are present in each patient, and contribute to an in-depth understanding. However, our position stresses the value of understanding the working motivational needs rather than a depth analysis of the basic personality processes alone (Wood, Rakusin, and Morse, 1962).

Other Approaches to Precipitating Events

At least three other approaches provide frameworks for understanding precipitating events, recent life changes, and motivational needs (cf. Adler and Bunn, 1963; Kalis et al., 1961):

THE STRESS-PRESSURE APPROACH

External precipitating events are understood as exerting stress and pressure sufficient to disrupt a state of psychic equilibrium (e.g., Adler and Bunn, 1963; Fenichel, 1945; Harris, Kalis, and Freeman, 1964; Kalis et al., 1961; Kalis, Freeman, and Harris, 1964). A breaking point is reached and the personality falls into a psychiatric state such as neurosis or psychosis. A precipitating factor, such as "having a pregnant wife," is then understood in terms of heightened tension-stress which overwhelms an unhealthy complement of defenses, culminating either in psychiatric illness and hospitalization (Peterson, 1954) or in a significant disruption of defenses—for better or for worse (Forer, 1963). The diagnostic search consists of an "exploration of the patient's current life situation and of the events which might have disturbed a previously maintained equilibrium" (Freeman, Kalis, and Harris, 1964, p. 414). (This approach arises out of the traditional medical-psychiatric model, yet the categories of precipitating stresses bear no systematic relationship with the traditional psychiatric diagnosis [Adler and Bunn, 1963]. Instead, the precipitating events are categorized in terms of the depth or severity of impact, disruption, or strain [cf. Forer, 1963, pp. 278–80]—rather than in terms of the nature of emergent or determining need.)

Our approach rejects concepts of pressure and stress, psychic equilibrium, crumbling defenses, and the like (Mahrer, 1967b). Recent life changes are understood, instead, in terms of the emergence of motivational needs.

THE SOCIAL REJECT APPROACH

Another approach shifts the focus onto the family, community, and society. The locus of precipitating change is in the surrounding social group rather than in the individual himself. Thus, for example, the road to hospitalization is initiated with a precipitating change in group tolerance of deviant behavior (Davis, Freeman, and Simmons, 1957; Freeman and Simmons, 1958a, 1958b, 1959). When the deviant behavior is no longer tolerated, the person is forced toward the hospital. Shifting the focus onto the social group emphasizes society's efforts to protect itself by imposing social restraint on disruptive individuals. (Szasz, 1957).

Our approach interprets the same events in terms of the person as the nexus of determining processes. Psychological constructs are employed to understand the person through his own mediating needs. Our construction of the same events allows for the person's *eliciting* of social rejection, his *inviting* the family to go beyond its tolerance, his *inducing* of restraint from the community. Or, when the social group restrains, rejects, or banishes him, our concern is with the manner in which the person *uses* the situation to feel anguished, alone, hurt, revengeful, mistreated, or the like. Thus, our approach provides a substantially different construction or interpretation of these events.

THE NATURAL-COURSE-OF-ILLNESS APPROACH

Another approach postulates various psychiatric illnesses and diseases with identifiable stages of development, more or less universal sequences through which the illness-disease progresses along a natural course of development (Mahrer, 1967b). Precipitating events hasten the movement along this sequence.

Such an approach would almost require that prodromal symptoms of illness and disease would appear prior to actual hospitalization. In direct contrast, however, Whitmer and Conover (1959) report a surprising absence of psychiatric psychopathology during the critical pre-hospitalization phase.

Our approach rejects the concept of a psychiatric illness or disease, and along with that the concept of an intrinsic, built-in series of stages (Mahrer, 1967c, 1967d). The impacts of precipitating events are understood not in terms of movement along a series of disease stages, but rather in terms of emergent motivational needs. The occurrence of changes in clinical behavior is a function of far more than a natural course of development of a presumed disease; "investigators had not, until recently, been consistently aware of the influence of the hospital society itself in creating some of the characteristics of what is often called the 'natural course' of behavioral disease" (Caudill and Stainbrook, 1954, p. 27).

The Need for Hospitalization

The next step toward hospitalization is the emergence of a specific need for hospitalization, i.e., concrete motivational needs which require the hospital setting (Mahrer, 1962a; Mahrer, Mason, and Pomeroy, 1965) for the achievement of significant goals, for the experiencing of the emergent need-state, for the playing out of the necessary feelings and experiences. We may properly refer to a *psychological need for hospitalization.*

PSYCHOLOGICAL NEED VERSUS PSYCHIATRIC ILLNESS-DISEASE

The person headed for hospitalization is in a psychological state characterized by drives, motivations, experiencings, and feelings, a state of movement or process. He is flooded with some kind of experiential feeling, asking for something, wanting and needing something, fearing and avoiding something. An awareness of the process nature of the psychological needs, goals, motivations, and feelings makes superfluous any assumption of the person's "illness," "psychiatric disease," or "psychiatric diagnosis," and focuses clinical attention upon such questions as "why the patient is requesting help at this time . . . what had brought the patient into treatment now" (Harris, Kalis, and Freeman, 1964). To understand the complex movement toward hospitalization in terms of sickness, illness, or psychiatric disease is to turn away from psychological principles for understanding behavior and to adopt what S. Asch, G. Allport, and others refer to as a dwarflike, caricatured, attenuated, impoverished image of man (Jessor, 1961, p. 28). In other words, we reject the notion that people move toward hospitalization "because they are sick," "because he became schizophrenic," or "because she became mentally ill."

Described in terms of his "psychiatric illness," a person may be labeled "a paranoid patient." But that same "paranoid" person may also be described in terms of psychological needs, for example, to perceive "most of the people in his world as being against him, bent on his humiliation and organized to a greater or less degree in a plan to see that his desires are thwarted" (Bullard, 1960, p. 137). It is his motivational need which invests hospitalization with meaning.

Hospitalization as goal-motivated behavior. Jackson's (1957) and Haley's (1963) work on the function served by a severely symptomatic child within the family setting has a larger implication for the hospital-directed function of given clinical behaviors: whatever the nature of the encompassing system of painful relationships, the movement toward hospitalization affords potential change. Although the prehospital situation ranges from discomfort to despair, the need for hospitalization is tantamount to an attempt to change the situation, an indication of a striving "in order to utilize sickness and hospitalization as a means of gratifying their respective needs" (Burstein, 1965, p. 214). From this point of view, for many patients at least, the need for hospitalization is hopeful and salubrious.

The patient's sole instrument for change is clinical behavior. Yet, in the traditional psychiatric approach, clinical behaviors are interpreted as signs of an illness or disease. Their occurrence, rather than being understood as a need-motivated striving, is labeled as the sign of a pathology. The need for hospitalization is seen as a disastrous portent. Hospitalization is the final defeat, the situation to be resisted at all costs, the ultimate failure in mental health.

Psychotherapy and hospitalization. Individual psychotherapists recognize patients' underlying powerful motivations for seeking treatment (cf. Alexander and French, 1946, p. 283) and for establishing a particular relationship with the therapist. In the same way in which psychotherapy patients are motivated toward the deeper, idiosyncratic meaning of the psychotherapeutic journey, other patients undergo the need for hospitalization. The same motivational needs which underlie the patient-therapist relationship also occur between the patient and the hospital, and are condensed into what we term the "need for hospitalization."

DEEPER MOTIVATIONAL NEEDS AND THE NEED FOR HOSPITALIZATION

The need for hospitalization does not exist alone in a patient's personality. Stated in one way, deeper motivational needs underlie the need for hospitalization; stated another way, hospitalization is a means of reaching toward subsequent goals. For example, hospitalization may serve as a means of preventing the threatened loss of a wife who is pulled at least to remain with the patient during his patienthood. But the deeper motivational need may be to exert severe control over females, so that the motivational need to prevent her threatened loss is understood as a means of severely controlling females in general. For another person, hospitalization serves to provide structure and control of, for example, aggressive impulses. But within a particular personality, aggressive impulses must be controlled because their expression would precipitate a homosexual panic; in other words, the need for hospitalized structure and control is itself determined by deeper motivational needs of a homosexual nature. An understanding of any patient's need for hospitalization calls for an understanding of the deeper motivational needs (and subsequent goals) which give rise to that particular need for hospitalization. There is as yet no systematic investigation of the deeper motivational needs which underlie any given need for hospitalization, and therefore each patient must be individually approached and understood.

The patient who comes to the hospital with acute nausea and vomiting, anxiety, hand tremors, and pressing suicidal thoughts, may be drawn by a need to seek external structure and control of violent rage reactions. Although hospitalization serves a motivational need for structure and control of violent rage reactions, the patient is to be understood from the perspective of deeper personality needs. What deeper motivational need (subsequent goal) is functionally related to the obtaining of structure and control? Some persons may be so closely bound to a mother that the death of the mother activates a deep motivational need to follow the mother into death; this leads the patient to undergo self-directed rage and motivational needs for structure and control. The immediate need for hospitalization is functionally understood in terms of a given patient's deeper motivational needs.

THE ROLE OF THE HOSPITAL

What is the role of the hospital relative to the need for hospitalization? How is the hospital equipped to implement the needs for hospitalization?

The psychological role of the hospital is to implement those needs which arise out of recent life changes. Rather than to "cure mental illness," the hospital serves a particular class of motivational needs. Even those who retain a concept of "mental disease" recognize that "it is important to note that mental hospitals care for more than the mentally ill. The unwanted, the aged, the indigent, the lonely, and others often enter public mental hospitals voluntarily" (Mechanic, 1962, p. 70). Instead of saying that hospitals "treat the mentally ill," we can now say that hospitals serve to implement the motivational needs of patients.

The low proportion of hospitalized patients who are, for example, married or whose parents are living might be taken as evidence of the kind of population prone to "psychiatric illness and disease" (Morgan and Johnson, 1957; Wanklin et al., 1955). In contrast, our approach understands the hospital as especially equipped to accommodate the motivational needs of the unmarried or of those without both parents —needs for withdrawal into the hospital, needs for a surrogate family, needs to be rejected, needs for basic human security.

Punishment-pain. Hospitalization is an effective means of implementing needs for punishment and self-directed pain. The person is now "a psychiatric patient," "mentally ill," "schizophrenic," "psychotic," with the full punitive brunt of these terms and of "being in a mental hospital." For implementing motivational needs for punishment-pain, society's legal-penal system is an effective agent, but hospitalization is also a powerful means of implementation.

Acceptance. The hospital may offer acceptance of the person's impulses, deviant behavior, and verging drives. Freeman and Simmons (1958a, 1958b, 1959) have emphasized the importance of familial tolerance or lack of tolerance as an instrumental factor in forcing a person toward hospitalization. Like the family, the hospital is often placed in the role of the acceptor of the patient's impulses or deviant ways, and the hospital is traditionally familiar with and equipped for such a role. In fact, the hospital may outdo spouse, family, friends, private psychotherapist, and clergyman in tolerating the most obnoxiously provocative behavior, from gross alcoholism to defiant stoical equanimity (Fenichel, 1954b, p. 34), from wild shouting to exhibitionism.

Structure and control. Some patients call upon the hospital's resources for providing containment, structure, and control. These resources often equip the hospital for this role better than a spouse, a family, a community, or even a penal system. Even in open-door hospitals special structure and containment is often called for with suicidal and highly aggressive patients, and those chronic individuals who manifest lack of contact and tend to wander off (Hurst, 1957). Rather than labeling such persons as mentally ill, our approach would see these persons as inducing the hospital to provide some form of structure and control.

Dependency. With regard to dependency, our cultural folklore considers this the supposed forte of the hospital system. The craving for all brands and varieties of dependency, strong in so many people, will lead an individual up one societal blind alley after another in search of gratification.

Avoidance-retreat. "Psychiatric" hospitalization offers one of the most effective means for a person to withdraw, to avoid, to retreat (Goldberg and Rubin, 1964). Persons under this motivational need may move toward religious retreats, aimless geographic wanderings, jails, or the aloneness and withdrawal of city life. But for many of these persons, long-term custodial hospitalization offers a full measure of avoidance-retreat.

Staff-patient "goodness-of-fit." Just as Jackson (1957) asserts that the family often is drawn together by the burden of taking care of the sick person, and a community pathologically needs its "sick" element (Cotts, 1954), in analogous fashion many hospitals may be aptly described as settings in which the personnel are drawn together by the job of taking care of patients. Hospital staff may be described as possessing distinctive attitudes and needs which either enhance or inhibit the "goodness to fit" between the hospital and the patients' needs for hospitalization (cf. Ellsworth and Stokes, 1963; Morimoto, Baker, and Greenblatt, 1954; Schwartz, Schwartz, and Staunton, 1951). The personnel will tend to facilitate or to inhibit patients' needs for dependency, protection, understanding, love, impulse-expression, structure, or other motivational needs. The personnel and patients align in some sort of goodness of fit.

Psychosocial role of the hospital. Hospitals settle into a role in the community and engender specific reputations (Greenblatt, Levinson, and Williams, 1957; Pratt, Giannitrapani, and Khanna, 1960; Woodward, 1955). If a hospital is known as custodian of the socially unfit and rejected, potential patients with needs to feel socially unfit and rejected will tend to that particular hospital. Mental hospitals have various specialties: alcoholics, the aged and the infirm, those in danger with the law, those who need protection from or punishment by the community, and the like. Distinctively different psychosocial roles will be assumed by hospitals which either see patients as sociological problems or in terms of psychological processes or as medicosomatic cases (Strauss et al., 1964). Some hospitals may function as the discipline arm of society, others as the extended hand of welfare, the sanctuary, the big brother, the bully, the camisole, the loving mother. Increasingly numerous and active mental hospitals of today (Barton, 1962) assume roles historically assigned to a variety of social institutions. The psychosocial role of the hospital is an important factor in whether or not it is to facilitate the motivational needs of given classes of potential patients.

Social class availability. The mental hospital varies its availability to different social classes and groups. What has been taken as evidence of heightened "mental disturbance" among the lower class (Rennie et al., 1957) or the urban population (Malzberg, 1956; Parker, 1958; Wanklin et al., 1955) may instead signify that these social groups utilize behaviors (symptoms) and "mental" hospitals in achieving what members of other social groups achieve in other ways. The lower-class man under a motivational need to induce others to keep him from his own self-destructive tendencies might move toward the community mental hospital which effectively prevents him from self-destruction. The upper-class man, equally motivated to induce others to keep him from his own self-destructive tendencies, might find himself negotiating some poor business contracts so that his associates are forced to assume effective control over his economic mandate, thereby implementing his need to force others into the role of keeping him from his own self-destructive tendencies. For some social groups the hospital route is more available and effective in achieving what the individual is motivated to obtain.

Clinical Behavior

Our examination has included recent life changes and associated motivational needs directed toward hospitalization. The stage is now set for the understanding of clinical behavior (symptomatology).

CLINICAL BEHAVIOR AND HOSPITAL ADMISSION

Clinical behavior is directed toward the immediate goal of achieving hospital admission. The candidate must manifest behavior sufficient to place him in the new status of patienthood, "entitled to treatment or help by virtue of his very disability" (Szasz, 1961, p. 188). It is clear "that becoming a 'patient' is not a simple act but represents a personal and social achievement" (Levinson, 1962, pp. 13–14). This achievement is a necessary first goal of clinical behavior under a motivational need for hospitalization.

Ordinarily, admission requires particular clinical behaviors which the psychosocial community recognizes as "sick," "emotionally ill," or characteristic of a "psychiatric disease." These behaviors vary according to the particular psychosocial community. Hospitals will deny access to patients unless they demonstrate defined clinical behaviors. Feeling rather low is ordinarily inadmissible; slicing a wrist is admissible. Suggestive prurient behavior toward a girl in a bar is inadmissible; that same behavior toward elementary school girls on a playground is admissible. Needs which carry a person into the hospital are generally strong and pressing. The patient whose dependency needs draw him toward hospitalization is generally under a motivation of greater magnitude than the fellow whose dependency calls for an occasional beer. The patient who is motivated toward hospitalization as a means of avoiding sexual threat is under more impelling need than the husband who avoids sexual relations through regular evening arguments. The requirements of the psychosocial community as well as the generally heightened impulsion of the motivational needs determine, as Diener and Young (1961) imply, that persons who come to hospitals should demonstrate dramatic and strongly motivated clinical behaviors as compared with persons who do not come to hospitals.

One with a strong need for hospitalization may try out various clinical behaviors before achieving admission. A woman, seeking hospitalization as a means of punishing her parents and forcing a hospital to care for her, might manifest a series of clinical behaviors before one culminates in admission. An inability to work might be initially manifested, directed toward both the punitive goal and that of gaining care from others. A subsequent forcing of friends and relatives to make decisions for her would serve as a punitive gesture as well as requiring others to provide care. Once the specific need for hospitalization takes shape, a series of sharp clinical behaviors would be targeted toward admission. Under the increasingly focalized need for hospitalization, several private therapists might be consulted. Profound depressive clinical behavior being manifested could prove successful when coupled with highly public and dramatic suicidal gestures.

The rising need for hospitalization may call up an extremely broad array of clinical behaviors before settling upon an effective clinical condition. Adler and Bunn (1963) report a high frequency of traditional "medical illness" just prior to the exhibiting of what they term "psychiatric" symptoms which actually eventuated in hospitalization. Our contention is that the "medical illnesses" are open to reinterpretation as a class of clinical behaviors directed toward hospital admission.

Continued experience in gaining hospital admission equips the would-be patient with an increasingly effective set of clinical behaviors. Mahrer and Katz (1963) found that number of hospitalizations and number of symptoms at admission were inversely correlated, which suggests that experienced admission-achievers have profited from their experiences.

In order for a clinical behavior to be successful in achieving hospitalization, it must possess visibility. As Mechanic (1962) asserts, if symptoms are not sufficiently visible, the person will not gain admission. Dancing nude in the city square is quite visible; attempting murder is visible. On the other hand, internal aches and pains, covert behaviors, private thoughts, internal feelings, and many physical changes are not visible and must be converted from internal to external clinical behavior. Stomachaches must be converted into complaints to a physician. Voyeurism must either disturb a neighbor, engage the attention of a concerned friend, or be communicated to the proper professional person as a self-report. Private thoughts of being Jesus Christ must be made public. Internal feelings of hopelessness and despair must be publicly displayed. All manner of bodily changes must be presented in the proper way to the proper authorities. For the "symptom" to be successful, "the patient's behavior must be extreme in its influence on someone else" (Haley, 1963, p. 5).

Patterns of hospital-directed clinical behavior. The above implies that the broad spectrum of hospital-directed clinical behaviors should occur in clusters or patterns which constitute major goal-directed behavioral avenues for achieving hospital admission. A factor analytic study of 150 hospital-directed clinical behaviors self-reported by 302 hospitalized male psychiatric patients yielded the following patterns: (1) Physical Complaints, including discomforts involving arms, hips, ears, total body, thinking, etc.; (2) Physical Debilitation, including physical malfunctionings, somatic incapabilities, loss of physical functionings, and bodily weaknesses; (3) Alcoholism; (4) Interpersonal Difficulties, including interpersonal rejection, vocational inadequacy, social incapability, and interpersonal verbal problems; (5) Marital Discord, including maritally focused emotional lability, tearfulness, and aggression; and (6) Aggression, including anger, irritation, hostility, and violence (Mahrer, Stewart, Horn, and Lind, 1967).

THE PSYCHODYNAMICS OF ADMISSION

Induced rejection by the hospital. Sometimes clinical behaviors are aimed not at gaining hospital admission, but rather in playing out other needs which do not require actual hospitalization. For example, a need to provoke rejection may induce the hospital to deny admission. Certain kinds of clinical behaviors bring about this rejection. "Certain patients and their families phrase requests or present problems in a manner which practically insures their not being fulfilled . . . . [In a given case, the patient's] behavior was part of a characterological pattern which functioned, by provoking rejection, continually to prove to him his own unworthiness" (Kalis, Freeman, and Harris, 1964, p. 267). The motivational need calls upon particular clinical behaviors to provoke rejection by the hospital.

Rejection of hospital admission. Some motivational needs are directed toward eliciting overtures for acceptance or help which are promptly rejected. Appropriate clinical behaviors elicit admission, after which the patients refuse to undergo hospitalization. Often these clinical maneuverings are aimed at instilling the hospital (and staff) with a sense of guilt, as if it were a bad mother who is now properly punished into worrying what it did "wrong," why the patient did not accept its offer, or why the patient dropped out prematurely.

THE POSTADMISSION STAGE OF HOSPITALIZATION

Postadmission changes in clinical behavior. The successful achievement of admission may be accompanied with a significant change in the motivational need which brought the patient to the hospital. Thus, significant changes in clinical behavior are often observed almost immediately following admission (Shapiro, 1961). Such changes in clinical behavior following admission appear inconsistent with an approach (Mahrer, 1967c) which interpreted clinical behavior as signs or symptoms of an underlying illness or disease with natural course of development along defined stages. Our approach would suggest that significant changes in clinical behavior should occur in the critical period immediately following admission whether these changes are measured in terms of intensity or severity of the symptoms-behaviors (Shapiro, 1961), changes in target symptoms or symptom clusters (Gorham and Overall, 1961; Mahrer, 1963; Mahrer and Mason, 1965), or changes in sheer amount of symptomatology or number of symptoms (Ellsworth and Clayton, 1959; Freeman and Simmons, 1959; Mahrer, Mason, Kahn, and Projansky, 1967). Mahrer and Mason (1965) found that significant behavioral changes occurred during this postadmission period; furthermore, admission appeared to exert the dual impact of both increasing and decreasing the amount of clinical psychopathology. A study of patient groups just before and after admission indicated that following admission there were increased frequencies of clinical behaviors associated with the side effects of chemotherapies, the pressure of sexual and aggressive impulses, and of general decline and impotence (Mahrer, 1963). Such results suggest that admission to the hospital is a significant event and may well determine sharp changes in motivational needs and associated clinical behavior.

Sick role vs. patient role. The distinction between clinical behavior directed toward hospital admission and clinical behavior subsequent to admission is reflected in Parsons's (1951a, 1951b; Burstein, 1965) distinction between the "sick role" and the "patient role." The former includes the major motivation of demonstrating a "sick" state, while the latter includes the acquiring of certain relationships to other patients, effecting staff interactions, avoiding certain ward pressures, etc. The kinds of clinical behaviors associated with the sick role are different from those associated with the patient role. Gaining hospital admission is a significant dynamic event which should be reflected in altered clinical behaviors.

Short-term dropouts. During the psychodynamically critical period immediately following admission, many patients abruptly leave the hospital, but not because they have been "treated." As Clausen observes (1956, p. 9), released patients often "are fully as ill as many patients currently in hospitals." Furthermore, short-term psychiatric patients do not seem to differ from long-term patients in symptomatic severity (Anker, 1962). At least two factors are paramount in accounting for discharge soon after admission.

The first factor is a change in the need for hospitalization. Once the need-state is significantly altered, the basis for the clinical behavior drops away and there is reduced need to remain in the hospital. The need for hospitalization may arise, for example, out of inexpressible aggression directed toward the wife's brother and his family, all of whom lived in the patient's home, exerting increasing pressures upon him. Collapsing into a depression, the patient's extreme withdrawal led him into the hospital. Hospitalization constituted a crisis which forced the intruders to leave. The need for hospitalization was thereby reduced and the depressed clinical behaviors abated, all shortly following admission and without benefit of traditional "treatment." Sheer admission was sufficient to correct the situation, and eliminate further the need for hospitalization.

When the need for hospitalization stems directly from family pressures and stresses, changes in clinical behaviors and leaving the hospital soon after admission are functions of change in the family pressures and stresses which initially created the need for hospitalization. "It is possible that these . . . patients who come to the hospital in large measure in response to pressures from their families are ready to leave more quickly than other patients—perhaps as soon as their families modify these pressures" (Wood, Rakusin, and Morse, 1962, p. 44). In response to family pressures, the need for hospitalization may be, for example, to accede, to declare a state of helplessness, or to fall into a dependent status. Admission has a direct effect upon the family, reducing the need for hospitalization, and culminating in the patient's leaving the hospital soon after admission (Wood, Rakusin, and Morse, 1960).

For other patients, the mere act of securing acceptance (i.e., being admitted) is all that is required for a particular motivational need. Following admission, these patients undergo a dramatic change in motivational needs and clinical behaviors, for their major need was merely to gain a gesture of acceptance from the hospital.

Frequently a patient's short-term relationship with the hospital may be predicted from his relationship with other people and institutions. These relationships often reflect a behavioral pattern or style of short, abortive contacts. The motivational need dictates that the contact must be brief; thus, a short hospitalization may be predicted from the duration of contacts with other external agents, especially social agents and institutions (Moran, Fairweather, and Morton, 1956).

A second factor for the abrupt discharge-withdrawal from the hospital involves a hospital's inability or refusal to implement the patient's needs. A person who desperately craves love and affection may be sorely disenchanted by the harsh realities of the hospital ward. Under these circumstances, the patient turns, disappointed, away from the hospital.

Other needs for hospitalization require, for example, an appropriate atmosphere for a complete collapse, a safe site for bizarre impulse-expression, or an accepting situation for manifest helplessness (Anker, 1962). These patients are sensitively cognizant that many hospitals are most intolerant of such behavior; that such behavior is to be "treated"; that the patient is to be given drugs to minimize this behavior; that it is unacceptable to fall further into that "condition"; that further demonstrations of such behavior are evidences of his "getting worse" or "becoming psychotic"; that such behavior is opposed by an unverbalized but explicit "primary goal . . . to return as many of our patients as possible to social usefulness. . . . The primary objective . . . must be to return the patient to a productive social role" (Felix, 1961, p. 15). Similarly, patients whose need for hospitalization calls for a "passive recipient" attitude on the part of the staff will likely experience a reduced need for hospitalization under a staff attitude shift toward "active participant" (Ellsworth and Stokes, 1963). For patients whose needs for hospitalization are left hanging or resisted by the hospital, their short stays and failure to return (Crandall et al., 1954) may be a function of need-frustration rather than "improvement" or "successful treatment" or "spontaneous recovery."

In order to understand the "early drop-out phenomenon" (Rogers, 1960), it is proposed that such factors as ego strength (Barron, 1953), low socioeconomic level (Meyers and Auld, 1955; Winder and Hersko, 1955), psychiatric diagnosis (Anker, 1962), or low intelligence and education (Hiler, 1958; Rubenstein and Lorr, 1956) might profitably be recast into (1) principles of the "poorness" of fit between the actual hospital situation and the patient's need for hospitalization and (2) principles of the significant changes in the recent life situations which generated the need for hospitalization.

GOAL-DIRECTIONALITY OF CLINICAL BEHAVIOR

Clinical behavior is motivated toward the immediate goal of hospital admission (or other goals involving acceptance-rejection by the hospital). Subsequent to admission, clinical behaviors are goal-directed toward what Freud (1955b, p. 54) terms the "paranosic gain" of an "illness." To state that clinical behavior (cf. "symptomatology") arises from motivational needs is to acknowledge its goal-directionality, its intent, its foundation of meaning and wish (Holt, 1915; Fingarette, 1963), its ability to mobilize others into action (Szasz, 1961, p. 130), and its openness to understanding and systematic study in terms of guiding, underlying motives (Leary and Gill, 1959). To assert that clinical behavior possesses a goal-directionality is to expand a narrow, closed,

and solely intrapsychic system into an open, motivated, behavioral interpersonal system (cf. Haley, 1963, pp. 108, 151–52). Clinical behaviors
are the means of reaching toward the goals associated with the need for
hospitalization. Thus, our view accepts "the premise that the behavior
of persons said to be mentally ill is meaningful and goal-directed—provided one is able to understand the patient's behavior from *his* particular
point of view" (Szasz, 1961, p. 59).

Alcoholism and periodic blackouts not only achieve admission, but
may place the person in a state of helplessness. A suicidal gesture may
be aimed at a wholesale reorientation of one's entire psychological environment so that he is the central focus of familial concern and attention.

Clinical behavior expresses the motivation which brought the person to the hospital. A need to identify with a father in the terminal
stages of cancer can be facilitated by necrophobia and a morbid preoccupation with one's own viscera. A need to be actively rejected may
lead to such clinical behaviors as excessive alcoholism or suicide attempts or ideas of reference (Fleischl, 1958) which bring about rejection (and hospitalization) from one's family, peers, or the community.
Motivation to avoid a threatening relationship may call up highly effective bizarre or "crazy" behavior, in accord with Haley's (1961, p. 344)
succinct statement that "The only way that a person can effectively avoid
forming a relationship with anyone is by behaving like a schizophrenic."
Motivation to escape from external sexual threat may be expressed in
such clinical behavior as fears of sexual deviation, a bursting pressure
throughout the head, excessive masturbation.

Clinical behaviors establish a meaningful and needed relationship
with the other patients, staff, personnel, or significant individuals outside
the hospital. For example, the need for a strong external disciplinarian
may occasion obnoxiously antagonistic behavior coupled with esoteric
peripatetic physical pains about which the patient incessantly complains.
A need to be ignored and rejected may be manifested in ward withdrawal, in a minimum of requests or overtures to others, and subtle cues
which induce others to withhold response (Schwartz, Schwartz, and
Staunton, 1951). Patients' clinical behaviors are aimed toward inducing
others to assume roles which complement their own (Spiegel, 1957),
and thereby to establish a desired relationship.

Some patients may seek special acceptance or evidence of special
worth through gaining "favors" from the hospital—being accepted into
psychotherapy or remaining in the hospital an especially long time
(Wood, Rakusin, and Morse, 1962). These special favors are granted
to patients manifesting certain winning characteristics and unexpected
behaviors, e.g., abrupt onset of agoraphobia in a personable and produc-

tive young executive, or a frightening "devil" delusion in a brilliant and attractive female. Such clinical behaviors provide the means for achieving needed relationships with the hospital.

Mahrer (1963) reported the increased frequency of postadmission clinical behaviors signifying the pressure of sexual and aggressive impulses, and general decline and impotence. Rather than regarding them as symptoms of disease processes or the effects of "institutionalization," these increased-frequency clinical behaviors may be interpreted in terms of their goal-directionality, i.e., as asking for something or needing something within the hospital context. For example, they may be means of seeking a safe sanctuary in which to give in to deteriorating pressures, or means of seeking structure, acceptance, or withdrawal from intolerable impulses.

In a study of "low-complainers" versus "high-complainers" (Mahrer, Mason, Kahn, and Projansky, 1966), low-complainers were characterized by self-concern, self-directionality, difficulties in simple psychobiological functions, and rather mild overall distress. In contrast, high-complainers were characterized by a concern with the interpersonal external world and a more seriously disrupted overall psychological state. These results suggest that patients with many complaints are under severe stress in relation to their external worlds whereas patients with few complaints are under motivational needs for self-preoccupation and self-concern. In a sample of veteran psychiatric patients, the strong skew toward low-complainers (Mahrer, Mason, Kahn, and Projansky, 1967) implies that these patients are characterized by motivational needs indicating relatively mild distress and strong self-directed concerns and preoccupations. It would appear that motivational needs are determinants of the sheer amount of clinical complaints presented by patients.

Clinical behavior, goal-directionality, and pain. The feelings accompanying clinical behaviors may be "good" or "bad." In other words, clinical behavior is aimed toward particular goals and is motivated by particular needs, but the attendant feelings are frequently quite painful (Mahrer, 1967a). The process of moving toward motivationally determined hospital goals is seldom accompanied with good feelings. Hospitalization may serve as a means of avoiding threat, punishing a family, containing an intolerable impulse, or acquiring dependency, but the clinical behaviors and the motivated goals are typically accompanied with feelings of inner turmoil, hurt, fear, tension, stress, and other kinds of psychological pain. We must carefully distinguish between motivated goal-directionality and the nature of internal feelings; the clinical behavior of hospitalized patients is, unfortunately, motivated toward goals whose successful achievement typically involves considerable feelings of hurt and pain.

Three rationales for hospital clinical behavior. There are at least three rationales for understanding hospital clinical behavior. Consider a patient who becomes quite violent in the ward. Our view is that the meaningful determinants include personality motivations, needs, and goal-directionalities. Becoming violent is a motivated behavior directed toward some goal. Another viewpoint understands hospital clinical behavior in terms of psychiatric illness, disease, symptoms of pathological processes, and the like, concepts rejected by our own approach. This second view might perhaps describe the patient's behavior as manifesting an aggressive reaction or psychosis. A third viewpoint sees clinical behavior largely as a function of the social system, the interplay of sociological variables. The patient's violence might reflect increasing stresses in the hospital social system. In contrast, our own view is that the causal determinants reside in the goal-directionality of the personality motivations and needs and that these personality processes invest the hospital and sociopsychological system with meaning and significance; we acknowledge the critical importance of the hospital social system (cf. Caudill, 1956, 1958; Caudill et al., 1952; Schwartz, 1957), but retain the personality processes as the determinants of the meaning of the psychological situation and clinical behavior.

Extended and chronic hospitalization. Remaining in the hospital a long time, or becoming a chronic hospital "repeater," is interpreted as a clinical behavior understandable in terms of personality motivations and goal-directionalities: (1) The content of patients' motivational needs determines whether hospitalization is to be long or short. For example, patients whose needs are to elicit and abruptly reject gestures of acceptance are destined for short hospitalizations, whereas motivational needs for parental care and nurture call for more extended hospitalization. (2) The absence of change in the need-state implies an extended hospital relationship. For example, the need for hospitalization as a means of avoiding sexual threat posed by a homosexual person at work will persist until there is either an internal or an external shift in the sexual threat. (The social psychological point of view axiomatically and accurately warns against the dangers of a patient returning to the very same extrahospital circumstances which exacerbated the initial need for hospitalization.) Thus, returning to work and being exposed to the initial sexual threat serves to maintain the need for hospitalization. (3) An extended or chronic hospitalization is determined in part by the "goodness of fit" between the needs of the patient and characteristics of the hospital. As long as the patient and the hospital continue to need each other, the situation is optimal for an extended relationship. In some settings, the relationship may flower into a highly personal interinvolvement (cf. psychotherapy) so that patients in this state may be expected to remain somewhat longer in the hospital (Wood, Rakusin, and Morse, 1962). Similarly, the progressive loss of other external resources (wife, job, family, etc.) will tend to heighten the goodness of fit between patient and hospital.

These principles of personality motivations, needs, and goal-directionalities underlying the clinical behavior of extended or chronic hospitalization incorporate such predictor variables as depth of pathology (Anker, 1962; Ellsworth and Clayton, 1959), ego strength (Barron, 1953), low economic level (Meyers and Auld, 1955; Winder and Hersko, 1955), low intelligence or education (Hiler, 1958; Rubenstein and Lorr, 1956), and psychiatric diagnosis (Anker, 1962). Such principles help to account for the findings that extended or chronic hospitalization is associated with single marital status, less evidence of "improvement" than in a short hospital duration (Ullman, 1957; Pascal et al., 1953), psychotic diagnosis, severe pathology, legal incompetence (Lindemann et al., 1959), a low proportion of living parents, and a low proportion of married patients (Morgan and Johnson, 1957); such principles explain that veteran psychiatric patients apparently cling to hospitals (Brody and Fishman, 1960) on the basis of need-motivations rather than parameters of psychiatric illness.

FUNCTIONAL SIMILARITY AMONG CLINICAL BEHAVIORS

Since the major characteristic of clinical behaviors is their goal-directionality (Mahrer and Young, 1962), similarity should be assessed and defined in terms of the goals they address; i.e., similarity is determined by the *function* of the clinical behaviors. Bizarre behavior, alcoholism, being unable to hold a job, and stomach pains appear phenotypically quite different. Yet, the function of each of these clinical behaviors may group them together as aiming at the same goal. Bizarre behavior may serve a need to be placed in a dependent, cared-for state within the hospital setting. Dependency may also be achieved by inability to hold a job. Stomach pains frequently are a means of making overtures to be cared for dependently.

Multiple goal-directionality. Any given clinical behavior may possess a number of potential goal-directed functions. "Blackouts" may be a primitive means of recoiling from sexual threat, an avenue toward complete helplessness, or a method of controlling others in the family. A tight, painful feeling in the chest region may be a means of containing anxiety-ridden behavioral tendencies as the patient seeks the added structure and containment of the hospital, or it may be a method of indicating the painful absence of nurturing. Any given clinical behavior may be directed toward multiple goals within the hospital setting. Thus, the same clinical behavior, in different patients, may be directed toward a number of different goals and arise from a number of different needs. The attributing of multiple goal-directionality to clinical behavior may well avoid Kanfer and Saslow's warning that "diagnosis by symptoms . . . is often misleading because it implies common etiological factors" (1965, p. 532).

A "delusion," for example, is a clinical behavior which may be directed toward a number of different goals. Our approach rejects a description of "the delusional" patient (cf. Boverman, 1953). Our approach is not able to provide general statements about "the delusional" patient: "They are particularly sensitive about their intellectual prowess. . . . These patients frequently have great difficulty in admitting their own errors" (Boverman, 1953, p. 149). The literature is saturated with general statements about "the compulsive," "the retarded," "the alcoholic," "the senile," "the depressed," and dozens of other behavioral groupings. Compulsive behavior and all other kinds of clinical behavior are, in our view, linked to a variety of goals and needs. The challenge to clinical analysis and research is to understand clinical behavior in terms of clusters of associated goals and needs.

DEEPER FOUNDATIONS OF HOSPITAL CLINICAL BEHAVIOR

The needs for hospitalization rest on a foundation of deeper personality needs. Vomiting may be a means of expelling explosive anger within the safety and acceptance of the hospital settings, but this immediate goal of an angry outburst may relate to deeper needs to experience anguish and hurt over loss of a parental agent. Depressive behavior may be directed toward the immediate hospital goal of removal from an intolerable family situation, but the deeper need may be to remove oneself from intolerable homosexual tendencies. The immediate goals of hospital-directed clinical behavior take on further significance when seen as pathways for deeper needs and goals. A patient's ward behavior, for example, may be understood as creating a particular role which itself is understood in terms of his deeper needs and goals. The patient may be the instigator of insurrection, the obnoxious child, a provoker of extra attention, or the favorite of the avuncular staff personnel. "The basic patterns evident in these relationships may be similar to or identical with those in the early family. That is, the patient tends to reconstruct in his 'ward family' significant relationships from his past and to employ techniques which encourage personnel and fellow patients into roles of past key persons" (Pinderhughes et al., 1966, p. 140; cf. Spiegel, 1957).

Hospital-specific clinical inferences. Not only does the clinical behavior emerge from a series of deeper needs, but interpretation of any clinical behavior should take into account the significance of the here-and-now specific hospital situation. The literature provides general inferences for understanding clinical behavior. Our approach requires that these general statements be refined by taking into account the clinical behavior's goal-directed components within the hospital setting.

For example, headaches in general have been understood as the release of repressed affect (Lustman, 1951), a precursor of a psychotic episode (Brenner, Friedman and Carter, 1949), unexpressed or repressed resentment (Grinker and Gottschalk, 1949), a response to excessive environmental demands and pressures (Friedman, von Storch, and Merritt, 1954), emotional stress (Alexander, 1950, p. 155; Weiss and English, 1949, p. 656), the strain of solving conflicts by "conscious rational thinking" (Grinker and Robbins, 1954, p. 109), a manifestation of sustained life stress (Wolff, 1953), inner tension (Fenichel, 1945, p. 253), and unconscious conflicts (Fenichel, 1945, p. 253). Alexander and French arrive at the general principle that "symptoms resulting from the frustration of an activity are likely to involve especially the organs which are most under tension at the moment of frustration" (1948, p. 242), e.g., the head.

In contrast to the above, the following inferences take into account the goal-directedness of headaches specifically within a hospital setting: (1) Headaches serve as part of a heightened multiplicity of complaints, disturbances, and difficulties aimed at the goal of achieving admission to hospitalization (Mahrer, Mason, and Rosenshine, 1966). (2) Headaches signify a state of heightened threatening sexuality in patients seeking hospitalization as a means of avoiding and withdrawing from the external threatening sexual situations. (3) Headaches signify pressing, internalized aggressive tendencies in patients whose need for hospitalization is a means of gaining added external structure, control, and containment.

In order to understand the specific motivational need behind a clinical behavior, such as a headache, general principles of unachieved gratifications (Freud, 1936, p. 17) or repressed wishes (Freud, 1955a, p. 14) must be concretized by acknowledging the importance of a specific situation (Diener, 1967; Rotter, 1955), such as the hospital. We conceive of a series of inferences, such as those suggested for headaches, applied to each clinical behavior in each situational context. An analysis of the same clinical behavior in different situational contexts should yield varying sets of inferences. Thus, clinical explanations of headaches should vary in a hospital situation as contrasted with a business setting, private practice, detention home, university setting, and the like. With varying motivations and goal-directionalities in varying situational contexts, "the behaviors defined as symptoms of an 'illness' may be as much characteristic of some particular situation or group setting as they are enduring attributes of persons" (Mechanic, 1962, pp. 67–68).

In a population of hospitalized male psychiatric patients, for example, aggressive behaviors-symptoms were found to interrelate in a single general cluster (Pomeroy, Mahrer, and Mason, 1965). Although these results may be taken as support of a unitary factor theory of aggression (Berkowitz, 1962; Buss, 1961; Feshbach, 1964), this conclusion must be restricted to the studied population, not only because of considerations of experimental design, but also because of a position that aggressive behavior in a hospital situation is motivated toward goals which are probably different from the goals associated with, for example, a military situation, a family setting, or a political convention.

Expectancy for improvement as clinical behavior. Patients' "expectancies" for improvement are also understood as clinical behavior, related to needs for hospitalization and directed toward given goals. The active and energetic young boy, eager to please the hospital, will manifest a high expectancy of improvement as a means of gaining favor. The reluctant patient, bent on eliciting rejection, will likely manifest a low expectancy of improvement as a means of defying anyone to reach or help him. Studies of expectancy of improvement (cf. Brady, Reznikoff, and Zeller, 1960; Friedman, 1963) are investigating another facet of clinical behavior, characterized by goal-directionality. A high or low expectancy for improvement is as need-motivated and goal-directed as insomnia, onanism, nail-biting, or any other clinical behavior.

THE MOTIVATED GOAL-DIRECTIONALITY
OF EXTREME CLINICAL BEHAVIORS

Our approach asserts that all extreme clinical behavior, traditionally included under such labels as schizophrenia, paranoia, severe psychopathology, psychosis, extreme deviance, psychiatric disease, or psychiatric illness, is conceptualized as motivated goal-directed psychological behavior. For purposes of understanding underlying motivational needs and goal-directionalities, the conventional psychiatric labels are not needed. The groundwork for such a position has been established in, for example, Haley's statement of the need to reconceptualize the motivational interpersonal behavior of persons labeled "schizophrenic": "Despite all that is said about difficulties in interpersonal relations, psychiatric literature does not offer a systematic way of describing the interpersonal behavior of the schizophrenic so as to differentiate that behavior from the normal person. The schizophrenic's internal processes are often described in terms of ego weakness, primitive logic or disassociative thinking, but his interpersonal behavior is usually presented in the form of anecdotes" (1963, p. 86).

BODILY PROCESSES AS CLINICAL BEHAVIOR

A construct approach to bodily events and processes. Clinical behavior is not restricted to external acts; it includes the entire realm of bodily processes, physical states and changes, aches and pains, internal and external bodily conditions (Mahrer, 1967e). The human body is open to understanding as psychological clinical behavior, using the motivational principles that apply to external clinical behavior. Motivational needs for hospitalization frequently utilize the human body for goal-directed purposes in the same manner as all other clinical behavior.

Our approach does not permit a reduction of psychological constructs to physiological constructs (cf. Burt, 1955; Rotter, 1954; Cantor and Cromwell, 1957; Kantor, 1953) any more than it allows physiological constructs to be reduced to psychological concepts. It insists on the accessibility of bodily phenomena to psychological description and understanding; as a neutral event (not basically physiological or chemical or psychological or whatever), the body is open to understanding and description from all relevant points of view (Kantor, 1942; Stevens, 1935). An ache in the head (or change in breathing rate or cramp in a muscle or numbness of an arm or occurrence of a pain, ulcer, baby, or tumor) is open to a full description by any system of constructs. In other words, "We contend that the designata of the mentalistic language are identical with . . . the designata of the neurophysiological language" (Feigl, 1953, p. 623). In accord with Aldrich's rejection of a dualistic division into functional and organic diagnostic explanations of bodily processes, our position is that bodily events have no intrinsic organic, psychic, chemical, neurological, or physiological nature. Just as bodily events are open to understanding in terms of physiological constructs, for example, our approach asserts that all bodily events are open to a full and complete understanding in terms of a system of psychological constructs.

The motivated goal-directionality of bodily clinical behavior. Bodily clinical behaviors are talismans of needs for hospitalization; i.e., bodily processes are behaviors directed toward specific hospital goals. The need to avoid sexuality may use a state of physical exhaustion, low back pains, or periodic blackouts as bodily means of avoiding a threatening sexual role. Other patients may use "little boy" bodily processes such as diarrhea and stomachaches to declare their immaturity and their unfitness for adult, male heterosexuality.

Patients who need hospitalization to escape punishment may develop all manner of bodily pains and conditions to avoid personal responsibility and punishment by placing the burden on his bodily condition. Thus, patients with guilt, who fear punishment and retribution from significant individuals or from society, may arrive at the hospital on stretchers, in a coma, in pools of blood, suffering from terrible pains, with all manner of bodily states and conditions. An "epileptic fit" may be a means of placing responsibility on a bodily condition when the patient mauls his younger brother or chokes his wife during an "attack"; the patient himself thereby avoids punishment.

Needs to deteriorate, to fall apart, are served by bodily clinical behavior involving a deterioration of bodily functionings, visceral collapse, a sheer falling apart of certain physical processes, all within the service of the powerful hospital-directed needs. Bodily clinical behavior may serve as means of asking for and securing structure, containment, and control of intolerable inner impulses and behaviors. Throat conditions, chills, trembling, serious muscle weakness, and varieties of joint pains may be direct overtures for the hospital to restrict and contain pressing inner rages and unexpressed aggressive outbursts. Other bodily behaviors aimed at the same goals include convulsions, traumatic physical insults, paralyses, headaches, and the like.

Motivational needs for withdrawal from internal impulses and behavioral tendencies may be instrumented through amnesic episodes and fugue states as the patient seeks total withdrawal in the hospital. In a bid for nurturant and dependent succor from the hospital, patients may use bodily clinical behavior to express a feckless inability to function; they turn mandate over to some external agent by means of dizziness, brain malfunctioning, the failure of vital body organs, total body collapse, incapacitating muscle and joint pains, and the like.

Bodily clinical behavior may be used to reach out for dependent concern and nurturing. For these motivational needs the patient is plagued with vague and mysterious complaints and ailments, hints at esoteric physical conditions and borderline bodily illnesses generally located deep within the body.

Psychological classification of bodily processes. The body has traditionally been classified and categorized on the basis of medical constructs. Our view holds that systems of psychological constructs are linked with reclassification and recategorization of internal and external bodily states, conditions, processes, and changes (Mahrer, 1962b,

1967b; Strauss, 1966). Neuroanatomical and biophysiological constructs have provided only one mode of understanding the body. Bodily processes, changes, manifestations, and behaviors may be systematically recategorized and reclassified on the basis of psychological constructs such as motivational needs.

Structural and functional bodily changes. Psychological clinical behavior occurs in the form of actual changes in bodily structure and function, both external and internal. Changes in the structure and function of the brain will accompany the development and growth of "tumors" in conjunction with needs to avoid pressing and overwhelming sexual tendencies. Strong needs to avoid external threat may be accompanied with changes in the structure and the function of the heart. Perceptible changes in muscle structure and function will manifest a need for total debilitation and decline. Actual changes in bodily structures and functions occur as behavioral changes in relation to motivational needs.

Complaint-value of bodily clinical behavior. The need for hospitalization may require that clinical behavior be directed toward the goal of an extended, prolonged hospitalization. For these purposes, little can rival the effectiveness of a deep-seated, mysterious bodily ache, pain, or "condition" which is not observable, but only accessible through the report of the patient. These pains are buried in the head, back, chest, legs, and so on. Nearly always, laboratory reports are equivocal. Such bodily clinical behavior is of high value because it is so potent and maneuverable by the motivational needs.

Some hospital-directed goals call for the patient placing himself in a position of power or control. For these purposes, a frightened insignificant little man can occupy the prominent position of interpreter-reporter on the current state of his bodily condition, thus placing him in the position of controlling the staff personnel. They are almost totally dependent upon him in determining the pain's nature, response to treatment, worsening or improvement.

It may be argued that a bodily "condition" offers the maximum potential for attracting concern, attention, and personal involvement, especially in a hospital situation, but also with regard to one's family and significant others. The concern and attention of a parent was most naturally elicited by means of bodily behavior. In our present culture, one's internal bodily state is a powerful site of sympathetic concern both from others and from oneself. Physical bodily pains effectively elicit concern and attention from a friend or parent, even from strangers, and especially from nurses, attendants, psychologists, and physicians in a hospital. Thus a motivational need for gaining the concern and attention of others easily includes a broad spectrum of bodily complaints.

The retreat into the body. A bodily state, condition, or pain may occasion desired retreat from a threatening external involvement. Thus, the patient who fears an external world which threatens to punish him catastrophically may turn this conflict inward and emerge with simple bodily malfunctionings such as excretory difficulties, urinary problems, loss of hearing, and the like. The body serves as a sanctuary or retreat from external conflict (Mahrer et al., 1966; Rickels, Downing, and Downing, 1966). The accomplishment of this retreat is another psychological goal of bodily clinical behavior.

Internal and external isomorphism. For some patients relationships with the external world are echoed within the body. A female patient's acrimonious feelings accompanying external sexual involvement will frequently be accompanied by internal bodily changes, for example, in the form of a chronic vaginal infection. If a patient recoils from a growing threat from the external world, his internal bodily processes may likewise face a growing internal threat, such as a tumor or a toxic state. The patient whose external clinical behaviors are frustrated attempts to secure attention and concern may maintain bodily states which demand the patient's own concern and care, as for example, in stomach ulcers. The rigid containing of pent-up aggression in the patient's external clinical life may be reflected in the internal bodily containment of feces, as in colitis. Internal bodily changes and responses to chemotherapeutic agents follow the same psychological principles as external behavioral changes and responses to external social-situational agents (Mahrer, Young, and Katz, 1960). Thus, it is consistent that patients with somatic complaints will demonstrate a heightened responsiveness and sensitivity in the related physiologic system (Malmo and Shagass, 1949). Both external and internal (bodily) behavioral changes follow the same psychological principles so that what is expressed externally is also being expressed internally. Internal bodily clinical behavior is isomorphic with external clinical behavior, and shares in the motivated directionality toward hospital goals.

Epilogue

The challenge remains one of understanding and treatment. Thus, the present chapter is a prologue to a system of personality classification for psychological change. Our focus of study remains on patients in hospitals; the understanding of such persons is to be taken as a specific application of a motivational theory of understanding other persons in general.

REFERENCES

Adler, R. A., and Bunn, D. Precipitating factors at a psychiatric emergency service. *Psychiat. Stud. and Projects,* 1963, **3**, 1–4.

Aldrich, C. K. The diagnostic process. *Lancet,* 1956. **76**, 59–64.

Alexander, F. *Psychosomatic medicine.* New York: Norton, 1950.

Alexander, F., and French, T. M. *Psychoanalytic therapy.* New York: Ronald, 1946.

Alexander, F., and French, T. M. *Studies in psychosomatic medicine.* New York: Ronald, 1948.

Anker, J. M. A note on the factor structure in the neuropsychiatric chronicity scale. *J. consult. Psychol.,* 1962, **26**, 198.

Barron, F. An ego-strength scale which predicts response to psychotherapy. *J. consult. Psychol.,* 1953, **17**, 327–33.

Barton, W. The future of the mental hospital: the portent of some current emphases. *Ment. Hosp.,* 1962, **13**, 368–69.

Bateson, G. The biosocial integration of behavior in the schizophrenic family. In N. W. Ackerman, F. L. Beatman, and S. N. Sherman (Eds.), *Exploring the base for family therapy.* New York: Family Service Ass. of America, 1961. Pp. 116–22.

Berkowitz, L. *Aggression: a social psychological analysis.* New York: McGraw-Hill, 1962.

Boverman, M. Some notes on the psychotherapy of delusional patients. *Psychiat.,* 1953, **16**, 141–52.

Brady, J. D., Reznikoff, M., and Zeller, W. W. The relationship of expectation of improvement to actual improvement of hospitalized psychiatric patients. *J. nerv. ment. Dis.,* 1960, **130**, 41–44.

Brenner, C., Friedman, A. P., and Carter, S. Psychological factors in the etiology and treatment of chronic headache. *Psychosom. Med.,* 1949, **11**, 1–26.

Brody, E. B., and Fishman, M. Therapeutic response and length of hospitalization of psychiatrically ill veterans. *A.M.A. Arch, gen. Psychiat.,* 1960, **2**, 174–81.

Bullard, D. M. Psychotherapy of paranoid patients. *Arch. gen. Psychiat.,* 1960, **2**, 137–41.

Burstein, B. Family dynamics, the sick role, and medical hospital admissions. *Fam. Process,* 965, **4**, 206–16.

Burt, C. *The subnormal mind.* London: Oxford University Press, 1955.

Buss, A. H. *The psychology of aggression.* New York: Wiley, 1961.

Cantor, G. N., and Cromwell, R. L. The principle of reductionism and mental deficiency. *Amer. J. ment. Def.,* 1957, **61**, 461–66.

Caudill, W. Perspectives on administration in psychiatric hospitals. *Admin. Sci. Quart.,* 1956, **1**, 155–70.

Caudill, W. *The psychiatric hospital as a small society.* Cambridge: Harvard University Press, 1958.

Caudill, W., Redlich, F. C., Gilmore, H. R., and Brody, E. B. Social structure and interaction processes on a psychiatric ward. *Amer. J. Orthopsychiat.*, 1952, **22**, 314–32.

Caudill, W., and Stainbrook, E. Some covert effects of communication difficulties in a psychiatric hospital. *Psychiat.*, 1954, 17, 27–43.

Clausen, J. A. *Sociology and the field of mental health.* New York: Russell Sage Foundation, 1956.

Cotts, G. K. A socially constructive type of psychopathologically determined activity. *Psychiat.*, 1954, **17**, 97–99.

Crandall, A., Zubin, J., Mettler, F. A., and Logan, N. D. The prognostic value of "mobility" during the first two years of hospitalization for mental disorder. *Psychiat. Quart.*, 1954, **28**, 185–210.

Darbonne, A. R. Crisis: a review of theory, practice and research. *Psychother.: Theor., Res. Pract.*, 1967, **4**, 49–56.

Davis, J. A., Freeman, H. E., and Simmons, O. G. Rehospitalization and performance levels among former mental patients. *Soc. Prob.*, 1957, **5**, 37–44.

Diener, R. G. Prediction of dependent behavior in specified situations from psychological tests. *Psychol. Rep.*, 1967, **20**, 103–8.

Diener, R. G., and Young, H. H. Factors contributing to requests for mental hygiene clinic treatment by veterans with psychiatric disorders. *J. clin. Psychol.*, 1961, **17**, 397–99.

Ellsworth, R. B., and Clayton, W. H. Measurement of improvement in "mental illness." *J. consult. Psychol.*, 1959, **23**, 15–20.

Ellsworth, R. B., and Stokes, H. A. Staff attitudes and patient release. *Psychiat. Stud. Projects*, 1963, No. 7, 1–6.

Feigl, H. The mind-body problem in the development of logical empiricism. In H. Feigl and M. Brodbeck (Eds.), *Readings in the philosophy of science*. New York: Appleton-Century-Crofts, 1953. Pp. 612–26.

Felix, R. H. Implications of goals of therapy. *Ment. Hosp.*, 1961, **12**, 10–15.

Fenichel, O. *The psychoanalytic theory of neurosis.* New York: W. W. Norton, 1945.

Fenichel, O. The concept of trauma in contemporary psychoanalytical theory. In Hanna Fenichel and D. Rappaport (Eds.), *The collected papers of Otto Fenichel: second series.* New York: W. W. Norton, 1954a. Pp. 49–69.

Fenichel, O. An infantile, preliminary phase of "defiance by lack of affect." In Hanna Fenichel and D. Rappaport (Eds.), *The collected papers of Otto Fenichel: first series.* New York: W. W. Norton, 1954b. Pp. 32–34.

Feshbach, S. The function of aggression and regulation of aggressive drive. *Psychol. Rev.*, 1964, **71**, 257–72.

Fingarette, H. Real guilt and neurotic guilt. *J. existent. Psychiat.*, 1962, **3**, 145–58.

Fingarette, H. *The self in transformation.* New York: Basic Books, 1963.

Fleischl, M. F. A note on the meaning of ideas of reference. *Amer. J. Psychother.*, 1958, **12**, 24–29.

Forer, B. A. The therapeutic value of crisis. *Psychol. Rep.*, 1963, **13**, 275–81.

Freeman, E. H., Kalis, B. L., and Harris, M. R. Assessing patient characteristics from psychotherapy interviews. *J. proj. Tech. and Pers. Assess.*, 1964, **28**, 413–24.

Freeman, H. E., and Simmons, O. G. Mental patients in the community: family settings and performance levels. *Amer. Sociol. Rev.*, 1958a, **23**, 147–54.

Freeman, H. E., and Simmons, O. G. Wives, mothers and the posthospital performance of mental patients. *Soc. Forces*, 1958b, **37**, 153-59.

Freeman, H. E., and Simmons, O. G. The social integration of former mental patients. *Int. J. soc. Psychiat.*, 1959, **4**, 264–71.

Freud, S. *The problem of anxiety.* New York: Psychoanalytic Quarterly Press and W. W. Norton, 1936.

Freud, S. Fragment of an analysis of a case of hysteria: prefatory remarks. In E. Jones (Ed.), *Collected papers.* Vol. 3. New York: Basic Books, 1955a. Pp. 13–21.

Freud, S. Analysis of a case of hysteria: I. the clinical picture. In E. Jones (Ed), *Collected papers.* Vol. 3. New York: Basic Books, 1955b. Pp. 22–77.

Friedman, A. P., von Storch, T. J. C., and Merritt, H. H. Migraine and tension headaches: clinical study of 2000 cases. *Neurol.*, 1954, **4**, 773–88.

Friedman, H. J. Patient-expectancy and symptom reduction. *Arch. gen. Psychiat.*, 1963, **8**, 61–67.

Goldberg, A., and Rubin, B. Recovery of patients during periods of supposed neglect. *Brit. J. med. Psychol.*, 1964, **37**, 266–72.

Gorham, D. R., and Overall, J. E. Dimensions of change in psychiatric symptomatology. *Dis. nerv. Syst.*, 1961, **22**, 1–5.

Greenblatt, M., Levinson, D., and Williams, R. H. *The patient and the mental hospital.* Glencoe, Ill.: Free Press, 1957.

Grinker, R. R., and Gottschalk, L. Headaches and muscular pains. *Psychosom. Med.*, 1949, **11**, 45–52.

Grinker, R. R., and Robbins, F. P. *Psychosomatic case book.* New York: Blakiston, 1954.

Haley, J. Control in psychotherapy with schizophrenics. *Arch. gen. Psychiat.*, 1961, **6**, 340–53.

Haley, J. *Strategies of psychotherapy.* New York: Grune & Stratton, 1963.

Harris, M. R., Kalis, B. L., and Freeman, E. H. Precipitating stress: an approach to brief psychotherapy. *Amer. J. Psychother.*, 1963, **17**, 465–71.

Harris, M. R., Kalis, B. L., and Freeman, E. H. An approach to short-term psychotherapy. *Mind*, 1964, **2**, 198–206.

Hiler, E. W. Wechsler-Bellevue intelligence as a predictor of confirmation in psychotherapy. *J. clin. Psychol.*, 1958, **14**, 192–94.

Holt, E. B. *The Freudian wish and its place in ethics.* New York: Holt, 1915.

Hurst, L. C. The unlocking of wards in mental hospitals. *Amer. J. Psychiat.*, 1957, **114**, 306–8.

Jackson, D. D. The question of family homeostasis. *Psychoanal. Quart.*, 1957, **31**, 79–90.

Jessor, R. Issues in the phenomenological approach to personality. *J. Indiv. Psychol.*, 1961, **17**, 27–38.

Kalis, B. L., Freeman, E. H., and Harris, M. R. Influences of previous help-seeking experiences on application for psychotherapy. *Ment. Hyg.*, 1964, **48**, 267–72.

Kalis, B. L., Harris, M. R., Prestwood, A. R., and Freeman, E. H. Precipitating stress as a focus in psychotherapy. *Arch. gen. Psychiat.*, 1961, **5**, 219–26.

Kanfer, F. H., and Saslow, G. Behavioral analysis. *Arch. gen. Psychiat.*, 1965, **12**, 529–38.

Kantor, J. R. Preface to interbehavioral psychology. *Psychol. Rec.*, 1942, **5**, 173–93.

Kantor, J. R. *The logic of modern science.* Bloomington, Ind.: Principia, 1953.

Leary, T., and Gill, M. The dimensions and a measure of the process of psychotherapy: a system for the analysis of content of clinical evaluations and patient-therapist interactions. In E. A. Rubenstein and M. B. Parloff (Eds.), *Research in psychotherapy.* Washington: Amer. Psychol. Ass., 1959. Pp. 62–95.

Levinson, D. The psychotherapist's contribution to the patient's treatment career. In H. H. Strupp and L. Luborsky (Eds.), *Research in psychotherapy.* Washington: Amer. Psychol. Ass., 1962. Pp. 13–24.

Lindemann, J. H., Fairweather, G. W., Stone, G. B., Smith, R. S., and London, I. T. The use of demographic characteristics in predicting length of neuropsychiatric hospital stay. *J. consult. Psychol.*, 1959, **23**, 85–89.

Lustman, S. The headache as an internalized rage reaction. *Psychiat.*, 1951, **14**, 433–38.

Mahrer, A. R. The psychodynamics of psychiatric hospitalization. *J. nerv. ment. Dis.*, 1962a, **135**, 354–60.

Mahrer, A. R. A preface to the mind-body problem. *Psychol. Rec.*, 1962b, **12**, 53–60.

Mahrer, A. R. Psychological symptoms as a function of psychiatric hospitalization. *Psychol. Rep.*, 1963, **13**, 266.

Mahrer, A. R. The goals of intensive psychotherapy. In A. R. Mahrer (Ed.), *The goals of psychotherapy.* New York: Appleton-Century-Crofts, 1967a. Pp. 162–79.

Mahrer, A. R. The goals and families of psychotherapy: summary. In A. R. Mahrer (Ed.), *The goals of psychotherapy*. New York: Appleton-Century-Crofts, 1967b. Pp. 259–69.

Mahrer, A. R. The goals and families of psychotherapy: discussion. In A. R. Mahrer (Ed.), *The goals of psychotherapy*. New York: Appleton-Century-Crofts, 1967c. Pp. 259–69.

Mahrer, A. R. The goals and families of psychotherapy: implications. In A. R. Mahrer (Ed.), *The goals of psychotherapy*. New York: Appleton-Century-Crofts, 1967d. Pp. 288–301.

Mahrer, A. R. The psychological problem inventory. *Psychol. Rep.*, 1967e, **20**, 711–14.

Mahrer, A. R., and Katz, G. Psychiatric symptoms at admission to hospitalization. *Psychiat. Dig.*, 1963, **24**, 23–30.

Mahrer, A. R., and Mason, D. J. Changes in number of self-reported symptoms during psychiatric hospitalization. *J. consult. Psychol.*, 1965, 265.

Mahrer, A. R., Mason, D. J., Kahn, E., and Projansky, M. High-complainers versus low-complainers: patterning of amount of self-reported symptomatology in psychiatric patients. *Psychol. Rep.*, 1966, **19**, 955–58.

Mahrer, A. R., Mason, D. J., Kahn, E., and Projansky, M. The non-Gaussian distribution of amount of symptomatology in psychiatric patients. *J. clin. Psychol.*, 1967, **23**, 319–21.

Mahrer, A. R., Mason, D. J., and Pomeroy, E. A psychological diagnostic system: outline of research-derived motivational categories for hospitalized psychiatric patients. *VA Newsltr. Res. Psychol.*, 1965, **7**, 23–24.

Mahrer, A. R., Mason, D. J., and Rosenshine, M. A headache syndrome in psychiatric patients: symptom clusters accompanying headaches. *J. clin. Psychol.*, 1966, **22**, 411–14.

Mahrer, A. R., Stewart, P., Horn, J., and Lind, D. Symptom patterns in psychiatric patients: a goal-directed approach to psychiatric symptomatology. *J. Psychol.*, 1967, **68**, 151–57.

Mahrer, A. R., and Young, H. H. The onset of stuttering. *J. gen. Psychol.*, 1962, **67**, 241–50.

Mahrer, A. R., Young, H. H., and Katz, G. Toward a psychological rationale for understanding the effects of anti-depressant medication. *Coop. Chemother. Stud. Psychiat.*, 1960, **5**, 131–34.

Malmo, R. B., and Shagass, C. Physiologic study of symptom mechanisms in psychiatric patients under stress. *Psychosom. Med.*, 1949, **11**, 25–29.

Malzberg, B. A. Statistical review of mental disorders in later life. In O. Kaplan (Ed.), *Mental disorders in later life*. Stanford: Stanford University Press, 1956.

Mechanic, D. Some factors in identifying and defining mental illness. *Ment. Hyg.*, 1962, **42**, 66–74.

Meyers, J. K., and Auld, F., Jr. Some variables related to outcome of psychotherapy. *J. clin. Psychol.*, 1955, **11**, 51–54.

Moran, L. J., Fairweather, G. W., and Morton, R. B. Some determinants of successful and unsuccessful adaptation to hospital treatment of tuberculosis. *J. consult. Psychol.*, 1956, **20**, 125–31.

Morgan, N. C., and Johnson, N. A. Failures in psychiatry: the chronic hospital patient. *Amer. J. Psychiat.*, 1957, **113**, 824–30.

Morimoto, F. R., Baker, T. S., and Greenblatt, M. Similarity of socializing interests as a factor in selection and rejection of psychiatric patients. *J. nerv. ment. Dis.*, 1954, **120**, 56–61.

Parker, S. A note on first admissions of the aged to mental institutions. *J. nerv. ment. Dis.*, 1958, **127**, 275–78.

Parsons, T. Illness and the role of the physician: a sociological perspective. *Amer. J. Orthopsychiat.*, 1951a, **21**, 452–60.

Parsons, T. *The social system.* Glencoe, Ill.; Free Press, 1951b.

Pascal, G. R., Swensen, C. H., Feldman, D. A., Cole, M. E., and Bayard, J. Prognostic criteria in the case histories of hospitalized mental patients. *J. consult. Psychol.*, 1953, **17**, 163–71.

Peterson, D. R. Predicting hospitalization of psychiatric outpatients. *J. abnorm. soc. Psychol.*, 1954, **49**, 260–65.

Pinderhughes, C. A., Goodglass, H., Mayo, C., Greenberg, R. M., and Friedman, H. L. A study of childhood origins of patients' ward relationships. *J. nerv. ment. Dis.*, 1966, **142**, 140–47.

Pomeroy, E., Mahrer, A. R., and Mason, D. J. An aggressive syndrome in hospitalized psychiatric patients. *Proc. 73d Amer. Psychol. Ass.*, 1965, 239–40.

Pratt, S., Giannitrapani, D., and Khanna, P.. Attitudes toward the mental hospital and selected population characteristics. *J. clin. Psychol.*, 1960, **16**, 214–18.

Rennie, T., Srole, L., Opler, M. K., and Langner, T. S. Urban life and mental health. *Amer. J. Psychiat.*, 1957, **113**, 831–37.

Rickels, K., Downing, R. W., and Downing, M. H. Personality differences between somatically and psychologically oriented neurotic patients. *J. nerv. ment. Dis.*, 1966, **142**, 10–18.

Rogers, L. S. Drop-out rates and results of psychotherapy in government aided mental hygiene clinics. *J. clin. Psychol.*, 1960, **16**, 89–92.

Rogler, L. H., and Hollingshead, A. B. *Trapped: families and schizophrenia.* New York: Wiley, 1965.

Rotter, J. B. *Social learning and clinical psychology.* Englewood Cliffs, N. J.: Prentice-Hall, 1954.

Rotter, J. B. The role of the situation in determining the direction of human behavior. In M. R. Jones (Ed.), *Nebraska Symposium on Motivation, 1955.* Lincoln: University of Nebraska Press, 1955. Pp. 245–68.

Rubenstein, E. A., and Lorr, M. A. Comparison of terminators and remainers in outpatient psychotherapy. *J. clin. Psychol.*, 1956, **12**, 345–49.

Schwartz, C. G., Schwartz, M. S., and Staunton, A. H. A study of need-fulfillment on a mental hospital ward. *Psychiat.*, 1951, **14**, 223-42.

Schwartz, M. S. Patient demands in a mental hospital context. *Psychiat.*, 1957, **20**, 249–61.

Shapiro, M. B. A method of measuring psychological changes specific to the individual psychiatric patient. *Brit. J. Med. Psychol.*, 1961, **35**, 151–55.

Speers, R. W., and Lansing, C. *Group therapy and childhood psychosis.* Chapel Hill: University of North Carolina, 1965.

Spiegel, J. P. Resolution of role conflict within the family. *Psychiat.*, 1957, **20**, 1–16.

Stevens, S. S. The operational definition of psychological concepts. *Psychol. Rev.*, 1935, **42**, 517–27.

Strauss, A., Schatzman, L., Bucher, R., Ehrlich, D., and Sabshin, M. *Psychiatric ideologies and institutions.* New York: Free Press, 1964.

Strauss, E. W. *Phenomenological psychology.* New York: Basic Books, 1966.

Szasz, T. S. Commitment of the mentally ill: "treatment" or social restraint? *J. nerv. ment. Dis.*, 1957, **125**, 293–307.

Szasz, T. S. *The myth of mental illness.* New York: Hoeber-Harper, 1961.

Tybring, G. B. A resource for the family complex. *Ment. Hosp.*, July 1962, 370–71.

Ullman, L. P. Selection of neuropsychiatric patients for group psychotherapy. *J. consult. Psychol.*, 1957, **21**, 277–80.

Wanklin, J. M., Fleming, D. F., Buck, C. W., and Hobbs, G. E. Factors influencing the rate of first admission to mental hospital. *J. nerv. ment. Dis.*, 1955, **121**, 103–16.

Weiss, E., and English, O. S. *Psychosomatic medicine.* 2d ed. Philadelphia and London: W. B. Saunders, 1949.

Whitmer, C. A., and Conover, C. G. A study of critical incidents in the hospitalization of the mentally ill. *Soc. Wk.*, 1959, **4**, 89–94.

Winder, A. E., and Hersko, M. The effect of social class on length and type of psychotherapy in a VA mental hygiene clinic. *J. clin. Psychol.*, 1955, **11**, 77–79.

Wolff, H. G. Life stress and bodily disease. In A. Weider (Ed.), *Contributions toward medical psychology.* Vol. 1. New York: Ronald, 1953. Pp. 315–67.

Wood, E. C., Rakusin, J. M., and Morse, E. Interpersonal aspects of psychiatric hospitalization. I. The admission. *Arch gen. Psychiat.*, 1960, **3**, 632–41.

Wood, E. C., Rakusin, J. M., and Morse, E. Interpersonal aspects of psychiatric hospitalization. II. Some correlations between the admission circumstances and the hospital treatment. *Arch. gen. Psychiat.*, 1962, **6**, 39–45.

Woodward, J. L. Changing ideas on mental illness and its treatment. In A. M. Rose (Ed.), *Mental health and mental disorder*. New York: Norton, 1955. Pp. 482–500.

9

MOTIVATIONAL THEORY: A SYSTEM OF PERSONALITY CLASSIFICATION

ALVIN R. MAHRER

The traditional psychiatric diagnostic system has had more than its share of criticism (cf. Ash, 1949; Foulds, 1955; King, 1954; Leary and Coffey, 1955; Rotter, 1954), so a new system of personality classification requires more than the echoing of criticism. The previous chapter laid the groundwork for a motivational theory different from the conceptions which underlie the standard psychiatric nomenclature. The present chapter proposes categories of motivational needs which constitute a personality classification for a single clinical population, viz., hospitalized psychological male patients. A specific set of classificational categories is applied to a specific clinical population as an example of a general principle, viz., that personality behavior may be meaningfully categorized and classified on the basis of motivational needs.

The psychiatric disease-illness model. Attempts to build a nomenclature often utilize items (e.g., symptoms or descriptive statements of pathology) taken from standard psychiatric textbooks or fabricated by clinicians committed to the rationale underlying the standard psychiatric system (Anker, 1962; Bryant et al., 1958; Guertin, 1962; Lorr, Klett, and McNair, 1963; O'Connor and Stefic, 1959; Trouton and Maxwell, 1956; Wittenborn, 1951). Unfortunately, these items are already quite heavily loaded with a standard psychiatric diagnostic orientation. For example: "In its construction, an attempt was made to design an instrument to measure traits which correspond as nearly as possible to the type of descriptive outline used by psychiatrists in examining their patients; consequently, the scale which was developed closely resembled a widely used form of the mental status examination" (Bryant et al., 1958, p. 167). Thus, when these items are allowed to regroup themselves (usually through clustering or factoring techniques), they naturally form limited variations on the same diagnostic categories from which they were originally extracted (cf. Bryant et al., 1958; Degan, 1952; Guertin, 1952; Lorr, O'Connor, and Stafford, 1957; Wittenborn, 1951, 1963). Such a procedure returns essentially to the very system from which it started.

A variation on the above approach utilizes ratings or judgments of psychiatric behavior. The psychiatric behaviors are then subjected to groupings, factorings, or clusterings. However, once again the items are heavily loaded, for they consist of *psychiatric* behavior. Furthermore, the emergent groupings are understood by traditional psychiatric nomenclature. Following such a procedure, Lorr and his co-workers, for example, have emerged with such classifications as manic excitement, paranoid projection, and melancholic agitation (Lorr, Jenkins, and O'Connor, 1955), concepts which are reminiscent of their psychiatric parentage.

A motivational theory approach begins instead with a set of personality motivations and needs, especially as these are descriptive of actual persons moving into the hospital situation. The personality conceptions underlying a motivational theory approach rejects any assumption of psychiatric diseases or illnesses. Our categories refer to psychological motivational needs rather than to types of mental illnesses, disorders, or diseases.

Formal criteria for classification constructs. Classification constructs should meet such formal criteria as logical relatedness, construct validity, clarity of meaning, minimum overlap, systematic interrelatedness, etc. Yet, as Reid points out (1957), the state of our knowledge is so loose and ambiguous that setting acceptably high standards of formalization and systematization for the categories will not necessarily improve the state of our knowledge nor the personality conceptions undergirding a system. Nevertheless, a motivational theory acknowledges formal systematic criteria as one important factor in assessing the adequacy of a system. On these formal criteria, the proposed motivational classification system is admittedly inadequate.

Sociological variables. Our approach makes no explicit attempt to incorporate sociological variables. Although current literature reflects the heightened tempo of sociological and social psychological studies of psychiatric hospitals, our approach recasts these variables into a psychological framework of motivational needs.

Single vs. multiple classification. In the psychiatric classificatory system, each category is a mental disorder. Seldom, if ever, is it expected that a person can be both "psychotic" and "psychoneurotic," both "manic depressive" and "paranoid schizophrenic." In an effort to circumvent such a constricted, single-disease, entity approach, Noyes and Kolb (1963) suggest a tripartite division into an etiological genetic component, a dynamic behavioral component, and a predictive clinical component. Our approach represents, perhaps, a further step away from single-diagnosis and toward "a conception of the psychiatric patient as characterized by a limited number of functionally independent processes which are reflected in observable symptomatology" (Overall, Gorham, and Shawver, 1961, p. 601). Within our system, each "process" refers to a motivational need, and there is no reason to expect that a person necessarily moves toward hospitalization under a single motivation. Instead, it is recoginzed that the process of moving toward hospitalization often reflects several major motivational needs.

Motivational categories, patients vs. nonpatients, neurosis vs. psychosis. All patients share one characteristic, viz., movement into the hospital. This directionality holds true whether the patient rushes in, wanders in, is forced in, or enters with any of a myriad of justifying "reasons." The complex act of actually coming to the hospital is the only distinction between those who are in the hospital and those who are not in the hospital. Motivational theory recognizes no other distinction between those who are in and those who are out except this single act.

Associated with movement toward the hospital are varying sets of motivations which comprise our system of classification. In no manner is it to be assumed that these motivations distinguish those in from those not in the hospital. In fact, our view would hold that these motivations are fully as characteristic of those out of the hospital as they are pertinent to those in the hospital. The difference lies not in the content or substance of the motivations, but in their leading to the critical act of movement toward the hospital.

Our thesis is that patients and nonpatients differ in clinical behavioral symptomatology only to the extent that patients will utilize a range of "hospital-directed" entry behavior; patients and nonpatients differ in underlying motivational needs only to the extent that a certain subsample of motivational needs is functionally linked to hospitalization; the major difference between these groups lies in the functional utilization of the hospital setting. Thus, our thesis is an extension of the historically recurrent theme, "namely, that the borderline between the nervous, normal and abnormal states is indistinct" (Brill, 1938, p. 177), without qualitative differences (Burt, 1955).

In terms of the proposed motivational needs for hospitalization and the goal-directionality of clinical behavior, the traditional qualitative distinction between neurosis and psychosis (cf. Maher, 1966) is not needed. Each of our motivational categories includes clinical behaviors which traditionally were included under neurosis or psychosis.

Treatment. It is beyond the scope of this chapter to discuss treatment modalities and programs associated with each motivational need category. Kanfer and Saslow have pointed out that "None of the currently used dimensions for diagnosis are directly related to methods of modification of a patient's behavior, attitudes, response patterns and interpersonal actions" (1965, p. 533). However, we hold as essential the requirement that a classification system provide explicit guides for treatment programming and methods, differentially associated with each category. Thus, each category refers to a motivational need for hospitalization, with the twin goals of understanding and treatment, in accord with the following propositions of our motivational theory: (1) The behavior of hospitalized psychological patients is a function of determining motivational needs. (2) The treatment of hospitalized psychological patients consists of a therapeutic resolution of the determining motivational needs.

Homogeneity vs. heterogeneity. In an examination of the psychiatric diagnostic system, King argues, "In the matter of composition, diagnostic categories are broad and heterogeneous, rather than restricted and homogeneous. Such a diversity of behavior is subsumed under diagnostic groups that one gets the impression, for example, that the difference between two schizophrenics can be as significant as the difference between a normal and a schizophrenic" (1954, p. 384). Although Zigler and Phillips (1961) seriously question homogeneity as a primary desideratum of a classificatory scheme, our aim is to propose a set of motivational categories whose contents (recent life histories and clinical behaviors) homogeneously reflect a single motivational need. In short, we accept the value of homogeneous categories.

Reliability. Zigler and Phillips define the reliability of diagnostic categories as follows: "Since the defining characteristic of most classes in psychiatric diagnosis is the occurrence of symptoms in particular combinations, the reliability of the system mirrors the specificity with which the various combinations of symptoms (syndromes) have been spelled out" (1961, p. 611). At the working level, any given clinical behavior or recent life history may be related to a *set* of motivational categories (Mahrer, Thorp, and Sternlicht, 1960). *Combinations* of clinical behaviors or precipitating histories should strengthen the linkages to one or more motivational categories (Mahrer and Young, 1961). Similar combinations of recent life histories and clinical behaviors should point toward similar motivational needs for hospitalization. In other words, our approach accepts the criterion of reliability.

Clinical behavior vs. etiology. Zigler and Phillips (1961) analyze underlying classificatory principles as organized primarily about either symptom manifestation or etiology. Of these two major principles, the authors argue that the future of classification lies in the careful use of the former. "What is needed at this time is a systematic empirical attack on the problem of mental disorders. Inherent in this problem is the employment of symptoms, broadly defined as meaningful and discernible behaviors, as a basis of a classificatory system" (p. 616). Recent notable attempts to search out other classification dimensions have begun with symptomatology (Eysenck, 1956; Lorr, Klett, and McNair, 1963; Overall, Gorham, and Shawver, 1961). Within the psychiatric system, the meaning of "symptom" derives out of the Kraepelinian search for symptomatic regularities to aid discovery of underlying, somatically based illnesses, sicknesses, and diseases; the etiological principle likewise refers to causal factors associated with the course of the illness, its onset, natural history, and development by stages, prodromal conditions, and the like. "The Kraepelinian system and portions of the 1952 APA classification emphasize etiological factors. They share the assumption that common etiological factors lead to similar symptoms and respond to similar treatment" (Kanfer and Saslow, 1965, p. 529).

Although our approach rejects the above medical-model meaning of "symptom" and "etiology," we presume that any given motivational need for hospitalization will be reflected both in identifiable clinical behaviors (cf. symptoms) and in identifiable recent life histories (cf. etiology). Within *these* meanings, we select *both* classificatory principles.

Motivational classification by clinical behavior and recent life history. The process of classification is one of describing the major motivational need(s) for hospitalization. To accomplish this, the previous chapter proposed two avenues which converge upon one or more motivational needs. Any given clinical behavior, especially a major presenting clinical behavior (cf. "symptom") contains a rich potential yield of motivational goal-directionality. In other words, any given clinical behavior points toward one or more motivational needs. A study of a patient's idiosyncratic clinical behaviors should theoretically establish linkages with one or more of the motivational categories.

Similarly, as proposed in the previous chapter, significant recent life histories also contain a vector or vectors which point toward one or more of our motivational categories. The final classification is established through a combination of these two avenues of data which converge on the major motivational needs for hospitalization in accord with

Kostlan's (1954) study of the rich yield from two sources of data: history and symptomatic clinical behavior.

Range of convenience. The standard psychiatric diagnostic system includes mental disorders and diseases with universal coverage, i.e., they may "attack" any and all persons. In contrast, our approach follows the late George Kelly's (1955) dictum that given personality theories and bodies of constructs may have somewhat different ranges of convenience, i.e., may cover different territories of prediction and usefulness. Accordingly, our specific categories refer and apply to (1) hospitalized psychological patients (rather than nonhospitalized groups), (2) males (rather than females), and (3) adults (rather than adolescents or children). A broader but weaker range of convenience includes that segment of the adult (both male and female) population which relates itself to "helping" resources such as social agencies, outpatient clinics, private practice, treatment centers, and the like. Confidence in and usefulness of the system would naturally reduce with each enlarged circle of potential range of convenience. Thus, it is clear that this is by no means a general cataloging of the motivational needs of all persons; it is strictly limited to those motivational needs which underlie the clinical functioning of our hospitalized, adult male "psychological" patients.

We may now turn to the system itself. The categories replace the mental diseases or disorders of the standard psychiatric nomenclature with sets of motivational needs for hospitalization (Mahrer, Mason, and Pomeroy, 1965). Each motivational need is defined and identified by its (1) characteristic clinical behaviors and (2) characteristic recent life histories. The clinical behaviors are motivated by the given need and are directed toward the given goals of hospitalization. They are the fruits of an intensive investigation of 322 actual male "psychiatric" adult patients admitted to a single hospital from 1958 to 1967. The recent life histories contain the emergence of the motivated need for hospitalization. They are also derived from the same patient pool. Each category represents an attempt to understand patients, not in terms of diseases, illnesses, or mental disorders, but in terms of deeply ingrained motivational needs, processes of reachings out, strivings, and goal-directed internal tendencies, all in relation to the broadly conceived hospital situation.

A PERSONALITY CLASSIFICATION SYSTEM OF MOTIVATIONAL NEEDS FOR HOSPITALIZATION

1. Avoidance of threat.
    a. Avoidance of sexual threat.

      b. Avoidance of the threat of loss of a significant figure.
      c. Avoidance of the threat of punishment.
      d. Avoidance of the threat of adulthood.
2. Punishment.
      a. Self-directed punishment.
      b. Externally directed punishment.
3. Acceptance of impulses.
4. Structure and control.
      a. Structure and control of primitive disintegration.
      b. Structure and control of aggressive impulses.
      c. Structure and control of sexual impulses.
5. Dependency.
      a. Nurturant dependency.
      b. Induced dependency.
      c. Instrumental dependency.
6. Identification.

Avoidance of Threat

For patients whose major need is to avoid psychological threat hospitalization is a means to reduce or otherwise avoid the threat. The hospital serves them as a sanctuary.

AVOIDANCE OF SEXUAL THREAT

Some of these patients are motivated to avoid, ward off, remove, or reduce a sexual threat which constitutes the dominant motif in their psychological worlds. The sexual threat may be localized internally in the form of rising behavioral tendencies, sexual drives, or overwhelming sexual needs. On the other hand, the sexual threat may appear in the form of external sexual figures and agents.

Hospitalization serves as a simple and direct means of avoiding the sexual threat. In addition, there are at least three expressions of the parent goal of avoiding the sexual threat: (1) sexual inadequacy, impotence, and incompetence; (2) childishness, immaturity, or infantilism; (3) "mental illness" or "mental disease."

If hospitalization is instrumental in avoiding the sexual threat, the patient's clinical state may change significantly following admission. The more the sexual threat is focused in a specific, concrete external agent, the greater is the likelihood that hospitalization will avoid the threat and result in clinical change.

Recent life histories

The following histories are characteristically associated with a need to avoid a sexual threat:

Increased sexual threat of a mother figure. The following are representative generators of a need to avoid the sexual threat of a mother figure: (1) A sexualized mother figure recently moved into the patient's household. (2) A sexualized mother figure is without a male partner. She is a capable, financially able woman who is currently making overtures for the patient's close assistance and companionship. (3) A sexualized mother figure is now alone in the world and the patient is experiencing pressures to care and provide for her. (4) The sexualized mother figure has divorced a number of men until the patient is currently the adult "man of the family." (5) After being without a male partner for many years, the sexualized mother figure marries and flaunts her sexual recrudescence to the patient. (6) The patient is a young man living at home in a sexual triangle with his mother figure and a father figure. (7) The patient is involved in direct sexual relationships with a mother figure.

Increased sexual threat of other female figures. The following themes are representative of one's engendering a need to avoid the sexual threat of other female figures: (1) The patient's daughter acts out sexually either toward the male patient or toward other men. (2) The patient is in close contact with a highly sexualized female. (3) The patient marries a woman with an adolescent daughter who constitutes a distinct sexual threat. (4) The wife is exerting increased pressures for the patient to be more virile, more aggressive, more heterosexual.

Sexual threat associated with loss or decline of the father figure. The following are representative precipitators of a need to avoid sexual threat associated with the loss or decline of a father figure: (1) Death has occurred recently to a father figure, bringing the (sexual) mother threateningly closer to the patient. (2) A formerly strong father figure is significantly declining with age or with debilitating or incapacitating physical illness. (3) The loss or decline of a father figure opens the way for the sexually threatening emergence of a powerful female (mother, aunt, older sister, etc.) who appropriates the power of the father figure.

Sexual threat of a male figure. The need to avoid sexual threat may be precipitated by a closer (sexual) involvement with other men. In addition to direct homosexual encounters, this need may be precipitated by the heterosexual acting out of a wife, sister, mother, daughter, or girl friend.

If the recent life history falls in the above categories, the major motivational need for hospitalization is to avoid an imminent sexual threat.

Clinical behaviors

The following clinical behaviors are motivated by the need to avoid sexual threat, and are directed toward the goal of avoiding the sexual threat by means of hospitalization.

Reduction of overwhelming sexuality. The following clinical behaviors are representative of those which avoid threatening sexuality by declaring that sexuality is overwhelming and out of control, or that internal sexual tendencies are highly threatening and must be escaped:

Sexual overpreoccupation, frightening erotic fantasies, extreme sexual anxiety, concerns with sexual deviateness, perversity and abnormality; episodic acting out of homosexuality and sexually deviate behaviors, sexual acting-out with children; intolerable sexual feelings; painful headaches encompassing the full head region, especially accompanied with a bursting feeling; excessive masturbation; panic-filled inner impulses to scream.

Avoiding a punitively threatening external world. The need to avoid sexual threat may utilize clinical behaviors which (1) indicate how threateningly punitive the external world has become; (2) manifest the patient's own sexuality beneath the verging external threat; and (3) aim toward avoiding the threatening external world by withdrawing into the hospital. Representative clinical behaviors include:

General feelings of threat from the external world; special and grandiose missions; fears of plots and conspiracies; feelings that others are talking about him, teasing him, rejecting him, excommunicating him, calling him "queer"; fears of punishment from others for his sexual thoughts or actions; vivid fantasies of being attacked as he falls asleep; fears that women will kill him, poison him, take his real property and psychic resources.

Avoidant withdrawal from the external world. Some clinical behaviors serve the need to avoid a sexual threat by moving the patient away from contact with the external world in general. The patient pulls into himself in an effort to avoid the (sexual) external world; hospitalization is an avoidant withdrawal. The following clinical behaviors are representative:

Depression; melancholy aloneness, generalized withdrawal, feelings of hopelessness; hermit-like or monastic existence; depressed suicidal gestures; depersonalization; overideational preoccupations such as excessive reading or writing.

Avoidance through impotence, inadequacy, and immature incompetence. The goal of these behaviors is to avoid the sexual threat by becoming unsexual, inadequate, immaturely presexual, physically incompetent, dependently nonsexual, somatically an impotent little boy. The following clinical behaviors are representative:

Generalized bodily weaknesses, overall physical exhaustion and physical decline; "paralysis" from waist down; lack of strength in specific body parts; generalized lack of energy; "little boy" physical ailments such as diarrhea or stomachaches; cessation of sexual activity; sudden, acute blackouts; confused thinking, inability to express himself, loose thinking, hearing loss, confusion and other evidences of inadequate intellectual functioning; reduced vocational competence (e.g., bankruptcy); increasing dependency on welfare and care-providing external figures and agencies.

Clinical behaviors in the above categories serve to implement the motivational need to avoid sexual threat by means of hospitalization.

AVOIDANCE OF THE THREAT OF LOSS OF A SIGNIFICANT FIGURE

These patients are motivated toward hospitalization as a means of avoiding, postponing, or forestalling the loss of a significant figure. Generally, the figure is a female who is threatening to leave the patient.

The clinical behavior is aimed toward bringing the "sick" state to the attention of this figure in order to avoid her loss. The major determinant of change in the patient's condition is the nature of the response by the significant other figure.

Recent life histories

The characteristic recent life history includes a bond to a parental figure who is threatening to disrupt the relationship. The need to avoid the threatened loss of the significant (female) figure is precipitated by such representative themes as the following: (1) The dependency-providing wife is threatening to leave or divorce the patient. (2) A parental figure (e.g., father, mother, older sister) who has been housing and caring for the patient is now threatening to leave him, evict him, marry, or seek other attachments.

Clinical behaviors

The goal of the clinical behaviors is to avoid the threat of loss of the significant figure by forcing a return of concern and care. The clinical behaviors are accompanied by feelings of frustration, anger, and rejection. Thus, the patient's clinical condition reflects both a passive dependency upon the abandoning figure and also anger at the threatened loss. The following clinical behaviors are representative:

Depression. The depression ranges from hopelessness and abject despair (e.g., suicide attempts) to depressed hostility and aggression (e.g., threats to kill public officials), all directed to the attention of the significant figure.

Dependency. Clinical behaviors of helpless dependency (e.g., chronic alcoholism) indicate the patient's incapacity to cope or fend for himself. These are overtures aimed in the direction of the significant figure.

AVOIDANCE OF THE THREAT OF PUNISHMENT

The patient is motivated toward hospitalization as a means of avoiding the threat of punishment. Punishment is imminent from society, from the family, from himself. The threat of punishment is reduced or avoided by indicating to society, his family, or himself that he is already suffering, and that the responsible element is his personality, his deep-seated conflicts, his "mental illness."

The critical determinant of change is the degree to which hospitalization is effective in avoiding or reducing the threat of punishment. Paradoxically, if hospitalization is effective in reducing the threat of punishment, a full-blown "clinical condition" may be held in readiness for use whenever the patient is again faced with an imminent threat of punishment.

Recent life histories

The motivational need to avoid a threatened punishment occurs along the following representative pathways:

Societal punishment. The patient has acted out against society and is under the threat of societal punishment. These acts range from those which are distinctly illegal (e.g., murder, pedophilia, writing bad checks, embezzling) to those extralegal gestures and activities which nevertheless threaten societal punishment.

Impulsive intolerable acts. Some acts are of a much more personal nature. They include highly impulsive actings out, catastrophically intolerable to the patient and bringing severe punishment. These acts include, for example: attempted rape; a homosexual outburst; an explosive, destructive physical rampage; preoccupation with thoughts of killing one's wife; sexual molesting of children; a highly impulsive attempt to choke a fellow worker; an act of poor judgment which brought the family business to near ruin. In each case, the person is now under a motivational need to avoid the threat of punishment.

Clinical behaviors

The following clinical behaviors serve to achieve the goal of avoiding the threatening punishment:

Anxiety and fear. Anxiety and fear indicate that the patient is undergoing internal punishment. The full brunt of the external punishment is avoided by partial inner experiencing of punishment. The clinical behaviors include the classically wide range of expressions of anxiety and fear.

Depression. The full brunt of external punishment is avoided by experiencing a significant measure of inner-directed depression. The patient withdraws into himself in a state of self-punishment, while the depressed state itself serves to ward off a full measure of external punishment.

Distanced responsible "condition." These clinical behaviors present a pathological condition to justify the actions leading to the threatened punishment. While the clinical behaviors indicate a serious pathological state, the patient himself feels detached from "his condition." He is relatively free of agony, pain or distress, although he presents, indicates, or describes an agonizing, painful, or distressing "condition." Representative clinical behaviors include:

Arriving on a stretcher, in a coma, in an amnesic, fugue, or dissociative state; describing—but not manifesting or demonstrating—all manner of signs and "symptoms" of psychiatric-medical-neurological illnesses and diseases (usually with a responsibility denying plea of "finding out why I did it"); sexual or aggressive acts carried out while the patient was under the influence of "epileptoid fits or seizures," alcohol, drugs, amnesias, dissociations, fugues, or transient "psychotic" states or blackouts.

AVOIDANCE OF THE THREAT OF ADULTHOOD

Adulthood is a state of relative maturity and responsibility generally reflected in a commitment to a vocation, achievement of adult heterosexuality, the abandonment of a child's relation to parental figures. The motivational need for hospitalization is to avoid the threat attendant either upon success or failure in achieving the general state of adulthood.

The patient needs a clinical state to justify avoidance of adulthood. Seldom is the threat manifested by a concrete, identifiable external figure or situation.

Recent life histories

The groundwork of recent life histories lies in primitively close early-life bonds with a father figure with problems of his own in the area of adulthood. Both components are required, viz., a father figure with conflicts about his own adulthood, and an especially close bond between the patient and the primitive father figure during early childhood. For example, during the patient's early childhood years the father figure may be involved in dependency conflicts, competition with his own father, rivalry with his older brother, adolescent struggles or fears of assuming an adult heterosexual role. The son's especially close primitive bonds with the father derive from the son's role as either the antagonist or protagonist of the father's conflicts about his own adulthood.

Death or decline of the father figure. Death or decline of the father figure places on the patient the new responsibility of head of the family, the "provider" for the mother. Or, with increasing age or physical decline, the competitive father figure is in gross deterioration. Or, father figures are absent early in the patient's life, setting the stage for serious threat when the patient is later faced with his own adult manhood. Or, the patient is in a new protective, paternal, adequate role in relation to the declining father.

Imminent success. The patient experiences the threat of imminent success in direct or indirect competition with the father figure. For example: the patient has risen past the father's level of achievement and is confronted with entering graduate school or accepting an extremely responsible position; the patient can no longer ward off marriage or sexual adulthood; the patient and his father figure have been in direct (sexual-physical-vocational) competition and the tide is turning in favor of the patient.

If the precipitating themes run along the above channels, the need for hospitalization is to avoid the threat of adulthood.

Clinical behaviors

The following clinical behaviors mark retreat from adulthood and are motivated toward avoiding the attendant threat:

Anxiety. Heightened anxiety proclaims fear of success or failure while avoiding the threat by means of hospitalization. These behaviors include: sleep difficulties; floor pacing; generalized agitation and shakiness; vague, global fears of people in general.

Fear of a threatening external world. The lost, deteriorated, or overcome father figure is replaced by a highly threatening external world (cf. a "paranoid projection"). The patient thus wards off adult manhood by recreating the symbolic external powerful agent. Complete withdrawal from this external threat is found in blackouts, fugue states, and amnesias.

Incapacitating depression. Depressive clinical behaviors incapacitate the patient and thereby keep him from the threatening state of adult achievement, success, and competence. These behaviors include: sudden depressed withdrawals from an imminently successful business; inability to make decisions; inability to work; sudden loss of confidence; fears of leaving a room, home, or immediate neighborhood; sudden withdrawal from people; suicidal thoughts (e.g., of driving off the road).

Guilt-ridden sexuality. Some behaviors are directed toward avoiding adulthood while expressing accompanying feelings of guilt-ridden sexuality. Representative behaviors include: masturbatory guilt; anxiety-laden sexual fantasies and preoccupations; sexually dominated excursions to houses of prostitution, "border" towns, or other countries; precipitous marriages; vasectomies, sterility; excessive masturbation which leaves the patient sexually incapable, ennervated, and temporarily less anxiety-ridden; body chills from the waist down, accidents to groin, knee, leg, and foot.

Punishment

The major motivation for hospitalization can be the experiencing of punishment, aggression, and hostility. Being hospitalized is an aggressive act bringing punishment onto oneself or others.

SELF-DIRECTED PUNISHMENT

The motivational need for hospitalization can be to punish oneself, to hurt, to feel painfully alone and rejected, to suffer, to experience pain. These patients seek a hospital situation for the experiencing of punitive self-torment. Sheer hospitalization may be sufficient to insure self-punishment. Often the patient uses the hospital as a setting for banishment, utter rejection, and punitive withdrawal; he feels ousted by family and society in an agony of self-directed punishment. Hospitalization is part of a depressed withdrawal from life, a self-punitive withdrawal into one's self.

These patients may induce hospital personnel to punish them, to reject them, to take away privileges, to restrict or isolate them, to dislike them, to punish them with aggressively tinged psychiatric diagnosis, to subject them to punitive medical "treatment" such as brain surgery and electric shock. The motivational need includes self-imposed misery, punitive self-beating, and self-flagellation. These patients are skilled at inducing other patients to reject them, to isolate them, to treat them as a ward goat, outcast, hated villain, or bully.

The meaningful psychological world shrinks away from the extra-hospital environment so that the patient is beyond the reach of changes in the external world. Changes in the clinical condition are largely a function of what happens within oneself and the immediate hospital environment.

Recent life histories

Recent life histories typically fall along three representative lines:

Loss of punitive figure. A major life relationship has been with a strong, punitively disciplining parental figure. This relationship is so central in the patient's life that dissolution of the relationship (e.g., through death of the dictatorial figure) precipitates a motivational need for a surrogate punitive agent.

Guilt-ridden actions. The patient carried out a singular, impulsive, totally unacceptable act or wish. For example, in stark opposition to his usual mode of behavior, the patient suddenly attacked his wife; secretly gambled away all his savings; tried to rape his older sister; nearly killed a neighbor. The need is to undergo self-imposed punishment for harboring and acting upon these intolerable wishes.

With some patients, the guilt-ridden behaviors may be ongoing for many years (e.g., a marriage marked by incest, sexual perversity or threatening sexual acting out), with the guilt occurring after completion of the action (e.g., divorce).

Generalized failure. A lifelong pursuit of highly valued capability, achievement, and success culminates in inescapable signs of failure—lack of productivity, being passed by, old age, etc.

For those whose recent life histories fall along the above lines, the motivational need for hospitalization is to experience self-imposed, self-directed punishment, suffering and pain.

Clinical behaviors

The following clinical behaviors are means of eliciting and experiencing self-directed punishment:

Guilt, depression, anxiety. The patient undergoes self-directed punishment by means of guilt, depression, and anxiety. Surrounding feelings are of misery, self-abnegation, melancholy, hopelessness, lack of worth, despair. Self-directed punishment is attained through loss of jobs, a sinking into ignominious vocations, or bankruptcy. An alternative route includes the pursuit of expiation through a sudden religious commitment, a total "giving" of oneself to religion, as if driven by guilt, depression, or anxiety.

Antagonistic superiority. The patient manifests obnoxious and antagonistic superiority in a manner which elicits the needed punishment from others. The air of superiority is generally coupled with efforts after intellectualization, grand schemes, high-flown life philosophies, hollow recountings of abilities and accomplishments. These behaviors only superficially ward off the underlying generalized failure while inducing punishment from others.

Patients' clinical behaviors of the above kinds are motivated toward bringing about self-directed punishment within the context of hospitalization.

EXTERNALLY DIRECTED PUNISHMENT

Hospitalization serves some as a passive means of punishing some (parental) agent. The patient is punishing (parental) figures who have mistreated him and who will suffer because he has fallen into such a miserable state. The figures include parents, siblings, spouse, hospital, community, anyone willing to assume the role of concerned parental figure. The patient aims to punish by being beyond help, unable to work, absent from the family, agonizingly unhappy, chronically unreachable, as rejecting of them as they have been of him.

For some patients the hospital is the weapon against the external parental figure. For others, the hospital itself is the bad parent, and the patient proves the hospital has failed to provide adequately, failed to help him, failed to satisfy his demands, failed to make him feel better.

Since the unimproved, recalcitrant, resistant clinical state is the major weapon, significant "improvement" is unlikely, especially if an external target is unresponsive or unavailable.

Recent life histories

This motivational need for hospitalization is not associated with characteristic recent life histories. Instead, it seems to arise early in life and to occur as a more or less consistent motivational need throughout the patient's life. For example, the rejecting aura of illegitimacy or parental desertion may lay the groundwork for a lifelong need to punish subsequent parental figures. Since patterns of punishing parental figures by passive means seem to be laid down early, hospitalization becomes merely another avenue toward the lifelong goal. Both recent and early life histories characteristically reflect behavioral patterns of punishing parental figures.

Clinical behaviors

The following behaviors serve as means of punishing an external agent-figure through the passive avenue of hospitalization:

Vagueness and subjectivity. The clinical picture is free of directly observable clinical behaviors, Instead, the patient himself vaguely and subjectively reports some problem or condition with reference to his thoughts, his feelings, his general state, his internal constitutional-physical condition, etc. Thus, the patient tells others about his homicidal or suicidal thoughts, but does not act them out. In extremes, the vagueness and subjectivity may take the form of a general loss of reality contact. These vague and subjective conditions and complaints are aimed punitively at the external figure.

Tantrum states. The patient punishes the external figure by falling into severe tantrums manifested by states describable as: "becoming psychotic," "losing control," "going to pieces," "falling apart," etc. The existence of the externally directed punitive component is shown in the typically direct link between these states and increased "pressure" or "stress" from the external parental agent. The tantrum may be somatically internalized as sharp abdominal pains, constipation, and diarrhea; these manifest angrily frustrated dependency needs, and are again means of punishing some external parental figure.

Passive-aggressive interpersonal relations. There is a punitive component to the patient's passive-aggressive relationships with parental agents. These include: nagging and badgering behavior; complaints of being rejected, mistreated; competing with his wife for the female role; passive-aggressively demanding care and attention.

To the extent that the clinical behaviors fall in the above categories, the need for hospitalization is to punish an external agent.

Acceptance of Impulses

These patients are in a state of flux, coping with overwhelming behavioral impulses which are new, alien, and frightening. The need for hospitalization is to seek a safe accepting atmosphere in which to express the pressing impulses, a situation in which it is all right to be radically different. These patients are motivated to act, feel, and express themselves without fear of recrimination or retaliation. Their need is for acceptance of their impulses.

A critical determinant of change is the degree of genuine acceptance offered by the hospital. The patient's psychological world is typically reduced to the hospital interactions, with heightened sensitivity to the hospital's accepting or unaccepting atmosphere. The uncertain and fluctuating reaction of the patient to his own emerging, changing impulses is reflected in the need for unconditional acceptance by the hospital.

Recent life histories

The recent life history is characterized by a traumatic upsurge of powerful behavioral impulses. For example, from early childhood a patient's life was inextricably intertwined with his father; when the father died, he required more than anything some accepting atmosphere in which to release his catastrophic anguish. Another patient lost his wife, unborn child, and his three children in an airplane crash, leading to a motivational need for a safe atmosphere for release of a massive collapse. A truck accident reduced a third patient to a mere torso and one arm; the immediate motivational need was for a safe atmosphere for acceptance of the ensuing impulses.

Clinical behaviors

The behaviors of such patients are characterized by crises, acuteness, extreme compellingness, and total involvement. They also radiate a devastating plea for external acceptance. Representative clinical behaviors include: profound weeping; retreat into a religiously oriented world; complete infantile regression; living in an idiosyncratic, delusional world with a deceased parent, spouse, or child; silent withdrawal into oneself; profound deterioration and collapse.

Such clinical behaviors indicate a need for the hospital as a safe, accepting atmosphere.

Structure and Control

The major motivational need is for structure and control of a pressing, internal behavioral tendency. The patient feels a pronounced impetus to act or behave in ways so threatening that the only means of coping is to call upon external sources of structure and control.

STRUCTURE AND CONTROL OF PRIMITIVE DISINTEGRATION

These patients are under the impetus of a complete and total disintegrative breakdown. Collapse of the total psychological world seems imminent, frequently accompanied by the outpouring of catastrophically disorganizing material. The need is for the hospital to represent basic security, to hold the patient together, to contain the crumbling process, to provide a stable basic structure and control. The hospital offers an anchor to solid reality.

The clinical state may change significantly if the patient receives the needed structure and control. In fact, this need for hospitalization may be so effectively implemented by sheer hospitalization that the patient's motivational need is only apparent near the time of discharge.

Recent life histories

The characteristic recent life theme is the abrupt loss of those segments of the patient's life which provided basic structure and stable control. In order to maintain psychological functioning, these patients require a certain degree of external anchorings to primitive structure and control. The following are representative changes which release tendencies toward primitive disintegration, collapse, and disorganization: sudden suicide of a figure (e.g., parent, friend, relative, sibling) who, since childhood, had represented basic structure and control for the patient; death of the oldest daughter, forced marriage of the younger, terminal hospitalization of his father, and divorce by the wife, in a patient who required the structure and control of an intact family; disruption of a long-term, highly stable life and family status by his children reaching young adulthood and the threat of family disintegration associated with their leaving; divorce from the wife and death of the father, the two figures who constituted an external stable reality link. To the extent that there has been a recent and sudden loss of these structuring life segments, the patient's need is for external structure and control.

Clinical behaviors

The following clinical behaviors indicate the verging disintegrative outpouring of catastrophic material and serve to elicit externally imposed structure and control. They are motivated toward the goal of gaining structure and control of primitive disintegration.

Structureless external world. Some behaviors make manifest an external world without basic order—a frighteningly capricious and unpredictable external reality. These behaviors include: terror of sudden catastrophe; sudden unpredictable delusions and hallucinations; sudden depression, loss of ambition, inability to work.

Loss of body integrity. These behaviors indicate that the body is becoming disorganized and losing control: absence of feeling throughout the body; loss of power in the limbs or throughout the entire body; chills or shaking; tightening of the throat; pounding sensations in the head, severe headaches, memory lapses, loss of train of thought.

STRUCTURE AND CONTROL OF AGGRESSIVE IMPULSES

The motivated goal is to achieve hospitalization as a means of structuring and controlling internal aggressive tendencies. These patients are coping with pressing aggressive behavioral impulses by seeking external control in the hospital. Such control prevents the acting out of aggressive behavioral tendencies either inwardly or externally.

The sheer presence of the hospital commonly provides the necessary structure and control, so that significant change may occur almost immediately after admission.

Recent life histories

The following kinds of recent life changes may be noted:

Aggression attendant to a given motivational need. Life changes tend to elicit behavioral expression of a motivational need which is highly intolerable to the patient, and which is therefore surrounded by aggressive feelings. For example, a wife's adulterous activities may touch off a patient's homosexuality—with accompanying feelings of violent aggression. Or, precipitating circumstances encourage the patient toward a dependent state, with a release of long-term aggressive feelings associated with his own dependency needs (e.g., a patient with a long-term history of rejection finally marries a woman with children, surrounding himself with a potential dependency-providing situation). Or, a wife becomes hopelessly alcoholic, forcing the patient toward providing strength and independence—an intolerable state accompanied with feelings of aggression.

Aggression directed toward a figure responsible for a loss. These represent some loss, releasing aggression toward the figure perceived as responsible: threatened or actual loss of a wife (mother, grandparents) upon whom the patient has been dependent releases aggression toward that figure; decline or death of the father figure releases rage hidden until then by an apparent identification (father and son had similar given names, vocations, life patterns, etc.); inability of a wife to conceive children may release contained aggression toward females; loss or failure of a business may release aggression toward the figure seen as responsible for the loss.

Aggression carried out by other figures. Outbreak of aggression in other figures induces the patient to seek control of his own aggressive tendencies. Generally, the aggressive outbreak is directed toward the patient himself. These events are representative: the patient is treated brutally and mercilessly by a business partner; the wife tries to kill her sister in the presence of the patient; a stepfather sends the patient vindictive and highly deprecatory letters; an adolescent son openly attacks the father.

Aggression carried out by the patient. The beginnings of the patient's own aggressiveness lead him to require control of a deeper rage.

Representative beginnings include: screaming at a supervisor in front of a number of co-workers; a sudden attempt at choking a pregnant wife; a highly atypical show of aggressive defiance toward the dominant older brother; becoming inflamed at the father and knocking him down.

Clinical behaviors

Uncontained aggression. Clinical behaviors manifest the beginnings of uncontained aggressive behavior and serve as overtures for imposed control. Representative behaviors include: attempting to kill oneself with carbon monoxide, slashing the wrists, shooting oneself; pressing suicidal ideation; turbulent impulses to kill another person; self-destructive "accidents" such as mashing the hands, slamming one's automobile into other cars, or falling down stairs; explosive aggressive outbursts such as tearing the house apart, beating up several people, throwing objects at windows or television sets, public nudity, breaking store windows, or dashing in front of cars; sensing aggression from the external world, such as terrors of being "hexed," or a conviction that others are plotting one's murder.

Physically contained aggression. Physical-somatic states indicate the containment of internal aggressive behaviors and the motivational need for further external control. These include: headaches; chills, bodily tremors and tremblings, numbness and tingling in extremities; fits, seizures, and convulsions; nightmares; paralyses of the limbs; incapacitating muscle weaknesses; vomiting, nausea, and diarrhea.

Distancing from aggressive tendencies. In seeking control and structure, some clinical behaviors are means of denying, avoiding, and generally distancing oneself from his own aggressive behavioral tendencies. Representative behaviors include: blackouts, fugue states, dissociative episodes, fainting spells, amnesias, and the like. The need to seek control is indicated by the placing of mandate in the hands of others; thus, these patients often are brought to the hospital by other figures such as a wife, policeman, hospital attendant, or friend.

STRUCTURE AND CONTROL OF SEXUAL IMPULSES

The motivational need for hospitalization is to secure external control of sexual impulses. Sexual behavioral tendencies give rise to a fear of uncontrollable acting out and verging collapse under increasing sexual pressures. Recent life histories document the increasing expression of sexuality, and clinical behaviors are motivated toward the goal of acquiring structure and control through hospitalization.

Internal sexual tendencies often are too deeply rooted to be affected by hospital resources for structure and control. It is as if the hospital can provide only the situational arena for the playing out of the patient's conflict between internal sexual behavioral tendencies and elements of structure and control.

Recent life histories

The patient's own actions are not directly instrumental in "sexualizing" the situation. Instead, an external figure exerts a disruptive influence on the structure and control of sexual tendencies. The following life changes are representative:

(1) After many years of being divorced, the patient's father rather suddenly remarries, disrupting the patient's own formerly controlled sexual tendencies. Or, an adult patient's mother quickly remarries following the recent death of the father. Or, after an on-and-off relationship with the mother figure during the early years, followed by periods of rare contact as an adult, the patient has an intense (and sexually arousing) involvement with the mother figure. (2) The patient undergoes a surgical operation in the groin, culminating in disruption of structure and control over the sexual impulses. (3) The patient has maintained a safe identification with the father figure (manifested in similar lines of work, similar interests in cooking or music, etc.), but this is dramatically changed (e.g., through death of the father figure or an explosive breaking of a business partnership), leaving the patient in a precarious new sexual environment (e.g., living alone with mother). (4) Following a "father absent" childhood and close involvement with the mother, patient marries and abruptly divorces a sexually overwhelming woman, leaving him in a threateningly "open" sexual state. The general theme is an extended adult period of essentially "nonsexual" relations, followed by involvement with a highly sexually oriented woman, releasing uncontained sexual impulses.

Frequently, the above precipitating themes release threatening and panic-ridden homosexual impulses intermingled with heterosexual impulses, all requiring external structure and control.

Clinical behaviors

The clinical behaviors reflect the pressure of sexual impulses and are motivated toward obtaining added structure and control. Representative behaviors include: homosexual panic, impulsive incestuous involvements, overwhelming sexual preoccupation, shaking and trembling, sexual exhibitionism, tension and perspiration; shoulder and back pains; head complaints such as headaches, buzzing and ringing in the ears, tightening of the throat, numbness, shooting head pains, facial pains and tics; fear of blackouts, phobia of heart attacks; outbursts of bizarre talk about God, religion; alcoholism.

Dependency

The major motivational need is for dependency, with the hospital serving as a potential source of dependency gratification.

NURTURANT DEPENDENCY

The motivational need is for the hospital to serve as a nurturant parental agent. The hospital is the direct provider of dependency. Nurturant dependency includes the following components:

Total dependent care. The need is to be taken care of, to be totally unable to function, unable to assume minimal responsibility, to be a helpless ward or burden.

Complaining dependency. The need is to establish a dependent relationship wherein the patient may complain and protest. In relationship to the hospital, the patient is motivated to be an unhappy child, to be mistreated and maltreated, to be insufficiently cared for, to be demanding, whining, nagging, protesting, and complaining. He needs to feel rejected and to place the hospital in the role of the parent whom the patient judges as helping or failing to help him.

Secure dependency. The patient needs the kind of nurturant dependency which provides a basic sense of security, a primitive sense of needed belongingness, a home. This is the basic security of the comforted child.

Nurturant guidance. The patient's need is to receive parental direction and guidance from the hospital. The patient is in the role of the child who looks to the parent-hospital for help, for kindly direction, for loving and concerned advice and guidance.

Parental rewards and punishments. The major need is to establish a child-parent relationship wherein the hospital praises the patient for his efforts, accomplishments, and achievements; the hospital rewards the patient for trying, for becoming a responsible person, for being a "good boy," for doing his chores, for earning the reward of parental approval and favor. Similarly, the hospital is to disapprove, criticize, withhold approval and praise, remonstrate and punish in the manner of a parent.

Magical dependency. The hospital is placed in the role of the magical provider, the overly idealized resource with special powers to restore the patient, to turn him into a man, to give him the will to live.

A major determinant of clinical change is the extent to which the patient and the hospital are able to effect the needed nurturant dependent relationship. Often, the need calls for a long-term, self-perpetuating relationship manifested by frequent readmissions, long-term hospitalizations, and custodial relationships. Within the hospital setting, changes frequently are from one type of nurturant dependency to another as the patient and the hospital work out a mutually need-satisfying relationship.

Recent life histories

The dominant theme is loss of a dependency-providing parental agent. For some patients, the chronic life theme may include a series of losses of dependency-providing parental agents alternating with the establishment of new parental figures. Other patients may have been preserved in such a relationship only to face a recent loss of the dependency-providing parental figures. The following recent histories are representative of the dominant theme:

(1) The dependency-providing mother figure died, became ill, or aged to the point of having to relinquish her accustomed role. (2) The patient, even as an adult, was held in a dependency-providing relationship with his family, but recently the parents died, separated, or divorced, or became debilitated. (3) The patient was maintained in a dependency-providing job for many years (e.g., a business partnership with his father and older brother, or a position in an established institution), but the patient was recently retired, lost his job, the business failed, etc. (4) A dependency-providing wife divorced the patient, became ill or unable to provide, began demanding another kind of relationship, offered her dependent resources to others, etc. (5) There is a loss of the surrogate-figure who early assumed the role of dependency-provider (e.g., adopted parents, a stepfather, grandparents, or others who raised the patient since childhood). Or, since childhood, father assumed the parental role when mother went to mental hospitals, and father recently died. (6) Since early childhood, the history includes a concatenation of dependency-providing agencies, institutions, families, hospitals, individuals, and social resources.

If the recent life history falls along the above lines, the motivational need is to gain nurturant dependency from the hospital.

Clinical behaviors

The following kinds of clinical behaviors are motivated toward the goal of gaining nurturant dependency from the hospital:

Helplessness and inability to cope. These clinical behaviors indicate that the patient is unable to cope or to provide for himself. Representative behaviors include: blackouts, epileptoid seizures, syncope, and dizziness; appeals for financial aid and support; inappropriate laughing and crying, wild and bizarre behavior; inability to reason or think through minimal tasks, problems, or decisions; abnormal and demented thought content and processes; weaknesses and aches in the legs.

Immature inadequacy. These clinical behaviors demonstrate a generalized immaturity, a need to be cared for as an inadequate child: alcoholism; chronic inability to hold a job; all-encompassing life decisions which the hospital is to resolve; generalized signs of inadequacy.

Complaining dependency. These clinical behaviors effect a negativistic dependency and use passive-aggressive means of enforcing nurturant dependency and parental rejection from the hospital: vague, generalized complaints of being vaguely "sick"; nonspecific, alcohol-ridden depressions; a fragile and easily disrupted personality state hanging on the ragged edge of reality; depressive behaviors complete with suicidal ideation and unhappy wailings of being inadequately appreciated or cared for; chest pains in the breast region, burning sensation in the abdominal area.

Loss of secure dependency. These clinical behaviors seek nurturant dependency by proclaiming a disruptive loss of security: feelings of losing the security of some supportive group, of being rejected or being "odd"; periods of wandering, homelessness; manifested feelings of decline, of loss of abilities, of deterioration; giving up a lifelong line of work; generalized fears of insecurity (e.g., fears of death); fearful anxieties tied to the sudden loss or decline of a vital organ (e.g., heart, brain, or sexual apparatus).

INDUCED DEPENDENCY

These patients find themselves thrust into a state of dependency, a new state induced or imposed by external conditions. The motivational need for hospitalization is to seek an acceptable situation for the sampling, adapting, experiencing, or "getting used to" the newly induced dependent state.

Clinical change is a function of the hospital experience in adapting to the newly acquired dependency status. The nature of the hospital experiences is often critical in determining the eventual adjustment to the induced dependency condition.

Recent life histories

At least two kinds of recent life histories culminate in an induced dependency state:

Gradual aging. The aging processes may gradually move a patient into a state of induced dependency. The slow onset of physical decline may place a foreman, a physically active businessman, an athlete, or any other vigorous individual in a new state of dependency. Gradual slowing of thinking processes may be sufficient to place others in a state of induced dependency, especially those who relied upon vigorously efficient thinking processes.

Physical traumas. Explosions, crashes, accidents, physical beatings, and other physical traumas may place an individual in a state of induced dependency by removing legs or arms, paralyzing major body parts, damaging hearing or speech or sight, or significantly impairing thinking abilities.

If recent histories fall along the above lines, the need for hospitalization is to adapt to or experience the state of induced dependency.

Clinical behaviors

The most conspicuous clinical behaviors demonstrate the absence or loss of a former state of capability and activity. The characteristic behaviors reflect a heavy component of either sad and melancholy dependency or agitated and frustrated dependency. The presence of these clinical behaviors is a gauge of the need for induced dependency to be experienced or adapted to in the hospital situation.

INSTRUMENTAL DEPENDENCY

The need is for hospitalization to serve as a means or pathway toward the achievement of dependency from extrahospital figures. Hospitalization is instrumental in the achievement of subsequent dependent gratification, rather than serving as the direct provider or resource. By becoming a hospital patient, the individual is thereby making dependent signs or overtures to some other agent or figure. Underlying the dependent overtures is, commonly, a layer of rejection feelings.

The critical determinant of the patient's clinical state is the reaction of the extrahospital agent or figure. Thus, significant clinical changes frequently occur more or less independently of the hospital circumstances and treatment programs.

Recent life histories

Threatened loss of dependency. Some change occurs which threatens to withdraw an external source of dependency gratification. The following are representative: the patient's dependency-providing wife has separated or divorced, and the patient requires some means of securing dependency from the father and mother; there is a threatened reduction (or possibility of an increase) in compensation, welfare, or aid, providing the patient's state justifies such a change; the patient's mother or wife is withdrawing the flow of dependency-provision; changes in the parental

Direct identification. The mother's or wife's hysterectomy may be reflected in genital-urinary difficulties; the mother's childbirth may be reflected in stomach and chest pains; a father's terminal cancer may be reflected in a state of physical collapse and somatic decompensation; an older brother's brain tumor and paralysis may be reflected in paralysis and near-death from a car accident.

Death identification. Death of the significant figure may be reflected in a deathlike hospital journey, fears of dying, morbid preoccupation with decaying viscera, or retreat into a dreamlike state out of contact with the real world.

Alternating identification. The route of identification may alternate from one kind of bond to another. A father's suicide by carbon monoxide may be reflected in hospitalization for bronchitis, asthma, or various lung ailments. This may suddenly give way to an acute episode of "seeing God" and screaming assent to becoming an instrument of God's will. Both sets of clinical behaviors are means of identification with the deceased father figure.

If the clinical behaviors are represented above, the need for hospitalization is to pursue identification with a significant other figure.

Epilogue

The above system of motivational needs is tentative and highly provisional, a first approximation which invites improvement, expansion, modification, and systematization. The next step—the real challenge—lies in the area of treatment. Our aim has been to propose a system of motivational needs for understanding the recent life changes and clinical behaviors of male veteran hospitalized patients. The next step is to describe the recent life changes, clinical behaviors, and determining motivational needs of other clinical groups (e.g., adolescents, college girls, children) in regard to other situations (e.g., outpatient clinics, private practitioners).

REFERENCES

Anker, J. M. A note on the factor structure of the neuropsychiatric chronicity scale. *J. consult. Psychol.,* 1962, **26**, 198.

Ash, P. The reliability of psychiatric diagnosis. *J. abnorm. soc. Psychol.,* 1949, **44**, 272–77.

Brill, A. A. (Ed.). *The basic writings of Sigmund Freud.* New York: Modern Library, 1938.

Bryant, J. H., Wurster, C. R., Hine, F. R., and Dawson, J. G. A factorial analysis of behavior ratings of hospitalized mental patients. *J. Psychol.,* 1958, **46**, 167–73.

Burt, C. *The subnormal mind.* London: Oxford University Press, 1955.

Degan, J. W. Dimensions of a functional psychosis. *Psychometr. Monogr.,* 1952, No. 6.

Eysenck, H. J. Neurosis and psychosis: an experimental analysis. *J. ment. Sci.,* 1956, **102**, 517–29.

Foulds, G. A. The reliability of psychiatric, and the validity of psychological diagnosis. *J. ment. Sci.,* 1955, **101**, 851–62.

Guertin, W. H. A factor-analytic study of schizophrenic symptoms. *J. consult. Psychol.,* 1952, **16**, 308–12.

Kanfer, F. H., and Saslow, G. Behavioral analysis. *Arch. gen. Psychiat.,* 1965, **12**, 529–38.

Kelly, G. A. *The psychology of personal constructs.* New York: Norton, 1955.

King, G. Research wtih neuropsychiatric samples. *J. Psychol.,* 1954, **38**, 383–87.

Kostlan, A. A. Method for the empirical study of psychodiagnosis. *J. consult. Psychol.,* 1954, **18**, 83–88.

Leary, T., and Coffey, H. Interpersonal diagnosis: some problems of methodology and validation. *J. abnorm. soc. Psychol.,* 1955, **50**, 110–26.

Lorr, M., Jenkins, R. L., and O'Connor, J. P. Factors descriptive of psychopathology and behavior of hospitalized psychotics. *J. abnorm. soc. Psychol.,* 1955, **50**, 78–86.

Lorr, M., Klett, C. J., and McNair, D. M. *Syndromes of psychosis.* New York: Macmillan, 1963.

Lorr, M., O'Connor, J. P., and Stafford, J. W. Confirmation of nine psychotic symptom patterns. *J. clin. Psychol.,* 1957, **13**, 252–57.

Maher, B. *Principles of psychopathology: an experimental approach.* New York: McGraw-Hill, 1966.

Mahrer, A. R. The psychological problem inventory. *Psychol. Rep.,* 1967, **20**, 711–14.

Mahrer, A. R., Mason, D. J., and Pomeroy, E. A psychological diagnostic system: outline of research-derived motivational categories for hospitalized psychiatric patients. *VA Newsltr. Res. Psychol.,* 1965, **7**, 23–24.

Mahrer, A. R., Thorp, T., and Sternlicht, I. The role of cues in psychodiagnosis. *J. gen. Psychol.,* 1960, **62**, 247–56.

Mahrer, A. R., and Young, H. H. The combination of psychodiagnostic cues. *J. Pers.,* 1961, **29**, 428–48.

Noyes, A. P., and Kolb, L. C. *Modern clinical psychiatry.* Philadelphia: W. B. Saunders, 1963.

O'Connor, J. P., and Stefic, E. C. Some patterns of hypochondriasis. *Educ. Psychol. Measmt.,* 1959, **19**, 363–71.

Overall, J. E., Gorham, D. R., and Shawver, J. R. Basic dimensions of change in the symptomatology of chronic schizophrenics. *J. abnorm. soc. Psychol.,* 1961, **63**, 597–602.

Reid, J. R. Logical analysis. *Amer. J. Psychiat.,* 1957, **114**, 397–404.

Rotter, J. B. *Social learning and clinical psychology.* New York: Prentice-Hall, 1954.

Trouton, D. S., and Maxwell, A. E. The relation between neurosis and psychosis. *J. ment. Sci.,* 1956, **102**, 1–21.

Wittenborn, J. R. Symptom patterns in a group of mental hospital patients. *J. consult. Psychol.,* 1951, **15**, 290–302.

Wittenborn, J. R. Distinctions within psychotic dimensions: a principal component analysis. *J. nerv. ment. Dis.,* 1963, **137**, 543–47.

Zigler, E., and Phillips, L. Psychiatric diagnosis: a critique. *J. abnorm. soc. Psychol.,* 1961, **63**, 607–18.

EXISTENTIAL PSYCHOLOGICAL STATES, INTEGRATION, AND A CLINICAL DIAGNOSTIC APPROACH

According to Thorne, personality classification is at a standstill. The reason is that there is no adequate rationale for an existential approach to psychological states and to the psychology of integration. Thorne aims to supply such a rationale and thereby to lay the basis for an adequate classification system. To begin with, the raw data consist of the specific mental states of the patient at a given moment—the continuing, conscious, feeling, thinking, acting self. Thorne stresses the assessment of the ongoing, here-and-now, adaptive, coping behaviors. Psychodiagnosis involves the assessment of the existential situation in which the person is involved. Particular attention is geared toward the evaluation of how well the person is managing his life and adjusting to the world about him.

To assess the central concept of the psychological state, Thorne offers a number of avenues. These include introspection, direct observation (including direct observation in the problematical situations), stream of life or case history, time studies, assessment of life adjustment skills, objective and projective test methods.

By studying the sequence of psychological states from the initiation to the completion of a total action, Thorne evaluates the degree of integration of the personality. Integration is assessed through measures of general adequacy, psychophysiological stability, mental context adequacy, life management skills, self concept, ego strength factors, and existential status.

Thorne has attempted to reject the Kraepelinian-psychiatric model,

309

to espouse an eclectic comprehensive personality system incorporating existential conceptions, and yet to retain a focus on practical diagnosis. The path which Thorne has set for himself requires the solution of a problem which many existentialist writers have thus far failed to resolve, viz., to bridge the gap between strongly held existentialist conceptions and the everyday practicalities of clinical psychodiagnostics. Thorne's approach moves toward a resolution of this problem by providing an array of clinical psychodiagnostic methods to assess the existential psychological state.

Thorne has selected to abandon Kraepelinian-psychiatric diagnostic conceptions and yet to provide a system which does all the jobs the traditional approach tries to accomplish.

10

DIAGNOSTIC IMPLICATIONS OF
INTEGRATIVE PSYCHOLOGY

FREDERICK C. THORNE

Introduction

The system of integrative psychology which we have outlined elsewhere
(Thorne, 1967) has entirely different implications, for clinical practice
in general and diagnostic processes in particular, from classic personality trait theory and all other systems emphasizing limited aspects of
behavior. Something is basically wrong with the theoretical rationale of
a presumed clinical "science" in which a multitude of conflicting systems
are competing for acceptance, and this is currently true of the status of
both clinical psychiatry and clinical psychology. Elsewhere (Thorne,
1961b), we have attempted to resolve the dilemma of the competing
claims of the different schools of psychology by making an operational
analysis of their various tenets, and demonstrating that the various
schools typically are dealing with different operational approaches to
different facets of behavior.

Each of the principal schools of psychology deals with important
levels of behavior phenomena such as learning, perceiving, retaining,
thinking, etc., but none of them comes up with universal etiological factors capable of explaining the entire gamut of behavior with which we
must deal. Only a comprehensive integrative psychology is capable of
evaluating and assigning the proper emphasis to all the levels of factors
underlying clinically important behaviors.

Our system of integrative psychology depends heavily upon the

This chapter consists of a revision and expansion of Chapters 9 and 10
taken from: F. C. Thorne, *Integrative Psychology* (Brandon, Vt.: Clinical
Psychology Publishing Company, 1967).

theory of the *psychological state* which is phenomenally, systematically, and methodologically a different unit for study than either the classic personality trait or the psychoanalytic mechanism. Every psychological state is a dynamic integrate whose organization reflects the unique pattern of psychological forces operating at any particular point in life.

Psychological state theory is more suited than personality trait theory or psychoanalytic dynamism theories for explicating many of the critical events which form the turning points of life, and which may provide the only clinical data worth knowing about the person. Every psychological state is a unique integrate. Life is a process of constant change during which no two points can be exactly identical. Consequently, the etiological dynamics of succeeding psychological states must involve changing patterns of integration. The unique events which are psychological states too often represent one-of-a-kind patterns, so that clinical methods must be attuned to diagnosing and measuring the factors organizing any particular pattern of integration and also those responsible for change. Psychological states are the phenomenal units of the stream of life. Clinical psychology must come to grips with the unique events which are psychological states for purposes of understanding, prediction, and manipulation.

Continuing clinical diagnosis of fluctuating psychological states is an absolute necessity and foundation for any system of integrative psychology. Clinical diagnosis, therefore, must be oriented to the study of *clinically important* psychological states and the factors organizing their integration. This means that when psychological states are in constant flux, clinical diagnosis must develop methods capable of uncovering the dynamics of change, and this cannot usually be accomplished in terms of classical personality trait theory which emphasizes constancy rather than change. Clinical diagnosis must be capable of dealing with change as well as constancy.

Integrative psychology is concerned primarily with the unfolding record of the growth and development of a person, with the moment-to-moment status of how this individual is running his life in the world. The crux of any psychological state is the *integrative milieu,* the psychological field of forces striving to gain prepotency and to organize the pattern of integration of the moment. Although psychological trait theory may outline the basic dimensions of humanness, it requires *psychological state diagnosis* to understand what is happening in any individual life. Indeed, studies of clinical judgment (Thorne, 1961a) indicate that very little of importance can be predicted from knowledge of static personality traits, since traits do not inevitably determine state outcomes. It requires individual study of the critically important psychological states which a person gets into to explain what he does in particular situations.

In the context of integrative psychology, clinical diagnosis has specific implications and methods suitable for the study of states as well as traits. Clinical diagnosis must deal both deductively and inductively with the raw data of specific psychological states, not only with reference to individuals, but also in relation to specific social situations. Integrative psychology studies the individual, *in vivo,* at clinically important moments of running the business of life. Although generalizations concerning personality traits in general can be made from the armchair, only continuing clinical study and life process diagnosis can clarify the dynamics of the individual.

What Are the Actual Data and Referents of Clinical Psychology?

Integrative psychology contends that psychological states are the prime raw data of all psychological study, whether reported introspectively, observed objectively, or measured instrumentally. Psychological states are the prime data no matter what the unit of measurement, and "behavior" is only a generic term for the life stream of psychological states.

Every act of clinical diagnosis takes place in reference to a particular psychological state at the moment when a judgment or measurement is being made. Every act of case handling (psychotherapy) takes place with reference to a psychological state which is the specific mental status of the client at the moment. The proper units for clinical diagnosis are the successive components of the unique streams of life which characterize individuals, and these can be understood only in terms of what the person is doing at that moment.

> Consider, for example, the act of lifting a cup toward the lips. The behaviorist may be able to describe the muscular movements involved objectively, but the act can be understood only through knowing what is in the cup. Much different implications reside in whether the cup contains water, milk, coffee, alcohol, or poison.

Although clinicians often refer to "personality study," "traits," "structures," "mechanisms," "factors," "scales," "profiles," etc., all these are semantic abstractions many levels removed from the raw data (psychological states) which are the actual units of study. Taken in isolation away from the specific events of individual lives, generalizations or measurements of personality traits, mechanisms, or factors have only theoretical relevance, and rarely have much predictive significance in relation to the psychological states which are the critical determiners of important acts in life.

Clinical diagnosis in the past has been too concerned with deductive attempts to apply popular theories to individual cases, and too little concerned with the inductive study of the actual phenomenal "givens" presented in the person's raw behaviors. Integrative psychology is concerned with the actual etiologic factors organizing any particular pattern of integration, and only secondarily with whatever theory may be applied validly to any particular case.

Recognizing that the prime existential motive is to maintain the highest possible levels of integration throughout life, the basic clinical question is, How well is the client doing with his life? and this can be resolved only by study of the factors organizing clinically important patterns of integration. The basic data for all clinical study consist of the status of the person running the business of his life in the world.

The Existential Relevance of Clinical Methods

The basic clinical questions underlying all case handling relate to (1) What is the psychological state of the client? and (2) How did he get that way? Even more specifically, such questions become relevant only when they are related to specific development phases and situational problems of life. The study of personality "traits" in isolation usually has little relevance to what the client is actually doing in life, which is a much more global issue. The importance clinical issue is: Which, if any, of the popular theories and measurement methods have any relevance to specific situational and existential questions?

Integrative psychology, with its eclectic insistence upon studying all levels of factors potentially organizing clinically important behaviors, is the only systematic position comprehensive enough to explain the whole gamut of behaviors characterizing the flux of psychological states occurring during any twenty-four-hour period, to say nothing of a whole life.

More broadly, psychodiagnosis must concern itself with the global unit of the-person-running-the-business-of-his-life-in-the-world. It must deal genuinely with existence, with Being, with the ultimate meanings of this particular life—with the uniquely individual nature of the person. Basic diagnostic questions relate to the questions of *what* the person is doing with his life, *why* he is doing it, *how* he is doing, *when* and *where* he is successful or failing, and *what* is his adaptability to important situations and his general social impact.

It is paradoxical that both clinical psychology and psychiatry have been content to make classificatory diagnoses, and to sidestep their existential and social implications. The democratic ideal is to mind one's own business and not to interfere in another life even though it is judged to be mismanaged. Thus, many diagnosticians have not concerned themselves with the existential and personal-social implications of their diagnoses. The tendency is to avoid diagnoses or prognostications which might tend to discriminate against the persons or to imply personal inadequacy.

Perhaps this is the reason why many of the clinical methods of the past have been proved invalid and unreliable for the purposes used. Existential questions require existentially oriented answers. Clinicians cannot avoid the implications of the questions as to how well a person is doing with is life and what needs to be changed.

Only a temporally oriented diagnostic approach, continuously studying the stream of life with its succession of psychological states, is capable of studying the process of living (Being, existing) across time. Thus, diagnosis must becomes a continuing process, continually alert to changes in the integrative milieu which reflect changing prepotencies of etiologic factors and consequent alterations of the psychological state of the person.

Basic Problems of Diagnosis

Much of the confusion associated with the nature and purposes of diagnostic process in the past may be resolved by clarifying the principal dimensions of factors under consideration. Four classes of considerations usually enter any diagnostic process: normative, etiologic, psychosocial, and legal. Additional considerations may be imposed by special statistical or institutional requirements. The following classification outline indicates the various dimensions arranged as bipolar factors.

I. Normative	Normality	vs.	Abnormality
(Personal status)	Typical		Atypical
	Conforming		Deviant
	Health and happiness		Pathology
	Morale		Demoralization
II. Etiologic	Integration		Disintegration
(Mental status)	Control		Loss of control
	Positive mental health		Illness
	Productivity		Disorder
	Creativity		Disease

III. Psychosocial	Adaptability	Inadaptability
(Social status)	Adjustment	Maladjustment
	Achievement	Disability
IV. Legal	Competence	Incompetence
(Legal status)	Responsibility	Irresponsibility

The clinician should make every effort to keep these diagnostic dimensions separate in order not to confuse issues. Different diagnostic systems have emphasized different dimensions, and this has resulted in confusion and misunderstanding due to communication difficulties. This system differentiates not only different diagnostic approaches but also the usages to which they are put.

Normative diagnosis relates to personal-existential status as compared to clinical or objective normative standards. It is concerned with whether the person is in full possession of faculties and functioning within normal limits.

Etiologic diagnosis relates to mental status in connection both with factors contributing to positive mental health at one extreme as well as with factors producing disintegration (loss of control) in pathological conditions. "Illness" is a generic term referring to a breakdown in functioning, whether due to organic or functional causes. "Disorder" usually refers to functional conditions which are reversible. "Disease" refers to conditions of organic nature involving established pathology, and usually irreversible.

Psychosocial diagnosis usually relates to various criteria of personal-social self-actualization, i.e., the degree to which the person is able to cope with life and its special situations. "Adaptability" refers to the flexibility and appropriateness of coping behaviors. "Adjustment" relates to adaptability in relation to specific social demands. "Disability" refers to degree of socioeconomic incapacitation.

Forensic diagnosis is concerned with the determination of mental (in)competence and legal responsibility as arbitrarily defined in law. This involves factors of conscious awareness, cognitive understanding of right vs. wrong, self-control, and self-insight.

In each dimension, it is understood that diagnostic evaluations can apply only to the psychological state of the person at the time of the examination except in those conditions with chronic or deteriorating pathological conditions where no improvement can be expected.

Diagnosis in Clinical Practice

Every act of clinical case handling, whether diagnostic or therapeutic, logically should be based upon the diagnostic indications or contraindications for doing any particular thing. This concept tremendously broadens our whole concept of what diagnosis involves. If case handling is to be a rational process, it must depend upon many levels of diagnostic activity, in each instance based upon identification of the etiologic (causative) factors underlying the particular integrative status under study.

The assumption that certain methods are applicable in all situations, i.e., have universal validity in all clinical situations, has been accepted as justification for applying special systems such as psychoanalysis or nondirectivism. Psychoanalysis postulates one dynamic system as applying to all cases, and thereby limits diagnosis to psychoanalytic applications. Nondirectivism, on the other hand, postulates emotional conflict and blocking as the underlying cause of all disorders, and thereby eliminates the necessity for any diagnostic activity. The dictum of Carl R. Rogers that diagnosis is not necessary or even contraindicated in nondirective case handling is of questionable validity and has set back progress in psychodiagnosis for more than twenty-five years.

Integrative psychology, on the other hand, with its postulation of an almost infinite number of psychological states succeeding each other in the process of living, regards diagnosis as essential in identifying the etiologic factors underlying any particular psychological state so that the flow of behavior can be understood. Diagnosis is essential and integral to the process of case handling stemming from integrative psychology.

Diagnosis and Clinical Judgment

Clinical judgment involves applied psychodiagnosis. Every act of clinical judgment logically should be based upon some type of diagnostic process, upon diagnostic data from which the indications and contraindications for any step in case handling stem. Clinical judgment is diagnostic judgment, enlarging the concept of diagnosis to include all steps of interpretation and decision resting upon differentiation of the etiologic factors underlying a condition *and* knowledge concerning the outcomes of various case handling methods (Thorne, 1961a).

Integrative psychology is totally dependent upon valid clinical diagnosis in identifying and clarifying the psychological states which determine critical events. The cookbook methodology of behaviorism, psychoanalysis, or personality trait psychology may have only very limited value in elucidating the factors organizing clinically significant patterns of integration.

Expanded concepts of the nature of clinical diagnosis must recognize that all acts of clinical judgment depend upon valid knowledge of not only etiologic factors but also the indications and contraindications leading to various outcomes. Diagnostic judgments intervene at all levels of case handling, and the clinician must be acutely aware of the reasoning process underlying his decisions.

The concept of moment-to-moment clinical diagnosis implies that the clinician assimilates each new piece of clinical data, every new thing which the client says or does, in an *inductive* clinical judgment process. *Diagnostically,* each new item of clinical evidence must be interpreted as to its significance, and then incorporated into the evolving diagnostic hypotheses, which must then be confirmed or altered in terms of whether new evidence is consistent or inconsistent with formulated hypotheses. *Therapeutically,* every step in case handling should stem from diagnostic judgments as to what should be done next (Thorne, 1968).

Clinical diagnosis is a process which involves more than matching clinical symptoms with standard diagnostic classifications. Clinical diagnosis as process must be operative continuously during all stages of case handling, since it provides the rational basis for clinical judgments. This viewpoint categorically denies the validity of (1) the nondirective theoretical assumptions that diagnosis is not necessary or even contraindicated for case handling, or (2) the deductive assumption that all case handling must depend upon the mechanical application of some master blueprint such as psychoanalytic theory or behaviorism. Whether the underlying diagnostic decisions are considered consciously or not, they are always present in any case handling methods and should be formulated clearly to permit validating appraisal.

Different Types of Diagnosis

Every kind of clinical judgment depends, basically, upon the validity and reliability of various levels of diagnostic process. In the past, the basic dependence of clinical judgment upon diagnosis has been often overlooked because of enthusiasm for some favored theoretical or cookbook approach.

Cookbook approaches take the judgment out of clinical decision processes by implying that all the clinician has to do is to follow the rules mechanically. However, the clinician should not overlook the two underlying assumptions that (1) the particular cookbook rules are demonstrably valid, and (2) that any particular clinician is applying the rules reliably. Actually, if cookbook rules were absolutely valid and reliable, there would be no need for clinicians, because all cases could be evaluated mechanically by computer methods.

A principal difficulty with the psychodiagnosis of the past has been that it was not broadly enough conceived, and had become prostituted to clinical statistical classification purposes and thereby became too limited and static to deal with behavior *in vivo*. The applications of integrative psychology require an expanded process of clinical diagnosis applied to every clinically important aspect of the stream of life and its constitutent psychological states. As developed within the context of integrative psychology, and utilized in our own clinical practice for over twenty years, we have expanded and applied the nature of diagnosis according to the following outline.

I. DIFFERENTIAL DIAGNOSIS. The differentiation and identification of various classes of etiologic factors. This might also be called *etiologic diagnosis* because the purpose is to discriminate the causal (etiologic) factors underlying a condition.
   A. *Trait Diagnosis*. The classic study of psychological traits as measured by factorial methods. Traits are commonalities which determine basic patterns of humanness but may not differentiate individuality.
   B. *State Diagnosis*. The study of the psychological states which are the units of experience.
      1. Mental status diagnosis. The psychiatric determination of normality or abnormality.
      2. Physical diagnosis. The medical diagnosis of the physical organism.
      3. Psychosomatic diagnosis. Diagnosis of the interaction of physical and psychological conditions.
II. CLINICAL PROCESS DIAGNOSIS. The diagnosis of moment-to-moment developments in the process of case handling. This type of diagnosis underlies clinical judgments of the significance of new developments in terms of the indications and contraindications of methods and conditions.
   A. *Integration Level Diagnosis*. The study of hierarchical levels of integration, the factors controlling them, their fluctuations, etc. The diagnosis of factors of positive mental health.
   B. *Disintegration Threshold Diagnosis*. The study of factors contributing to breakdown, the levels at which breakdown is occurring, the dynamics of disintegration. The dynamics of psychopathology.

III. EXISTENTIAL STATUS DIAGNOSIS. The integrative dynamics of self functioning.
   A. *The Self Concept.* The self reacting to itself.
      1. The actual self.
      2. The ideal self.
      3. Actual-ideal self discrepancies.
   B. *Reality Contacts.*
   C. *Self Executive Functions.* The evaluation of levels of self-control.
   D. *Success-Failure Status.* The evaluation of morale.
      1. Existential meaning status. The existential vacuum.
      2. Levels of morale. Morale vs. demoralization.
      3. Motivation levels.
IV. LIFE MANAGEMENT STATUS DIAGNOSIS. The study of how well the person is running the business of his life in the world. The evaluation of behavior in terms of social-situational requirements. The diagnosis of adjustment or adaptation levels.
   A. *Educational Adjustment Diagnosis.*
   B. *Vocational Adjustment Diagnosis.*
   C. *Sexual and Marital Adjustment Diagnosis.*
   D. *Social Adjustment Diagnosis.*
   E. *Financial Management Diagnosis.*
   F. Other special social role-playing adjustment diagnoses.
 V. CLINICAL CLASSIFICATION DIAGNOSIS. The differentiation and classification of conditions according to standard nomenclatures and statistical systems.
VI. PROGNOSTIC DIAGNOSIS. Predicting future outcomes.

The reader should note that the classic functions of diagnosis, namely, clinical classification diagnosis, are listed at the end of this outline, thus emphasizing their relatively slight importance as compared with the dynamic integrational diagnosis of ongoing life processes.

The Diagnosis of Individuality

Classic diagnostic methods often have failed to differentiate individuality because of overemphasis on common factors such as personality traits or mechanisms which turn out to be so universal that they do not differentiate anybody. The real significance of a person consists not in physical or personality trait differences but rather in terms of what each person is doing with his life.

Constitutional physical and psychological differences may limit what any person can accomplish but do not necessarily predict what will be achieved. Within the limitations of humanness, infinite possibilities for variation exist, and what actually happens can be discovered only from study of the life record of each person.

It is for these reasons that the diagnosis of individuality depends far more on life management and existential status diagnosis than upon differential or classification diagnosis. Differential diagnosis and clinical process diagnosis provide the necessary background information for existential and life management diagnosis in making possible clinical judgments concerning the degree to which native endowment is actualized in pertinent achievements.

The study of individuality requires answers to a much broader range of questions than is customarily provided in psychological and psychiatric examinations. We are interested in knowing more than the person's IQ, temperamental traits, or whether he is neurotic or psychotic. To really know *how* a person is doing, it is necessary to know how well he is playing the important roles of life, the nature of his social strivings, his life style, and, above all, his existential status. All these factors determine integrational status, so diagnostic processes should be geared to investigate all pertinent factors contributing to genuine self-actualization and positive mental health.

Personality Trait Diagnosis

In our experience, classic "personality" trait measurements are most useful in cases where such factors are so prepotent and inflexible as to limit and structure behavior in constant patterns. The critical issue is whether measurable traits actually determine clinically significant behaviors. Ideally, in spite of inevitable trait structures or composition, the normal person should be able to cope with life so flexibly and adaptively that behavior patterns are constantly changing to adjust to changing conditions of existence. The fact is that different "personality" or "trait" types under normal conditions are able to cope with and solve identical problems albeit by different methods. The critical issue is not the presence of the trait but the degree to which it facilitates or inhibits coping behaviors.

Trait diagnosis has the objectives not only of differentiating trait loadings and patterns but also of establishing how they facilitate or inhibit coping behaviors. Many traits are clinically neutral, contributing to style but not to outcomes. Traits become significant only when they become positive assets or negative liabilities as behavior determiners.

The difficulty with predictions based on trait measurements or profiles is that people with different trait patterns may achieve the same problem solutions while people with the same traits may behave differently in different situations. The important clinical fact is that traits often are not the most important determiners of outcomes, so that many other classes of factors (such as motivations, situational reactions, etc.) must also be taken into consideration. The same comments apply to personality "structure" and "mechanism" approaches which may apply in single cases at specific times but have not been proven to have universal validity.

The Limitations of Personality Trait Diagnosis

A basic axiom of clinical diagnosis is that measurements have significance only to the degree that they predict clinically important factors and outcomes. The history of clinical psychology clearly demonstrates that it is possible to make many types of objective measurements which, unfortunately, are not valid predictors of clinically important factors. Indeed, the history of clinical psychology records a long succession of tests and methods which have proved invalid (even though reliable) in predicting clinically important outcomes. In summary, most of the clinical methods of the past have been proved invalid and unsuccessful in measuring existential status.

A good example of the shortcomings of contemporary clinical methods involves personality trait diagnosis, which is based on the unproved assumption that "personality" traits can predict clinically important factors. The difficulties start primarily with the concept of "personality," which is a semantic abstraction with exactly the same validity as the concept of "mind." Personality theory involves all the inadequacies of any structural psychology, in this instance utilizing the concept of personality "traits" as the basic units of personality "structure." The fact that certain behaviors show constancy across time leads to the conclusion that there must be some underlying constant structure which is "personality." Unfortunately, few of the alleged "traits" thus far discovered turn out to have very high predictive validity.

Most behavior constancies turn out to be caused by emotional reactions, ideas, purposes, or motivations which achieve prepotency over relatively long temporal periods but do not necessarily imply "structures." In such cases, the inferred traits are conceptual artifacts whose valid interpretations may be entirely different. "State" psychology provides much more valid interpretations than "trait" psychology in explaining the organization of many integrational states.

An excellent example of the difficulties with trait psychology may be cited in the concept of extraversion-introversion. Jung's original introduction of the terms was met with a wave of popular acceptance because of the face validity of the concept. Scales purportedly measuring E-I were constructed uncritically and the resulting measures were considered to reflect important personality "types." Only gradually was it discovered that true types apparently do not exist, and that everyone shows a mixture of the so-called traits, and that even the same person can show very different situational reactions.

The concept of E-I was resurrected with the advent of factor analysis which, in the hands of Eysenck (1953), reported a superfactor of E-I, which thereby became a prime personality dimension. Disregarding for the moment serious criticisms relating to the validity of Eysenck's factorial methods and structural interpretations, E-I measurements turn out to be substantially noncritical as predictors of important clinical outcomes. These may be called "So what?" measurements in that what they measure turns out to be nonsignificant.

Even more serious criticisms may be directed toward "traits," "structures," "types," or "profiles" derived from scores based on empirically derived and nonfactorially pure items which are summated to result in some measure such as "neurotic tendency." The history of clinical psychology has been replete with instances of tests and measures having impressive face validity but no predictive validity. Before any trait is assigned predictive validity, it must be demonstrated to be actually organizing pertinent states of integration.

Mental Status Diagnosis and the Psychological State

Traditional psychiatric mental status diagnosis always has stressed that the psychological state of a person is in a constant process of change so that any diagnostic conclusions must be related specifically to the time of the examination. Standard psychiatric practice requires a series of mental status examinations to follow the psychological status of the patient as it changes during case handling. Thus, the whole mental status concept postulates change as a natural phenomenon and properly provides for its successive measurement.

In contrast, many clinical psychologists tend to depend upon "personality" measurements given on a single occasion. This practice stems from personality trait theory, which assumes a relatively stable "personality structure" and, consequently, relatively constant trait or factor measurements. Also, most standard personality inventories are not designed for repeated administration of the same test with the same subject, and several alternate forms of any test are not generally available. The point here is that conventional personality testing procedures based upon personality trait and structure theories are not adapted to the measurement of changing mental status.

Integrative psychology with its emphasis on mental life as consisting of changing psychological states is completely consistent with the psychiatric mental status concept. Indeed, we would insist that the central problem of all clinical psychology and psychiatry is to study the changing patterns of psychological states in order to differentiate various levels of factors organizing integrated states.

Our expanded system of diagnosis actually involves an elaboration and extension of the psychiatric mental status examination beyond the more limited objective of determining mental (ab)normality *at the moment* to the broader objective of studying all levels of factors contributing to the integrative patterns determining what the person is doing with his life in the present. This enlarged concept requires active consideration of many levels of factors such as ideological/attitudinal composition, role playing, social status factors, life style patterns, and existential status factors not previously systematically considered.

Since the psychological state of the moment actually involves the person's status of *being in the world,* all evaluations of psychological states must deal with the frame of reference of the person-running-the-business-of-his-life-in-the-world. This insistence on global existential orientation in the expanded mental status examination goes far beyond static personality trait or structure descriptions. Such existential evaluations must necessarily involve some orientation to adaptation and adjustment problems since the clinician is always concerned with practical outcomes.

It is no longer acceptable simply to make classificatory or descriptive statements indicating the presence of mental retardation, psychosis, personality traits, etc. Existential diagnosis also requires an elaboration of how such factors actually are influencing a particular life in terms of past development, present mental status, and future prognosis. For these reasons, diagnosis must be a continuing process, following the development of integrational dynamics literally from birth to death in order to keep abreast of existential developments.

Differential (Etiologic) Diagnosis

The term *differential* has had slightly different meanings in clinical medicine and in psychometrics. *Differential diagnosis* in medicine refers to the attempt to discriminate the type of pathology, i.e., the differentiation of the disease entities which might cause a given clinical condition. More basically, it involves the differentiation of possible classes of etiologic factors in order to discriminate the etiologic equation operating in any particular case. The concept of the etiologic equation is necessary in order to identify all pathological factors and to assign proper weights and sequences to their modes of operation. (See Thorne, 1967, Ch. 8.) Operationally, this involves listing all possible etiologic factors (types of disorder), and then eliminating the improbable and untenable factors, until finally the true causes are identified.

Although the types of pathology and etiologic factors occurring in psychological disorders is different from the medical model of physical disease, with its emphasis on gross and microscopic (cellular) pathology, the basic objectives and approaches of differential diagnosis are equally applicable to both mental and physical conditions. All natural phenomena must have natural causes, and the subject of etiology is dedicated to the study of causation, utilizing appropriate classifications of etiologic factors for any particular modality.

In clinical psychology, the term *differential* has been applied to the study of individual differences on measurable variables. In clinical practice, the differential approach attempts to measure how the individual scores on standard measures to make possible comparison with norms.

Actually, both the medical and psychological meanings of the term *differential* have relevance for the study of psychological states and their underlying integrational status. Certain broad questions arise immediately in relation to every clinical condition. Is it innate or acquired? Hereditary, constitutional, or learned? What etiologic factors are involved? What levels of integration are involved? How does this person compare in relation to norms or standards? What is the personal-social significance of the condition? What criteria are to be utilized in judging this person clinically?

Psychological differential diagnosis probably involves more complex problems and interrelationships than medical physical diagnosis because it must deal with the global unit of the person in the world. This involves a tremendous complexity of personal-existential, social-cultural, situational-adjustive factors whose influence must be differentiated and weighted in an etiologic equation referring to any particular psychological state. And then the whole process must be repeated for all succeeding psychological states which are clinically important.

The process of differential diagnosis involves consideration of all personal, social, situational, and existential factors determining any particular integrational milieu. The basic question is: What are all the important classes of etiologic factors requiring to be integrated (unified) in terms of what the person is attempting to do with his life, and how he is going about it, and how is it coming out? Although everything which can be known about a person is potentially relevant, the immediate clinical problem always is to explicate the causation of particular clinically important psychological states.

The Diagnosis of Hierarchical Levels of Integration

The clinical problem is to discriminate the hierarchical factors contributing to any integrational pattern, either *positively* in support of integration, or *negatively* to produce disintegration. In our own diagnostic plan for analyzing integrational patterns, the first step is to identify the approximate level of integration reflected in the psychological state of the moment. This is accomplished by utilizing a checklist of factors at progressively higher levels of factors organizing integration in relation to what the person is doing at the moment.

> For example, an adult male patient is heatedly abusing his wife and charging her with gross infidelities incident to a divorce action. Is this behavior conditioned by neurotic hatred for his mother, cumulative frustrations in marriage, inadequate sex role playing, frustrated social status strivings, cumulative lacerations of his ego, or a peak of existential demoralization? Such factors are completely unique in each individual case, and no standard formulations apply to all cases.

The second step is to try to formulate an *etiologic equation* representing all the factors prepotent in any particular integrational milieu. Most behaviors are more complexly determined than has been traditionally accounted for. Too often, standard interpretations based on some theory such as psychoanalysis have been glibly applied without reference to their actual validity. We would insist that an individual etiologic equation must be made for each separate psychological state to reflect the dynamics of each situation of the person running the business of his life in the world.

The third step is in weighting the relative contribution of all classes of participating factors in the causation of clinically significant behaviors. Each individual life has its own particular dynamics and it is necessary to come up with etiologic formulations and diagnosis which reflect this individuality. This can only be accomplished by proper representation of the relative priorities of all factors involved in any particular psychological state.

> Most homicidal acts are committed during unique psychological states in which all the necessary elements leading to the violent act happen to be represented in such prepotency as to surpass the

threshold necessary for such an act to occur. For example, how to explain an episode of homicidal rape committed by a respectable family man with several children who has always had a satisfactory sexual relation with his wife? Only a careful study of the psychological state of the moment can explain how such an act could have been committed.

Finally, we always attempt to relate the circumstances of any particular psychological state to the general sequence of what the person had been doing with his life. It is necessary to relate all pertinent developments to the life plan in general in order to discriminate the meanings which give specific behaviors significance. Personality traits or mechanisms, taken in isolation, usually shed little light on the dynamics of what the person is doing. In contrast, psychological states are an integral part of what a person is doing; hence they constitute raw data of the highest importance for diagnosis.

Diagnosing Critical Psychological States

Perhaps the most important decision of case study relates to the choice of *what* to investigate. One of the most significant conclusions from studies of clinical judgment is that only a relatively few types of measurements have much practical clinical significance (Thorne, 1961a). The history of clinical psychology is replete with examples of promising new measurement methods which turned out to be invalid because not related to clinically significant factors. The critical issue always involves establishing the relevance of measurement methods to diagnostically important factors. This issue cannot be taken for granted and is not widely enough understood among clinicians.

The fact is that of all the variety of psychological measurements which have been devised, only a very few have much clinical significance and established predictive validity. Perhaps the three best examples of clinical invalidity due to irrelevance of measurement methods relate to (1) the attempt to measure intelligence by brief tests involving single factors such as memory, (2) the general failure of personality "trait" and "structure" measures to predict outcomes, and (3) the general invalidity of projective applications of psychoanalytic theory applied blindly on the basis of supposedly universal applicability.

The only unit which has relevance for clinical measurement and study is the psychological state of the person at the time when critical incidents of life occur. It is only through the analysis of critical incidents that the clinician can discover what was actually happening in the life of the person to cause him to do clinically significant things. This means that the classic measurements of clinical psychology and psychiatry can have relevance only if they actually relate to factors organizing clinically significant integrational patterns. In other words, the classic personality traits, structures, mechanisms, etc., have valid application only when they can actually be demonstrated to be organizing clinically important psychological states.

In the clinical method outlined in our applied integrative psychology (Thorne, 1967, 1968), the first step consists in identifying the critical incidents which involve genuinely important turning points of life. Not everything which a person does has much clinical significance. We must discriminate that which is important to study.

The second step consists in identifying the particular psychological state (expanded mental status examination) which the person was in at the time of commission of clinically important acts. This usually involves the direct examination and introspective reporting by the client of *how* he felt at that moment, and *why* he did what he did. This involves the intensive study of states of being.

A third step *may* involve the collection of psychological test data relating to such traits, factors, structures, or mechanisms as probably have relevance to what has actually occurred. Only those measurements which have existential relevance will have much value here.

Finally, an attempt is made to relate specific critical incidents with the whole existential pattern of the person as revealed by past history and what the person is attempting to do in life. It cannot be stressed too strongly that critical incidents in a life almost always devolve from the dynamics of regnant psychological states.

> Consider, for example, the dynamics of suicide attempts. Attempts to explain suicide in terms of general theories such as Freudian life-death instincts, aggressive tendencies directed inwards in psychotic depressions, etc., have not proven to have much predictive validity. It is only by studying the psychological state of the person at the time of the suicidal impulses that the actual dynamics of what was occurring can be demonstrated. Usually, suicide is precipitated by progressive states of frustration, existential despair, and situational stress which finally culminate in an irresistible impulse which may disappear completely once the psychological state changes.

Prediction becomes possible only when it is demonstrated that recurring patterns of the same etiological factors tend to reproduce the same psychological states. It is axiomatic that homogeneity of psychological states is prerequisite for behavior constancy, and this requires that identical etiologic patterns keep recurring. One of the best examples of the dependence of overt behaviors on underlying psychological states is in reference to patterns of sexuality. Sexual excitement is a prototypal psychological state phenomenon. Sexual excitement fluctuates directly in relation to purely "state" factors which can change dramatically, e.g., frigidity can follow a sex trauma. It cannot be taken for granted that the psychological state will remain unchanged. Only the continuing study of psychological states can discover what is actually happening in integrative dynamics.

Diagnosing Integrational Status

The prime motive of existence is to maintain the highest possible integrational status because disintegration in any form always involves some type of loss of control. Psychologists and psychiatrists often refer glibly to "personality" integration without specifying operationally what is involved or how it is to be measured. The background theory of integrative psychology stated elsewhere (Thorne, 1967) interprets underlying integrative processes as underlying all types of controls, so that the diagnostic problem becomes one of identifying the patterns of faulty integration or disintegration underlying control defects.

The first step in diagnosing the status of integration levels consists in making a clinical judgment concerning the general level of global integration, i.e., the level of *integration of integrates* involving the global integration of integrated subfunctions. Broadly speaking, the concept of "integration of integrates" refers to the highest level integrational unit existing at any moment, organized and supported by many lower level integrates (e.g., psychophysiological supporting functions). This includes the integration of component affective, cognitive, and conative subfunctions into an internally consistent and relatively unified state which adequately supports the global motivational unit of *the person working out the business of life in the world*.

The second step consists of a diagnosis of the integrative process directed toward discovering (1) faulty patterns of integration which prevent the highest level integrations from being organized, or (2) factors actively producing disintegration of previously established integrations. We are concerned here with the factors which prevent or distort the highest level "integration of integrates" and thereby inhibit the highest levels of being and existential achievement.

The third step in integrational diagnosis involves identifying specific psychological state syndromes, which we have classified and described elsewhere (Thorne, 1967). This system of psychological state diagnosis makes possible consideration of many "state" syndromes never previously classified or described and tremendously extends the diagnostic armamentarium. For example, the traditional psychiatric diagnostic systems have never explored intensively the large area between psychological normality and psychiatric disorder which includes many clinically significant eccentricities and psychologial state reactions.

The fourth step consists in making clinical judgments concerning the positive or negative mental health implications of various integrational patterns evaluated in terms of concepts of adaptation and adjustment. It is evident that many patterns of integration are not socially acceptable or healthy, i.e., the confidence man or swindler may be highly integrated by socially undesirable factors. Ultimately, it is necessary to formulate clinical judgments concerning whether any integrational pattern is adaptive, adjustive, and healthy or maladaptive, maladjustive, and unhealthy. This is not an easy problem, and the various issues are discussed later.

Clinical judgments concerning global integrational status depend primarily on the study of the sequence of psychological states comprising a motivational unit from start to completion (action sequence). This overall diagnosis requires clinical evaluation of the attributes of integrated behavior as follows:

1. *Unification.* Unity is the phenomenal result of integration. Phenomenally, dynamically, and meaningfully, the integrational unit is intact, unified, purposeful, and directed. The person is doing something and what he is doing is to the point.

2. *Organizational complexity.* The highest level integrations are enormously complex and should be recognized as such.

3. *Internal consistency.* Consistency dynamically implies the absence or resolution of conflict.

4. *Phenomenal completeness.* Integrated states at the highest levels of organization are so perfectly coordinated and manifestly directed as to give the phenomenal appearance of being highly integrated, i.e., the person looks integrated and the clinician can recognize the presence or absence of the integrated state after brief observation. Integrated states are gestalts in which the whole is greater than the sum of the parts.

5. *Manifest competency.* Integrated states at their highest reflect levels of perfection of controls whereby performances are highly efficient and to the point. The person knows what he is doing and accomplishing it efficiently.

6. *Correlated manifestations.* Correlation of psychological measures is the mathematical expression of integration. The more broad the correlation of factors, the higher the level of integration.

The basic state of being integrated is an important clinical consideration entirely apart from the meanings or composition of its factorial contents. Integrations are positive when they enhance existential actualization or negative if they are self-destructive. However, the presence or absence of integration has to be ascertained before its content and significance can be assessed.

Psychopathology and the Diagnosis of Disintegration

Disintegration always involves the absence or breakdown of the factors normally organizing integrated states. States of disintegration are recognized clinically by the exact opposites of the signs listed above as characteristic of integration—namely, lack of unity, lack of organization, inconsistency, incompleteness, incompetency, disorganization of consciousness, lack of correlatedness, and generally chaotic nature. The central phenomenal manifestation always is loss or deficit of some type of essential controls.

An enlarged system of psychopathology is necessary to incorporate all the levels of factors potentially producing disintegration. Our own personal professional development has been marked by the continuing search for expanded systems of psychopathology and psychodiagnosis presented first in our basic *Principles of Psychological Examining* (1955) and later developed in our *Diagnostic Classification and Nomenclature of Psychological States* (1964). Both of these sources outline the directions for future broad extensions of the science of psychopathology to include many levels of factors never previously systematically considered.

Powerful arguments may be cited to the effect that all of psychopathology must relate to problems of integration/disintegration. Although factors on different levels of integration may involve different etiologic agents and dynamic principles, their influence is always on the process of integration/disintegration. Psychoanalytic type mechanisms are an example of explanatory principles which, although providing valid interpretations of certain levels of integrative patterns, do not have the universal applicability originally assumed in Freudian theory as applying to all behavior.

The Issue of Relativity in Clinical Diagnosis

Diagnostic practices depending upon medical models of disease have come under severe critisicm from Szasz (1961), Adams (1964), and others on the grounds that mental disease is a myth and analogies from the medical model of physical disease are invalid because most psychological disorders stem from disturbed personal relationships. It is argued that the standard diagnostic classifications of the American Psychiatric Association are largely invalid and that such concepts as "schizophrenia" or "psychoneurosis" are simply catch-all devices to include a variety of heterogeneous conditions of uncertain etiology. It is argued that many of the classic diagnoses are simply logical artifacts or statistical conveniences utilized solely for expedient classification purposes.

Studies of clinical judgment (see Thorne, 1961a) tend to support the contention that current diagnostic practices, classification systems, case handling methods, psychological measurement methods, and even systematic foundation theories are invalid, unreliable, and grossly inefficient. In our opinion, much of the error stems from invalid and obsolete theoretical approaches involving personality "trait" and "structure" theories which have long since been discredited but which are still clung to tenaciously by defenders of proprietary interests in the various schools of psychology and psychiatry.

It is our contention that only the eclectic approach is capable of discriminating the contribution of all the classes and levels of etiologic factors which may organize integrational patterns, and that more limited approaches, as exemplified by the special schools, all involve the error of being too limited, restrictive, and incapable of encompassing all the known factors commanding consideration. Classic structural approaches (including psychoanalysis) must be abandoned in favor of the flexible, eclectic approach of integrative psychology.

Many of the errors underlying invalid clinical judgments appear to stem from the failure to consider the principles of psychological relativity in evaluating behavior data and the outcomes of actions. The standards and criteria for making many types of clinical judgments are relative to many kinds of psychological, sociological, and cultural factors which must be properly represented to achieve valid etiologic equations. Wide disagreements exist concerning the criteria of normality vs. abnormality. The etiology of many conditions is either unknown or incompletely understood. There is no general agreement as to the role and weighting of various classes of factors underlying mental disorders. Most clinical decisions are intuitive, unreliable, and demonstrably invalid for predictive purposes. Clinicians too often find themselves in diagnostic or therapeutic quicksand where nothing holds up.

Many of these difficulties disappear when the clinician limits himself to the study of significant psychological states, analyzing them in terms of the eclectic approach of integrative psychology, which seeks to discover the etiologic equation reflecting the organization of any integrational pattern. Within this frame of reference, all diagnostic and case handling questions are related specifically to particular problems or life situations. Clinical answers and decisions are related to specific situations, and further studies are made to keep abreast of changing psychological states.

Usually it is possible to obtain a consensus of clinical judgments concerning *relative* (defined in terms of specific criteria) normality/abnormality, adaptability, adjustment, illness, or disability. Differences in individual clinical judgments usually can be resolved by more exact definitions and criteria, by discussions of differences, or by the adoption of arbitrary procedures.

Psychological State Measurements

The diagnosis of psychological states always depends upon *in vitro* observations and measurements related specifically to specific psychological states. *Psychological state diagnosis* is concerned with the actual raw behavior data, with the phenomenal "givens" which are the succession of psychological states constituting Being. The clinical endeavor is to objectify the nature of psychological states as completely as possible, specifying the situations or conditions in which they occur, and attempting to discover the etiologic equations underlying them. This approach is facilitated by getting as close to the raw data as possible.

Introspective reporting is the prime method for discovering what a person is experiencing. The most direct approach is simply to ask the subject what he is experiencing. With highly verbal subjects, introspective reporting provides the richest data but is less successful with uncommunicative clients.

Direct observation. The skilled professional observer often can not only identify psychological states but can also interpret situational dynamics not susceptible to indirect methods of examination. *Empathic* understanding conveys the nature and significance of emotional and feeling states.

Situational analysis in which the clinician directly observes the client behaving in the situations wherein he is maladjusted may be the only method of directly observing the dynamics of interpersonal difficulties.

Stream of life diagnosis was developed by Adolf Meyer (1948) to objectify longitudinal developments by graphically recording critical incidents of development and experience.

Time investment diagnosis utilizes time studies of behavior to discover the temporal distribution of prevailing patterns of organization of the integrational milieu. A simple tabulation of how any person spends his time provides important evidence concerning what the person is doing (or not doing) with his life.

Life management diagnosis involves applied psychological efficiency engineering to discover how well the person is performing the essential roles of civilized living with special regard to work efficiency, family adjustment, marriage and sex, financial management, etc.

Objective state measurements may be obtained from successive administrations of the classical personality inventories or more particularly from tests specifically designed to elicit state measurements. This author has devised the *Integration Level Test Series* involving eight tests specifically designed to sample ideological/attitudinal, role playing, social status, life style, and existential meaning factors not hitherto investigated (Thorne, 1966–1967).

Projective methods may be utilized to uncover the nature of underlying psychological states in clients who are unable to communicate introspective life easily.

Clinical Classification Diagnosis

This topic has been left to the last because we regard it as having only secondary importance in the diagnostic process. Suffice it to state that current diagnostic classifications are largely invalid and grossly unsatisfactory for clinical prediction purposes. It should be understood clearly that recurring attempts on the part of professional groups such as the American Psychiatric Association to establish standard classification systems have done much to introduce confusion and obfuscation into the field of psychodiagnosis. The official diagnostic classification of the American Psychiatric Association is premature in the sense that we don't know enough to arrive at any final classification, obsolete in that many of its categories are demonstrably invalid, inadequate in that many syndromes are either ignored or improperly described, distorted in that it often forces improper classifications for administrative or statistical convenience, illogical in that it utilizes mixed criteria for establishing different categories, static in that dynamics often are ignored, and in many other ways generally unsatisfactory. Many official categories such as "schizophrenia" or "sociopath" are wastebasket classifications including many disparate conditions of unknown etiology.

The theory of integrative psychology with its emphasis on the stream of psychological states which constitutes experience (Being) is basically incompatible with classic classification systems emphasizing symptoms, syndromes, personality traits, and structures. It is impossible to classify psychological states with any rigid system which ignores situational and existential considerations. Integrative psychopathology requires a new and much more complex classification system based on the psychological state, which we have outlined in more detail elsewhere (Thorne, 1964).

However, in spite of the inadequacies of the classical classification systems, there is some advantage in retaining such categories or dimensions as have some demonstrated validity for the purpose of indicating the general coordinates of the field of clinical psychopathology. If they are redefined in terms of the dimensions of "state" psychology, many of the classic terms have real relevance. Indeed, many of the classic categories take on new meanings when redefined in terms of "state" concepts. Basic constructs include the following:

"Personality" is redefined as the characteristic integrative pattern underlying individuality.

Correlations between behaviors reflect common integrative factors.

The factor analytic findings of general, group, and specific factors reflect different degrees of generality of integrative functions.

General intelligence is redefined as cortical integrative quality and capacity.

Perception, learning, memory, feelings and emotions, concept formation, and creative thinking reflect different levels of the integration of integrates. Perception involves the integration of informational input with existing mental (associative) context.

Higher level integrations make possible higher levels of controls. Conversely, disintegration always involves loss of controls.

The prime motive is to maintain the highest possible integrational status.

Ego strength is redefined as high level integrative stability or strength.

The subject of psychopathology also may be redefined from the viewpoint of integrative psychology. The diagnostic problem becomes one of differentiating the levels of organization at which integration fails to be achieved or breaks down.

The unitary factor in all mental disorder involves defects of, or loss of, integration resulting in progressive loss of controls. The one common factor in all mental disorder is integrative defect.

Endogenous mental deficiency involves defects or deficits of psychophysiological supporting structures and functions, which prevent normal growth and maturation and thus prevent the development of higher level integrations.

In exogenous mental deficiency, organic injuries damage the structures upon which higher level integrations depend.

Psychosomatic syndromes involve disordered functions in component organ systems which disrupt higher-level integrations by loss or disorder of lower-level supporting systems.

Conditioned behavior disorders involve inappropriate redintegrations.

Anxiety states involve the imminent or actual breakdown of defensive integrations against fear, hostility, guilt, or conflict.

Psychoneurotic states involve disintegrations of part functions while maintaining general integration. (Self functioning still intact.)

Psychotic states involve general disintegration disrupting self executive functioning.

Hysteria and hysteroid states involve dissociative integrations in which conflictual factors are kept in functional isolation.

Schizophrenic reactions, in general, involve associative disorders preventing integration of affective and cognitive life.

Paranoid states involve pathological defensive reorganizations, rationalizing personal inadequacies and projecting causes of failure onto the environment. A type of negative reintegration.

Conditioned behavior disorders reflect negative integrations learned by imitation from asocial peers.

Neurotic conduct disorders involve negative integrations expressing frustration and unresolved conflict.

Sociopathies involve conditioned negative integrations based on maladaptive life styles.

Existential neuroses involve personality reactions to frustration and failure where integrative patterns fail to produce sufficient success or meaning to life. Existential anxiety is a reaction to the imminent breakdown or failure of integrative patterns.

Demoralization reactions occur when cumulative failure destroys the motive to maintain the struggle for integration.

Gross traumatic or degenerative central nervous system defects occurring in later life (organic brain disease) result in progressive impairments of established supporting systems, resulting in personality disintegration.

Transient psychophysiological disorders involving diffuse biochemical or toxic disruption of functioning cause temporary decompensations and disintegration, reversible when normal conditions resume. These include the toxic states.

Affective over- or under-drive tends to disrupt or prevent higher level cognitive integrations, i.e., intrusive emotions, excitements, depressions, furors, etc.

Mental context limitations due to educational deprivation tend to limit the range and complexity of what is integrationally possible on higher levels of organization of behavior. Severe affective trauma or experiential deprivations tend to limit the possibilities for higher level integrations.

Fixations or regressions of integration may be observed where growth is blocked by internal conflicts or external pressures.

"Negative" integrations in an otherwise healthy individual may reflect the natural consequences of error, superstition, untenable beliefs, value distortions, etc. Here, the symbolic content or existential meanings of any integrational pattern may be called in question in terms of personal-social inadaptability.

Compensatory "reintegrations" may occur in reaction to thwarting of natural outlets, or in attempts at conflict resolution.

The acquisition of newer and more refined controls makes possible the escape from mechanistic determination of behavior through higher level integrations maintained consciously and voluntarily.

Existentially, full-humanness results from the individuation stemming from the highest level integrative patterns.

In summary, integrative psychology is concerned with the struggle of the organism to maintain the highest levels of integration. The fields of general psychology and psychopathology need to be reinterpreted in terms of phenomena relating to the achievement, maintenance, and breakdown of integration. The psychological state is the basic unit of experience with which integrative psychology deals. Every psychological state is a resultant of an integrational milieu which can be objectified in terms of an etiologic equation in which all pertinent factors are represented.

Case Illustrating Diagnostic Process

Cause of Referral: Husband complains of progressive withdrawal from family life, ignoring of household duties, sexual frigidity, and increasing neuroticism.

Demographic Data: Mrs. V, age 27, American born, married eight years, two children. College sophomore when married. Considered a brilliant student. IQ WAIS, 126.

CLINICAL DATA	DIAGNOSTIC INFERENCES
Husband complains that for last two years, Mrs. V has become progressively more emotionally unstable and failing in her marital duties. Spends most of her time in bed, ignoring the children, refusing to interact with her husband, and apparently brooding about her problems. He claims that she has deteriorated markedly in caring for her-	Based on the husband's complaints, this appears to be a severe psychoneurotic or even a prepsychotic condition. The habit deterioration, withdrawal from reality, and ignoring of family duties suggest an insidious schizophrenic reaction. The husband's story seems to indicate a relatively serious disorder;

self or in trying to fulfill her duties. He claims that she has not submitted to marital relations for three years. He believes that she is mentally disordered since she seems to have withdrawn from the world.

Mrs. V agreed to cooperate with psychotherapy and came for an interview voluntarily. She is an attractive young matron who appears in good contact with reality. No psychotic behavior elicited. However, she admitted all her husband's complaints that she was spending most of her time in bed and escaping from her duties.

however, the clinician makes a mental note not to be overinfluenced by it.

This client certainly is not overtly psychotic since she drove to the interview by herself, is normally oriented, shows no association disorder. No delusional material or hallucinations elicited. Emotionally, she appears unstable and perhaps slightly depressed. Well educated and cultured. Diagnostic impression altered to "Not psychotic—schizoid tendencies at most."

Sessions 2–6   First week

Conducted nondirectively. Mrs. V spent most of the time telling how unhappy she is. She describes horrible feelings of being unable to face life. "I would cry all the time if I didn't stay in bed. . . . Everything seems too much for me. . . . The kids drive me crazy. I can't stand their noise. I try to get up and do things but I can't seem to manage."

Because Mrs. V appeared so distraught emotionally, interviews 2–6 were conducted on successive days. She would come to the office, complain and cry for an hour, and then go home to bed.

Patient obviously is very frustrated and demoralized over her inability to perform her roles and duties.

During this recital of complaints, Mrs. V acted like a little girl crying over broken toys. Her manner is definitely immature and childish.

Simple catharsis and ventilation were experimented with to see how much relief she would get.

Sessions 7–11   Second week

No change in her condition. Still spending much time in bed neglecting duties. Her train of association now more concerned with describing her "terrible" feelings. "I don't know how long I can go on this way. I feel so miserable. All I can think of is myself. I feel weak and shaky all the time. . . ."

Appears agitated and depressed but not psychotically. When her attention is distracted from herself, she is able to joke and laugh.

Sessions 12–16 Third week

Mrs. V obviously is under much pressure from her husband to start functioning again. Mr. V openly requests that she be psychiatrically hospitalized. Mrs. V is panicked by this suggestion and becomes even worse. She now cries most of the time.

"Please don't send me to a mental hospital. I am not crazy. My mind is all right, it's just that I can't get a hold of myself. I hate to be this way but I can't help it."

Observing the interactions of Mr. and Mrs. V, and considering his impatience with her and his demand for her hospitalization, it is apparent that Mr. V is quite impatient, hostile, and aggressive toward her. She is totally unable to cope with his critical attitudes.

Apparently never too well integrated, her current psychological state is one of general paralysis of functioning by constant emotional instability.

Sessions 17–19 Fourth week

Up to this time, Mrs. V has never openly expressed her feelings about her husband. The therapist gently directs her attention to their interactions. "I suppose I have been afraid of him since even before we were married. . . . He was always much more eager than I was to get married. . . . I almost didn't marry him because I had a premonition what it was going to be like. . . . He is much more bossy and aggressive than I am."

Co: What about sex?

Cl: I guess that is the worst problem. It never has been any good.

Co: He doesn't seem to understand you?

Cl: I don't know what is the matter. All I know is I get nothing out of it whatsoever. Nothing.

Co: It leaves you cold?

Cl: That's right. All the other girls are talking about how exciting it is and I can't get with it.

Co: You've never had a climax?

Cl: I wouldn't know what that is. It's more or less like rape and it always has been. When he wants

Since the husband obviously is a major cause of her instability, the diagnostic decision was made that this area had to be opened up.

More evidence of an immature woman unable to stand up for her rights against an older and more domineering husband.

In view of her husband's complaints about her frigidity, this subject was opened up to get her side of it.

A state of sexual frigidity probably caused by the interference of the stronger emotions of fear and anger.

The first bold statement of her resentment over sexual aggressions. She does not know how to express it he just takes it. Sometimes I feel I could scream.

Co: How did you come to marry him anyway?

Cl: I've asked myself that often. I guess I just don't know. He was always so certain of himself and he seemed to think he knew just what was right for me and I guess I was flattered by such attentions and got swept off my feet.

Co: And now you feel trapped.

Cl: I guess that's completely right. I'm trapped. I've got these kids and we haven't much money and my family is not too sympathetic with me and I'm just trapped. Nowhere to turn.

Co: Well, what are you going to do about it?

Cl: You've got me. I just don't know.

Sessions 20–22   Fifth week

Co: Do you feel that you've got it in you to get hold of yourself and gradually get things under control again?

Cl: I truly don't know. What do you mean?

Co: There is no easy way out of this except to recondition yourself and learn to handle some of the things you have been failing with.

Cl: I'll do anything I can.

Co: All right. We will work out a program for you, one thing at a time. The first week I want you to stay out of bed no matter how you feel. All right, so you feel like crying. Go into the bathroom and have your cry and run cold water over yourself but don't go to bed. This is an absolute must.

------

her own resentments outwardly, hence they turn inwards and paralyze her.

Another expression of feelings of immaturity and inadequacy.

Her emotional agitation is now seen to be a helpless protest against stronger forces which she feels unable to cope with.

The decision to institute retraining through task therapy and behavior therapy is made.

The patient is confronted with the issue that she must start the fight to regain control over herself.

The first step is to tolerate her own emotional instability and not retreat into bed.

Sessions 23–25   Sixth week

Mrs. V has done better this week, spending almost no time in bed. However, she still feels agitated and unstable emotionally.

Co: Let's get back to your husband. How do you really feel about him?

Cl: Oh, I suppose I love him. At least I think I do. He is so good and patient with me.

> Ambivalence toward Mr. V stated for the first time.

Co: Do you mean you love him or only that you think you should?

Cl: Now, that is a good point isn't it? No, now that you mention it, I don't really love him. In fact, I don't really care for him at all. I do respect him, though.

> This is probably the core problem, faced for the first time.

Co: If this is true, how did you come to have three children?

Cl: I have two children. He wanted to have children as quick as possible. He said it would bring us closer together.

———

Seventh to tenth weeks

This was a very unstable period. It started when Mrs. V's parents intervened and insisted that she should leave her husband and return home to live with them. They also insisted that she be seen by another therapist. There was an open family quarrel when Mr. V insisted that his wife should remain at home. Mrs. V had a transient relapse in which she returned to bed and started crying again.

> Her newly found integration collapsed under increased stress.

The impasse was broken when it was agreed that Mrs. V should return to her parent's home and take treatment with a female psychoanalyst known to her parents.

After four weeks' treatment with the analyst, Mrs. V felt strong enough to face her problems again

> The psychoanalyst's main contribution appears to have consisted in reassuring her that she was not psychotic. The analyst also frankly interpreted her immaturity in trying to escape from hostility and aggression in the husband.

and return to her husband and family. She had not been happy living with her parents, who blamed her for being weak and not standing up to her husband.

Sessions 26–29 Eighth to twelfth weeks

On returning home, Mrs. V did surprisingly well with her duties. She rarely went to bed, handled the children better, and seemed better resigned to facing her problems.

Cl: You know, I have been thinking. I know I have been cold with my husband, but I don't really think I'm a frigid person.

Co: How is that?

Cl: It came to me when Dr. D (the analyst) asked me what I thought about when I went to bed. Of course, most of the time I would be thinking about my troubles. But some of the time I would be having romantic daydreams about other men.

Co: Who for instance?

Cl: Never my husband. It would be screen actors or men that I met.

Co: It would mean quite a lot to you to find out whether you are really frigid.

In succeeding interviews, Mrs. V began to explore her sexual reactions more intensively, recalling that she had been frightened and perhaps mishandled on her wedding night, and that her husband was definitely not her romantic ideal.

Sessions 30–42 Thirteenth to twenty-sixth weeks

This was a very difficult period for all concerned. Mrs. V suddenly blossomed into a much more at-

---

Her psychological state is much healthier.

This represents one of the first tentative steps on the part of Mrs. V to reconstitute her self concept and resume a more positive attack on life.

Probably a true insight that her frigidity might be only situational and that she could be normally reactive with another man.

Insightful reorientation to her own sexual nature and reactions.

Changing self concepts and orientations to life have produced a profound alteration of her psycho-

tractive and aggressive young woman. She threw herself into an active flirtation with a handsome man about town who kept it from ripening into an open affair only because he was a business associate of her husband's and could not afford a scandal. Mrs. V openly invited him to take her off on a weekend. It appeared that Mrs. V was striving to prove herself as a woman.

logical state and integrational patterns.

Cl: I make no bones about it. I'm crazy about Charlie and I don't care who knows it. I know that I could respond to him. I just feel it in me.

Her newfound determination to prove herself is an encouraging sign.

Co: You feel that you have to prove that you're not frigid?

Cl: Now I *know* I'm not frigid. I know from my feelings when I think about Charlie that I could be perfectly normal with him.

Co: Well, be that as it may, you can't just throw things over and run off with Charlie. Even you must know that's impossible.

Some restraint is indicated to keep her reactions within the limits of what is realistically possible.

Cl: Nevertheless, I intend to do it if I can.

Co: Maybe you ought to pull in your horns a little. Knowing Charlie, I don't think he would do it even if he could afford to do it. Maybe you can prove yourself without tearing your whole life apart.

Cl: I don't care what anybody else thinks. I have decided that I have to be myself. That is more important than anything else.

She is beginning to develop stronger self executive functioning.

Co: Well, you can be yourself without tearing everything to pieces.

Cl: That's what I have to find out for myself. I'm going to run my own life for a change.

Mrs. V actually proposed to her

Many clients seem to have to

friend Charlie that they have an affair. She offered to do anything or go anyplace he wanted. Charlie wisely refused. Mrs. V then experimented with several other men but nothing developed.

carry things to extremes before they return to the middle of the road.

Sessions 43–49 Twenty-seventh to thirtieth weeks

This continued to be a very difficult period. Mr. V was counseled to be very patient and tolerant of his wife until she found herself. Fortunately, he was strong enough to tolerate her experiments with other men.

Eventually Mr. and Mrs. V worked out a tolerable if not ideal relationship. Mrs. V never came to regard her husband as an ideal lover, and probably never really was able to love him; however, she respected his good qualities and also resolved to do her duty by her children. She was able to resume a limited sexual life, usually not responding, but occasionally coming to climax particularly when she had been drinking.

The marriage continued under conditions of limited compatibility.

Gradually, Mrs. V began to compensate for the shortcomings of her marriage by developing community interests and becoming more interested in the development of her children as they became older and were less of a threat to her.

Summary: This case provides an interesting example of the study and treatment of what was essentially an existential problem. The diagnostic and therapeutic approach consisted in attempting to understand the psychological state of Mrs. V as it changed dramatically in different phases of case handling. Viewed as a problem of reorganizing integrational patterns and self concepts, a reconstruction of coping behaviors was accomplished.

REFERENCES

Adams, H. B. Mental illness or interpersonal behavior? *Amer. Psychol.*, 1964, **19**, 191–96.

Eysenck, H. J. *The structure of personality.* New York: Wiley, 1953.

Meyer, A. See Leif, A. *The commonsense psychiatry of Adolf Meyer.* New York: McGraw-Hill, 1948. Pp. 418–22, 492–94.

Szasz, T. S. *The myth of mental illness.* New York: Hoeber-Harper, 1961.

Thorne, F. C. *Principles of psychological examining.* Brandon, Vt.: Journal of Clinical Psychology, 1955.

Thorne, F. C. *Clinical judgment.* Brandon, Vt.: Journal of Clinical Psychology, 1961a.

Thorne, F. C. *Personality.* Brandon, Vt.: Journal of Clinical Psychology, 1961b.

Thorne, F. C. Diagnostic classification and nomenclature. *Clin. Psychol. Monogr.*, 1964, No. 17.

Thorne, F. C. An analysis of Szasz' "Myth of Mental Illness." *Amer. J. Psychiat.*, 1966, **123**, 652–56.

Thorne, F. C. *Integration level test series.* 8 tests. Brandon, Vt.: Clinical Psychology Publishing Company, 1966–1967.

Thorne, F. C. *Integrative psychology.* Brandon, Vt.: Clinical Psychology Publishing Company, 1967.

Thorne, F. C. *Psychological case handling.* 2 vols. Brandon, Vt.: Clinical Psychology Publishing Company, 1968.

BEYOND DISORDER, TOWARD TRANSACTIONS

Psychodiagnostic systems, assert Pratt and Tooley, are derived from explicit or implicit personality models, approaches to taxonomy, and underlying philosophies of man. The word "psychodiagnosis" has been linked to the medical model of personality, which discusses man in terms of disorder, illness, and psychopathology. Yet the traditional psychodiagnostic system is merely one taxonomy derived from one philosophy of man.

Pratt and Tooley lay a conceptual framework for a significantly different taxonomy of man. In contrast to the conventional medical model, Pratt and Tooley see the essence of man in his capacity to make transactions or promises, to form contractual relationships, to develop means-ends instrumentalities for the creation and exchange of human values. Most such mutual obligations are not consciously assumed, but psychological meaning arises from the transactions at all levels, from intrapsychic to international. Analysis of such contracts is made in terms of interpersonal, intrafamilial, and intergroup relations.

The authors take issue with those who believe that psychodiagnosis should relate to psychopathology, to neurosis and psychosis, to "clinical" groups. Their approach focuses on none of these areas, nor do they propose a variation or modification in our present diagnostic system, for they abandon the medical psychiatric model of man and urge a reconceptualization of personality. Their position raises a number of questions. Does their approach help us to understand a given individual and his problems? Does it place him in any category? Does it uncover

347

his uniqueness? Does it suggest differential means for treatment? Does it incorporate research findings? Does it provide means of evaluating and assessing individuals?

Pratt and Tooley assert that a serious consideration of advances in personality classification *must* begin with drastically different personality models. Their transactional-contractual system provides a groundwork for a taxonomy based not on categories of illness and disease, but rather on means-ends instrumentalities, interpersonal and intergroup contracts and transactions. They question the very purpose and underlying model of a personality classification system and take what may prove to be fruitful steps in a new direction.

11

TOWARD A METATAXONOMY OF HUMAN SYSTEMS ACTUALIZATION: THE PERSPECTIVE OF CONTRACT PSYCHOLOGY

STEVE PRATT   JAY TOOLEY

Metataxonomy: What Taxonomies and Taxonomies for What?

The given topic, the title of this book, is *New Approaches to Personality Classification*. We would like to introduce a few notions, which we hope would be of heuristic value, that might be taken into consideration in regard to both the use of current systems and the prospects for some radically new approaches. Our purpose is not to present a critique of past or present psychodiagnostic systems or nosologies—such critiques in the current literature almost outnumber extant systems. Nor is our aim to deliver a single definitive system as such—many workers are engaged in this task and much of their work would fit at least parts of our purpose very well. Our emphasis here is on *metataxonomy* or theory of taxonomies, to provide a conceptual context for both the design and development of taxonomies and for the *ordering* of taxonomies, for taxonomies of taxonomies. From this perspective, we will be citing examples of current classification procedures and systems as being particularly useful for "getting at" (ordering) different levels, domains, and dimensions of human systems (structure, functioning, and dysfunctioning).

As one basic aspect of a new approach we use the term "taxonomy" (or better, "taxonomies") instead of "psychodiagnostic." There are two reasons for this semantic preference. First, we do not wish to be constrained by the prefix which might imply that our concern is exclusively within-the-person. Not that this "intrapsychic" level is unimportant, but rather that it is too important to be treated reductionistically. The second concern relates to another question of orientation, namely,

that alternatives to the term "diagnostic" (with its derivative procedures) deserve a hearing in order to provide an opportunity for the
development of concepts that avoid exclusive preoccupation with pathol-
ogy-centered nosologies. Even here we would not necessarily argue one
as opposed to the other, though we frequently have done so (Pratt,
1961; Pratt and Tooley, 1962a, 1964), because ultimately these are
questions requiring empirical resolution. But alternatives do need to
have a chance to be tried out in order to be tested.

In terms of allowing fully for conceptual alternatives, a review of
the literature will reveal that even when alternatives to psychopathology-
centered nosologies are adduced, they are usually still *dis*order-oriented.
A major controversy, considered by some authorities to be the central
controversy between nosologies, hinges on the assumption of *continuity*
vs. *discontinuity* between normal and abnormal (disordered) behavior
(Eron, 1966; Menninger, 1963; Wolman, 1965). The assumption of
continuity between disordered and normal behaviors automatically projects the positive end of the continuum, even though operationally it is
characteristically ignored. Likewise, discontinuity theory logically demands a dichotomous classification that must, at least by implication,
posit a positive though separate side of the coin, which again is treated
as more or less irrelevant. Thus there has traditionally been little choice,
with both kinds of nosologies (continuous-discontinuous) focusing on
the disorder as the primary subject (Jahoda, 1958).

Setting aside for the moment the continuity-discontinuity controversy, we would like to *reverse* this primary-secondary relationship, to
conceptualize disorder as secondary and human systems actualization as
primary. Again, our purpose is simply to provide for comparative evaluation in order to make it possible to determine, empirically, the most
productive approach. Thus, some new approaches might well look at a
few of the major problems and potentialities inherent in sketching out
possible frames of reference adequate to the development of taxonomies
of human systems actualization. It may turn out that such functional
taxonomies will prove to be a precondition to resolving the continuity-
discontinuity controversy and essential for any useful understanding of
psychosocial disorders per se.

Our aim is to raise some of these crucial theoretical problems and
possibilities and to present the preliminary outlines of one possible frame
of reference for new taxonomies: *contract psychology*. It is our assumption that any and every taxonomy of human systems, of behaviors, or
of any aspect of human conduct explicitly or implicitly invokes a *model
of man* and thus, more generally, a model of the human enterprise (Pratt
and Tooley, 1964). This means that the level of accounting sufficient for

comprehensive taxonomies of human conduct (effective behavior and disorders) within adequate taxonomies of human psychosocial systems generally, must derive from a philosophy of man. An adequate *systematic* philosophy must incorporate an explicit epistemology and ontology. These questions cannot be avoided.

Taxonomies, at whatever level of generality or specificity, that ignore such *systematic* considerations can only function as relatively closed systems assumed to be free from outside ecological determinants. Taxonomies can get by with this just as long as the contextual field remains relatively constant, but any time the field changes genotypically such taxonomies must inevitably break down. Thus, systematically misconstruing *what is* as well as what is *becoming*, they will miss the variance in both change and stability within change. Social-behavioral science taxonomies cannot be limited to static entities but must be concerned with both stability and flexibility, with rigidity and with conduct undergoing change in a changing world.

Human actions, whether actualizing or counteractualizing (effective or ineffective), involve human systems at a variety of *levels* of human organization. For instance, community, institution, family, person are all *systems,* and to deal with any one of them we need a systems theory. As each of these different systems can only be understood or classified in relation to the others, to study any one of these systems nothing less than a *general* systems theory can be adequate.

Taxonomies are designed to track down systems, system functioning (or dysfunctioning), and system change. Thus, as does its subject matter, a metataxonomy requires a general systems theory. Our "special" general systems theory is contract-system theory, i.e., contract psychology. Out of this systematic weltanschauung it should be possible to construct a heuristic metataxonomy adequate to encompass the many kinds of taxonomies necessary to man's purposes and to deal with the problems and possibilities connected with the development of open-system taxonomies designed to function as *instrumentalities* for human systems actualization.

Contract Psychology's Epistemology of Ontology

All taxonomies try to get at some slice of the world and, within our extended metataxonomy, also may serve as instruments in shaping reality to man's purposes. From contract psychology's perspective, knowing proceeds through the "participation-observation-intervention" of "man in the universe." Thus we speak of the *epistemology* of *ontology,* of knowing and the existential reality of the knower and the known, of *becoming* and the "to be known." Metataxonomy is shaped by epistemology and ontology, whose basic assumptions, explicitly or implicity, reach through each and every taxonomy (Barber, 1960; Handlon, 1960; Newbury, 1958; Van Kaam, 1958).

Epistemology refers to the process of knowing, to the relationship of the knower to the known, to man's reflexive study of man and his surroundings (Grene, 1966). Scientific inquiry, social action, the humanities, and the arts are all aspects of the human endeavor and thus part of the historical purview of psychology. As all of the social-behavioral sciences are ultimately based on human behavior and human relationships, psychology becomes, as Stevens (1936) said, "the *propaedeutic* science." In his compelling call for theories of complexity and prodigality, "Psychological Science Versus the Science-Humanism Antinomy: Intimations of a Significant Science of Man," Koch (1961) put epistemology in psychology's lap: "It is, incidentally, my growing conviction that many problems still allocated to epistemology will receive little further clarification until they are recognized for the psychological problems they are" (p. 637).

We have elsewhere presented, as have others (Cantril et al., 1949), a taxonomy of epistemologies which takes the position that all epistemologies can be ordered into one or another of three fundamental types: (1) *auto*-actional epistemologies, (2) *inter*-actional epistemologies, and (3) *trans*-actional epistemologies (Pratt and Tooley, 1967b). The choice between these three epistemological positions is crucial both for metataxonomic theory and for the construction of specific taxonomies. The conceptual advantage of the transactional approach is being increasingly recognized for psychology, psychiatry, communication theory, education, biosocial sciences, and for science generally (Bauer, 1966; Bentley, 1935, 1954; Bertalanffy, 1952; Cantril and Bumstead, 1960; Dewey and Bentley, 1949; Grinker et al., 1961; Miller, 1965a). In *Explorations in Transactional Psychology,* edited by Kilpatrick (1961a, p. 3), we find the following:

Our work has been aimed at a systematic examination of such problems [i.e., in the field of perception], and out of this examination there has been developed a basic formulation concerning the nature of knowing and of observation. . . . This basic theory is one which has elsewhere been called "transactional." According to this view, living is an enormously complex evolving process which includes space and time and environment, as well as the organism, in an indissoluble whole. A segment in time of this process may be labeled a "transaction" (Dewey) or "occasion" (Whitehead) in which all aspects of the process are contained, including purposes, past experience in the form of assumptions, and the future in the form of expectancies. Cantril (1950, p. 59) explains this position in the following way: "Each transaction of living involves numerous capacities and aspects of man's nature which operate together. Each occasion of life can occur only through an environment; is imbued with some purpose; requires action of some kind, and the registration of the consequences of the action. Every action is based upon some awareness or perception, which in turn is determined by the assumptions brought to the occasion. All of these processes are interdependent. No one process could function without the others."

Epistemological consideration of the total relevant contractual-field as *transactional* precludes polar reductionism, whether intrapsychic as in psychoanalytic or cultural as in absolute cultural relativism (the person as putty). Transactional epistemology, by requiring that *meaning* be derived from the nature of the transaction itself, also precludes both the mechanistic and the reductionistic misinterpretations of whole and part processes characteristic of traditional taxonomic theory and practice (Cantril, 1964; Hayakawa, 1955; Kilpatrick, 1961b).

Our regnant construct (i.e., contract or contract-system) represents the conceptualization of an exclusively human form of transaction. Contract psychology employs a transactional epistemology, which it extends into a *"field*-theoretical" approach, and thus into an explicit transactional-*field* epistemology which, then, for human systems (at all levels of organization) becomes the *contract-system-field*.

Now to shift to the problem of ontology. For ontology, the search is for the most useful key conceptual tools and schemata with which to explicate and articulate the nature of "being, of being-in-the-world," of the "world-to-be-known," and of the "world-becoming." To put it pragmatically: What are the most useful ways for laying out flexible patterns of reality, of the ever-changing world-we-live-in? How to weave a conceptual net to catch all the necessary existential-normative-nomological variance?

Contract psychology puts together all the major pieces of the pattern through the conceptual architecture of its *heuristic-normative-nomological network*. This is not a simple construction, but it is most economical considering what it covers.

This level of accounting *links* ontology with epistemology through the common ground concept of "transactional-field" which they substantively share. The transactional-field (contractual-field for human systems) encompasses the human enterprise through the concept of contract-system levels. This construct of *levels* has its conceptual and methodological roots in several significant theories and constructs. These include: Feibleman's (1954) theory of "integrative levels"; Novikoff's (1945) concept of "levels of organization"; Weaver's (1948) "theory of complexity"; Kantor's (1953, 1959) "levels of participant-observation" and "levels of interpersonal interaction"; and Kaplan's (1964) "levels of abstraction." Within the total contract-systems field, we are concerned with human systems at all levels, from interior intrapsychic contract-system space to international contract-system space. As systems at the various levels are transactionally interrelated, change in any one may be contingent upon change in related systems. As each different system can only be understood in relation to others, to study (or change) any one system at a given level nothing less than a *general systems theory* can be adequate. Thus, our contractual-field concept combines theories of levels with general systems theory.

Another basic epistemological-ontological problem is reflected in the need for conceptual tools with which to link *theories* with *empirical events,* at all levels of organization. Since Bergman and Spence's (1941) excellent discussion of the theoretical and empirical components of science appeared over twenty-five years ago, several theoreticians have conceptualized the complementary interrelationships of science's empirical and theoretical elements in various forms. Margenau (1950), for instance, has elaborated a spatial paradigm formed by blending planes of existence, the inferential or Conceptual Plane (C-Plane) connecting with the empirical, observable or Protocol Plane (P-Plane). Dealing with the same problem, Feigl and Scriven (1956) first introduced the notion of a "nomological net" to encompass and relate the various levels of *theoretical constructs* with their referential *events.* These schemata, including Kaplan's (1964) "empirical-theoretical continuum," can be selectively combined and then used in connection with Northrop's (1947) concept of "epistemic correlation" which provides for "indices of correspondence" between C-Plane and P-Plane, i.e., between theoretical constructs and empirical events.

Contract psychology gives high priority to the incorporation of questions of human purpose—*the axiology of praxiology* (Kotarbinski, 1965). Value theory and action theory are conceptualized as transactionally coupled and as an inextricable part of the total transactional-field. We extend Feigl and Scriven's nomological net to incorporate hierarchical levels of *ends-means* configurations. Thus, the nomological net becomes a *normative*-nomological network. By combining the nomological net with the normative net, we place the theoretical-empirical components of existence (Margenau) within an ends-means context: the normative-nomological network. Thus we can also extend to value theory Northrop's construct of "epistemic correlation," which defines the degree of correspondence (validity) between theory and its empirical referent.

If one posits a transactional relationship between ends and means, then ends-means must be treated as inseparable (irreducible) configurations. Scientific inquiry, the arts, ethics, and the humanities can be considered as *ends-means* activities. Churchman, in *Prediction and Optimal Decision* (1964), and Rapoport, in *Operational Philosophy: Integrating Knowledge and Action* (1953), have each developed this argument in great detail with an emphasis on experimental, mathematical, and operational constructs. They both present an excellent analysis of ends-means taxonomies. Kluckhohn and colleagues (1962) have done likewise and have also covered much of the current thinking on the complex interrelationships (if not "identity") of "fact" and "value."

In discussing the relationship between normative and existential (i.e., nomological) propositions Kluckhohn agrees with Lepley (1943, p. 395), who in his paper "The Identity of Fact and Value" points out:

The belief that valuative statements as expressive of means-end relations are inherently different from scientific propositions as denoting cause-effect relations has apparently risen, as has the view that valuative sentences are less verifiable than factual statements, from failure to see that the whole gamut of events and relations can be referred to by both forms of statement.

Kluckhohn (1962, p. 389) also concurs with the Cornell value-study group:

The concept "value" supplies a point of convergence for the various specialized social sciences, and is a key concept for the integration with studies in the humanities. Value is potentially a bridging concept which can link together many diverse specialized studies—from the experimental psychology of perception to the analysis of political ideologies, from budget studies to economics to aesthetic theory and philosophy of language, from literature to race riots. . . .

Sophisticated use of value-theory can help to correct the wide-spread static-descriptive bias of the social sciences. The pervasive emphasis, for example, upon static-equilibrium theories in economics; upon "social structure" in sociology; upon static "need-reduction" theories of personality in psychology.

Epistemologically speaking, all *knowing,* including scientific inquiry as a course of action, proceeds through explicit or covert ends-means activities involving a complex series of valuations or judgments, e.g., decision to investigate in the first place, formulation of any given problem, selection of methodology, decisions regarding significance levels, utilization of feedback to modify theory and methodology (Smith, 1954). Recent experimental literature reflects a new and growing interest in the empirical investigation of ends-means attributable sources of variance (McGuigan, 1963; Riecken, 1962; Rosenthal, 1963a, 1963b; Sarason, 1951; Tooley, Pratt, and Rosenthal, 1964).

Historically, traditional experimentalists have characteristically given intrusive value-variance the ostrich treatment, frequently to their embarrassment. They have tried to control it directly, or to control it statistically—to "partial it out." Again, trying the opposite tack, we have indicated methodologies through which ends-means variance could be purposively "partialed in" and put to work. Also, in addition to showing how "experimenter variance" and "experimental situational demands" (Orne, 1962) can be exploited, we have pointed out how such shibboleths as subjects' "knowledge of hypothesis" or "personal stake in outcome" can be made an explicit part of the design in "participant-social-action-research" (Pratt and Tooley, 1968b; Tooley, Pratt, and Rosenthal, 1964). Whether one wishes to avoid the embarrassment of value-connected variance cropping up as unwelcome "error variance," or whether one plans to exploit ends-means variance by putting it to work—in either case it must be identified for what it is. Thus, all ends-means derived sources of variance (whether associated with subjects, experimenters, or other "situational demands") must be made explicit for all scientific inquiry, in laboratory or *in situ*. We have labeled this methodological requirement "the principle of axiological specification" (Pratt and Tooley, 1968b; Tooley, Pratt, and Rosenthal, 1964).

Particularly in the social-behavioral sciences, the cost of ignoring ends-means sources of variance has been exorbitant. This is not a conjectural conclusion but an empirical matter of fact. It could readily be argued that, historically, the part played by social science in the prevention of scientific (and social) progress in large part stems from epistemologically untenable amputation of means from ends (Barber and Hirsch, 1962; Borman, 1963; Horowitz, 1963, 1964b; Pratt and Tooley, 1963, 1968a). If we must have stereotypes perhaps the time has come to replace the myth of the disinterested, dispassionate scientist with the picture of the socially conscious social scientist *engagé*.

In any case, the most productive kind of objectivity is that which best accounts for the most (maximum) relevant sources of variance. Thus there is the peculiar paradox that "objectivity" precludes objectivity—meaning that a pseudo-objectivity that eschews ends-means parameters (values, significances, consequences) as potential sources of variance may in the name of "rigorous objectivity" exclude significant (sometimes the most significant) sources of variance.

An epistemology-ontology that incorporates axiology and praxiology is considered crucial for theories of action or change-agentry for systems theory generally, and thus for all taxonomies of human systems actualization or disorder. It is for this reason that the objectivity-deline-ating nomological net must be enlarged into a *normative*-nomological network encompassing explicit value-system parameters.

When we lay out a pattern for reality, we set a net to snare the variance. For scientific inquiry, variance is the *femme fatale;* the name of the game is *cherchez la variance.* Now we have said that our network was to be a *heuristic* network. We want to work the notion of a heuristic model for all it is worth—to find new ways to get purchase on the variance problem. By heuristic we mean ways in which to engage reality, ways to get at reality from several perspectives:

1. *What is* (the basic phenotypic-genotypic descriptive process)
2. *What can be* (given what is, under existing circumstances)
3. *What could be* (contingent upon genotypic or radical change: "if so, then so")
4. *What ought to be* (relatively "intrinsic" to highly relative)
5. *Emergent nomological conditions* (substantive, process, events)
6. *Emergent ends-means configurations* (within open-ended hier-archical ends-means systems)
7. *Emergent potentialities* (as contrasted with the Aristotelian con-cept of potentialities invariably being preset, intrinsic to the organism or system)
8. *Creation of new existential realities* (normative and nomo-logical)

This heuristic attack serves to discover or approximate what is, to ex-plore what can or could be, to stimulate innovation, and continuously to create new psychosocial realities.

In our version of a heuristic model we consider "discovery" and "invention" to be transactionally related aspects of social action or scientific inquiry which are carried out within the context of the larger, relevant transactional-field. Though Asher's (1964, p. 88) distinction is semantically somewhat arbitrary, it is conceptually sound:

There is a distinction between *discovery* and *invention* which should be discussed. Discovery seems to refer to a new concept which gives fresh understanding to an existing structure such as Harvey's concept of how blood-circulation functioned. The discovery of a new concept for some aspect of an existing structure or existing system transforms that which was invisible into something which is visible. And once visibility is achieved with the new concept experiments can be designed to test the veracity of the proposed concept. Invention is to create structures or systems which were not previously in existence such as Edison's electric light or Bell's telephone. For psychology, both discovery and invention are relevant directions of work but the latter should be more predominant. For example, if we are interested in how behavior functions, this research activity results in discovery. If we want to *evoke* or even modify human behavior, this will require invention.

Tart and Creighton (1966, p. 3) shift the emphasis even further when they state that "The basic philosophical or existential assumption is that *we do not discover our answers in life, we create them.*" Schaefer (1967, p. 1) states that "Modern science can affect life patterns in two ways: (1) by an analysis of human behavior, and (2) by creating new conditions of life."

From the heuristic viewpoint, the representation of "present" reality (including taxonomic representation) is conditioned by potentialities for change: change through expected or unexpected emergents or through participant intervention. Again as Lewin said, one can only understand a system by changing it. And (by Gödel's theorem, 1963) one can only change a "closed" or complex system by transcending it: the conceptual-methodological breakthrough. Only the new can complete the definition of the old, of what is known, of what is. "Hard facts" can never be treated as anything more than systems of inferences derived from sets of assumptions, often hidden. The hardest of hard facts are still approximations of approximations, frequently upended by unpredicted emergents or restructuring of the relevant genotypic field.

In the social-behavioral sciences as in the physical sciences, the heuristic approach takes into account and attempts to exploit not only the concept of "degrees of freedom" but also the concept of the totally unpredictable "surprise," of qualitative change where quantitative change was predicted (Bronowski, 1956; Heisenberg, 1958; Oppenheimer, 1956). This heuristic open point of view provides for evaluation of degrees of system openness and of the relationships between closed and open systems. The concepts of "transcendence" and "teleology" can be meaningfully redefined and the "variance potential" of "futures" can be formulated as hypotheses (often as "outrageous hypotheses") to be empirically tested sequentially over time (Murphy, 1963). It is interesting that two decades ago, from a behavioristic learning theory orientation, Shaw (1948, 1949a, 1949b) introduced the concept of "bringing home" future consequences. He used this notion of connecting distant or long-range consequences with present conduct as the key concept for his theory of psychotherapy. The failure to make or maintain time-binding connections between positive and negative future consequences and present actions was central to his taxonomy of psychological disorders (Mowrer, 1947; Mowrer and Ullman, 1945).

We have presented a brief overview of contract psychology's epistemology of ontology. The whole point has been not to overlook any major or crucial sources of variance; to cover the maximum relevant sources of variance that can be put to work for human purposes; and to treat these purposes themselves as an integral part of the total variance picture. "Representativeness of circumstances" and investigative-inter-ventive-inventive design are formulated through the *heuristic-norma-tive-nomological network*. This conceptual synthesis represents a far more comprehensive frame of reference than the original construct of nomological net, and makes possible a qualitatively new, higher order, and optimally inclusive use of the important constructs of "ecological validity" and "epistemic correspondence." This comprehensiveness is not to complicate scientific or social inquiry but to simplify it, to make it at the same time increasingly more effective, powerful, and efficient. For scientific inquiry, including metataxonomy, and for specific taxo-nomies, conceptual-methodological *power* is generated through search-ing out or creating, potentiating, and exploiting the maximum sources of variance (as in $E=mc^2$). Efficiency is increased by optimal exploitation of only the *most relevant* sources of variance used selectively out of the total network—screened and weighted, as in a regression equation. For taxonomizing, this represents a pragmatic but prodigal reductionism, a knowledgeable bias, and a more sophisticated shave with Occam's razor.

Contract Psychology: A Context for Taxonomies

As we have indicated, one must try for a systematic philosophy that includes an adequate model of man. This requires a general systems theory to encompass the human enterprise. This level of accounting is essential if we want to look beyond a given taxonomy (or "nosology") to consider any one, or all, taxonomies within their ecological contexts, or if we wish to develop taxonomies of degree-and-kind of actualization as well as taxonomies of underactualization, e.g., of degree-and-kind of psychosocial disorder, disorganization, or "psychopathology."

Recently we have introduced and have begun to elaborate con-tract psychology as providing the skeleton of a systematic philosophy sufficient to the human endeavor. This comprehensive and comprehen-sible heuristic model for modern man encompasses and brings into sharp focus the distinguishing essence of man.

Contract is at once an ancient phenomenon and a relatively modern one. . . . All this is to be expected. For to make and break promises is an exquisitely human faculty. Nietzsche, who so strongly influenced Freud, even suggested that "to breed an animal that is able to make promises . . .

is the task which Nature set for herself." The result is man. So far as
we know, no other animal has this capability (Szasz, 1965, p. 108).

My first proposition is one which I believe all will accept. It is that as soon
as man learned to talk, became able to think about the future and acquired
a moral sense, he had all of the equipment essential for making and
keeping promises. Each of these faculties, you will perceive, is rather close
to the core of what makes humanity human (Havighurst, 1961, p. 12).

Thus man as *socius* is cast in irreducible form on the stage of life.
From the perspective of contract psychology the distinguishing essence
of human beings and of the human enterprise, of individuals, and of
societies is the capacity for the development, expression, and exchange
of human values.

*The fundamental postulate of this system asserts that the essence of
man consists of, and is expressed by, his unique capacity to form contractual relationships;* this applies to man-in-the-universe, whether taken
individually, intrapsychically, interpersonally, in primary or sociopolitical
groupings, internationally, or in outer space.

Our contract systems—explicit or implicit, conscious or unconscious, unilateral or consensual, voluntary or coercive—constitute warp
and woof of personal and social life. The integrative function for all
human relationships at all levels of social organization can be conceptualized as contractual: contracts are the glue that holds each man, and
the man-made world, together. Contracts make the human world and
make the world go round. We make contracts with ourselves and others,
while others make contracts that affect every aspect of our lives.

We are both the creatures and creators of our contractual world.
"From birth to death every human being is a Party" (i.e., as a party to
the *Societal Contract* and within the contract spheres of living) "so that
neither he nor anything done or suffered can possibly be understood
when it is separated from the fact of participation in an extensive body
of transactions—to which a given human being may contribute and
which he modifies, but only in virtue of being a partaker in them"
(Dewey, 1948, p. 198). We *are* our contract systems (particularly the
ones we make and what we make of them), operationally defined by the
totality of our patterns of contractual transactions. As we have said,
Contraho ergo sum!

The career of man, the career of societies, through the ages and
today, can best be apprehended in terms of the nature and dialectics of
the *Societal Contracts* characterizing each transitional society. In sum-
marizing the significance of the concept of contract throughout the history of man, the economist von Mises (1949, p. 198) concludes that

"Human civilization as it has been known to historical experience is preponderantly a product of contractual relations." For Hayakawa (1967, p. 213), the general semanticist, contractual agreements comprise the sine qua non of society: "What we call society is a vast network of mutual agreements. . . . Without such agreements there would be no such thing as society."

The Societal Contract that defines each society can be represented by the *contract spheres* of human endeavor. These contract spheres have been approached by those arbitrary conveniences called the social sciences and can be selectively seen as the political sphere, economic sphere, etc.; or as contract spheres studied by political science, sociology, economics, psychology, law, education, etc. (Koch, 1963; Lynd, 1939; Mills, 1959).

From the contractual perspective, man is *in* society and society *in* man (Frank, 1951; Popper, 1945). The concept of psychosocial contract systems makes it possible to fill in the long-lost "missing link" between the personality level (intrapsychic or personalistic) and the social (or societal) level. The career of each man in his own time, through the social stages and crises of his unique life (Allport, 1962; Allport, 1955; Erikson, 1959; Parad, 1965), can best be appreciated in terms of the interpersonal, ideological, and situational contracts to which he commits himself and to which he is committed. Kinds of contracts are as diversified as the ever-changing, emerging, kinds of contract spheres, major and minor, that constitute the total human enterprise. Consider the range of reciprocal role- and status-defining contracts such as the marital contract, the parent-child contract, the employer-employee contract, the teacher-student contract, the citizen-politician contract, ad infinitum. All social relationships represent contractual transactions in the major contract spheres of living—political, economic, professional or vocational, avocational, primary or secondary group, marital, parental, or whatever.

We, of course, use the concept of contract not only in its legal, but in a broad social sense, in the etymologically most generic, richest, denotative and connotative usage (Mandler and Kesson, 1959; Nash, 1964). Contracts represent (are) reciprocal arrangements, agreements, promises, understandings, expectancies, commitments, compacts, covenants; they are ends-means *instrumentalities* for the creation and exchange of human values. They can, of course, be either creative and actualizing, or constraining and counteractualizing.

Contracts occur among *parties*—between a person and a group, organization, or country; between groups, organizations, or social systems of any size; or conversely between any such social system and its own subsystems (e.g., between an organization and its constituent departments, and within departments), between any system or subsystem and individual members. Furthermore, and this is particularly significant, human systems have the unique capacity for contractual transactions with themselves—for *reflexive* (system-with-itself) contracts. This capacity for reflexive contracts obtains at all levels of organization for human systems, from individual (intrapsychic) self-system to international systems, from a reflexive New Year's resolution to the United Nations' "Universal Declaration of Human Rights." Philosophically and psychologically, all contracts between parties are actually secondary to each party's primary reflexive contract (i.e., subjective decision) to enter into the interparty contract.

For human systems, the language of contract psychology is *contractual,* requiring that meaning be derived from the nature of the contractual transaction itself—but the transaction is invariably considered within the context of the total relevant *contractual-field*. Again, this applies for human social systems at all levels, intrapsychic to international. Language itself, in the generic sense, is based on contract, on the reciprocal agreement to accept specified conventions (meanings)—signs, signals, word symbols, and syntax. Communication and communication theory invariably involve language, however abstracted or analyzed, and exchange is also conceptualized as a domain (an aspect) of contract theory.

For the two inextricable purposes of understanding the human enterprise and actualizing human systems, we have conceptualized the concept of contract as *the regnant construct.* As the highest-order theoretical construct, contract covers such basic concepts as contract systems, organizational contracts, contractual transactions, and thus incorporates as key subsidiary or derivative constructs: *transaction, exchange, organization, levels of organization, reflexivity,* and *commitment.* Also incorporated are concepts that designate specific contract-system arrangements: *institution, role,* and *status;* and of course all contractual or related terminology: contract "conditions," "terms," "negotiations," "bargaining," "obligations," "rights," "benefits," "penalties," "cooperation," "competition," "power," "conflict," "costs," etc. As systematic philosophy, contract psychology likewise encompasses translated extant theoretical systems: general systems theory, field theory, communication theory, personality theory, learning theory, games theory, value theory, etc. By translate we mean to adopt, adapt, or redefine all such concepts or theories (their referential content, process, and context) to order them as componential theoretical systems within the more comprehensive contract psychology purview.

The most significant advance in the social-behavioral sciences today is the movement toward systematic integration of the social-behavioral sciences (as against fractionation, reductionism, mechanization, and dehumanization). Particularly relevant is the integrative work of the exchange theorists, Adams (1965), Blau (1964), Homans (1961), Kuhn (1963), Levine and White (1961), the transactional psychologists (previously cited), and the "interactional" theorists in sociology and social psychology, e.g., Brown (1942), Cooley (1902), Faris and Dunham (1939), Kantor (1959), Mead (1934), and Sells (1963).

THE LANGUAGE OF CONTRACT

A contract can be defined as an arrangement providing for (or allowing for) the *exchange of obligations and benefits.*

Parties to contracts can be variously defined as the individual, persons, or groups, participating directly or indirectly in the contractual exchange or secondarily, if so specified, as those affected by the exchange. The exchange may take place in the present or future and may take the form of reciprocal *expectancies,* e.g., reciprocal role expectancy. When contracts extend over time, and when future expectancies are involved, contracts become "time-binding," "time-connecting," or "time-scheduling" (Berne, 1961; Frank, 1942; Fraser, 1966; Korzybski, 1933; Mowrer and Ullman, 1945). For instance, under the feudal *Societal Contract,* as it included the "law of primogeniture," all status-derived prerogatives, including real property and serfs, automatically passed to the eldest son. However, too many instances did not fit (e.g., no son), and the *will* as a contractual instrumentality was introduced to accommodate diversified wishes and to assure that these wishes would be carried out after one's death, reaching from one generation into the succeeding generation (Havighurst, 1961; Hoebel, 1954; Maine, 1861).

Contracts cover the entire range of human exchange. This includes the exchange of commodities or "goods" (an etymologically significant value term) and the exchange of behaviors, expectancies, reinforcements (positive and negative), values, ideas, feelings, contingencies, rights, and responsibilities—whatever "currency" serves human purposes. Contractual exchange occurs *within* and *between* all levels of organization for human systems, and within and between all of the domains or contract spheres of living. Contractual exchange characterizes subjects as diverse as "social institutions" (institutional behavior and the behavior of institutions) and learning theory (including "behavior modification" or operant conditioning procedures).

In modern society, from cradle to grave, every individual is directly or indirectly involved in organizational and institutional contracts (Pratt and Tooley, 1967a; Pugh, 1966; Schein, 1965). Social contracts define institutions and organizations: their values, purposes, policies, rules, and sanctions; their resources and resource allocation systems; their external and internal systems of exchange, including obligations (e.g., tasks, demands, duties, work, responsibilities), benefits (e.g., rewards, rights, privileges, remuneration), and stipulated sanctions for execution of contract and for breach of contract or negotiation of fraudulent contracts. These personal-organizational-societal contracts are ends-means instrumentalities that continually connect sets of *consequences* with sets of *actions* (formally and informally); they are reciprocal give-and-take, give-get, do-receive, to-from systems of contractual exchange.

The dictionary definition of exchange is "to give and receive reciprocally." Institution is defined first as, "an established law, custom, practice, system, etc."; and, differentially, it is also defined as, "an organization having a social, educational, or religious purpose, as a school, church, hospital, reformatory, etc." Thus Levinson and Gallagher (1964) use the language of contract and of contractual exchange (rights and obligations) in their taxonomic conceptualization of both institutional role and the role of institutions (particularly mental hospitals, prisons, and residential schools):

The client thus becomes a client-member, an inmate of a community that not only offers specific services but also makes manifold *claims* upon him. His membership in the hospital involves a distinctive *contract* (Durkheim, 1957; Parsons, 1957; Bidwell and Vreeland, 1963) that defines his *rights* and his *obligations*. . . . (p. 34). The "socializing" institution has a "*commitment* to society; it has a formal obligation to foster the recovery of its patients, and every patient whatever his motivation, takes on a *contractual obligation* to *work* toward this end" (emphasis ours; p. 39).

Using this contractual exchange conception of role as the connecting link, these authors have coupled a psychological analysis with a sociological-anthropological approach: "We have examined the socio-cultural system from the perspective of its psychological meaning, and have examined the individual personality from the perspective of its engagement in the social environment." This provides a basis for comparative study "of various therapeutic-educative-corrective systems, seen from the viewpoint of their client-inmate members" (p. 244). This is an excellent example of one way in which taxonomies can be constructed from the viewpoint of the target population itself.

All role theory that intentionally or by default, attempts to study role or role process per se, disregarding content or context, can have little meaning or generality. Here "context" of course refers to the *contract-system field,* including relevant contract-systems at all levels from societal to intrapsychic. This caveat regarding "empty theories" (pseudo content-free) and out-of-context (pseudo *in vacuo*) theories applies equally to all social-behavioral theories, e.g., communications theory, learning theory, decision theory, and likewise to all social-behavioral classification systems or taxonomies. This again points up the fact that taxonomic systems cannot escape the requirements of general systems theory. As long as contextual stability obtains, that is, stability of the transactional-field, a conceptually narrow taxonomy may work quite well. However, to the degree that relevant content and/or context are ignored, crucial sources of variance may be overlooked. Taxonomies can "get by" treating a "thin slice" of reality *as if* it were stable, static, self-contained, *in vacuo,* or absolute only at the risk of basic misconstruction, with the further risk of conceptual catastrophe in the face of germane genotypic field change or restructuring. In each case the risk is of missing the (variance) boat (Kagan, 1967).

In our recent review of *Patienthood in the Mental Hospital: An Analysis of Role, Personality and Social Structure* (Pratt and Tooley, 1967a), we have provided an indication of the conceptual power of the language of contract in providing a higher-order construct with which one can relate and thus explicate subsidiary concepts in the critical review and evaluation of current literature. Under the title "Flattery Will Get You Somewhere: Styles and Use of Ingratiation" (Jones, 1965), we find a similar illustration of the use of the language of contract in a substantive overview of a significant book (Jones, 1964). Consider a sample from the section headed "Breaking the Social Contract":

But how do we determine when behavior is "legitimate"? Relationships and associations involve, in normal circumstances, an unstated *contract* between the actors. Different authorities describe this *contract* in different ways. Sociologist Erving Goffman (1959), in his book *The Presentation of Self in Everyday Life,* emphasizes what he calls "ritual elements" in social interaction. Goffman believes that not only does communication take place in its usual sense but that the communicators also engage in a "performance" —each transmits and receives clues about his definition of the situation, his view of himself, and his evaluation of the other. Mutual adjustment occurs. Perhaps most important the actors enter into a silent *compact* to help each other save face. Each becomes involved in "face-work"—*give-and-take* actions that smooth over potentially embarrassing threats, lend mutual support, and make for coherent and consistent performances. Each person has a "defensive orientation toward saving his own face and a protective orientation toward saving the other's face." Within this frame of reference, the ingratiator may be seen as exploiting this *contract* while seeming to support it. He neither violates the *contract* openly, nor merely fulfills it. Rather, he keeps sending out reassuring signals that he accepts the *terms of the contract;* but all the while he is actually working toward other goals (emphasis ours; Jones, 1965, p. 20).

H. A. Murray intended his "Personology" (Sahakian, 1965) to be a science of men and a method of inquiry. He conceptualized personality as a "temporal integrate of mutually dependent processes (variables) developing in time"; and explanation of a single one of these variables involves the recognition of a large number of others and their reciprocal relations (p. 210). Murray used the language of contract extensively, as in his conception of the "Ego system":

Everyone has experienced "resolving to do something" or "selecting a purpose." . . . Decisions and intentions of this sort—"accepting a goal," "planning a course of action," "choosing a vocation," as well as *promises, compacts* and "taking on responsibility" . . . all of them (are) related to time-binding and the establishment of expectations and levels of aspiration. . . . We should say that such conscious fixations of aim were organized to form the "Ego system." The concept of Ego emphasizes the determining significance of conscious, freely-willed acts: making a *resolution* (with oneself) or a *compact* (with others) or *dedicating* oneself to a life-long vocation, all of which "bind" the personality over long periods of time. . . . One index of the degree of structuration or strength of the Ego is the ability of an individual to "live by" his *resolutions* and *compacts* (emphasis ours; p. 236).

Hittelman has developed aspects of contract psychology for critical and experimental application to the prediction of changes in interpersonal attraction (1966a), to T-group theory and practice (1966b), and to major sociological and psychological theories of psychosocial deviance (1966c). He emphasizes reciprocal behavioral expectancies: "A contract is the mutually agreed upon (explicitly or implicitly) expectations for behavior between two or more parties with the rewards (and sanctions) for meeting (or violating) that expectation. It implies not only the behavior expected, but also the conditions and reservations under which the expectations are held" (1966b, pp. 4–5).

Contemporary learning theorists, suffering from a legacy of self-imposed conceptual constraints, are currently turning to the language of contract to liberate even the most "operational" *operant* conditioning procedures from the triple cul-de-sac of an "atheoretical" stance, a "value-free" posture, and an "empty organism" (S-R versus S-O-R) paradigm.

Sulzer (1962), for instance, must feel that he has found conceptually strange bedfellows when he joins Menninger (1958) and Szasz (1965) in writing extensively about the "therapeutic contract." Though in this instance followed by something of a non sequitur, Rickard and Dinoff (1965) likewise make explicit use of the language of contract in their case histories: "Perhaps the prime techniques used in eliciting adaptive behavior from Bill was emphasis upon the *terms of the contract*. Whenever Bill refused to take part in activities or to comply with camp regulations alternate channels were pointed out to him and the expected behavior was clearly labeled in a nonpunitive nonjudgmental manner" (p. 327).

The training films produced by Krasner and his colleagues showing their work with autistic children vividly present the contractual negotiation and exchange process, including specification of conditions, choice, and reciprocal action-consequence sequences: "You give me that and I'll give you this; If you do that, I'll do this; If you do that then you'll get to do this." A structured series of contractual exchange events proceed in a manner designed to evoke and reinforce desired behaviors. Reciprocal expectancies are generated for child and "therapist"—when the child gives or does (contingency behavior) he finds that he has a right to expect to get, or to get to do (reinforcing behavior or event). Both parties are reinforced—the child gets (gets to eat) the piece of candy and the therapist gets to play his game and to believe in his hypotheses through action confirmation.

As Krasner (1964), Ferster (1965), Homme (1965), and several others (Ullmann and Krasner, 1965; Ulrich et al., 1966) have done, Goldiamond has made major theoretical and empirical contributions toward a more enlightened and sophisticated behavior theory, particularly in such underdeveloped areas as reflexive- or self-reinforcement and self-control, and the connection of contingencies and consequences with value theory and ethics. Goldiamond (1965a) states unequivocally that "The aim in behavioral modification of the type we have been using is to alter those behaviors about which a *contractual agreement* has been made implicitly or explicitly" (p. 254).

Addison and Homme (1966) employ the language of contract in extending operant conditioning concepts into a comprehensive motivational system that includes the concept of "coverants" in the self-management of contingencies. They use the terms "contracting systems," "contractor," and "contingency contracts" to specify the operational relationships between "contingent behaviors" and "reinforcing events" (a conceptual alternative to the limiting construct "reinforcing stimulus"). In a recent essay, "Contingencies of Reinforcement in the Design of a Culture," Skinner (1966) emphasizes the role of reinforcing events and contingent behaviors in optimizing human systems at individual and societal levels. The discovery and development of reinforcing properties is equated with the "history of the discovery of human potentialities" both positive and negative (p. 163). Skinner stresses the actualizing role of contingent behavior in carrying out the work of the world:

Men are happy in an environment in which active, productive, and creative behavior is reinforced in effective ways. The trouble with both affluent and welfare societies is that reinforcers are not contingent on particular forms of behavior. Men are not reinforced for doing anything and hence they do nothing. This is the "contentment" of the Arcadian idyll and of the retired businessman. It may represent a satisfaction of needs, but it raises other problems. Those who have nothing important to do fall prey to trivial reinforcers. . . . Only when we stop using reinforcers to allay needs can we begin to use them to "fulfill man's nature" in a much more important sense. Contingencies of reinforcement are far more important than the reinforcers they incorporate, but they are much less obvious. Only very recently, and then only under rigorous experimental conditions, have the extraordinary effects of contingencies been observed. . . . The experimental analysis of behavior thus has a very special relevance to the design of cultures. Only through the active prosecution of such an analysis, and the courageous application of its results to daily life, will it be possible to design those contingencies of reinforcement which will generate and maintain the most subtle and complex behavior of which men are capable (p. 166).

It can readily be seen that for behavior theory the concept of contract covers the exchange of *obligations* and *benefits* which are translated as *contingencies* (operant behavior) and *consequences* (reinforcing events). The traditional proclivity of behaviorists for protean forms of S-R reductionism can be ruled out when behaviors are analyzed at the level of the "contractual unit" (as irreducible within the relevant contractual-field).

When behaviorists use the term "operant," they are by definition referring to a *means,* a behavioral means to effect certain environmental consequences. As all means are inextricably connected with ends and all ends represent values, operant psychology becomes an ends-means psychology with a primary and inescapable normative component. Without exception, all of the specific operational *referents* of the term "reinforcement" are value-defined. By operational definition, contingency contracts are invariably contingency-consequence contracts, they are contingency (means)-consequence (ends) contracts, and therefore ends-means contracts. The reinforcement-obtaining values of contingencies or of contingency behavior are learned through the individual's contractual transactions with himself and others, or, more mundanely, through his transactions with his world (environment). If not for rats at least for man as *socius,* reinforcement valence is largely *ascribed* ("cathected") rather than exclusively intrinsic to given stimuli or events (Koch, 1963). Thus reinforcement valence cannot be accepted as an invariant *given* but must be treated as *preferential behavior* involving questions of decision theory, value theory, and changing degrees of freedom for choice and action (Becker and McClintock, 1967).

These considerations crucially qualify and must be explicitly dealt with in all behavior theory taxonomies that attempt the "classification of behavior (*or behavior disorders*) in terms of maintaining consequences" (p. 57, Goldiamond, 1965b; Ferster, 1965).

Contract Systems: Levels and Taxonomies

From our metataxonomic perspective, taxonomies are directed at the delineation of human systems at all levels, at their actualization, and at "hitches" in actualization. These ends-means hitches are often conceptualized as psychosocial problems, e.g., political, sociological, economic, or psychological disorders. The contract-system-*field* approach to actualization or "hang-ups" requires analysis not only at the level of organization at which the problems are most discernible, but also at relevant levels above and below. This implies that members of those disciplines concerned with the scientific study and resolution of these problems not only function as specialists, but also retain (or in many cases acquire) the capacity to function as generalists in order to keep in perspective and appropriately weigh the higher- and lower-level determinants which create or contribute to, and maintain target problems (Gardner, 1964; Pratt and Tooley, 1965). It is not a question of whether we would like to look beyond the traditionally constricted confines of our arbitrarily defined specialties, but that we must do so, or else miss the point entirely. The very nature and scope of the substantive problems faced by the social-behavioral sciences discredit the artificial barriers or definitions set up between the social sciences. We can no longer beg the question with the seemingly "objective" and modest (but actually arrogant) excuse that consideration of those parameters is outside our area of competence and thus to be left to "others" while we proceed *as if* such determinants can be ignored or accepted as unquestionable givens. As Ackoff (1963) has chided: "We must stop acting as though nature were organized into disciplines in the same way that universities are" (p. 346). Also acknowledging the complexity and interdisciplinary nature of current psychosocial problems Mills (1959, p. 142) has insisted:

To state and to solve any one of the significant problems of our period requires a selection of materials, conceptions, and methods from more than any one of these several disciplines. A social scientist need not master the field in order to be familiar enough with its materials and perspectives to use them in clarifying the problems that concern him. It is in terms of such topical "problems" rather than in accordance with academic boundaries, that specialization ought to occur.

Not only is multilevel analysis essential to understand the systems that we study, but, more important, to change these systems it is often mandatory to intervene from different levels of organization, as Sanford (1965) has indicated: "In order to induce change in personality it may sometimes be necessary first to change the role structure in the organization in which the individual lives or works. By the same token, since we deal with a dynamic interaction between personality and social system, it may sometimes be necessary to change certain personalities in order to change the social system" (pp. 194–95). Sanford also emphasizes the need for theoretical concepts which bridge levels of organization such as the self-system level and social system levels. These necessary conceptual links, which articulate the transactional relationships between individuals and social systems within and between levels, are essentially contractual.

A variety of conceptual schemata representing the organization of human systems is available and useful according to different purposes. Some are institutionalized social-political schemata (e.g., international, federal, state, county, municipal, neighborhood), others are theoretical-empirical formulations such as Marney and Smith's (1963) elegant taxonomy of open systems, and Ruesch's (1966) richly heuristic, multi-level formulation of social processes. Other elaborate taxonomic schemata which *order* phenomena from inorganic to superorganic levels of organization include the various general systems theories (Bertalanffy, 1950; Feibleman, 1954; Miller, 1963, 1965b, 1965c; Novikoff, 1945) and, most recently, the culmination of Floyd Allport's (1967) ambitious thirty-year effort to formulate problems of organization and disorganization which, in his words, "constitute the major forms of 'enestruolysis,' or 'pathology' of organic beings; and they all seem to occur at all levels of organic or collective aggregates from the germ cell to nations or world organizations. And as such they are the targets of all the 'therapies,' medical, psychological, material and social that have been devised by men" (p. 23).

Boulding (1956) presents an equally comprehensive taxonomy in "General Systems Theory—The Skeleton of a Science." His schema (p. 201) is somewhat unique in that it differentiates levels of organization in terms of their "predominant emergent characteristics":

1. The static structure—a level of framework, the anatomy of a system; for example, the structure of the universe
2. The simple dynamic system—the level of clockworks, predetermined necessary motions
3. The cybernetic system—the level of the thermostat, the system moves to maintain a given equilibrium through a process of self-regulation
4. The open system—level of self-maintaining systems, moves toward and includes living organisms
5. The genetic-societal system—level of cell society, characterized by a division of labor among cells
6. Animal systems—level of mobility, evidence of goal-directed behavior
7. Human systems—level of symbol interpretation and idea communication
8. Social system—level of human organization
9. Transcendental systems—level of ultimates and absolutes which exhibit systematic structure but are unknowable in essence

Levels of human systems organization can be construed as *interlocking* contract systems. To gain purchase on a given target problem at whatever level it appears, all levels must be systematically considered in order to formulate the problem appropriately and empirically to check out possible sources of relevant variance. An adequate taxonomy of human (psychosocial) systems should accommodate the following *levels,* however, one chooses to label them:

1. Self-system or individual contract systems
2. Interpersonal, primary, or small group contract systems
3. Organizational and institutional contract systems
4. Community contract systems
5. National or sociocultural contract systems
6. International contract systems and the "world community's" social contract

These levels form a hierarchy of organizational complexity ranging from individual contract systems (within the *interior* contract space) through international contractual arrangements. Events at all of these levels potentially have repercussions at all other levels. In Ashby's (1960) term these levels are composed of "richly joined environments": systems in which every variable is functionally related to all other variables, such that a change in one variable may affect (however minimally) the values of all other systemic variables (Heider, 1967; Kagan, 1967). Currently most scientific inquiry, including taxonomic and interventive endeavors, focuses upon *intra*level events to the exclusion or neglect of other levels (Lippitt et al., 1958).

A metataxonomy must provide for taxonomies capable of *linking* these levels in order more adequately to delineate systems within levels, and also to bring interlevel as well as intralevel determinants to bear on system change or actualization. For this descriptive-valuative-interventive purpose, three basic types of human system taxonomies can be logically differentiated, and all available psychosocial taxonomies can in turn be ordered within these categories:

Type I Taxonomies: Structure-process taxonomies of human systems and subsystems

Type II Taxonomies: Normative taxonomies of systems actualization-underactualization

Type III Taxonomies: Methodological investigative-interventive procedures (e.g., "participative-social-action research") taxonomies of intervention

These three *classes* of taxonomies are treated as logical "abstractions of convenience" because they are invariably abstracted from and represent a part of the heuristic-normative-nomological network. Ultimately these three taxonomic types represent interdigitated aspects of the total relevant transactional-field, for human systems of the total relevant contract-system field. While all taxonomies can be ordered to one or another of these three categories, it must be appreciated that types I, II, and III are inextricably interrelated. Inevitably, consideration of any one of these nomological, normative, or methodological taxonomic types (or of any given taxonomy) automatically invokes consideration of the other two types. The purpose is to gain purchase on optimal sources of variance. The grand purpose of course for all metataxonomic activity is the illumination, articulation, and actualization of human systems at all levels-of-organization from international to intrapsychic.

REFERENCES

Ackoff, R. L. *Behav. Sci.,* 1963, **8**, (No. 4), 346.

Adams, J. S. Inequity in social exchange. In L. Berkowitz (Ed.), *Advances in experimental social psychology.* Vol. 2. New York: Academic Press, 1965. Pp. 133–75.

Addison, R. M., and Homme, L. E. The reinforcing event (RE) menu. *Nat. Soc. Prog. Instruc. J.,* 1966, **4** (No. 1), 8–9.

Allport, F. H. A structuronomic concept of behavior: individual and collective. I. Structural theory and the master problem of social psychology. *J. abnorm. soc. Psychol.*, 1962, **64**, 3–30.

Allport, F. H. A theory of enestruence (event-structure theory): report of progress. *Amer. Psychologist*, 1967, **22** (No. 1), 1–24.

Allport, G. W. *Becoming: basic considerations for a psychology of personality*. New Haven: Yale University Press, 1955.

Ashby, W. R. *Design for a brain*. New York: Wiley, 1960.

Asher, J. J. Toward a neo-field theory of behavior. *J. Human Psychol.*, 1964, **4** (No. 2), 85–94.

Barber, B. Resistance by scientists to scientific discovery. *Scient. Manpower*, 1960, **1**, 35–47.

Barber, B., and Hirsch, W. (Eds.). *The sociology of science: the role and responsibilities of the scientist—discussed as social phenomena*. New York: Free Press, 1962.

Bauer, R. A. Social psychology and the study of policy formation. *Amer-Psychologist*, 1966, **21** (No. 10), 933–42.

Becker, G. M., and McClintock, C. G. Value: behavioral decision theory. *Annu. Rev. Psychol.*, 1967, **18**, 239–86.

Bentley, A. F. *Behavior, knowledge, fact*. Bloomington, Ind.: Principia Press, 1935.

Bentley, A. F. *An inquiry into inquiries*. Boston: Beacon Press, 1954.

Bergman, G., and Spence, K. W. Operationism and theory. *Psychol. Rev.*, 1941, **48**, 1–14.

Berne, E. *Transactional analysis in psychotherapy: a systematic individual social psychiatry*. New York: Grove Press, 1961.

Bertalanffy, L. The theory of open systems in physics and biology. *Science*, 1950, **111**, 23–29.

Bertalanffy, L. *Problem of life*. London: Watts, 1952.

Bidwell, C. E., and Vreeland, R. S. College education and moral orientation: an organizational approach. *Admin. Sci. Quart.*, 1963, **8**, 166–91.

Blau, P. M. *Exchange and power in social life*. New York: Wiley, 1964.

Borman, L. D. Action social science: its implications for psychology. Paper presented as part of the symposium, The Psychologist as an Agent of Change, Amer. Psychol. Ass., Philadelphia, August 1963.

Boulding, K. E. General systems theory—the skeleton of a science. *Mgmt. Sci.*, 1956, 200–202.

Bronowski, J. *Science and human values*. New York: Harper, 1956.

Brown, L. G. *Social pathology*. New York: Crofts, 1942.

Cantril, H. *The "why" of man's experience*. New York: Macmillan, 1950.

Cantril, H. The human design. *J. Indiv. Psychol.*, 1964, **20**, 129–36.

Cantril, H., Ames, A., Hastorf, A., and Ittelson, W. Psychology and scientific research. Part III. The transactional view in psychological research. *Science*, 1949, **110**, 517–22.

Cantril, H., and Bumstead, C. H. *Reflections on the human venture*. New York: New York University Press, 1960.

Churchman, C. W. *Prediction and optimal decision: philosophical issues of a science of value*. Englewood Cliffs, N.J.: Prentice-Hall, 1964.

Cooley, C. H. *Human nature and the social order*. New York: Scribner, 1902.

Dewey, J. Common sense and science: their respective frame of reference. *J. Phil.*, 1948, **45**, 197–208.

Dewey, J., and Bentley, A. F. *Knowing and the known*. Boston: Beacon Press, 1949.

Durkheim, E. *Professional ethics and civic morals*. London: Routledge & Kegan Paul, 1957.

Erikson, E. H. Identity and the life cycle. *Psychol. Issues Monogr.*, 1959, **1** (No. 1).

Eron, L. D. (Ed.). *The classification of behavior disorders*. Chicago: Aldine, 1966.

Faris, E. L., and Dunham, H. W. *Mental disorders in urban areas*. Chicago: University of Chicago Press, 1939.

Fiebleman, J. K. Theory of integrative levels. *Brit. J. Phil. Sci.*, 1954, **5**, 59–66.

Fiegl, H., and Scriven, M. (Eds.). *The foundations of science and the concepts of psychology and psychoanalysis*. Minneapolis, Minn.: University of Minnesota Press, 1956.

Ferster, C. B. Classification of behavioral pathology. In L. Krasner and L. P. Ullmann (Eds.), *Research in behavior modification: new developments and implications*. New York: Holt, Rinehart & Winston, 1965.

Frank, L. K. *Nature and human nature: man's new image of himself*. New York: Rutgers University Press, 1951.

Fraser, J. T. *The voices of time: a cooperative survey of man's views of time as expressed by the sciences and by the humanities*. New York: George Braziller, 1966.

Gardner, J. W. *Self-renewal: the individual and the innovative society*. New York: Harper, 1964.

Gödel, K. *Gödel's theorem: on formally undecidable propositions*. New York: Basic Books, 1963.

Goffman, E. *The presentation of self in everyday life*. Garden City, N.Y.: Doubleday, 1959.

Goldiamond, I. Justified and unjustified alarm over behavioral control. In O. Milton (Ed.), *Behavior disorders: perspectives and trends*. Philadelphia: J. B. Lippincott, 1965a. Pp. 237–62.

Goldiamond, I. Training in behavior modification. In preconference materials: Conference on the Professional Preparation of Clinical Psychologists, Amer. Psychol. Ass., Washington, D.C., 1965b.

Grene, M. *The knower and the known*. New York: Basic Books, 1966.

Grinker, R. R., MacGregor, H., Selan, K., Klein, A., and Kohrman, J. *Psychiatric social work: a transactional case book*. New York: Basic Books, 1961.

Handlon, J. H. A metatheoretical view of assumptions regarding the etiology of schizophrenia. *Arch. gen. Psychiat.*, 1960, **2**, 43–60.

Havighurst, H. D. *The nature of private contract*. Evanston, Ill.; Northwestern University Press, 1961.

Hayakawa, S. I. Foreword to the special issue on transactional psychology. *Etc.: Rev. gen. Semantics*, 1955, **12** (No. 4), 243–44.

Hayakawa, S. I. The language of social control. In E. P. Hollander and R. G. Hunt (Eds.), *Current perspectives in social psychology: readings with commentary*. 2d ed. New York: Oxford University Press, 1967. Pp. 210–17.

Heider, F. On social cognition. *Amer. Psychologist*, 1967, **22** (No. 1), 25–31.

Heisenberg, W. *Physics and philosophy*. New York: Harper, 1958.

Hittelman, E. A comparison of the adequacy of Newcomb's abx model and contract theory for the prediction of changes in interpersonal attraction. Unpublished manuscript. Columbia University, 1966a.

Hittelman, E. A study of contract: T-group theory and practice. Unpublished manuscript. Columbia University, 1966b.

Hittelman, E. Deviance: Major sociological and psychosocial theories of deviance compared with a contractual hypothesis. Unpublished manuscript. Columbia University, 1966c.

Hoebel, E. A. *The law of primitive man: a study of legal dynamics*. Cambridge: Harvard University Press, 1954.

Homans, G. C. *Social behavior: its elementary forms*. New York: Harcourt, Brace & World, 1961.

Homme, L. E. Perspectives in psychology XXIV: Control of covenants, the operants of the mind. *Psychol. Rec.*, 1965, **15**, 501–11.

Horowitz, I. L. Establishment sociology: the value of being value-free. *Inquiry*, 1963, **6**, 129–40.

Horowitz, I. L. *The new sociology*. New York: Oxford University Press, 1964.

Jahoda, M. *Current concepts of positive mental health. Joint commission on mental illness and health monograph series*, No. 1. New York: Basic Books, 1958.

Jones, E. E. *Ingratiation*. New York: Appleton-Century-Crofts, 1964.

Jones, E. E. Flattery will get you somewhere: styles and uses of ingratiation. *Trans-action*, 1965, **2** (No. 4), 20–23.

Kagan, J. On the need for relativism. *Amer. Psychologist*, 1967, **22** (No. 2), 131–42.

Kantor, J. R. *The logic of modern science*. Bloomington, Ind.: Principia Press, 1953.

Kantor, J. R. *Interbehavioral psychology: a sample of scientific system construction*. Bloomington, Ind.: Principia Press, 1959.

Kaplan, A. *The conduct of inquiry: methodology for behavioral science*. San Francisco: Chandler, 1964.

Kilpatrick, F. P. (Ed.). *Explorations in transactional psychology.* New York: New York University Press, 1961a.

Kilpatrick, F. P. Personality in transactional psychology. *J. Indiv. Psychol.,* 1961b, **17**, 12–19.

Kluckhohn, C. Values and value-orientations in the theory of action: an exploration in definition and classification. In T. Parsons and E. A. Shils (Eds.), *Toward a general theory of action.* New York: Harper & Row, 1962. Pp. 388–433.

Koch, S. Psychological science versus the science-humanism antinomy: intimations of a significant science of man. *Amer. Psychologist,* 1961, **16**, 629–39.

Koch, S. (Ed.). *Investigations of man as socius: their place in psychology and the social sciences.* Vol. VI. *Psychology: a study of a science.* New York: McGraw-Hill, 1963.

Korzybski, A. *Science and sanity.* Lancaster, Pa.: Science Press, 1933.

Kotarbinski, T. *Praxiology: the science of effective action.* New York: Pergamon Press, 1965.

Krasner, L. Behavior control and social responsibility. *Amer. Psychologist,* 1964, **17**, 199–204.

Kuhn, A. *The study of society: a unified approach.* Homewood, Ill.: Irwin, 1963.

Lepley, R. The identity of fact and value. *Phil. Sci.,* 1943, **10**, 124–31.

Levine, S., and White, P. E. Exchange as a conceptive framework for the study of interorganizational relationships. *Admin. Sci. Quart.,* 1961, **5**, 583–601.

Levinson, D. J., and Gallagher, E. B. *Patienthood in the mental hospital: an analysis of role, personality, and social structure.* Boston: Houghton Mifflin, 1964.

Lippitt, R., Watson, J., and Westley, B. *The dynamics of planned change: a comparative study of principles and techniques.* New York: Harcourt, Brace & World, 1958.

Lynd, R. S. *Knowledge for what: the place of social science in American culture.* Princeton, N.J.: Princeton University Press, 1939.

Maine, H. *Ancient law.* London: J. M. Dent & Sons, 1861.

Mandler, G., and Kesson, W. *The language of psychology.* New York: Wiley, 1959.

Margenau, H. *The nature of physical reality.* New York: McGraw-Hill, 1950.

Marney, M. C., and Smith, N. M. The domain of adaptive systems: a rudimentary taxonomy. Multilith report. Research Analysis Corporation, 1963.

McGuigan, F. J. The experimenter: a neglected stimulus object. *Psychol. Bull.,* 1963, **60**, 421–28.

Mead, G. H. *Mind, self and society.* Chicago: University of Chicago Press. 1934.

Menninger, K. The contract: the psychoanalytic treatment situation as a two-party transaction. In *Theory of psychoanalytic technique*. New York: Basic Books, 1958. Pp. 15–48.

Menninger, K. *The vital balance*. New York: Viking, 1963.

Miller, J. G. The individual as as information processing system. In W. S. Fields and W. Abott (Eds.), *Information storage and neural control*. Springfield, Ill.: Charles C Thomas, 1963.

Miller, J. G. The organization of life. *Perspect. Biol. Med.*, 1965a, **9** (No. 1).

Miller, J. G. Living systems: Basic concepts. *Behav. Sci.*, 1965b, **10** (No. 3), 193–237.

Miller, J. G. Living systems: Structure and process. *Behav. Sci.*, 1965c, **10** (No. 4), 337–79.

Mills, C. W. *The sociological imagination*. New York: Oxford University Press, 1959.

Mowrer, O. H. On the dual nature of learning—a reinterpretation of "conditioning" and "problem-solving." *Harv. Educ. Rev.*, 1947, **17**, 102–48.

Mowrer, O. H., and Ullman, A. D. Time as a determinant in integrative learning. *Psychol. Rev.*, 1945, **52**, 61–90.

Murphy, G. The psychology of 1975: an extrapolation. *Amer. Psychologist*, 1963, **18** (No. 11), 689–95.

Nash, H. The role of metaphor in psychological theory. *Behav. Sci.*, 1964, **8** (No. 4), 336–46.

Newbury, E. The significance of assumptions and philosophic operations in psychological methodology. *J. gen. Psychol.*, 1958, **59**, 185–99.

Northrop, F. S. C. *The logic of the sciences and the humanities*. New York: Macmillan, 1947.

Novikoff, A. B. The concept of integrative levels and biology. *Science,* 1945, **101** (No. 2618), 209–15.

Oppenheimer, R. Analogy in science. *Amer. Psychologist*, 1956, **11**, 128–35.

Orne, M. T. On the social psychology of the psychological experiment: with particular reference to demand characteristics and their implications. *Amer. Psychologist*. 1962, **17**, 776–83.

Parad, H. J. (Ed.). *Crisis intervention: selected readings*. New York: Family Service Ass. of America, 1965.

Parsons, T. The mental hospital as a type of organization. In M. Greenblatt, D. J. Levinson, and R. H. Williams (Eds.), *The patient and the mental hospital*. New York: Free Press, 1957. Pp. 108–29.

Popper, K. R. (Ed.). *The open society and its enemies*. London: Routledge & Kegan Paul, 1945.

Pratt, S. Of myth and models: an agonizing reappraisal. Paper presented as part of the symposium, The Psychologist and the Mental Hospital, Amer. Psychol. Ass., New York, September 1961.

Pratt, S., and Tooley, J. How differing concepts of the nature of psychological disorders lead to differing practices in the hospital, the clinic, and the community. Paper presented as part of the symposium, Mental Illness: Is There Any Such Thing? Amer. Psychol. Ass., St. Louis, September 1962.

Pratt, S., and Tooley, J. Psychic psoriasis: the role of the psychologist in the prevention of progress. Invited address, Colorado Psychol. Ass., Denver, June 1963.

Pratt, S., and Tooley, J. Contract psychology and human actualization. Paper presented as part of the symposium, Psychological Views: Man and His Potentialities, Kansas Psychol. Ass., Hays, Kansas, April 1964.

Pratt, S., and Tooley, J. Contract psychology and training contracts. Invited paper presented as part of the symposium, The Role of Psychologists in Training the Non-Professional. *Proceedings,* 15th Conference of Psychology Program Directors and Consultants in State, Federal and Territorial Mental Health Programs, Chicago, September 1965, 21–26.

Pratt, S., and Tooley, J. A "contract psychology" review of "patienthood in the mental hospital: an analysis of role, personality and social structure." *Amer. J. ment. Def.,* 1967a, **71** (No. 4), 645–47.

Pratt, S., and Tooley, J. Contract psychology and the actualizing transactional-field. In O. H. Mowrer (Ed.), *Morality and mental health.* Chicago: Rand McNally, 1967b. Pp. 396–416. Also published in Spec. Ed. No. 1 (Theoretical Aspects and Research). *Int. J. soc. Psychiat.,* 1964, 51–69. Portions of this paper presented at the First International Congress of Social Psychiatry, London, August 1964.

Pratt, S., and Tooley, J. I. Action psychology and social action. In *Action psychology. J. Psychol. Stud.,* 1968a, **15**, Whole No. 3.

Pratt, S., and Tooley, J. Some methodological considerations and the research contract. In *Action psychology. J. Psychol. Stud.,* 1968b, **15**, Whole No. 3.

Pugh, D. S. Modern organization theory: a psychological and sociological study. *Psychol. Bull.,* 1966, **66** (No. 4), 235–51.

Rapoport, A. *Operational philosophy: integrating knowledge and action.* New York: Harper, 1953.

Rickard, H. C., and Dinoff, M. Shaping adaptive behavior in a therapeutic summer camp. In L. P. Ullmann and L. Krasner (Eds.), *Case studies in behavior modification.* New York: Holt, Rinehart & Winston, 1965. Pp. 325–28.

Riecken, H. W. A program for research on experiments on social psychology. Vol. 2. In N. F. Washburne (Ed.), *Decisions, values and groups.* New York: Macmillan, 1962.

Rosenthal, R. Experimenter attributes as determinants of subjects' responses. *J. proj. Tech. Pers. Assess.,* 1963a, **27** (No. 3), 324–31.

Rosenthal, R. On the social psychology of the psychological experiment. *Amer. Scient.,* 1963b, **51** (No. 2), 268–83.

Ruesch, J. Social process. *Arch. gen. Psychiat.,* 1966, **15**, 577–89.

Sahakian, W. S. (Ed.). *Psychology of personality: readings in theory.* Chicago: Rand McNally, 1965.

Sanford, N. Will psychologists study human problems? *Amer. Psychologist,* 1965, **20** (No. 3), 192–202.

Sarason, S. B. The psychologist's behavior as an area of research. *J. consult. Psychol.,* 1951, **15**, 278–80.

Schaefer, H. Can science develop an ethics? Paper presented at German Soc. soc. Resp. Sci., Frankfurt, February 1967.

Schein, E. H. *Organizational psychology.* Englewood Cliffs, N.J.: Prentice-Hall, 1965.

Sells, S. B. An interactionist looks at the environment. Presidential address, Southwest. Psychol. Ass., Dallas, Texas, April 1963.

Shaw, F. J. Some postulates concerning psychotherapy. *J. consult. Psychol.,* 1948, **12**, 426–31.

Shaw, F. J. A program of research on behavior changes. Unpublished manuscript. Purdue University, 1949a.

Shaw, F. J. The role of reward in psychotherapy. *Amer. Psychologist,* 1949b, **4** (No. 6), 177–79.

Skinner, B. F. Contingencies of reinforcement in the design of a culture. *Behav. Sci.,* 1966, **11**, 159–66.

Smith, M. B. Toward scientific and professional responsibility. *Amer. Psychologist,* 1954, **9**, 513–16.

Stevens, S. S. Psychology: the propaedeutic science. *Phil. Sci.,* 1936, **3**, 90–103.

Sulzer, E. S. Research frontier: reinforcement and the therapeutic contract. *J. counsel. Psychol.,* 1962, **9**, 271–76.

Szasz, T. S. *The ethics of psychoanalysis: the theory and method of autonomous psychotherapy.* New York: Basic Books, 1965.

Tart, C. T., and Creighton, J. L. The bridge mountain community: an evolving pattern for human growth. *J. human. Psychol.,* 1966, **6** (No. 1), 53–67.

Tooley, J., Pratt, S., and Rosenthal, R. Who watches the brain-watchers?: with rejoinder by R. Rosenthal. *Behav. Sci.,* 1964, **9**, 254–57.

Ullmann, L. P., and Krasner, L. (Eds.). *Case studies in behavior modification.* New York: Holt, Rinehart & Winston, 1965.

Ulrich, R., Stachnik, T., and Mabry, J. *Control of human behavior.* Glenview, Ill.: Scott, Foresman, 1966.

Van Kaam, A. L. Assumptions in psychology. *J. Indiv. Psychol.,* 1958, **14**, 22–28.

von Mises, L. *Human action: a treatise on economics.* New Haven: Yale University Press, 1949.

Weaver, W. Science and complexity. *Amer. Scient.,* 1948, **36**, 536–44.

Wolman, B. B. Mental health and mental disorders. In B. B. Wolman (Ed.), *Handbook of clinical psychology.* New York: McGraw-Hill, 1965. Pp. 1119–39.

SUMMARY

THE QUESTION OF PSYCHODIAGNOSIS

Albee questions the very foundations of psychodiagnosis. Psychodiagnosis is based upon a medical model which presumes that disturbed or disturbing behavior is separate, discrete, and discontinuous from normal behavior. If, on the other hand, disturbed or disturbing behavior is *continuous* with normal behavior, then the medical model and its psychodiagnostic ventures are unnecessary barriers to progress in the field of psychology. Albee further submits that one of the central uses of psychodiagnosis is to locate the person who is potentially dangerous, thereby risking permanent damage to him by so labeling and by institutionalizing him. Why, he pointedly inquires, does psychology want its own system in the first place? There is more to the question of psychodiagnosis than just personality theory, research investigation, and treatment programming. Society assigns considerable power to the profession which owns the accepted psychodiagnostic model.

Although each earlier contributor to this book has offered his own approach, Albee questions the very worth of the entire venture. He raises a fundamental question—whether a personality classification system may be based on a nonmedical personality model, one which has no place for normal vs. abnormal behavior, no place for abnormality, illness, disease, or similar medical psychodiagnostic notions. Is it possible to throw out the whole question of normal-abnormal, and still retain a diagnostic system, but one which looks nothing like the medical diagnostic one?

The contributors would agree that the present diagnostic system is used to locate persons considered potentially dangerous and thereby risks harming them, but there are *new* diagnostic systems which have altogether different purposes and functions never even possible with the present system. Whole new ranges of persons may be constructively aided by classification systems which bear little or no relation to the medical system of which Albee speaks. According to the contributors, Albee is referring to a medical diagnostic system, based upon a medical personality model, and addressed to medical administrative and treatment purposes. Let us retain the concept of a system of categories and either vigorously modify or completely replace the medical categories, the medical personality model, and the medical uses and functions.

The contributors acknowledge that power (and, they would hasten to add, responsibility) accrues to the profession which owns the generally approved diagnostic systems. Some of the systems proposed here are designed to reappraise and reorganize the theoretical structure of personality subsystems, e.g., to reconceptualize psychosis. But most of them are geared toward treatment programming and personality change, enterprises which do indeed imply both responsibility and power for the professions involved.

12

NOTES TOWARD A POSITION PAPER
OPPOSING PSYCHODIAGNOSIS

GEORGE W. ALBEE

When I accepted Dr. Mahrer's invitation to prepare a chapter for a volume emphasizing new approaches to psychodiagnostic systems, I believed that there was an urgent need for a new approach to this subject based on psychological science. But since then I have come to the conclusion that *any* formal psychodiagnostic system will be a millstone around psychology's neck, and so I find myself in the uncomfortable position of wanting to honor a moral commitment to write on a subject which now strikes me as an inappropriate effort for psychology.

Because this conclusion has grown slowly, and represents more of a feeling than an intellectually defensible position, it is doubly difficult to write, in the conventional scholarly way, a paper in formal opposition to psychodiagnosis. What follows, therefore, represents some working notes toward a vaguely formulated position opposing the use of diagnostic systems, from whatever origin, by psychology.

A conventional diagnostic system generally carries the clear-cut implication that either etiology or treatment or both are identifiably different for the separate categories. In the traditional medical sense a diagnosis is made in order to dictate the choice of treatment and in order to make significant prognostic statements. Also, because of tradition, and of contemporary experience, diagnostic efforts tend to focus on current inner pathology or weakness. Despite the fact that it is only behavior which forms the raw material from which our diagnostic systems in psychopathology are developed, we keep inferring inner processes and inventing intervening variables to account for the behavior we observe. By thus focusing our attention on the development of a conceptual model with a clear set of implications, widely understood by society, we create a set of rigid restrictions and role definitions for our field.

It seems to me that for our field of clinical psychology the fundamental question that gradually comes into focus asks whether disturbed and disturbing behavior is continuous with normal behavior, or whether separate, discrete, discontinuous mental conditions exist. If the latter is the case then efforts at a nomenclature based on psychological variables are justified and appropriate. But if disturbed human behavior is continuous with normal behavior then whatever system we use to describe normal behavior will apply equally well to exaggerations of the normal. We do not use, in psychology, a nomenclature or diagnostic system for normal behavior, and if we agree that disturbed behavior is continuous with normal behavior it seems inappropriate to try to formulate a nomenclature for disturbance.

I have carried on an extensive correspondence recently with an obstetrician who shares many of my views about the inappropriateness and unreliability of the use of psychiatric diagnosis for disturbed behavior, and who argues that many of the "diseases" that the nonpsychiatric physician diagnoses and treats are themselves describable as normal continuous processes. He has raised the intriguing question of whether there may not be some completely normal human processes that have been turned into iatrogenic illnesses by calling the individuals undergoing these processes "patients" and by bringing them into hospitals for intervention. The best example here, of course, is pregnancy and childbirth. In an overwhelming proportion of cases, and for most of the women of the world, this is a normal process, not usually requiring medical intervention. In the Western world, since the Victorian era, pregnant women have been turned into semi-invalids, and the fearful preparation of the expectant mother, who is taught to look forward to a difficult and painful time during labor, has had the effect of increasing the amount of difficulty associated with this natural process and creating a whole new population of "patients." The analogy to our "treatment" of normally disturbed people is clear. The subject matter with which we are concerned in approaching the field of behavioral deviations is always behavior. We do not even have a "normal" discontinuity, such as pregnancy, to identify. While there are certain relatively unimportant exceptions to the rule, in general it is only behavior which we observe, which we classify, and which we use in making our "diagnosis." In the case of nearly every real disease, there is some objectively identifiable pathological discontinuity on which a diagnosis can be based.

All too often the labeling of a pattern of disturbed behavior as a disease or diagnostic category has even more serious effects than a decision to call the pregnant woman sick. The role of the mental patient is much more deeply ingrained as socially unacceptable and so this label is often permanently damaging. We may cause a pregnant mother unnecessary suffering by treating her as a victim, but her sentence is relatively brief and she can resume her place as a normal member of society within a few short months. The person we label a mental case, on the other hand, is sentenced to a lifetime of discrimination by others and to permanent feelings of self-doubt and inadequacy.

Still another unfortunate encounter with the magic of diagnostic labels, which should be a clear warning to psychologists, is to be found in the field of mental subnormality. After more than half a century of experience with mental measurements, psychologists should know better than anyone else that most measurable human traits, including intelligence, are distributed in a bell-shaped normal curve. We should be reasonably certain, for example, that slightly less than 2½ percent of all children born will have IQs between 50 and 70 (where the mean is 100 and the standard deviation 15). These children, who fall between two and three standard deviations below the mean, are no more deserving of the label "abnormal" or "ill" than unusually short or unusually tall children, because intelligence, like height is dependent on the normal distribution of polygenic factors in the population. Yet we have allowed ourselves to fall into the trap of dividing these normally slow children into diagnostic categories which have quickly become reified. While we no longer use the terms *idiot, imbecile,* or *moron* we have accepted a conceptual system which makes necessary a variety of new categorical labels. Despite the fact that it can be demonstrated with reasonable scientific certainty that most intellectually subnormal persons are not damaged, in any discontinuous sense, we sit idly by and let the medical profession dominate the whole new federal program to construct university-affiliated research facilities for the mentally retarded. Even our own textbooks on abnormal psychology devote long sections to such topics as cretinism, Down's Syndrome, hydrocephaly, and phenylketonuria, despite the fact that all of these organic, discontinuous conditions put together do not represent more than 10 percent of all retarded children. Such is the magical power of symbols, diagnostic categories, and conceptual models.

It is possible to argue that the diagnostic labeling of disturbed behavior represents an undeserved value judgment on the part of society, except in those rare instances where the individual's behavior seems so threatening as to be imminently harmful to others. In his monumental essay *On Liberty* John Stuart Mill (1863, pp. 26 ff.) expressed the opinion that:

. . . the sole end for which mankind are warranted, individually or collectively, in interfering with the liberty of action of any of their number, is self-protection. But the only purpose for which power can be rightfully exercised over any member of a civilized community, against his will, is to prevent harm to others. His own good, either physical or moral, is not a sufficient warrant. He cannot rightfully be compelled to do or forbear because it will be better for him to do so, because it will make him happier, and because, in the opinion of others, to do so would be wise, or even right. These are good reasons for remonstrating with him, or reasoning with him, or persuading him, or entreating him, but not for compelling him, or visiting· him with any evil in case he do otherwise. To justify that, the conduct from which it is desired to deter him must be calculated to produce evil to someone else. . . . Over himself, over his own body and mind, the individual is sovereign.

This argument suggests that the only really important diagnostic judgment necessary from a social point of view involves the question of whether the individual exhibits behavior which marks him as dangerous to others. Considerable attention ought to be paid by psychologists to this argument.

While persons in this country are occasionally arrested on suspicion, or for investigation, the time they can be held without being charged with a crime is relatively brief, and they are practically never incarcerated because of a judgment that they are potential criminals. On the other hand many "mentally ill" individuals are deprived of their liberty and of their civil rights on the basis of the professional judgment that they may be dangerous to themselves or to others. Research is needed to determine the level of validity of such judgments. One might imagine a controlled study in which every second person adjudged dangerous, for psychological reasons, was released but followed up. At some point in time it would be necessary to make a judgment about the relative social gain to be realized from the incarceration of a large number of people in mental hospitals in order to prevent what might turn out to be a relatively small number of aggressive acts.

There is already research evidence which indicates that former mental patients actually commit a smaller number of crimes than control nonmental cases. (See Scheff, 1966, pp. 72 ff.) There are probably more compelling arguments for putting drunken drivers into state hospitals than for committing the average mental case, if protection of others is the primary criterion. The same argument applies to the secondary criterion in which society insists on its responsibility for protecting the individual from himself. It should be possible to develop a convincing case that drunken drivers are more likely to kill themselvs than is the average mental case.

To return to an earlier point, there is real danger, in using diagnostic categories, that serious, and sometimes permanent, damage occurs to the individual branded with a socially unacceptable label. Many clinicians are reluctant to call children schizophrenic for this reason. There is a similar reluctance on the part of psychiatrists to diagnose members of their own social class as schizophrenic, even though the behavioral symptoms may be identical with the behavior of lower-class individuals on whom this label is attached with relatively less reluctance. The terms moron and imbecile quickly acquired such damaging connotations that these terms are now taboo. The words themselves are innocent; it is the reaction of society to the individual defined by these words that is frightening. How long will it be before the words "trainable" and "educable" elicit similar taboo reactions from society?

Because of the social damage done by bad labels, the use of such labels cannot be treated lightly. Great care is taken in the tradition of English and American law to make certain that no innocent man is found guilty. Often (although the ideal is somewhat tarnished occasionally in reality) the view is defended that it is better for 1000 murderers to be freed than for one innocent man to hang. We reduce these odds somewhat in science but we still fear Errors of the First Kind much more than Errors of the Second Kind. (It is one of our laboratory caveats that it is far worse to reject the null hypothesis when it should be accepted than to accept it when it should be rejected.)

But our value systems in law and in science are not appropriate as a value system in medical diagnosis. It has been shown that physicians are more likely to diagnose disease or pathology where there is in fact none, than to find health where there is indeed disease. (See Scheff, 1966, Chapter 4.) Undoubtedly members of society prefer this situation as it is. A misdiagnosis, where a serious condition is overlooked, is more unforgivable, as a general rule, than the suspicion of disease where there is none. Because psychiatry is part of medicine it has generally followed this pattern. Any good psychiatrist can find psychopathology in practically anyone. The best example of this situation is the frequent report of findings of psychopathology in a majority of samples of the population interviewed carefully and diagnosed by psychiatrists and other psychiatric workers.

Unhappily, the fate of the misdiagnosed mental case is often most unfortunate and irreversible. Being diagnosed a psychotic, for example, can result in a loss of freedom, of civil rights, and of human dignity and can lead to months or years of living hell in one of the monstrosities we call state hospitals. Yet Scheff (1966, Chapters 4 and 5) has shown that psychiatrists in tax-supported public settings such as probate courts diagnose "mental illness" in a very large proportion of cases brought before them despite relatively brief interviews. In one particular study he reports nearly two-thirds of the individuals adjudged dangerous or helpless, and committed to a public institution, were actually neither dangerous nor helpless.

Obviously, then, one of the most important questions to be asked about a psychological diagnostic system concerns the use to which it is to be put. Psychologists have amused themselves and each other for years developing typologies, many of which were dichotomous. Intelligent lay conversation today is larded frequently with references to introversion and extroversion, to dominance and submission, to authoritarian and equalitarian values. Professional conversation may contain references to more polychotomous systems involving "the anal type," "the aesthetic type," or "an elevated neurotic triad." In most cases psychologists know perfectly well that these "types" represent names applied to extremes in a normally continuous distribution, and probably little harm is done, even by those who do not understand the properties of the normal curve. Psychologists also know that traits are more meaningful descriptive categories than types, and trait theory is certainly more respectable than type theory, at least since the work of Hartshorne and May (1928) done half a century ago. Psychologists have also known for a long time that traits are not absolute invariant qualities of the individual but appear and disappear, and change dramatically, depending upon a number of interacting variables, including the social situation. Yet we keep talking about the need to develop our own rigid diagnostic system for classifying disturbed behavior.

It is appropriate for behavioral scientists to be interested in every identifiable kind of human behavior. And being human, they will find that certain aspects or components of human behavior interest them more than others, and so there will be specialists in identifiable kinds of behavior. For many the behavior usually called abnormal holds a genuine fascination and for a smaller number certain kinds of abnormal behavior are even more intensely interesting. Thus are experts developed, and as the experts seek to order and classify behavior in which they are especially interested, classification systems grow out of relatively narrow ranges of behavioral observation and experience. Because the classifiers are those who know the most about their small circumscribed areas, it is difficult to argue with them, and the intelligent public tends to accept the classification systems of recognized authorities, or is occasionally bemused by arguments about which system is better.

It is only when we back off from the trees that the continuity of the forest becomes discernible. With some distance perspective, or time perspective, we may glimpse the inappropriateness of highly refined classification systems that have as their raw material nothing objective beyond observable human behavior.

More than two centuries ago the *Gentleman's Magazine* (1769, p. 1062) of London printed a letter from a physician who said, "When I first dabbed in this art, the old dystemper called Melancholy was exchang'd for *Vapours,* and afterwards for the *Hypp,* and at last took up the now current appellation of the *Spleen,* which it still retains, tho' a learned doctor of the west, in a little tract he hath written, divided the *Spleen* and *Vapours* not only into the *Hypp,* the *Hyppos,* and the *Hyppocons;* but subdivided these divisions into the *Markambles,* the *Moonpalls,* the *Strong-Fives* and the *Hockogrokles.*"

In the first half of the nineteenth century, in the United States at least, there was a relatively sparse literature concerned with the differential diagnosis of disordered behavior. But in the decades following the first waves of immigration from Europe there was a rapid disappearance of the widespread concept of moral insanity, and of small nonpublic institutions operated by clergymen or by religious orders, and a concomitant increase in public-supported minimum care of the insane with a parallel increase in explanations of insanity that emphasized illness. Some writers have attributed this change in approach to the unwillingness, or the inability, of society to accord sympathetic and humane care for the large number of foreign immigrant psychotics whose disturbed behavior, together with their unfamiliar language, seeming coarseness, and lack of financial resources, made them less attractive candidates for gentle moral persuasion. At the same time there was less general resistance to labeling these foreigners as hopelessly ill. Most of the Yankee physicians who had been able to extend a kind of Quaker fellowship to the insane found themselves unable to deal with the "foreign pauper insane" who had inundated the retreats in the latter part of the nineteenth century.

By 1872, John P. Gray, recently appointed editor in chief of the *American Journal of Insanity,* said (Bunker, 1944, p. 210) that he fully believed "what Maudsley is 'tempted sometimes to think,' that insanity occurs only as the result of physical causation—that a necessary antecedent to madness is a distorted physical state of the brain—that it never occurs in a person of sound brain."

In arguing against the social usefulness of psychological diagnosis, the most immediate and obvious counterargument emphasizes the important differences between *psychological* descriptions of disturbed people and categorization of people as having various specific sorts of illnesses. While the distinction is valid, the consequences resulting from the use of either system often seem indistinguishable.

Many of the categories of the nomenclature of the American Psychiatric Association are not illnesses, in any conventionally accepted sense, and few thoughtful psychiatrists would argue, in private discussion, at least, that people so labeled are sick. But because these categories constitute an official, and often legal, diagnosis, sometimes required for commitment to hospitals, or for the incarceration of juveniles, the public stance of psychiatry must be that only a physician is qualified to make these, or any other diagnosis in the system. The official position of many state and local clinics and hospitals restricts "psychiatric diagnosis" to the physician. The point is not whether behavioral science might be able to formulate a more valid and heuristic set of categories, but rather that the very process of diagnosis per se is so inextricably associated both with the folkways and the legal structure of our society as to bid us be cautious.

While this argument sounds as though political considerations were being used to influence scientific freedom this is certainly not my intention. Rather there is the danger that the choice of a model through which to approach an empirical problem—the diagnostic or typology model—occupies our attention because of its social success in strengthening professional hegemony. I fear that psychologists want their own diagnostic system not only because they see the scientific inadequacies of the official one but also because they see the power that has been assigned by society to the profession that owns a diagnostic model.

It is interesting in this context to note that the psychoanalytic diagnostic system contains relatively few formulations that derive from a sickness model, or from dependence on biological bases. While Freud occasionally acknowledged the biological basis of behavior, specifically in the origin of the instincts and libido, the whole formulation of developmental, topological, and dynamic aspects of the theory has been almost strictly psychological. Despite this, and despite more recent psychoanalytic emphases on the area generally understood to be encompassed by the term "ego psychology," psychoanalysis continues to exude a strong biomedical aura. The point is that a psychological diagnostic system will not necessarily free psychology from the distasteful experience of being found guilty by association. Diagnosis and diagnostic approaches suggest the medical or clinical model, and that model is an unnecessary barrier to real progress in our field.

I have discovered that opposition to the sickness explanation of disturbing behavior has been around for years and has been well articulated by many people. But somehow today the climate seems more ready to nurture this position. A number of years ago Julian Rotter (1954, p. 29) argued eloquently for the position that psychology does not need "a new classification but the elimination of the disease entity concept in psychology." Rotter discussed the various languages of psychology in terms that are highly relevant to the present issues.

It is one thing to classify people and another to classify behavior into categories. I believe there is an important difference between the statement "He exhibits neurotic behavior," and the statement "He is a neurotic." Persons may exhibit behavior which can be called neurotic or psychotic, but these same persons also exhibit a wide range of other behavior not different or remarkable from that of most of their peers. Somehow when a person is stamped as being psychotic we surround him with an aura which affects our response to him as a person, which eventually affects his own self-concept, and which may further damage his ability to relate to people.

It is possible, of course, to classify disturbed human behavior into meaningful, logical categories, and to determine what sorts of behavior go together. Of the various approaches that have been used with disturbed behavior, my own preference is for the sort of factor analytic studies done by Maurice Lorr and his associates (1962) where relatively independent categories of behavior have been isolated, and can be rated objectively. Such criteria will certainly be useful in epidemiological studies, prognostic studies, and similar research efforts.

My reservation about such systems derives primarily from the fact that they focus on behavioral symptoms adjudged disturbed and thereby lend, perhaps unwittingly, support to the illness model. In interviewing a human being who is in a mental hospital because of some behavioral disturbance, a search is made for symptoms in each of several categories. This means that the selective attention of the examiner focuses on pathological behavior. Indicators of strengths, of interests, of intact and effective behavior, are not attended to because of the demands of the system for identifying disturbance.

This situation is reminiscent of Sidney Jourard's (1967) warning that we should "stop seeing others as 'mentally ill,' as poor, benighted, trapped people." Jourard's argument goes on: "If you invite somebody to behave in a mad way, he will behave in a mad way. That is what psychiatry is about. But if we purge our minds of the idea that he is 'sick' and see him as just another person and invite him to tell us about his life, he accepts and becomes a human being again."

The point is important. In looking for indicators which will enable us to make a diagnosis we fall into the trap of defining prematurely the rules of the game. If there must be a diagnostician and a patient, then there is strong social conditioning to define and limit the proper role for each player. There is also pressure to identify behavior in the patient indicative of underlying pathology. And because there is almost always *some* evidence of underlying disturbance in everyone the evidence can be found in anyone. Most industrial psychologists are familiar with the common phenomenon that occurs when a clinical psychology student, or even an experienced clinical psychologist, is asked to assess normal people referred for evaluation by industry. Almost invariably the clinician finds all sorts of underlying conflicts and indicators of serious disturbance in persons who are functioning normally and doing reasonably effective jobs. Because we have tuned our assessment devices to the static we pay no attention to the music.

In summary, most nomenclatures imply a kind of typology, or a fixed set of negative traits, where the most usual utilization with respect to a person exhibiting disturbed behavior is to provide a type-label to hang on him. Thus, to label someone becomes the most important consideration influencing our reactions to him. The label colors all our observations and perceptions of the individual. But normal people do not wear such labels well, and it is hard to make them stick, because our relationships with our peers are not cast in the same kind of conceptual and hierarchical mold as our relationships with "patients." Our approach to the study of disturbed people, if we accept a continuity position, should not be any different than our approach to the study of normal personality, with as much attention to positive, constructive behavior as to behavior judged disturbed.

REFERENCES

Albee, G. The relation of conceptual models to manpower needs. In E. Cowen et al. (Eds.), *Emergent approaches to mental health problems.* New York: Appleton-Century-Crofts, 1968.

Bunker, H. A. American psychiatric literature during the past one hundred years. In American Psychiatric Association, *One hundred years of American psychiatry.* New York: Columbia University Press, 1944.

Gentleman's Magazine, London, 1769.

Hartshorne, H., and May, M. *Studies in deceit.* New York: Macmillan, 1928.

Jourard, S. Mimeographed paper. Presented at Annual Meeting, American Psychological Association, 1967.

Lorr, M. Measurement of the major psychotic syndromes. *Annals N.Y. Acad. Sci.* 1962, **93**, 851–56.

Mill, J. S. *On liberty.* 2d ed. Boston: Ticknor and Fields, 1863.

Rotter, J. *Social learning and clinical psychology.* New York: Prentice-Hall, 1954.

Scheff, T. J. *Being mentally ill: a sociological theory.* Chicago: Aldine, 1966.

PRESENT TRENDS AND FUTURE DIRECTIONS

ALVIN R. MAHRER

This chapter offers a summary of the ten approaches and a set of implications drawn from the ideas advanced by the contributors, an overview of present trends and future directions.

 Present Trends

VARYING FUNCTIONS OF PERSONALITY CLASSIFICATION

Clearly, there are a number of purposes or functions for personality classifications. These functions transcend disease or mental illness (Harrower; Leary; Mahrer; Thorne), and are by no means confined to psychopathology, *psychiatric* conceptions of personality, or *psychiatric* clinical groups (cf. Albee). Instead, there seem to be three distinguishable kinds of approaches:

Structural approaches. Operating within an explicit personality framework, one approach probes into the structure of personality to uncover its mode of organization and searches out underlying natural groupings, factors, communalities, nexuses, and dimensions (Cattell; Horn and Sweney; Lorr). By revealing the deeper organizational structure of personality, this approach is able to suggest better building blocks and elements for the further construction of its parent theory. For example, such an approach would inquire into the structural types which comprise the concept of psychosis (Lorr). This approach is dedicated to the description of the deeper structure of personality.

Functional approaches. Whereas structural approaches probe deeper into a personality theory, functional approaches put a personality theory to work on some defined and explicit task. Structural approaches are systematic and analytic; functional approaches are useful and practical. For example, functional approaches include a set of scales for placing persons into groups based upon their potential for responding to psychotherapy (Fine; Harrower) or potential success in a given training program. This approach aims at providing a practical working assistance for particular tasks.

Comprehensive approaches. A comprehensive approach (Eysenck; Leary; Mahrer; Pratt and Tooley; Thorne) provides a broad set of classes or dimensions for the deep understanding of persons in general. Unlike the structural approaches, these emphasize the understanding of persons rather than the component structure of some area of personality. Unlike the functional approaches, these not only highlight understanding, but also are oriented toward comprehensive aims rather than specific and defined functions.

VARYING RANGES OF APPLICABILITY

Approaches vary widely in their referent or target groups. Some are aimed at persons in general—all persons and under all circumstances (Eysenck; Horn and Sweney; Leary; Pratt and Tooley; Thorne). Some are designed for specific groups—persons in hospitals (Lorr; Mahrer), candidates for (private) psychotherapists (Fine; Harro; undergoing crises, children, psychotics. The conventional psychiat system has a range of applicability defined and limited by a dimension of psychopathology (Albee). Each approach has its own range of applicability, its own clinical group to which it is most appropriately applied.

Determinants of the range of applicability. A number of factors determine the range of applicability of a given system:

The range of applicability is determined in part by the nature of the approach, viz., whether it is structural, functional, or comprehensive. If an approach seeks to uncover the dimensions underlying psychosis, its range of applicability is thereby restricted to psychotic persons. If an approach is addressed toward the practical function of predicting therapeutic response to chemotherapy, its range of applicability is thereby limited to patients who may be treated with chemotherapeutic agents. The purpose of the approach, i.e., whether it is structural, functional, or comprehensive, serves as one important determinant of the range of applicability.

A second major determinant of the range of applicability is the nature of the underlying personality theory. In order to direct itself toward "psychotic" persons (Lorr), the underlying theory must rest on a concept of "psychosis." Not every personality theory includes such a concept (Mahrer). Similarly, in order for the system to apply to the range of "normal," "neurotic," and "psychotic," the underlying personality theory must contain these concepts, and again, some do (Cattell; Eysenck; Fine) and some do not (Leary; Pratt and Tooley; Mahrer).

Any consideration of the issue of continuity-discontinuity or normality, neurosis, and psychosis implicitly or explicitly accepts the Kraepelinian-psychiatric theory (Mahrer, 1967b, pp. 272–73, 276). The question may be whether normality is continuous or discontinuous with abnormality (Albee; Eysenck; Fine), or whether psychosis and neurosis are structurally composed of a number of underlying dimensions which crisscross each other (Cattell; Eysenck). As long as one inquires into the intertwinings and convolutions of normality, abnormality, neurosis, and psychosis, these concepts are solidly preserved and one is operating within a conceptual variant of the Kraepelinian-psychiatric system.

Other classification approaches are based upon personality theories free of the concepts of normality, neurosis, or psychosis (Leary; Mahrer; Pratt and Tooley). These three concepts, together with the issues pertaining to their interrelationships, are meaningful solely within the Kraepelinian-psychiatric diagnostic system and are not meaningful issues for all approaches. Thus, only the conventional psychodiagnostic approach labels certain persons as neurotic, psychotic, mentally ill, or psychiatrically diseased. Some of the approaches described in this book apply to the same individuals, but within a different conceptual net which identifies these persons as motivated toward hospitalization (Mahrer), instrumenting ends-means relationships (Pratt and Tooley), manifesting given traits, states, processes, and types (Horn and Sweney), possessing a given degree of mental health potential (Harrower), or engaging in given existential-transactional relationships (Leary). Thus, there may be considerable overlap among various ranges of applicability, depending upon the personality theory. By no considerations whatsoever are these ten systems limited to what the psychiatric diagnostic system labels as the mentally ill.

The third major determinant of the range of applicability is the degree to which a given system has been conceptually, pragmatically, and experimentally worked out with regard to one given class of persons rather than another. One system (Lorr) is based upon a set of psychotic dimensions and derived types. The concepts were worked out with regard to the class of so-called psychotic patients; the system has actually been tried out repeatedly with psychotic patients and is based upon considerable research with psychotics. Although the system is potentially applicable to normals and neurotics as well as psychotics, its actual range of applicability is limited to psychotics because of these conceptual, pragmatic, and experimental considerations.

Another system (Mahrer) is based upon a set of motivational needs. Although the concept of motivational needs potentially applies to all persons, the specific set of motivational needs was the product of conceptualization, actual clinical experience, and experimental research with persons in hospitals. Thus, the potential range of applicability includes all persons whereas the actual system targets upon persons in hospitals.

PRACTICAL, WORKING DESIDERATA OF PERSONALITY CLASSIFICATION SYSTEMS

The ten approaches proposed in this book have practical requirements. The following are intended to complement and supplement more abstract, theoretical, and methodological desiderata of an adequate system:

Increased sense of understanding. A system should provide an increased understanding of the person such as, for example, his probable response to psychotherapy (Fine; Harrower), the motivational needs underlying his major problem, or the etiological threads which organize his clinical history (Mahrer; Thorne).

Idiosyncrasy. A system should uncover the idiosyncratic uniqueness of each individual, his distinctive and characteristic motivational needs (Mahrer), source traits (Cattell), drives (Horn and Sweney), dimensions or heterogeneity of performance (Harrower). Indeed, the system should be equipped to face each person, as Eysenck says, as a fresh experimental problem or unique human being.

Defined purpose or function. A system should clearly define itself (e.g., as structural, functional, or comprehensive). It may aim to predict success in psychotherapy or to probe the types of neurosis, but in any case its use, aim, or purpose should be specifically identified (e.g., Fine).

Defined range of applicability. Each system should define its own target group, reference group, "range of convenience" (Kelly, 1955), or applicability. Some are aimed at children, psychoanalytic candidates (Fine), schizophrenics, or those in hospitals (Lorr; Mahrer). The specific clinical group for which it is intended should be clearly identified.

A guide to psychological change. The system should offer some link to psychological change; it should provide a program toward accomplishing some action or therapeutic change. It may offer a prediction regarding success or failure in some enterprise, or it may provide a comprehensive array of avenues toward accomplishing therapeutic goals. Even structural approaches are directed toward telling us what we may do about some issue. In contrast, the conventional psychiatric approach is regularly accused of being much ado about nothing; all diagnosed patients are generally given similar sorts of treatment regardless of the attached psychiatric label.

Incorporation of research findings. A system should take account of relevant experimental findings (e.g., Eysenck). While not oversensitive to slight evidence, neither should a system be isolated from accumulated bodies of research findings. "Our search for a proper classification . . . is basically a search for understanding vast amounts of data that requires synthesis" (Robbins, 1966, p. 35). The relative imperviousness of the present psychiatric taxonomy to growing bodies of experimental findings should stand as a warning to emerging new approaches.

At the practical, working level, the contributors offer the above as further desiderata of good systems of personality classification.

NEW PERSONALITY CONCEPTIONS UNDERLYING CLASSIFICATION SYSTEMS

The conventional psychodiagnostic classification is based upon a Krae-pelinian-psychiatric personality model. More recent conceptions and models of personality call for expression in new classificatory approaches. The following examples are representative of new personality conceptions which underlie the systems of the contributors. New classification systems will reflect and express changes in personality theory and personality models:

The situation. There is a growing understanding and recognition of the role of the psychological situation as a determinant of personality behavior (Horn and Sweney; Leary; Mahrer; Thorne). Theories of personality are incorporating the situational context as a central variable. When the underlying theory includes the situation as an important determinant, the associated classification system incorporates in its taxonomy the role of the uniquely changing situation.

The interactional relationship. Some underlying personality conceptions place central importance on the relationship between the individual and other persons—on the interaction, the transaction, the contractual relationship (cf. Leary; Mahrer; Pratt and Tooley; Thorne). If personality behavior is regarded as a function of this interactional relationship, the derived system is built around varying classes of interactional relationships.

Personality building blocks. Contemporary personality theories offer new building blocks for the structural organization of personality.

Sets of conditioned behaviors (Eysenck), sets of motives and drives (Horn and Sweney), sets of abilities and source traits (Cattell), and sets of motivational needs (Mahrer; Pratt and Tooley) are replacing the building blocks of the traditional psychiatric model. The new systems reflect these new structural components of personality.

Behavioral conditioning. In one approach (Eysenck), behavioral psychopathology is conceptualized as a function of autonomic responses conditioned to neutral stimuli. The basis of conditioning includes the excitation of thalamocortical portions of the reticular formation which mediate inhibition. The associated classification system must then express these autonomic-based conditioning variables.

Need-motivated clinical behavior. Behavior may be understood as directed toward goals and motivated by needs (Mahrer). These motivational needs engender behavior to express a given state of integration among basic needs and to experience the more basic needs. A personality model characterized by goal-directionality and motivational needs will require a classification system with appropriate parameters.

Homeostasis. A personality model may be explicitly built around a central concept of homeostasis, in which motivation relates to disruption of the homeostatic state (Horn and Sweney). The associated system is thereby called upon to utilize dimensions and categories on the basis of states of homeostasis.

Personality dimensions versus disease entities. The conventional psychiatric diagnostic system utilizes sets of disease entities. Each category is a mental illness, a disease. The rules of the Kraepelinian-psychiatric model are such that a person may have one mental illness. He is a "paranoid schizophrenic," or a "dissociative reaction," or a "sexual deviate." Furthermore, the "paranoid schizophrenic" cannot also have a "character disorder." Each disorder is separate.

The present trend in personality classification approaches has almost uniformly rejected the concept of separate disease entities. New approaches are based on personality models which provide sets of dimensions along which persons may range. A person may fall at different points along a number of these personality dimensions. For example, one dimension may range from normality to abnormality, with persons distributed at any or all points along the continuum. Another approach utilizes a number of factor-analytically derived personality dimensions in which an individual is described on the basis of his position on relevant dimensions (Cattell; Horn and Sweney; Lorr). Still another approach (Mahrer) understands individuals in terms of varying combinations of motivational needs. Although the number and the nature of the personality dimensions differ in the new systems, these dimensions have become an identifying hallmark of the current trend.

Introversion and extraversion. The old concepts of introversion and extraversion take on a new meaning in some of the current behavior modification theories (e.g., Eysenck). These concepts are significant as determinants of the nature and degree of conditionability. Accordingly, systems based upon conditionability would be organized around these two central concepts.

The existential self. Some new approaches organize persons on the basis of a conscious, feeling, thinking, enduring self (Leary) which possesses varying degrees of self-actualized or self-defeating integration (Thorne). The use of this central concept calls for a significant expression in the associated system.

Mental health potential. The theoretical underpinnings of one new approach go beyond the psychiatric personality model by adding an assumption of a positive side to personality, i.e., a mental health potential (Harrower). Accordingly, the conventional classifications must be reorganized with a series of additional categories to reflect categories of mental health potential.

Nonneurophysiological psychoanalysis. Psychoanalytic conceptualizations have been reflected in (and also restricted by) the present psychiatric diagnostic system. One approach (Fine) has cleanly severed psychoanalysis from unnecessary neurophysiological foundations, specifically with a functional approach geared toward the evaluation of potential for psychoanalytic treatment.

A neurophysiological foundation. At the other extreme, another personality approach (Eysenck) explicitly rests upon a neurophysiological base with an especial emphasis upon inherited differences in the ascending reticular activating system, the cortex, and the visceral brain. It may be expected that such a personality theory would give rise to a classification system reflecting the contours of its neurophysiological foundation.

Patternings of traits. Another approach rests upon trait theory (Cattell; Horn and Sweney). Abnormality refers to deviations on common traits, to particular traits, and to patternings of common traits. These traits and patterns of traits provide the basis for the new categories.

The emergence of new personality models and theories calls for equally new approaches to personality classification. No longer can the one conventional category system be expected either to serve or to reflect the burgeoning trends of new personality models, theories, and conceptualizations.

THE BRIDGING OF GAPS

The proposed systems reflect the bridging of at least the following three gaps:

The doers and the methodologists. Some of the contributors (Cattell; Horn and Sweney; Lorr) have focused on the gap between those primarily involved with the applied psychology of patient care and treatment and, on the other hand, those primarily involved in methodology, theoretical psychometrics, and factor analytic techniques. Some of the proposed approaches have specifically focused on bringing together experimental methodology and clinical application into new systems of personality classification.

The patient and the therapist. The conventional psychiatric diagnostic system has no place for the patient-therapist relationship in its exclusive emphasis upon the patient's mental illness. New approaches bridge the gap between patient and therapist by explicitly focusing on the interaction between the inner world of both patient and therapist (Leary), the patient's therapeutic readiness (Fine), and underlying motivational needs for treatment (Mahrer).

Theoretical advances and clinical techniques. Some of the new systems have attempted to link advances in personality theory with advances in clinical techniques. Advances in modern learning theory, for example, and advances in the clinical techniques of conditioning are being bridged in the new nosologies (Eysenck).

PERSONALITY EVALUATION

The conventional psychiatric model assigns one person the role of patient-subject and the other the role of diagnostician-observer. The diagnostician generally utilizes the "clinical interview" and the psychological "test" to provide data from which he draws inferences about the subject. The new approaches offer additional avenues for personality evaluation:

Specific clinical behaviors. Psychological diagnostic assessment has generally steered clear of applying careful systematic principles of inference construction to the realm of specific clinical behaviors. This phenomenon is less understandable as a scientific procedure than as another instance of "professional territoriality" whereby some psychiatrists try to claim the patient's clinical behavior as a psychiatric domain and consign the patient's "test responses" as the clinical psychologist's domain. Unfortunately, some clinical psychologists have accepted such arbitrary professional territoriality. However, the present trend is overcoming this deficit, and many of the proposed approaches are heavily concentrating on the careful and precise assessment and evaluation of specific clinical behaviors, symptoms, or complaints (Cattell; Horn and Sweney; Lorr; Mahrer), including laboratory behavior related to conditioning processes (Eysenck).

Self-report. Conventional interviewing and testing places the individual in the role of subject observed as he does something, e.g., tells a story fitting a picture-card or puts blocks together or counts backward from one hundred by sevens or explains the meaning of a proverb. Some of the new approaches take the individual out of the role of subject or object. Instead, he is encouraged to report about himself and what he says is awarded the stature of valid data. Nor is the individual asked to report about himself so that a diagnostician may interpret the pathological manner in which the person organizes, projects, or imposes his own special structure on essentially ambiguous material. Furthermore, there is no disguising of the purpose or aim. Instead, the person is guided to provide explicit, straightforward information about himself and his world. Personality inferences are drawn directly from these self-report data (Horn and Sweney; Mahrer).

One approach (Leary) represents a next step by specifically instructing the individual how to study and to report significant and meaningful data about himself. Instead of subject and observer, a working partnership is established with the aim of eliciting, organizing, and making cooperative sense out of self-reported data.

Submitting to the naturally occurring data. Conventional diagnostic evaluation occurs in an artificial situation, removed from the individual's natural life, limited to an hour or so of observations in which he is professionally manipulated into exhibiting pathological symptoms or test responses. In contrast, the new approaches suggest that the clinician submit *himself* to the naturally occurring data (Leary). This may involve being with the individual at his home, his work, or other naturally occurring situations (Horn and Sweney). It may involve being with the individual as he lives through a problem situation such as fearing a closed elevator or finding himself withdrawing from an adolescent daughter. Furthermore, the new approaches acknowledge the need for representative sampling of naturally occurring data by continuing the process over a period of time and throughout an adequate sample of natural situations (Cattell; Leary; Thorne).

A variation on the above theme is the creation of miniature situations which genuinely sample the natural occurrences of the person's life. In close approximations to the natural situation, the individual is given opportunities to manifest his problematic behaviors. By submitting to the naturally occurring data, new approaches to relevant information are opened.

Direct access to the internal domain. Another avenue for personality evaluation offers direct access to the individual's inner, private world (Leary), opening the way for systematic personality evaluation of the individual's internal processes. In conventional psychodiagnosis, either the diagnostician is supposed to possess extraordinary skills of clinical interpretation or the tests are hopefully endowed with special powers to "tap the basic personality processes." New approaches seek more direct access to the private world of the inner domain by at least three avenues: (1) chemicals may open up direct access to deeper levels of consciousness; (2) the realm of deeper feelings may be approached by clinical sensitivity training and specialized techniques for the individual to manifest directly his deeper feelings; (3) dreams may be systematized to provide data for personality evaluation.

The clinician as a source of data. In conventional psychodiagnosis, the clinician is assigned the role of external observer. In general, his own personality is regarded as a confounding intrusion. Some of the new approaches, however, allow for the clinician himself to serve as a useful source of data (Leary). These approaches highlight the relationship, the transaction (Pratt and Tooley), the contract, the interaction. The clinician fully inserts himself into the situation and uses the emergent data (e.g., I am induced to fight him; I feel like taking his part; I want to protect him; she leaves me sexually aroused). Carefully understood and utilized, the clinician's own feelings and reactions are valuable for personality inferences about the patient.

The systematic clinical history. The new approaches revivify the Adolf Meyer tradition of the clinical history as a source of data (Mahrer; Thorne). Conventional psychiatric histories have failed to utilize systematic methodology. It is curious that psychological tests have stoutly excluded the clinical history as useful data (more than likely another example of clinical psychology's ready acceptance of the social worker's and psychiatrist's professional territoriality). In contrast, the new approaches place high value on the clinical psychological history as a rich source of systematic and useful data.

The present trend is toward increasing utilization of the above six sources of data for personality assessment.

THE ASSESSED VARIABLES

In the standard psychiatric system, the categories of mental illness determine what variables are to be assessed. The diagnostic interview and tests concentrate upon certain kinds of variables: brain damage, mental retardation, sexual deviation, degree of depression, psychotic indicators, etc. The new approaches offer a multitude of dimensions and categories which call for assessment. A partial list includes the following: the ease of conditionability, introversion-extraversion, the array of adaptive-coping behaviors, various kinds of temperaments and styles, the ability to establish a therapeutic relationship, scales of homogeneity and heterogeneity of performance in an assessment of mental health potential, arrays and combinations of the several source traits, degree of openness to the inner life, intelligence, motivational needs, sets of abilities, the dimensions comprising neurosis and psychosis, socioeconomic status, levels of consciousness, the nature of the existential state, the self-concept, life management skills, experiential reality, the degree of disintegration. These variables supplement, complement, or replace the traditional ones and call for new methods of assessment.

Future Directions

With full recognition of the potentially enormous error and bias, the following glimpse may be taken into the future of the field of personality classification and psychodiagnosis.

MULTIPLE SYSTEMS OF PERSONALITY CLASSIFICATION

Psychology, psychiatry, and the related disciplines have functioned under essentially one diagnostic system. Although this system is struggling to maintain its universal acceptance, the future seems to promise the passing of the grand old single-system approach. Three considerations suggest the future of multiple systems:

The need for function-specific systems. The future need is for a series of separate systems, each serving a specific function. The trend is away from a few all-purpose therapeutic modalities and toward sets of defined programs which require their own functional systems. In the recent past, clinical groupings have been gawkishly large and loose: neurotics, psychotics, children, adults; treatment modalities have been equally large and loose: "psychotherapy," chemotherapy, custodial treatment, etc. The present trend is toward increasing differentiation. Thus, the future may see a specific system for the function of assessing appropriateness for long-term existential treatment, separate systems for the efficacy of specific chemotherapies for adults, distinctive systems for therapeutic programming of persons in crisis or emergency situations. There likely will be separate systems for the concrete functions of predicting success in varying kinds of training programs—from remedial reading programs for children to special training programs for adults, all utilizing their own functional sets of personality parameters and dimensions. Programming of community change will call for a system based upon emerging sociopsychological theories rather than the old Kraepelinian-psychiatric approach. Programs of self-actualization, growth and development, and constructive behavior modification will require a classification system able to reflect and assess individual potential and avenues of change.

The increased power of structural systems. The future should see the formation of an alliance between structural systems and statistical techniques such as factor analysis. With this coalition for plumbing the depths of the structure of varieties of personality classifications and dimensions—from homosexuality to autistic children, from alcoholism to incarcerated adolescents—leading to a further likelihood of multiple systems.

The development of comprehensive personality theories. The future should see the further development of a number of comprehensive personality theories. These will not only find the conventional diagnostic nomenclature unsuitable, but will present their own comprehensive systems so that, once again, the future includes the distinct likelihood of multiple systems.

FUTURE DIRECTIONS AND THE CONVENTIONAL PSYCHIATRIC DIAGNOSTIC SYSTEM

Present trends augur two major changes in the conventional psychiatric diagnostic system:

Structural reorganization. One future direction will retain the skeletal theoretical framework of the Kraepelinian-psychiatric system while computerized factor analytic approaches bring about an increased tightening and systematization of the total system. Cattell, Lorr, and their respective co-workers are already well into such research investigation. The results should include gross structural reorganizations both in breadth and in depth so that any given category (such as anxiety reaction, schizophrenia, or paranoia) will be reorganized in terms of statistically and clinically more appropriate dimensions and emergent subtypes. In addition to these changes in depth, changes in breadth will occur across the major rubrics, so that even such major conceptual categories as neurosis and psychosis will be assimilated into new primary classifications based upon more methodologically derived dimensions and types.

Dissolution of the conventional psychiatric conceptualization. The present conventional psychiatric system rests on a fractionated coalition of personality theories with internally inconsistent basic assumptions

(Mahrer, 1967a, pp. 262–69). At the present time, psychoanalytic theories are developing along one direction, while neurophysiological conceptualizations are proceeding along another. Existential psychiatry, ego psychology, behavior modification, experiential psychology, social psychiatry, and other burgeoning personality developments are threatening Kraepelinian psychiatry. The future may well see the vigorous development of several psychological-psychiatric personality theories and associated classification systems out of the present loose psychodiagnostic conceptualizations.

FUTURE COMPREHENSIVE PERSONALITY CLASSIFICATION SYSTEMS

On the basis of the present trends, the future holds the possibility of at least two comprehensive classification systems associated with two comprehensive personality theories:

Biopsychological classification system. One system will derive from a biopsychological personality theory which rests on a foundation of biological, neurological, and psysiological factors and processes (Mahrer, 1967a, pp. 262–64). Central roles in this system will be held by inherited differences, autonomic responses, the reticular activating system, constitutional endowments, and the cortex. The system will incorporate dimensions of biopsychological personality and will present a comprehensive typology rooted in its biological, neurological, and physiological personality foundations.

Psychological classification system. A second system will derive from a psychological personality theory in which "the basic, fundamental structure of personality resides in and is derived from *psychological* processes, variables and properties, with no presumption of a substratum composed of some other kinds of processes, variables or properties (e.g., biological, genetic, physiological or constitutional)" (Mahrer, 1967a, p. 265). It will include basic concepts of integration-homeostasis and self-actualization (Pratt and Tooley). The building blocks of personality will be seen in drives, motivations, and needs. Emphasis will be placed upon the role of the uniquely changing situational field, including the contextual perimeter surrounding the individual and the clinician.

FUTURE FUNCTIONAL CLASSIFICATION SYSTEMS

A number of functional systems addressed toward specific tasks, purposes, and jobs will emerge. These smaller systems will be highly utilitarian, with defined target groups.

The function of crisis intervention, emergency treatment, and suicide prevention should emerge with its own useful nomenclature which assesses the appropriate dimensions for treatment programming.

Each emergent approach to individual psychotherapy will be accompanied by its own classification system designed to evaluate candidates, provide understanding of the person, and serve as a guide for treatment programming. Adlerian, social learning, psychoanalytic, behavior modification, motivational, and experiential psychotherapies will be equipped with their own appropriate classification systems.

Omnibus treatment centers will employ personality classification systems for the practical function of fitting patients with appropriate treatment programs. On the basis of the functional classification, patients will be given certain drugs or given sanctuary from external stresses or provided with necessary legal assistance or guided through defined therapeutic experiences or placed in a carefully organized group therapy.

Functional systems will continue their usefulness in predicting success and guiding decision-making with regard to graduate school, entrance into military programs, executive placement in business, scientific research teams, and many kinds of training programs. The present trends suggest a vigorous future for such functional systems. They will assess readiness to undergo positive personality change, self-actualization, constructive behavior modification, growth and development, movement in the direction of optimal functioning.

THE SOCIAL SIGNIFICANCE OF PSYCHODIAGNOSTIC LABELS

At the present time, Kraepelinian-psychiatric labels (e.g., psychotic, mental patient, paranoid schizophrenic, psychopathic, "sick") constitute aggressive ammunition (Albee). The social significance of these labels is such that placing a person in a category can harm him.

The future holds promise of a distinct change in the social significance of classification constructs. In place of a single category for an individual (he is a paranoiac; he is manic-depressive), the individual would be described as falling at various points along a series of dimensions. Even more importantly, however, the entire aura of psychiatric disease and illness will be replaced with an array of nonmorbid types, categories, and dimensions. Psychological labels will regain a humanistic aura, if only by freeing themselves of the connotations of psychiatric disease.

At present the conventional labels refer to psychiatrically ill patients, especially those in mental hospitals and those requiring psychiatric care. In the future, personality classifications will be applied to any and all kinds of groups, dispelling the morbid gloom of the implied conventional mental hospital. Nor would the purposes be confined to treatment of mental illness; instead, personality classification will cover a multitude of functions, many of which will not have the slightest whisper of disease to them.

THE FUTURE OF PERSONALITY ASSESSMENT-EVALUATION

What does the future hold for the workhorses of today's testing-measurement assessment methods—the Rorschach, TAT, MMPI, intelligence tests, tests of brain damage, and the all-purpose clinical interview? What is the future of personality assessment and evaluation?

Psychological assessment in functional personality classifications. There will be new assessment instruments for use in functional personality classification. For example, systems for crisis-emergency problems will include a given set of variables and dimensions. Specific clinical instruments will likely be designed to measure precisely those variables and dimensions. In a similar way, other test-evaluation measures will be constructed for explicit functional purposes—to assess readiness for graduate school, government training programs, Jungian psychotherapy, sensitivity training, experiential psychotherapy, or other function-specific enterprises which will arise in the future.

The Rorschach, TAT, MMPI, intelligence, and brain damage tests have accompanied the need to measure the gross variables of the conventional psychiatric system. As specific functions call for measurement and assessment, these traditional devices will lose their meaning. Other instruments will be evolved to measure relevant variables and dimensons for new functions.

Psychological assessment in a comprehensive biopsychological personality classification. As a comprehensive biopsychological system emerges, it will require tests which directly assess neurological, physiological, and psychophysiological variables. For example, sets of tests will be needed to measure autonomic conditionability. Since none of our standard repertoire of tests is specifically suited for such purposes, new instruments will be required. Similarly, new tests will be needed to measure neuropsychological, biopsychological, and physiopsychological variables. For these purposes, the standard testing batteries will likely be replaced by precise laboratory instruments designed to measure variables not presently assessed by our Rorschach, TAT, MMPI, intelligence, or brain damage tests.

Open-face testing. Instead of the conventional meaning of the word "test," the devices will have the connotation of aiding and assisting both the individual and the clinician in coming to know and to understand more about the individual himself. It will become typical for the individual to possess knowledge about the real aims of the tests themselves. Instead of mysterious instruments for probing the inner world of the patient, they will become openly recognized systematic information-providers. The mystery and the magic will be assimilated into the ability of the clinician to make penetrating sense of the information. There will be no hiding, no indirection, no masking of purpose or methods, no counting on fooling or trapping the individual, no laying the groundwork for "projection" or removed external observation of the individual's pathology at work. Evaluation will become an open-face procedure, with a premium on a working collaborative relationship between individual and clinician.

Veridical self-report data. The individual will be instructed and guided in providing the clinician with veridical self-report data. For example, if the classificational approach calls for an analysis of the individual's sexual behaviors, the psychological significance of the assessment-understanding process and the role of the clinician will be conducive to an acceptance of the self-report data as legitimate and credible. The individual may be assisted by providing him with an inventory of specific, concrete sexual items; or the clinician may be invited into the individual's ongoing life so that the self-report data are in the nature of self-commentaries and observations of his own behaviors and accompanying inner feelings more or less in the live situations. It remains the clinician's role to make psychological sense of the data awarded to him, but the data will have been in the form of veridical self-report.

Entry routes into the inner world. The future should see the systematization of new routes into the individual's inner world. Instead of catching roundabout peeks through devious indirection, there will occur an opening of direct routes. Chemicals may hold the key to the opening of direct access to deeper levels of consciousness. It is expected that dreams will become rediscovered as systematic data-pools for personality evaluation. A third avenue of direct access will include techniques of critical experiencing, of sensitivity training, of specific techniques for expressing the world of internal experiencings, needs, and feelings. The role of the clinician will be twofold: to be knowledgeable in the several routes of entry (including the role of guiding and training the individual in their use) and in making constructive use of the emerged material.

The clinician as a data-pool. The future should see a systematic utilization of the clinician as a legitimate source of data. Instead of crowding himself into the unnatural role of the removed observer, he will make full use of the contract, transaction, and relationship with the individual as a source of data. Reactions, induced feelings, countertransferences, and responses on the part of the clinician will serve as a legitimate base for inferences about the individual. Conceptual changes will guide us in making far fuller use of the clinician as an assessment tool.

Natural situations. It is expected that personality evaluation will take much fuller cognizance of the role of natural situations as determinants. In the future, the clinician will likely recognize a time perspective by coming to understand the person's life more fully both in breadth and depth. That is, he will become far more familiar with the individual's family, his acquaintances, his social groups, the play of many situations in the individual's life. By the same token, assessment should occur over a stretch of time as a sort of time sampling procedure.

The clinical history. Both functional and comprehensive personality evaluation will provide new ways of understanding relevant historical material. Personality theories will identify the significant components of history and will also serve as guides in drawing systematic clinical inferences. Research methodology will impose a needed organization upon the realm of historical data. Such a wealth of information will be utilized differently by different functional and comprehensive approaches, but the future will likely see the careful and systematic use of clinical historical information as a central mode of assessment and evaluation.

Specific clinical behaviors. Psychological evaluation will provide means of assessing specific clinical behaviors. Sets of psychological inferences will be linked to each of the specific clinical behaviors so that a personality picture will emerge from the combination of inferences from sets of specific clinical behaviors.

In closing, I would like to give expression to two messages I have sensed throughout the writings of the contributors. One is a sense of an emerging understanding of personality; this is not yet fully articulated, but is seeking expression in such different approaches as experiential, behavior modification, factor analytic, dimensional, motivational, existential, and other models of personality. The second message is that there is a restless urgency to apply psychological knowledge and understanding to the promotion of individual, community, and social change. Personality classification and psychodiagnosis are means of organizing information necessary to begin movement toward personality change. These new approaches convey tangible eagerness to facilitate optimal functioning and constructive personality change in oneself, in one's fellowman, and in one's society.

REFERENCES

Kelly, G. A. *The psychology of personal constructs.* New York: Norton, 1955.

Mahrer, A. R. The goals and families of psychotherapy: summary. In A. R. Mahrer (Ed.), *The goals of psychotherapy.* New York: Appleton-Century-Crofts, 1967a. Pp. 259–69.

Mahrer, A. R. The goals and families of psychotherapy: discussion. In A. R. Mahrer (Ed.), *The goals of psychotherapy.* New York: Appleton-Century-Crofts, 1967b. Pp. 270–87.

Robbins, L. L. A historical review of classification of behavior disorders and one current perspective. In L. D. Eron (Ed.), *The classification of behavior disorders.* Chicago: Aldine, 1966. Pp. 1–37.

INDEX OF NAMES

Abott, W., 377
Ackerman, N. W., 269
Ackoff, R. L., 369, 372
Adams, H. B., 331–32, 345
Adams, J. S., 363, 372
Addison, R. M., 367, 372
Adler, R. A., 245, 253, 269
Albee, G. W., 383–85, 394, 397, 398, 399, 410
Aldrich, C. K., 265, 269
Alexander, F., 122, 132, 135, 248, 263, 269
Allport, F. H., 361, 370, 372–73
Allport, G. W., 23, 75, 247, 361, 373
Alpert R., 221, 232n, 236
Ames, A., 352, 373
Ammons, H., 114, 115
Anker, J. M., 255, 257, 261, 269, 277, 305
Aristotle, 174
Asch, S., 247
Ash, P., 277, 305
Ashby, W. R., 371, 373
Asher, J. J., 357–58, 373
Atkinson, J. W., 87, 96
Auld, F., Jr., 257, 261, 274

Baggeley, A. R., 67, 68, 95
Baker, T. S., 251, 274
Ball, G. H., 104, 115

Ballard, P. B., 63
Bannister, D., 169, 204
Barber, B., 352, 356, 373
Barron, F., 134, 135, 257, 261, 269
Barton, W., 251, 269
Bateson, G., 242, 269
Bauer, R. A., 352, 373
Bayard, J., 261, 274
Beatman, F. L., 269
Becker, G. M., 369, 373
Bellak, L., 132, 135
Bennett, J. L., 107, 115
Bentley, A. F., 352, 373, 374
Bergman, G., 354, 373
Berkowitz, L., 264, 269, 372
Berne, E., 363, 373
Bertalanffy, L., 352, 370, 373
Bidwell, C. E., 364, 373
Bieber, I., 133, 135
Bjerstedt, A., 12, 50
Blackwell, B., 195, 206
Blalock, H. M., 49
Blau, P. M., 363, 373
Bleuler, E., 192
Boisen, A., 132, 135
Borman, L. D., 356, 373
Boulding, K. E., 370–71, 373
Boverman, M., 262, 269
Boyer, L. B., 132, 135
Brady, J. D., 264

415

Brammer, L. M., 140, 164
Brand, H., 96
Brenner, C., 263, 269
Brill, A. A., 279, 306
Brill, H., 128, 136
Brodbeck, M., 270
Brody, E. B., 260, 261, 269
Bronowski, J., 358, 373
Brown, L. G., 363, 373
Brown, R., 59, 95
Bruner, J. S., 60
Bryant, J. H., 277–78, 306
Bucher, R., 251, 275
Buck, C. W., 249, 251, 275
Buhler, C., 184–85, 204
Buhler, K., 184–85, 204
Bullard, D. M., 247, 269
Bumstead, C. H., 352, 373
Bunker, H. A., 391, 394
Bunn, D., 245, 253, 269
Burstein, B., 248, 255, 269
Burt, C., 265, 269, 279, 306
Buss, A. H., 264, 269
Butcher, J., 56, 95

Caffey, E. M., Jr., 107, 115
Cantor, G. N., 265, 269
Cantril, H., 352, 353, 373
Carr, A., 125, 136
Carter, S., 263, 269
Cattell, M. D., 16, 50
Cattell, R. B., 6–9, 11, 12, 15, 16, 19,
    20, 23, 26–29, 32, 33, 35, 36, 38, 39,
    43, 47, 49–52, 54–56, 60, 64, 67, 68,
    71, 74, 76–80, 82–84, 93, 95–97,
    182–83, 188–89, 204, 397–400, 402–5,
    408
Caudill, W., 246, 260, 269–70
Cave, R., 107, 116
Churchman, C. W., 355, 374
Claridge, G., 177, 188, 190, 191–92,
    205
Clark, R. A., 87, 96
Clark, W. H., 235
Clausen, J. A., 123, 136, 255, 270
Clayton, W. H., 255, 261, 270
Clemans, W. V., 64, 95
Clyde, D., 26
Coffey, H., 277, 306
Cole, J. O., 107, 115

Cole, M. E., 261, 274
Colquhoun, W. P., 195, 204
Conover, C. G., 246, 275
Cooley, C. H., 363, 374
Copernicus, 221
Corcoran, D. V. J., 195, 204
Cotts, G. K., 250, 270
Coulter, M. A., 43, 50
Cowen, E., 394
Cowie, V., 185, 204
Crandall, A., 257, 270
Creighton, J. L., 358, 379
Cremerius, J., 171, 204
Cromwell, R. L., 265, 269
Cronbach, J. L., 104, 115
Cross, K., 78, 80, 95

Darbonne, A. R., 242, 270
Davis, C., 90–91, 95
Davis, J. A., 242, 246, 270
Dawson, J. G., 277–78, 306
Degan, J. W., 278, 306
Delhees, K. H., 19, 43, 50
Devadasan, K., 178, 204
Dewey, J., 352, 360, 374
Diamond, L. S., 107, 115
Diener, R. G., 252, 263, 270
Dinoff, M., 367, 378
Downing, M. H., 268, 274
Downing, R. W., 268, 274
Dubin, S. S., 19, 20, 50
Dunham, H. W., 363, 374
Durkheim, E., 364, 374

Eber, H. W., 16, 20, 47, 50
Ehrlich, D., 251, 275
Ellsworth, R. B., 251, 255, 257, 261,
    270
English, O. S., 263, 275
Erickson, C. W., 63, 96
Erikson, E. H., 361, 374
Eron, L. D., 170, 207, 350, 374, 414
Eysenck, H. J., 17, 50, 124, 165–206,
    281, 306, 323, 345, 398–405
Eysenck, S. B. G., 172, 177–78, 201,
    205, 206

Fairweather, G. W., 256, 261, 272, 274
Faris, E. L., 363, 374
Fechner, G. T., 233

Feibleman, J. K., 353, 370, 374
Feigl, H., 265, 270, 354, 374
Feldman, D. A., 261, 274
Felix, R. H., 257, 270
Fenichel, H., 270
Fenichel, O., 240, 245, 250, 263, 270
Ferster, C. B., 367, 369, 374
Feshbach, S., 264, 270
Fields, W. S., 377
Fine, R., 117–21, 125, 126, 133, 134, 136, 398–400, 403, 404
Fingarette, H., 241, 257, 270
Fisher, G., 232n, 235
Fishman, M., 261, 269
Fleischl, M. F., 258, 271
Fleming, D. F., 249, 251, 275
Foa, U., 220, 235
Forer, B. A., 245, 271
Forgy, E. W., 104, 115
Foulds, G. A., 102, 115, 277, 306
Frank, L. K., 361, 363, 374
Frank, T. V., 107, 115
Fraser, J. T., 363, 374
Freedman, D., 122, 136
Freeman, E. H., 240, 242, 245, 247, 254, 271, 272
Freeman, H. E., 242, 246, 250, 255, 270, 271
French, T. M., 248, 263, 269
Freud, A., 67
Freud, S., 9, 58–60, 67, 68, 124, 125, 129, 130, 132, 136, 170, 185, 231, 233, 257, 263, 271, 359, 392
Friedman, A. P., 263, 269, 271
Friedman, H. J., 264, 271
Friedman, H. L., 262–63, 274
Friedman, S. H., 114, 115
Fruchter, B., 11, 50

Galen, 172
Gallagher, E. B., 364, 376
Galton, F., 9
Gardner, J. W., 369, 374
Gaylin, W., 125, 136
Giannitrapani, D., 251, 274
Gill, M., 227, 235, 257, 272
Gilmore, H. R., 260, 269
Giovacchini, P. L., 132, 135
Gleser, G. C., 104, 115
Gödel, K., 358, 374

Goffman, E., 365, 374
Goldberg, A., 250, 271
Goldberg, L. R., 46, 50
Goldberg, S. C., 107, 115
Goldiamond, I., 367, 369, 374
Goodglass, H., 262–63, 274
Gorham, D. R., 255, 271, 279, 281, 307
Grasberger, J. C., 107, 115
Gray, J. P., 391
Greenberg, R. M., 262–63, 274
Greenblatt, M., 225–26, 235, 251, 271, 274
Grene, M., 352, 374
Grinker, R. R., 263, 271, 352, 374
Gottschalk, L., 263, 271
Guertin, W. H., 277, 278, 306
Guilford, J. P., 15, 16, 25, 51
Gurdjieff, G. I., 222
Guttman, L., 70, 96

Haley, J., 241, 242, 247, 253, 258, 264–65, 271
Hall, D. J., 104, 115
Handlon, J. H., 352, 375
Harman, H. H., 11, 51
Harris, C. W., 23, 51
Harris, M. R., 240, 242, 245, 247, 254, 271, 272
Harrower, M., 117, 137–38, 139, 140, 146, 147, 164, 397, 398, 399, 400, 403
Harshbarger, T. R., 51
Hartshorne, H., 390, 395
Hastorf, A., 352, 373
Hathaway, S. R., 51
Havinghurst, H. D., 360, 363, 375
Hayakawa, S. I., 353, 361, 375
Heider, F., 371, 375
Heisenberg, W., 358, 375
Hendin, H., 125, 136
Henry, G., 2, 3
Henrysson, S., 11, 51
Herman, L., 107, 115
Hersko, M., 257, 261, 275
Hewlett, J. H. G., 198, 206
Hildebrand, H. P., 187, 190, 206
Hiler, E. W., 257, 261, 272
Hine, F. R., 277–78, 306
Hirsch, W., 356, 373
Hittelman, E., 366, 375

Hobbs, G. E., 249, 251, 275
Hoebel, E. A., 363, 375
Hollander, E. P., 375
Hollingshead, A. B., 242, 274
Hollister, L. E., 107, 115
Holt, E. B., 257, 272
Homans, G. C., 363, 375
Homme, L. E., 367, 372, 375
Horn, J. L., 6, 15, 16, 19, 25, 51, 53–54,
    55, 56, 60, 64, 75n, 83, 84, 95, 96,
    254, 273, 397–405
Horowitz, I. L., 356, 375
Horst, P., 103, 115
House, A. M., 88–89, 96
Hovland, C. I., 62
Humphreys, L. G., 70, 96
Hundleby, J. D., 33, 51
Hunt, M., 134, 136
Hunt, R. G., 375
Hurley, J. R., 78, 96
Hurst, L. C., 250, 272

Ingham, N., 187, 206
Ittelson, W., 352, 373

Jackson, D. D., 241, 247, 250, 272
Jahoda, M., 350, 375
James, W., 233
Janet, P., 186
Jenkins, R. L., 278, 306
Jessor, R., 247, 272
Johannsen, W. J., 114, 115
Johnson, N. A., 249, 261, 274
Jones, E., 129, 136, 271
Jones, E. E., 365–66, 375
Jones, M. R., 96, 274
Jourard, S., 393, 395
Jung, C. G., 30, 51, 68, 173, 186–87, 233

Kagan, J., 365, 371, 375
Kahn, E., 255, 259, 268, 273
Kalis, B. L., 240, 242, 245, 247, 254,
    271, 272
Kanfer, F. H., 262, 272, 280, 281, 306
Kannas, M., 51
Kant, I., 172
Kantor, D., 225–26, 235
Kantor, J. R., 265, 272, 354, 363, 375
Kaplan, A., 354, 375
Kaplan, O., 273

Karvonen, M. J., 26, 51
Katz, G., 253, 268, 273
Keller, H., 133
Kelly, G. A., 282, 306, 400, 414
Kerenyi, A., 194, 206
Kesey, K., 226, 235
Kesson, W., 361, 376
Kety, S., 131, 136
Khanna, P., 251, 274
Kilpatrick, F. P., 352, 353, 376
King, G., 277, 280, 306
Kinne, S., 226, 229, 232n, 235
Klein, A., 352, 374
Klerman, G. L., 107, 115
Klett, C. J., 106, 107, 115, 116, 196,
    206, 277, 281, 306
Kluckhohn, C., 355, 376
Koch, S., 352, 361, 368–69, 376
Kohrman, Jr., 352, 374
Kolb, L. C., 279, 306
Komlos, E., 16, 19, 43, 50
Korzybski, A., 363, 376
Kostlan, A. A., 281–82, 306
Kotarbinski, T., 354, 376
Kraepelin, E., 54, 119–20, 121, 124,
    129, 131, 168, 192, 281
Krasner, L., 367, 376, 378, 379
Kretschmer, E., 30, 51, 173, 192–93,
    194, 195
Kuder, G., 18
Kuhn, A., 363, 376

Lang, P., 203
Langner, T. S., 136, 251, 274
Lansing, C., 241, 275
Lasky, J. J., 107, 115, 116
Lawlis, F., 91–92, 96
Leary, T., 165, 209–11, 220, 221, 226,
    227, 229, 232n, 235–36, 257, 272,
    277, 306, 397, 398, 399, 401, 403–6
Lefever, D. W., 184–85, 204
Leif, A., 345
Leighton, A., 123, 136
Leitschuh, T. H., 114, 115
Lepley, R., 355, 376
Levey, A., 199–200, 206
Levine, S., 363, 376
Levinson, D., 251, 252, 271, 364, 376,
    377
Lewin, K., 358

Lieberman, D. M., 169, 204
Lind, D., 254, 273
Lindemann, J. H., 261, 272
Lingoes, J. C., 32, 51, 104, 116
Lippitt, R., 371, 376
Little, K. B., 56, 75n, 96
Loevinger, J., 170, 206
Logan, N. D., 257, 270
London, I. T., 261, 272
Lorr, M. A., 6, 99, 101, 104–9, 116,
  196–97, 206, 220, 236, 257, 261, 274,
  277, 278, 281, 306, 393, 395, 397,
  398, 399, 400, 402, 404–5, 408
Lowell, E. I., 87, 96
Lubin, A., 103, 116, 177, 206
Luborsky, L., 272
Lustman, S., 263, 272
Lynd, R. S., 361, 376

McClelland, D. C., 87, 96
McClintock, C. G., 369, 373
McDougall, W., 75, 83, 96
MacGregor, H., 352, 374
McGuigan, F. J., 355–56, 376
McKinley, J. C., 51
McNair, D. M., 106, 116, 196, 206, 277,
  281, 306
McQuitty, L. L., 51, 104, 116
Mabry, J., 367, 379
Magoun, H. W., 199, 200–1, 206
Maher, B., 280, 306
Mahler, M. S., 241
Mahrer, A. R., 136, 165, 239, 240–42,
  245–47, 253–55, 259, 261, 263–68,
  272–74, 280, 282, 306, 385, 397–402,
  404–5, 406, 408–9, 414
Maine, H., 363, 376
Malmo, R. B., 268, 273
Malzberg, B. A., 251, 273
Mandler, G., 361, 376
Margenau, H., 354, 376
Marney, M. C., 370, 376
Mason, D. J., 247, 255, 259, 263, 264,
  268, 273, 274, 282, 306
Mattsson, N., 107, 115
May, M., 56, 93, 97, 390, 395
Mayman, M., 122, 136
Mayo, C., 262–63, 274
Maxwell, A. E., 179–80, 207, 277, 307
Mead, G. H., 363, 376

Mechanic, D., 249, 253, 264, 273
Meehl, P. E., 31, 51, 103, 116
Menninger, K., 2, 3, 122, 129, 136, 350,
  366, 377
Merritt, H. H., 263, 271
Messick, S., 57, 96
Mettler, F. A., 257, 270
Metzner, R., 221, 226, 229, 232n, 235,
  236
Meyer, A., 333, 345, 405
Meyers, J. K., 257, 261, 274
Michael, S. T., 136
Mill, J. S., 388, 395
Miller, J. G., 26, 52, 352, 370, 377
Mills, C. W., 361, 369–70, 377
Milton, O., 374
Moran, L. J., 256, 274
Morgan, N. C., 249, 261, 274
Morimoto, F. R., 251, 274
Morse, E., 245, 256, 258, 261, 275
Morton, R. B., 256, 274
Moseley, E. C., 107, 115
Mowrer, O. H., 358, 363, 377, 378
Murphy, G., 358, 377
Murray, H. A., 366

Nash, H., 361, 377
Nesselroade, J. R., 19, 26, 27, 50, 51
Newbury, E., 352, 377
Newcomb, T. M., 77, 96
Nietzsche, F. W., 359–60
Norman, W. T., 16, 51
Northrop, F. S. C., 354, 377
Novikoff, A. B., 353, 370, 377
Nowlis, H., 26
Nowlis, V., 26
Noyes, A. P., 279, 306

O'Connor, J. P., 107, 116, 277, 278, 306,
  307
Offer, D., 131, 136
Opler, M. K., 136, 251, 274
Oppenheimer, R., 358, 377
Orne, M. T., 356, 377
Osburn, H. G., 103, 116
Overall, J. E., 45, 51, 255, 271, 279,
  281, 307

Palmai, G., 195, 206
Parad, H. J., 361, 377

Parker, S., 251, 274
Parloff, M. B., 235
Parsons, T., 255, 274, 364, 376, 377
Pascal, G. R., 261, 274
Pasteur, L., 16
Pavlov, I. P., 199, 200
Pawlik, K., 33, 51
Payne, R. V., 198, 206
Peak, H., 67–68, 96
Peterson, D. R., 245, 274
Pfister, O., 128, 136
Phillips, L., 280, 281, 307
Pinderhughes, C. A., 262–63, 274
Pomeroy, E., 247, 264, 273, 274, 282, 306
Popper, K. R., 361, 377
Porter, R., 16, 51
Pratt, S., 165, 251, 274, 347–49, 350, 352, 355–56, 363–65, 369, 377–79, 398, 399, 401, 402, 406, 409
Presnell, M., 226, 229, 232n, 235
Prestwood, A. R., 245, 272
Projansky, M., 255, 259, 268, 273
Pruyser, P., 122, 136
Pugh, D. S., 363–64, 378

Rachman, S., 200, 201, 206
Radcliffe, J. A., 56, 60, 68, 84, 95
Radhakrishnan, B. K., 104, 108, 116
Rakusin, J. M., 245, 256, 258, 261, 275
Rao, C. R., 189–90, 206
Rapoport, A., 355, 378
Rappaport, D., 270
Redlich, F. C., 122, 136, 260, 269
Reid, J. R., 278, 307
Reik, T., 123
Rennie, T. A. C., 124, 136, 251, 274
Reznikoff, M., 264, 269
Rickard, H. C., 367, 378
Rickels, K., 20, 51, 268, 274
Ricks, D. F., 27, 52
Riecken, H. W., 355–56, 378
Robbins, F. P., 263, 271
Robbins, L., 2, 3, 401, 414
Robinson, J. O., 187, 206
Rogers, C. R., 43, 317
Rogers, L. S., 257, 274
Rogler, L. H., 242, 274
Rorschach, H., 140–41
Rose, A. M., 276

Rosenblum, M. P., 107, 115
Rosenshine, M., 263, 273
Rosenthal, R., 355–56, 378, 379
Rothstein, C., 107, 115
Rotter, J. B., 263, 265, 274, 277, 307, 393, 395
Rubenstein, E. A., 235, 257, 261, 274
Rubin, B., 250, 271
Ruesch, J., 370, 378

Sabshin, M., 131, 136, 251, 275
Sahakian, W. S., 366, 378
Salman, P., 169, 204
Sandoval, J., 94
Sanford, N., 370, 379
Sarason, S. B., 355–56, 379
Saslow, G., 262, 272, 280, 281, 306
Saul, L., 126, 136
Saunders, D. B., 19, 50
Saunders, D. R., 104, 108, 116
Schaefer, H., 358, 379
Schaie, K. W., 16, 51
Schatzman, L. 251, 275
Scheff, T. J., 388, 389, 390, 395
Scheier, I. H., 26, 43, 50, 52, 183, 188–89, 204
Schein, E. H., 363–64, 379
Schucman, H., 104, 108, 116
Schumer, F., 170, 207
Schwartz, C. G., 251, 258, 275
Schwartz, M. S., 251, 258, 260, 275
Schwitzgebel, R., 225–26, 229, 232n, 235, 236
Scriven, M., 354, 374
Sechehaye, M., 133, 136
Selan, K., 352, 374
Selesnick, S., 122, 135
Sells, S. B., 363, 379
Selye, H., 133, 136
Shagass, C., 194, 206, 268, 273
Shapiro, M. B., 204, 206, 254, 255, 275
Shaw, F. J., 358, 379
Shawver, J. R., 279, 281, 307
Sheldon, W. H., 30, 52
Sherman, S. N., 269
Shields, J., 193, 206
Shils, E. A., 376
Shostrum, E. L., 140, 164
Shotwell, A. M., 78, 96

Simmons, O. G., 242, 246, 250, 255, 270, 271
Skinner, B. F., 367–68, 379
Slack, C., 225–26, 236
Slater, E., 193, 206
Slater, P., 176, 177, 187, 189–92, 206
Slovenko, R., 136
Smith, M. B., 355, 379
Smith, N. M., 370, 376
Smith, R. S., 261, 272
Sneath, P. H., 32, 52, 197, 207
Sokal, R. R., 32, 52, 197, 207
Solomon, D., 235
Specht, L. L., 20, 36, 50
Speers, R. W., 241, 275
Speisman, J., 3
Spence, K. W., 354, 373
Spiegel, J. P., 258, 263, 275
Srole, L., 136, 251, 274
Stachnik, T., 367, 379
Stafford, J. W., 107, 116, 278, 306
Stainbrook, E., 246, 270
Staunton, A. H., 251, 258, 275
Stefic, E. C., 277, 307
Sternlicht, I., 280, 306
Stevens, S. S., 30, 52, 265, 275, 352, 379
Stewart, P., 254, 273
Stokes, H. A., 251, 257, 270
Stone, G. B., 261, 272
Stone, L., 132, 136
Strauss, A., 251, 275
Strauss, E. W., 266–67, 275
Strong, E., 18
Strupp, H. H., 272
Sullivan, H. S., 125, 129, 132
Sullivan, W. P., 52
Sulzer, E. S., 366, 379
Sweney, A. B., 6, 16, 19, 25, 33, 52, 53–54, 56, 60, 68, 82, 84, 93, 95–97, 397–405
Swensen, C. H., 261, 274
Szasz, T. S., 101, 116, 134, 136, 173–74, 207, 246, 252, 257, 258, 275, 331–32, 345, 359–60, 366, 379

Tapp, J., 68, 97
Tart, C. T., 358, 379
Tatro, D. F., 16, 19, 20, 43, 50
Tatsuoka, M., 16, 50
Taylor, C. W., 235

Thorne, F. C., 135, 136, 165, 309–11, 312, 317, 318, 325, 327–29, 331, 332, 334, 335, 345, 396, 397, 399, 400, 402, 404, 405
Thorp, T., 280, 306
Thurstone, L., 15, 25
Tooley, J., 165, 347–49, 350, 352, 355–56, 363–64, 365, 369, 377–78, 379–97, 398, 400, 401, 405, 408
Toops, H. A., 103, 116
Torgerson, W. S., 56, 59, 97
Trouton, D. S., 179–80, 207, 277, 307
Tybring, G. B., 242, 275
Tyler, F., 3

Uhr, L., 26, 52
Ullman, A. D., 358, 363, 377
Ullman, L. P., 261, 275, 367, 378, 379
Ulrich, R., 367, 379

Van Egeren, L. F., 26, 52
Van Kaam, A. L., 352, 379
Venables, P. H., 114, 116
Von Mises, L., 360–61, 379
Von Storch, T. J. C., 263, 271
Vreeland, R. S., 364, 373

Wagner, A., 16, 50
Wanklin, J. M., 249, 251, 275
Warburton, F., 35, 39, 47, 50
Ward, L. B., 62
Washburne, N. F., 378
Watson, J., 371, 376
Weaver, W., 353–54, 379
Weil, G., 226, 229, 232n, 235, 236
Weiss, E., 263, 275
Wenar, S., 126, 136
Wenig, P., 33, 52
Werts, C. E., 46, 50
Wessman, A. E., 27, 52
Westley, B., 371, 376
White, P. E., 363, 376
Whitehead, A. N., 352
Whitmer, C. A., 246, 275
Wilder, R. L., 135, 136
Williams, C. M., 45, 51
Williams, J. R., 26, 33, 52, 78, 80, 81, 97
Williams, O., 63

Williams, R. H., 251, 271, 377
Wilson, R. N., 123, 136
Winder, A. E., 257, 261, 275
Wittenborn, J. R., 277, 278, 307
Wolberg, L., 133, 136
Wolff, H. G., 263, 275
Wolman, B., 136, 170, 207, 350, 379
Wolpe, J., 201
Wood, E. C., 245, 256, 258, 261, 275
Woodward, J. L., 251, 276
Wundt, W., 172, 207

Wurster, C. R., 277–78, 306

Young, H. H., 252, 261, 268, 270, 273, 280, 306

Zeigarnik, B. V., 63
Zeller, W. W., 264, 269
Zigler, E., 280, 281, 307
Zilboorg, G., 2, 3, 122, 136
Zimmerman, W., 16, 25
Zubin, J., 170, 207, 257, 270

SUBJECT INDEX

Actuarial prediction: clinical prediction, 46–47
Adulthood, 288

Behavior: and diagnosis, 220; change of, 226; conditioning, 402; goal-directionality of, 257; hospital admission and, 252; measurement of, 222–24, 227, 404; multiple goals and, 261
Body: classification and, 266; complaint value of, 267; consciousness and, 231; construct approach to, 265; motivations and, 265–66; structural vs. functional changes, 267

Classification system: comprehensive approaches, 165; criteria, 40, 174, 278; dimensions of, 55, 172–73, 315, 319, 399; functional approach, 117; functions, 396; future directions, 406; homogeneity vs. heterogeneity, 280; life history and, 281; personality conceptions and, 401; philosophy of, 211, 387, 390–91; present trends, 397; range of convenience, 282, 317, 398; reliability, 280; single vs. multiple, 278; sociological variables and, 278
Clinical judgment, 332
Comprehensive approaches: future directions, 408–9; present trends, 398

Conflict, meaning of, 81–82
Consciousness: diagnosis and, 232; levels of, 231; measurement of, 231; vs. behavior, 214–15
Contractual relationships, 360; behavior theory and, 367–68; language of, 363; society and, 362

Defense mechanisms, meaning of, 93
Delusions, goals of, 262
Dependency, 299; induced, 301; instrumental, 302; nurturant, 299
Diagnosis: behavior and, 386, 393; case illustration, 337; clinical methods of, 314–15, 317; mental illness and, 388; misused as social labels, 389–90, 410; need for, 385; secrecy of, 214; differential diagnosis, 324–25

Epistemology, 352, 355
Ergs, 18, 74–75, 85
Expectancy of improvement, 264

Factor analysis: features of 10–14; P-technique, 23–24; Q-technique, 32, 41; R-technique, 26; uses of, 15
Functional approaches: future directions, 407, 409; present trends, 398

Hallucinations, meaning of, 233

423

Headaches, clinical goals of, 263
Heterogeneous scale, 144
Homeostasis, 402
Homogeneous scale, 143
Hospitalization: admission dynamics, 254; chronic, 260; dropout, 255; need for, 247–48; patients vs. nonpatients, 279; postadmission, 254
Hospitals: clinical behavior and, 260, 262; roles of, 249–50

Identification, 303
Impulses, acceptance of, 293
Individual differences: diagnosis of, 320; factor analytic meaning of, 22–25
Integration, diagnosis of, 326, 329
Interactional relationship, 400
Internal vs. external, 215, 217
Introverts vs. extraverts, 199–200, 401

Life history, 328, 405
Loss of significant figure, 286

Mental health potential, 403; classification, 159
Mental status, 323
MMPI, 35–38
Motivation: basic personality and, 244; major motivations, 69–71, 243–44; meaning of, 57–58; measurement of, 58–69; recent life changes and, 239–40
Motivation Analysis Test, 84–88, 91

Natural data, 212
Neurosis, subdivisions of, 186
Neurotic vs. psychotic, 20, 175, 179, 182, 185
Normal vs. pathological, 19–20, 39, 129, 131, 187, 191, 350, 386, 391, 397

Personality dimension vs. disease entities, 402
Personality evaluation, 404; clinician's role, 406; future directions, 411; natural data, 405; self-report and, 405
Precipitating events, approaches to, 245–46
Primitive personality, 241

Process, factor analytic meaning of, 27–28
Psychiatric diagnostic system: criticism of, 1, 43, 101, 119–24, 129, 131, 140, 167, 169–71, 334, 392; future directions, 408; history of, 2; social philosophy of, 392
Psychological pain, goal-direction and, 259
Psychological states: description of, 312; diagnosis of, 312–13, 327, 333; factor analytic meaning of, 26, 27
Psychological tests, philosophy of, 230
Psychological types, 29–32, 102–3; vs. clinically derived groups, 111–12; typological analysis, 104
Psychopathology: psychological states and, 331; quantitative meaning of, 20–21
Psychosis: acute types, 108–13; factor analytic meaning of, 21–22; goals of, 264; measurement, 105, 107; subdivisions of, 192, 195; treatability of, 132; typology for, 105–6
Psychotherapy: accessibility, 125, 127, 133; diagnosis and, 201–3, 318; goal of, 125, 221; hospitalization and, 248; and religion, 128; therapist behavior, 229
Punishment, 287; externally directed, 292; self-directed, 290

Reality: contract psychology and, 358; experiential meaning of, 216–17
Research, philosophy of, 219
Rorschach records and diagnosis, 147–50, 153–54, 161–64

Schizophrenia, 133
Self: existential, 403; in factor analysis, 76; sentiment, 75, 85–86
Sexual threat, 283
Sick role vs. patient role, 255
Situation: analysis of, 78; role of, 77, 401
Structural approaches, 6, 397; future directions, 408
Structure and control, 294; aggression and, 295; sexual impulses and, 297
Symptom vs. complaint, 101

Syndrome, meaning of, 102

TAT and diagnosis, 151
Taxonomy: vs. psychodiagnosis, 349; types, 372
Tests, validity of, 88

Therapist, patient and, 404
Traits: diagnosis of, 321–22; factor analytic meaning of, 25, 33; meaning of, 102, 403; source traits, 14–15, 19, 32, 35; surface traits, 15, 32, 35; vs. psychological states, 314